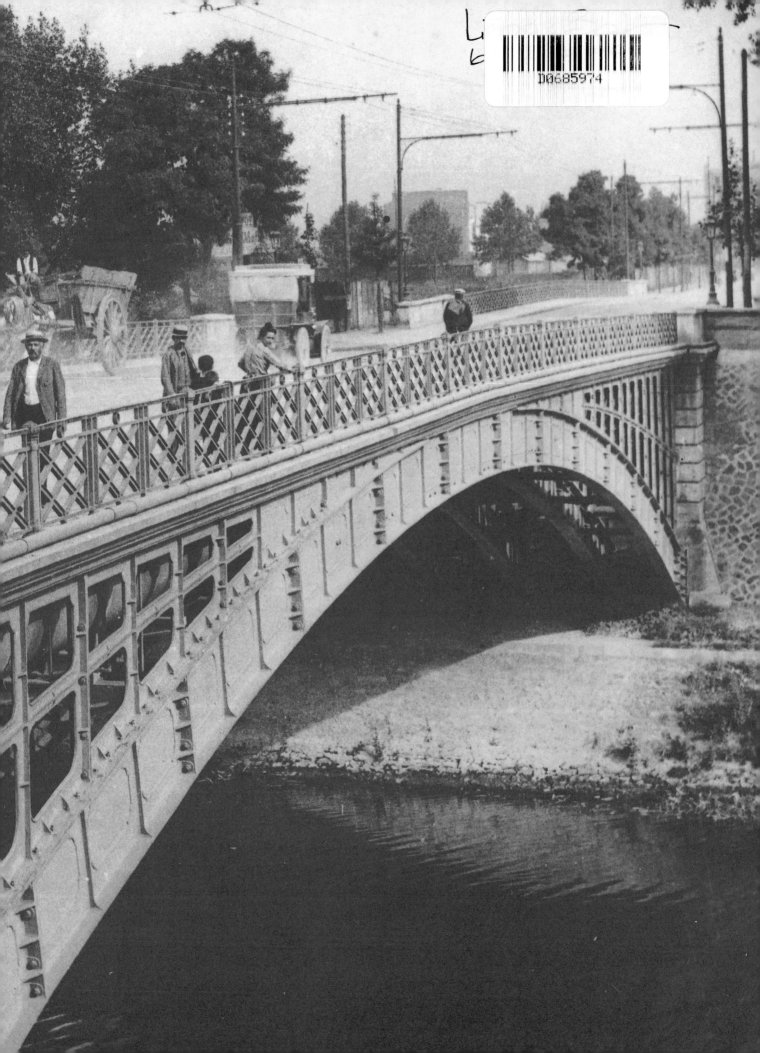

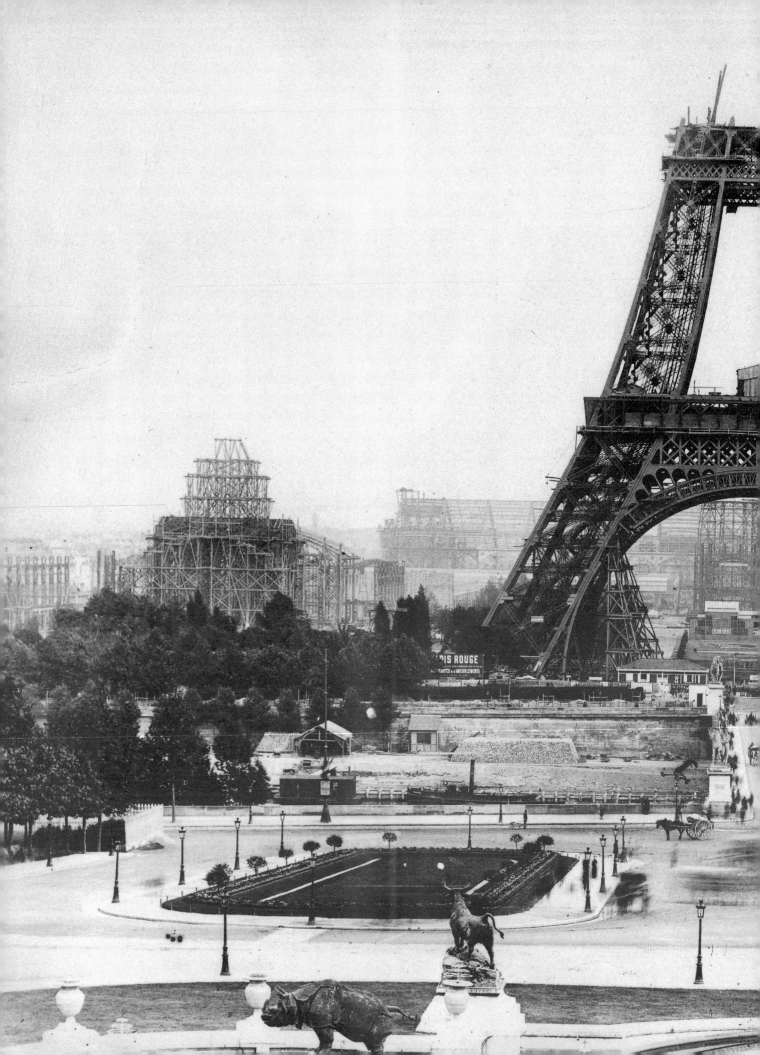

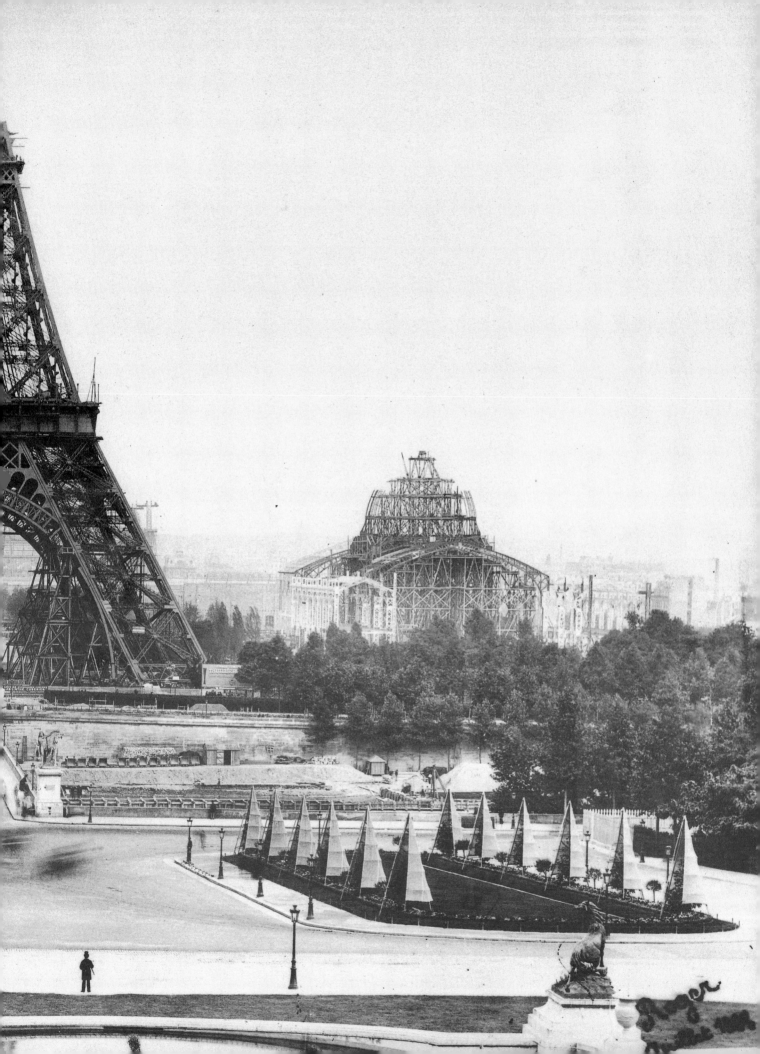

THE CHRONICLE OF IMPRESSIONISM

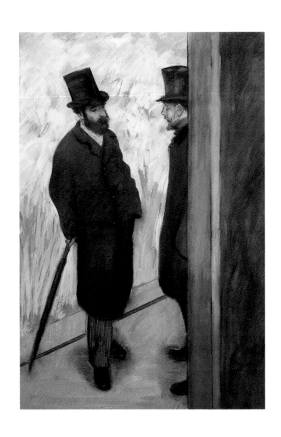

BERNARD DENVIR

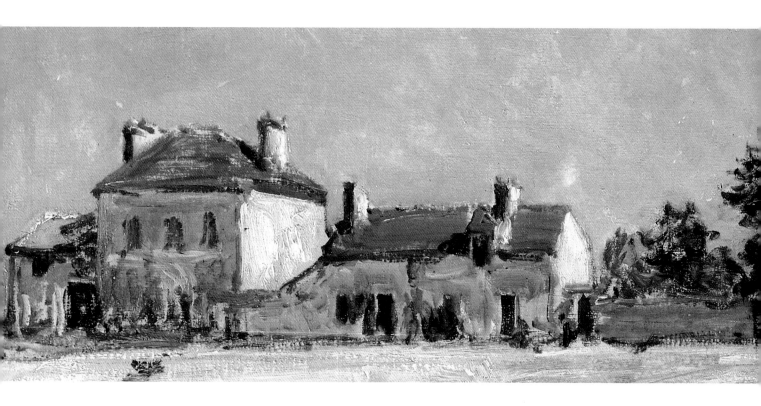

With over 400 illustrations, 203 in color

THE CHRONICLE
OF IMPRESSIONISM

AN INTIMATE DIARY OF THE LIVES AND WORLD OF THE GREAT ARTISTS

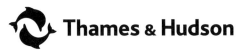
Thames & Hudson

OUTER ENDPAPERS: (*front*) Le Pont de Clichy, Hauts-de-Seine, Asnières. Photo Roger-Viollet; (*back*) L'Avenue du Bois de Boulogne, Paris. Photo Collection Sirot-Angel.

INNER ENDPAPERS: (*front*) Construction of the Eiffel Tower, July 1888. Photo Roger-Viollet; (*back*) La rue des Abbesses et la rue Lepic, Paris. Photo Roger-Viollet.

HALF-TITLE: Edgar Degas *Ludovic Halévy and Albert Boulanger-Cavé*, 1879

FRONTISPIECE: Alfred Sisley *Beside the Loing, Saint-Mammès* (detail), 1890

© 1993 and 2000 Thames & Hudson Ltd, London

Published in paperback in the United States of America in 2000 by Thames & Hudson Inc.,
500 Fifth Avenue, New York, New York 10110

Library of Congress Catalog Card Number 99-69563
ISBN 0-500-28214-5

Printed and bound in Singapore by Star Standard Industries (Pte) Limited

How to Use this Book

The core of this volume is a diary-style chronology of events, spanning the 1860s to the present day, which traces the entire development of Impressionism and its legacy, revealing the inside story of the artists' daily lives: their travels, exhibitions, sales, patrons, friends, lovers, families, finances and aspirations – a kaleidoscope of facts through which you may follow your own lines of enquiry.

For each year contemporary world events are also highlighted, both to illuminate the artists' milieu and to put their movement into the context of a rapidly changing environment.

This vast bank of information is complemented by a range of special features, which fall into four broad categories, each flagged with a different symbol for ease of reference:

 IMPRESSIONIST EXHIBITIONS

Full descriptions of the most exciting series of exhibitions ever held: the planning, the venues, what was shown and how it was received.

 IMPORTANT PEOPLE

Intriguing accounts of the lives of those collectors, dealers and writers who had a profound influence on the course of the movement.

 DOCUMENTS

Letters, diaries and articles in which you may hear the voices and opinions of the artists, their friends, patrons and critics.

 THEMES AND EVENTS

Detailed and entertaining commentaries on wider aspects of Impressionism – an overview of the day-to-day developments.

These handy devices are the key to cross-referencing the information in the book. When a point appearing in the chronology is followed by one of the above, you may discover more about the subject by turning to the feature with the appropriate symbol on the page given.

Over two hundred Impressionist masterworks are reproduced throughout the book in full colour and, together with a mass of drawings, prints, photographs and contemporary ephemera, these provide a simultaneous visual narrative that animates the artists' world with cinematographic clarity.

Starting on p.255, you will find an extensive 'Reference Data' section. This directory of Impressionism includes everything a student of the movement could need: a biographical index of the artists and other important figures; maps and descriptions of the principal Impressionist locations; a table of contemporary developments in the art of the Western world; an extensive gazetteer of major Impressionist collections; a detailed list of illustrations and a bibliography.

Contents

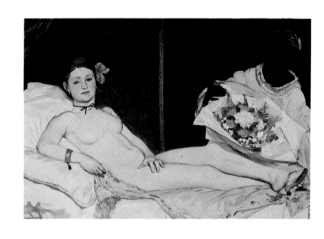

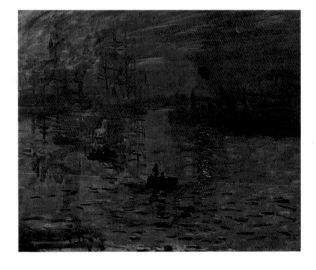

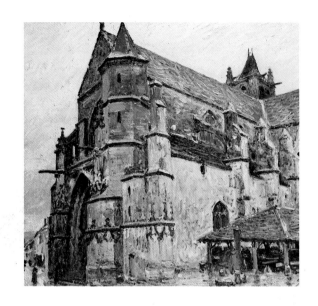

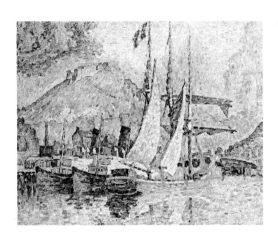

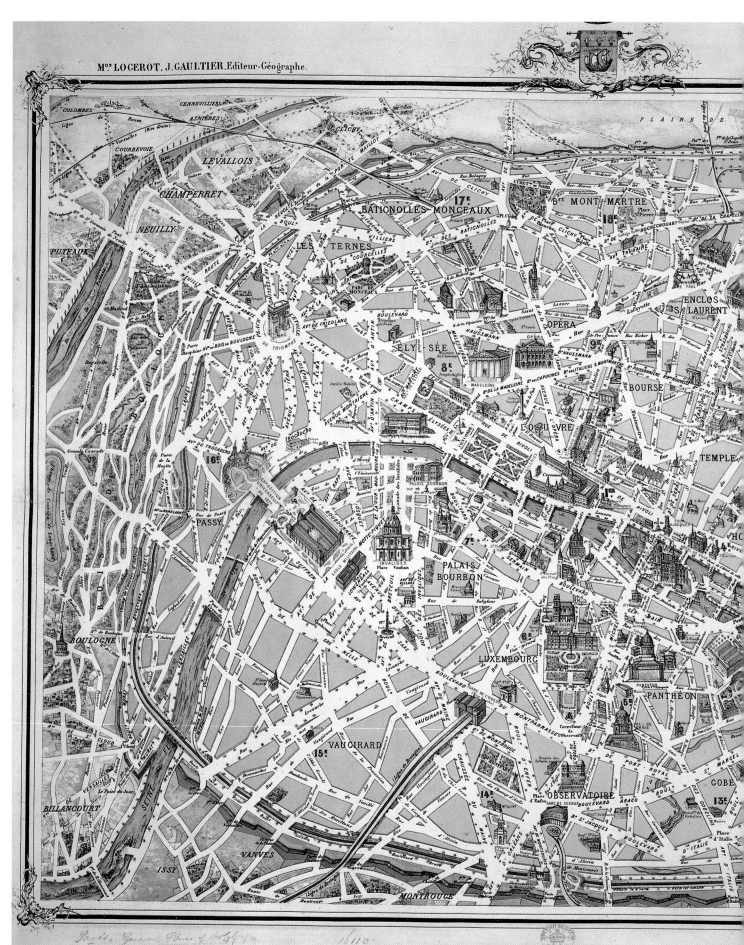

PARIS EN 1878.

SOUVENIR DE L'EXPOSITION UNIVERSELLE.

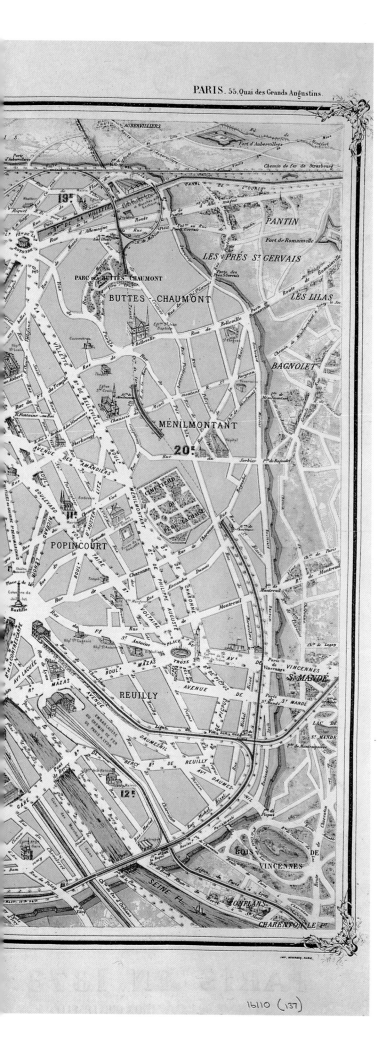

INTRODUCTION

The Impressionists' World

A souvenir map from the Paris Universal Exhibition of 1878
by Logerot and J. Gaultier.

The Impressionists' World

Seldom in the history of European painting has a single movement had so profound an impact as Impressionism. Within little more than a century its exponents have become household names in the global village of today, and the prices fetched by their paintings equal and often surpass those of the Old Masters. If a comparison must be found for their achievement it is only with the Renaissance, the period in which Man first believed in a universe that he could order and even control, determining what he saw and expressed not in terms of a transcendental scale of values but by the laws of perspective.

The Impressionists carried the process one step further, liberating art from its dependence on dogma and attempting to paint not what they thought they saw, nor what they thought they ought to see, but what they did see. From this emancipation was to come the art of the twentieth century, in all its varied manifestations.

The Impressionist movement was particularly remarkable in that it was achieved by some twenty artists, all of them familiar with each other, all based in one city, Paris, and all children of their time, the product of a unique cultural environment, which moulded them as much as they influenced it.

MANET
Civil War
1871–3

It is likely that Manet intended this lithograph to complement a proposed painting on the civil war – a project that was never realized. According to Duret, Manet saw the body of a dead National Guard lying 'at the corner of the rue de l'Arcade and the boulevard Malesherbes, and made a sketch on the spot.'

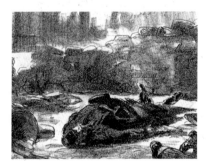

Political Allegiances

Between the birth of Pissarro in 1830 and the death of Monet in 1926, France experienced a variety of governments and constitutions; it was involved in two major wars, several minor ones, and a brief civil war that culminated in the brutal crushing of the Commune. It also gained an empire in Africa and the Far East, and was transformed from an agricultural country to a primarily industrial one, the basis of power passing to the predominantly mercantile middle class, which was becoming larger and more varied.

Nevertheless, despite the privations suffered during the siege of Paris
▲ (p.67), the horrors of the Commune and its suppression, the fierce passions roused by the Dreyfus affair, and the persistent waves of financial scandal that swept the country, the Impressionists – except for Pissarro, who was a Socialist with strong anarchist leanings – did not show much active political commitment.

Manet, it is true, was what might be described as an upper-class Republican, and his political sensibilities are occasionally evident in his work. His contempt for Napoleon III found poignant expression in his paintings of the execution of the Emperor Maximilian of Mexico ◆ (pp.56–9) – which by showing the firing squad in what looked like French army uniforms suggested, quite rightly, that the whole imbroglio had been brought about by Napoleon's devious policies. Also, out of all the Impressionists, Manet was the only one to leave a record of the horrors of 1871, in the form of a few drawings and lithographs showing scenes from the suppression of the Commune (opposite). His criticisms of authority were, however, muted by a desire to be accepted. 'Monsieur Manet has never wished to protest,' he wrote in the preface to the catalogue of his one-man exhibition of 1867 ▲ (p.45), and the fact that he never participated in any of the Impressionist exhibitions seems to have stemmed from a reluctance openly to defy the establishment. Monet too was a Republican, though not a very aggressive one, his sentiments owing something to his friendship with the politician Georges Clemenceau (p.18).

Renoir and Degas, on the other hand, were out-and-out reactionaries. 'Education', Renoir once remarked to Julie Manet ▲ (pp.193, 199 and 224), 'is the downfall of the working classes.' Both artists strongly believed in the panacea-like benefits of religion, although neither of them were actually practising Christians; they also regarded the inferiority of women as axiomatic; and were blatantly anti-Semitic. As for Cézanne, despite his excitable character and his 'total disregard for the dictionary of manners' ▲ (p.196), once he settled down to provincial life in Aix-en-Provence, the stirrings of youthful rebellion faded, and he became a confirmed conservative and a devout Catholic.

The Artists' Origins
The Impressionists were all either *grands* or *petits bourgeois* in origin, and none of them came from the peasantry or the proletariat. The fathers of Manet and Berthe Morisot were from the upper ranks of the judiciary and the civil service, Bazille's from a rich wine-growing family, Degas' from the minor Italian aristocracy and banking. Sisley's father, until his bankruptcy, was a well-to-do English businessman, settled in Paris; Pissarro's family were rich colonial merchants; and Caillebotte's had made their money in textiles, and augmented it by dabbling in real estate during the redevelopment of Paris in the 1860s. Monet's father and Renoir's – who came from the lower echelon of the bourgeoisie, the one being a merchant, the other a tailor – both made enough money to be able to retire to the countryside in their sixties. Cézanne's father ▲ (p.111), having started his business career as a hatmaker in Aix-en-Provence, developed into banking and became one of the city's most influential citizens.

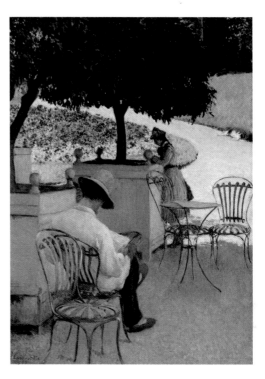

CAILLEBOTTE
The Orange Trees
1878

Caillebotte's painting of his brother Martial and cousin Zoé in the garden of their family estate at Yerres exudes an atmosphere of affluent domestic tranquillity.

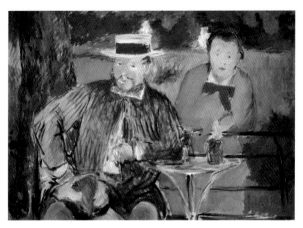

MANET
Ernest Hoschedé and His
Daughter Marthe at
Montgeron
1876

Owner of a chain of department stores, Hoschedé ◆ (pp.146–7) was an enthusiastic patron of the Impressionists prior to his bankruptcy in 1878.

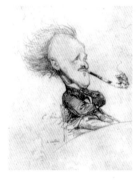

A caricature of Dr Gachet (*c.*1887) by Charles Léandre. The doctor was not only a committed supporter of the Impressionists but also gave them medical advice.

Patrons and Collectors

Equally obvious were the bourgeois origins of the patronage that the Impressionists received. Although many of the surviving aristocrats were wealthy, few of them – apart from the de Wagrams, who were of inferior Napoleonic nobility, and the Bibescos, who were Romanians – showed the enterprise displayed by the *nouveaux riches*. The acquisition of a collection of paintings provided the upwardly mobile with a visible symbol of their enhanced social standing; and it was the bourgeoisie and professional classes who imposed their taste on the art of the time.

Among the Impressionists' main patrons and collectors there were doctors such as Gachet (below left) and de Bellio; teachers such as the Abbé Gaugain; musicians such as Chabrier and the baritone Jean-Baptiste Faure ● (p.81); and civil servants such as the customs official Victor Chocquet ▲ (p.224). There were also businessmen such as Ernest Hoschedé (above), the department-store owner whose widow married Monet; Henri Rouart ■ (pp.131–2), an enterprising engineer who pioneered refrigeration machinery as well as being a talented painter; Paul Berard ● (p.231), the banker and diplomat at whose house at Wargemont Renoir so frequently stayed; Eugène Murer, the restaurateur and hotelier who gave free dinners for the Impressionists during the 1870s; and François Depeaux, the Rouen merchant who for a long time virtually supported Sisley.

An Expanding World

One consequence of industrialization was vastly improved transport. Between 1850 and 1900 the railways in France expanded from approximately 3000 kilometres (1850 miles) of track to 13,000 kilometres (8000 miles). When Cézanne first came up to Paris from Aix-en-Provence in 1861, the train journey took three days; when he paid his last visit to the capital in 1893, it took him only a day. The Impressionists were able to travel on a scale unknown to their predecessors. Monet, for example, not only explored and painted various aspects of the valley of the Seine and the Channel coast ▲ (p.33) but was able to travel to places as diverse as Normandy and Brittany, the Creuse valley ▲ (pp.171–2), Holland, Norway ▲ (p.203), Venice ▲ (p.92) and London ◆ (p.229). The whole of France was now available as a visual

MONET
The Railway Bridge
at Argenteuil
1874

Before 1840 Argenteuil was a small agricultural village on the Seine. The arrival of the railway, which brought it within 15 minutes of the Gare St-Lazare, also brought industry and tourism to the area. The railway bridge was therefore a symbol of progress, and an ideal subject for an artist committed to Realism.

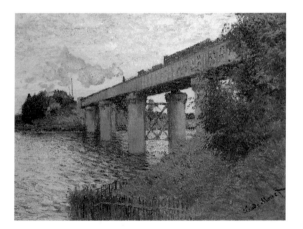

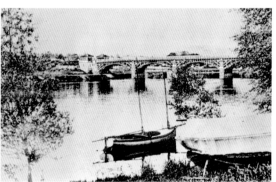

A contemporary photograph showing the second bridge at Argenteuil.

playground – places such as Argenteuil, Chatou and Asnières that feature so prominently in Impressionist paintings having been made easily accessible by the railways, which themselves became favourite images in the iconography of Manet, Monet and Pissarro. The opening of transalpine tunnels improved access to Italy, and the establishment of regular cross-Atlantic steamer services made it possible for enterprising dealers such as Paul Durand-Ruel (*see* p.162) to have easy access to the American art market, thus allowing the wealth and initiative of a new generation of collectors in the New World ▲ (p.167) to redress the aesthetic deficiencies of the old.

The Impact of Technology
Technological developments helped to promote new artistic ventures in a multitude of different ways. The invention of malleable-lead paint tubes in the 1840s facilitated open-air painting; the discovery of a new range of dyes extended artists' colour ranges; and the researches of chemists such as Eugène Chevreul gave rise to theories about the optical combination of colours that became fundamental to the techniques of Impressionism, Pointillism and Divisionism ◆ (p.107).

The development of photography ◆ (p.160) in increasingly sophisticated and versatile forms reinforced the Impressionists' concern with what Degas ▲ (p.204) called 'magical instantaneity'. Moreover, it made possible the proliferation of accurate reproductions of works of art, thus promoting visual literacy among an ever larger number of people. In the 1850s the photographer Adolphe Braun started to specialize in reproductions of works of art, which he sold for 15 francs each. Every year a couple of hundred pictures from the Salon were added to the list, and by 1896 his firm's catalogue contained approximately 20,000 reproductions. It was not so much that this process publicized the work of the Impressionists, but it did make an increasing number of people realize that the naturalistic realism of traditional art was not the only acceptable visual idiom.

The *Premier cercle chromatique* from Eugène Chevreul's *Des Couleurs et de leur application aux arts industriels.*

The Impressionists and the Press
New printing processes and methods of reproduction created an explosion in the number of papers and periodicals available to a population whose literacy figures quadrupled during the course of the century. The appetite for journalistic writing about art was enormous. 'Today', fumed Monet in 1883, 'nothing can be achieved without the press; even intelligent connoisseurs are sensitive to the least noise made

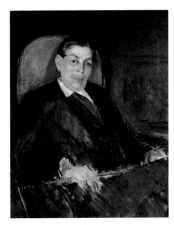

MANET
Portrait of Albert Wolff
1877

In a letter to Wolff dating from the year of this work, Manet wrote: 'Perhaps you do not yet like this kind of painting, but you will.' He was wrong. Wolff's dislike of the Impressionists was to be implacable.

by newspapers.' Indeed the very name Impressionism caught on because Louis Leroy, in a review of the exhibition held by the Société Anoyme des Artistes (*see* p.79) at Nadar's old studio in 1874 ■ (pp.86–7), hit on the device of making Monet's *Impression: Sunrise* the butt of a piece of journalistic whimsy ▲ (p.88).

Artist, engraver, playwright and critic, Leroy was typical of a whole tribe of failed or aspiring poets, novelists and dramatists who supplemented their incomes by writing reviews. Albert Wolff (left), for example, became art critic of *Le Figaro* – a position of such power that Manet virtually insisted on painting his portrait, despite Wolff's almost invariable hostility to the work of the Impressionists. A good deal of bribery and intrigue went on in the world of art criticism. Artists and dealers paid for fulsome introductions to catalogues; and galleries found that papers and periodicals were more likely to review exhibitions favourably if they advertised in their columns. Even Manet's portrait painting seems at times to have been used to reward services rendered. Among those whose portraits he painted were virtually all the critics who had been favourable to him – including Émile Zola ● (p.53), Zacharie Astruc ● (p.37), Théodore Duret ▲ (pp.145, 167 and 199), author of the first book on the Impressionists, the poet Stéphane Mallarmé ◆ (pp.220–1), who was one of Manet's most loyal supporters ▲ (p.99), and George Moore ◆ (p.46), the Irish novelist who was also a staunch defender of Impressionism.

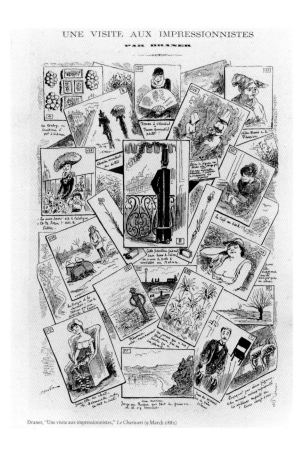

UNE VISITE AUX IMPRESSIONNISTES

Draner, "Une visite aux impressionnistes," *Le Charivari* (9 March 1882)

Some of the paintings shown at the fourth Impressionist exhibition ■ (p.115), caricatured by Draner in the magazine *Le Charivari* (March 9th, 1882).

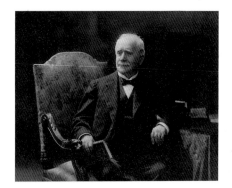

A photograph of the influential art dealer Paul Durand-Ruel (1910).

Art Dealers
The promotional machinery that dealers and artists could now command was extremely sophisticated, and had clearly benefited from the marketing and public relations methods developed by commerce and industry. In 1861 there were 104 firms of picture dealers in Paris (by 1958 the number had risen to 275), plus a number of smaller dealers, such as Père Tanguy ● (p.192), who sold works of art as a sideline. This increase was no doubt partly due to the fact that many of the dealers now offered their artists and clients a wide range of services, acting as bankers and promoters rather than mere stockists.

The most prominent of these new entrepreneurs was Paul Durand-Ruel, who played a vital role in promoting Impressionism. His father, Jean-Marie-Fortuné Durand-Ruel, had inherited a stationery shop, and he expanded into art dealing almost by accident, accepting his customer's works in exchange for brushes, pigments and materials, and <u>hiring them out for students and academies to copy</u>. When <u>Paul Durand-Ruel took over</u> the business after his father's death in <u>1865,</u> he adopted a more adventurous policy and started selling works by artists such as Delacroix, Corot, Daubigny and Courbet, and other painters of the Realist and Barbizon schools. On the outbreak of the Franco-Prussian War he moved to London – at the same time establishing an agency in Brussels ◆ (pp.214–5) – and opened a gallery in New Bond Street. Introduced by Daubigny to Monet ▲ (pp.182–3) and Pissarro, he exhibited their work in London; and on his return to Paris they introduced him to their colleagues and friends.

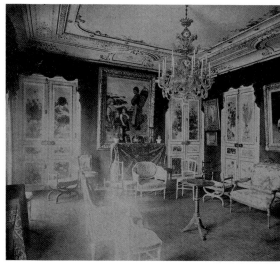

A contemporary photograph of the richly-furnished salon in Durand-Ruel's home at 33 rue de Rome.

Durand-Ruel's energy was boundless, and virtually the rest of his professional career was dedicated to making a success of the new movement. He sent the Impressionists' works to exhibitions all over France; he sent them to Belgium, Britain, Germany, Holland, Italy and Norway; and above all he sent them to the United States ▲ (p.153), where he opened a branch in New York and was the first European dealer to exploit the potential of the market ▲ (p.167). <u>Durand-Ruel's approach</u> was to establish a virtual <u>monopoly</u> over the work of certain artists by building up a stock of their pictures, bidding up their prices at auctions and promoting them by every publicity device then known. He produced a lavishly illustrated catalogue of his stock ▲ (p.80), published publicity magazines such as the *Revue Internationale de l'art et de la curiosité* (left), and maintained contact with a wide range of potential clients.

Nevertheless, Durand-Ruel received only a modicum of gratitude from his artists, who kept on temporarily abandoning him for other dealers and frequently attempted to avoid paying him commission by selling their work direct. The sort of problems he encountered are strikingly illustrated by the machinations over the collection of the Abbé Gaugain. Son of an illiterate labourer, Gaugain had risen to become headmaster of a private school in Paris. He developed a passion for Impressionism and became a regular client of Durand-Ruel. In 1901 Gaugain put his pictures up for sale – including works bought directly from Pissarro and Renoir. Durand-Ruel sent the catalogue to Renoir, pointing out that it included works which hadn't passed through his hands. Shamefacedly, Renoir confessed: 'I was weak enough to be unfaithful to you on several occasions, and dealt directly with the Abbé…but I have had enough of collectors, and I will not let myself be persuaded again.' Durand-Ruel bought Gaugain's entire collection for 101,000 francs; and both Renoir and Pissarro persisted in their devious habits.

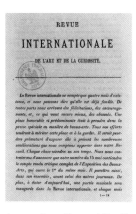

A page from Durand-Ruel's publicity magazine the *Revue Internationale de l'art et de la curiosité* (1869).

The New Paris

By the end of the nineteenth century, although few people would have foreseen the prestige Impressionism was to confer on French art, Paris was universally recognized as the art capital of the world. Moreover, during the course of the century the city had been transformed into a spaciously laid out modern metropolis, with 50 kilometres (30 miles) of new boulevards and a splendid variety of cafés ◆ (pp.46–7), restaurants and concert halls, catering for every class of customer. Grandiose public buildings seemed to be springing up everywhere – including the great

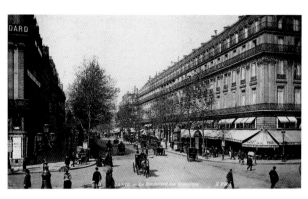

The boulevard des Capucines, photographed by Roger-Viollet (1900), which was one of the new thoroughfares of Baron Haussmann's Paris.

railway termini such as the Gare de Lyon and the Gare St-Lazare, which was the subject of a series of paintings by Monet, and the massive cupolas of the Sacré-Cœur, which gradually rose above the Batignolles Quarter and Montmartre – the area where Renoir and many other painters lived or had studios. Another feature of the new Paris was the opening of popular department stores, such as Bon Marché, where the women of the lower classes that appear in so many Impressionist paintings were able to buy cheap but attractive clothes. Even more noticeable were the architectural legacies of the Universal Exhibitions that took place in 1855, 1867, 1878, 1889 and 1900: huge halls such as the Palais de l'Industrie and the Grand and Petit Palais, and that icon of Paris – the Eiffel Tower.

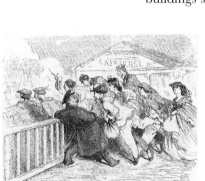

A cartoon by Gustave Doré (1861) showing excursionists arriving at Asnières. The village was one of a number of new Parisian resorts made accessible by the railway.

The Universal Exhibitions

Besides contributing to the prosperity of Parisian life, these vast exhibitions helped to spread the fame of French art abroad – something Courbet and Manet were clearly aware of when they staged their own one-man shows just outside the Universal Exhibition of 1867 (*see* pp.42–3) – but it was only in 1900 that the Impressionists were invited to exhibit within the Fine Arts section of an official show.

All the Universal Exhibitions included large sections devoted to the French colonies, which exposed the French public in general and artists in particular to the appeal of non-European cultures – encouraging Renoir, for instance, to pursue a fascination with pictorial motifs from North Africa that was originally derived from Delacroix. The Universal Exhibition of 1889 was especially rich in artefacts from Polynesia and the Far East, with whole areas laid out to display the largely unknown cultures of Polynesia, Java and Cambodia;

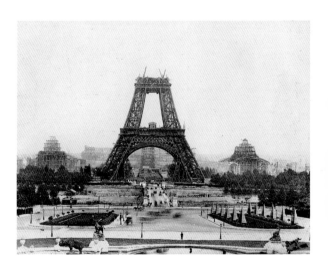

A photograph of the Eiffel Tower under construction (1888). The monument was built in a year, and was the highlight of the Universal Exhibition (*see* pp.168–9).

and, in addition to the evident effect these revelations had on Gauguin, they helped to stimulate a reaction against Impressionism among those who yearned for more emotive forms of art ◆ (p.243).

'Les Japonais'

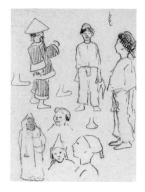

The riches of Oriental life and art, as displayed at the Universal Exhibition of 1889, had a profound effect on many French artists, including Gauguin, who produced these *Studies of Figures in Costume* during a visit to the exhibition.

But exotic artefacts had begun to appear in Paris much earlier. Monet claimed that he bought his first Japanese prints from ships in Le Havre in 1856; and by the 1860s Baudelaire, Whistler, Bracquemond, Zola and Manet were patronizing shops such as La Porte Chinoise and L'Empire Chinoise, which were selling oriental bric-à-brac, including contemporary prints. At the Universal Exhibition of 1867 the vogue for things Oriental was given added impetus by the participation of Japan, which had been opened up to international commerce thirteen years earlier by the American warships of Commodore Perry. The impact of the prints of Hokusai and Hiroshige on Manet was immediately apparent – both in his graphic work and in paintings such as *Olympia* (p.36), which possessed geisha-like undertones. In fact, the influence of Japanese art ▲ (p.80) soon permeated the whole movement to such an extent that, before they were known as the Impressionists, the group of painters working in the Batignolles area and acknowledging the leadership of Manet were sometimes referred to as 'les Japonais'.

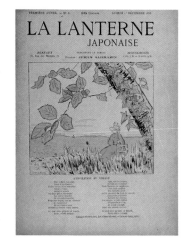
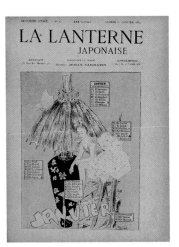

La Lanterne Japonaise was a periodical produced by the Divan Japonais – a café in Montmartre, where the waitresses dressed in kimonos and the walls were hung with silks and fans.

Official Patronage

The Impressionists lived in a city remarkable for the wealth and access-ibility of its art, and this was constantly being added to. In 1879, for example, the creation of the Musée des Monuments Français gathered together in one place the treasures of medieval France, and in 1890 the house of the Duchesse de Galliera was converted into the Musée des Arts Décoratifs.

Nor was contemporary art neglected. When in 1818 the famous series of paintings of Marie de Médicis by Rubens in the Luxembourg Palace was moved to the Louvre, it was decided that the Luxembourg should be devoted to contemporary French paintings acquired by the Government, mostly from the annual Salon – then if they became famous enough, they would be transferred from the Luxembourg to the Louvre five years after the artist's death. This honour was highly regarded by some – though others, such as Degas, were contemptuous of it, and it could provoke controversy. When part of the Caillebotte bequest ◆ (pp.197–8) was finally accepted by the State, a great deal of hostility was aroused among the more conservative elements of the art world, who viewed official recognition of the Impressionists as the final surrender to artistic anarchy. There was a similar scandal when in 1907, thanks to Monet exerting pressure on Clemenceau, Manet's *Olympia* ▲ (p.179) was transferred from the Luxembourg to the Louvre, where it was hung next to Ingres' *Grande Odalisque*.

The first work in any way connected with Impressionism to be acquired by the State was Eva Gonzalès' *The Little Soldier*, painted in 1870, which was purchased at the Salon of that year largely because her father had friends in high places. But the fact that a painting was bought by the State did not necessarily mean it would be hung in the Luxembourg – and after its official acquisition *The Little Soldier* was almost immediately consigned to the *mairie* of Villeneuve-sur-Lot, where it languished in a cellar until it was rescued from obscurity in 1960.

Official patronage was often wasted on mediocre academic paintings and until well into the twentieth century the Impressionists received precious little of it, though it did exist on a generous enough scale. In 1885 it was estimated that the value of the works of art owned by the Municipality of Paris was more than 12,000,000 francs, while those belonging to churches and other institutions were worth a further 8,000,000 francs.

Apprenticeship for Art

The glory of Paris was of course the <u>Louvre,</u> and echoes of its masterpieces reverberate throughout the works of the Impressionists, who found it a marvellous source of learning and inspiration. As Renoir observed, 'It is in the museum that one must learn to paint. One must make the paintings of one's own time, but it is there in the museum that one develops the taste for painting, which nature alone cannot provide.' Permission to copy works in the museum's galleries was relatively easy to obtain. Applicants had to have a card signed by some reliable person, preferably connected with the art establishment. Manet – who was to be one of the most assiduous frequenters of the Louvre, copying works by Delacroix, Titian, Tintoretto and Velázquez – was sponsored by his teacher, the academician Thomas Couture. Renoir's first card, issued in January 1860, was signed by Abel Terral, a picture restorer in the Musée de Versailles; and the following year he received permission to work in the Print Department of the Bibliothèque Impériale on the strength of a recommendation from his teacher, Charles Gleyre (*see* opposite). Degas had received permission to copy works in the Louvre seven years earlier, on the grounds that he was a pupil at the Lycée Louis le Grand and had taken the degree of Bachelor of Letters. He was to continue working in the museum for the next thirty years, copying works by painters such as Delacroix, Giorgione, Holbein, Mantegna, Poussin and Sebastiano del Piombo.

There were many ways of becoming an artist in Paris, but all of them involved working in the Louvre, usually under the tuition of an

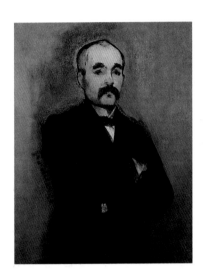

MANET
Portrait of Georges Clemenceau
1879–80

This is the second of two portraits Manet painted of Clemenceau during this period. He took great pains over this version, asking the politician to sit forty times and probably also referring to a photograph. Although it was shown at the Louvre, Clemenceau did not like the portrait and generally preferred Monet's work.

established artist to whose *atelier*, or studio, one became in effect apprenticed – a relationship basically not very different from the master-apprentice relationship that had operated since the Middle Ages. The stages preliminary to this could be various, as is amply illustrated by the diversity of Renoir's early career. After attending a Christian Brothers' school, where he was taught the rudiments of drawing, at the age of 13 he was apprenticed to a firm of porcelain painters, Lévy Frères et Compagnie, whose workshops were near the Louvre. At the same time, he took drawing lessons from the sculptor Callouette, who was Director of the École Gratuite de Dessin in the 3rd arrondissement. After serving his apprenticeship as a porcelain painter, he worked for a M. Gilbert, who described himself as a manufacturer of 'blinds of all sorts', including 'monumental and artistic blinds', blinds for steamboats, and 'perfect imitation stained glass' for churches. Then in 1860 he enrolled as a student of Charles Gleyre.

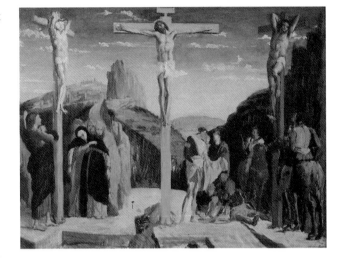

DEGAS
The Crucifixion,
after Mantegna
1861

During his formative years Degas copied extensively works from a large range of artistic periods, but always returned to the Italian artists of the early Renaissance. In this he was following his father's belief that 'the masters of the fifteenth century are the only true guides'.

The Atelier System

Gleyre's studio was one of many run by well-known painters, and in the course of his teaching career, which began when he took over the studio of Paul Delaroche in 1843, he taught some six hundred pupils, including Bazille, Monet, Renoir, Sisley and Whistler. Considered something of an eccentric, he emphasized the importance of originality. Indeed Bazille commented that, thanks to Gleyre's teaching, 'I shall at least be able to boast that I have not copied anybody.'

Students drew and painted from life (usually a male model one week, female the next), and the model would be posed by the leading student, known as the *massier*, who was responsible for the finances and management of the studio too. In addition, the students had to copy drawings, engravings and paintings by Old Masters, either directly in the Louvre or from reproductions. There were normally about thirty students in Gleyre's studio, but the fees were very low (only 10 francs a month), which may explain why in 1864 Gleyre found himself in serious financial difficulties and had to close the studio.

Art Schools

For those who did not want even the light degree of supervision exercised in a studio such as Gleyre's, there was the Académie Suisse – founded by a retired model of David's (presumably a Swiss) – which had no teaching but provided accommodation and a life model. This was attended by Cézanne, Guillaumin, Guillemet, Ludovic Piette, Pissarro and, for a short time, Monet.

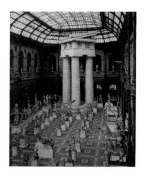

A contemporary photograph of the glazed sculpture court of the École des Beaux-Arts.

No other city in the world had as many art schools as Paris (in 1872 there were already twenty for women), and the city was awash with foreigners – mainly American, British and Dutch – pursuing some kind of artistic curriculum. This was largely due to the fact that since the reign of Louis XIV there had existed an elaborate State system for the control and encouragement of art. So far as artistic education was concerned, in nineteenth-century France the most prominent feature of this system was the École des Beaux-Arts (*see* p.26), originally founded in 1648. Theoretically, entrance to the École des Beaux-Arts was open to anyone of French birth aged between 15 and 30. But in reality nomination by a patron was necessary, and this was followed by an entrance examination. When Degas sat the examination in March 1855, he came thirty-third out of eighty; Renoir, who sat it in 1862, fared less well, coming sixty-eighth out of eighty.

The Monopoly of the Salon

The crown of the official system was the Salon – originally the annual exhibition of the Académie Royale de Peinture et Sculpture, which was held in the Salon Carré of the Louvre. But in 1791 it was thrown open to all artists (at the same time the awarding of medals was initiated) and soon, because of the increase in the number of exhibits, a selection procedure had to be introduced. In 1848 the official jury system was replaced by a committee chosen by the exhibiting artists; but as this resulted in more than 5000 paintings being hung, the experiment was immediately discontinued. Various reforms, intended to liberalize the selection procedure, followed: for example, in 1852 Napoleon III decreed that half the seats on the jury should be given to artists. Nevertheless, the jury system continued to cause a great deal of resentment, culminating in the flood of complaints that led to the Salons des Refusés of 1863 (*see* pp.24–5).

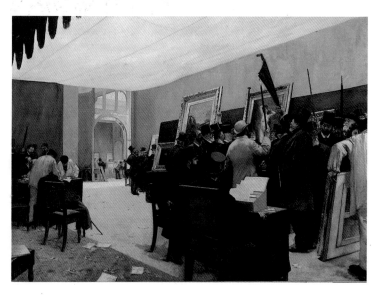

GERVEX
The Jury for Painting,
Salon des Artistes Français
1865

Henri Gervex became well known for his portrayals of Parisian life, typified by this painting of a Salon jury making their selection.

The Salon, which usually opened during the first week of May, was the most important event in the French art calendar, and from 1856 it was held in the splendid Palais de l'Industrie (p.25). It was also the supreme selling place, where artists' reputations could be made and the prices obtainable for their pictures determined. The careers of Manet, Renoir and Monet were considerably advanced by the success of works exhibited at the Salon, and before the formation of the Société Anoyme des Artistes (*see* p.79) all the Impressionists had endeavoured to get work hung there. As Renoir explained in a letter to Durand-Ruel in March 1881, 'There are scarcely fifteen collectors capable of liking a painting without the backing of the Salon. And there are another 80,000 who won't buy so much as a postcard unless the painter exhibits there. That's why every year I send in two portraits, however small. The entry is entirely of a commercial nature. Anyway, it's like some medicine – if it does you no good, it will do you no harm.'

Attendance figures were remarkable. The Ministry of Fine Arts estimated that in 1863 on Sundays, when admission was free, 30,000 to 40,000 people visited the Salon; and in 1876 the total number of visitors amounted to 518,892. No less significant was the coverage the Salon attracted in the press. The exhibition of 1863 was the subject of twelve articles by Ernest Chesnau in *Le Constitutionnel* and thirteen by Théophile Gautier in *Le Moniteur universel*; articles or drawings relating to it by Louis Leroy featured in eighteen issues of *Le Charivari*; and a total of 137 items appeared in other periodicals and newspapers, including the *Fine Arts Quarterly Review* and *The Times* in London.

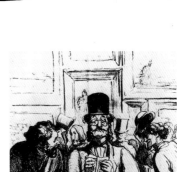

A caricature by Daumier entitled *The Critic*, which appeared in *Le Charivari* (June 24th, 1865).

The monopoly exercised by the Salon was one of the main factors that impelled the Impressionists to band together. What they objected to about official art was not so much its style as its machinery: the fact that in the Paris of the 1860s the Salon offered the only outlet for little-known artists, and there were virtually no opportunities for them to exhibit their work in public without having to submit it to a jury. A vital tenet of the Impressionists' creed was that the artists who subscribed to their exhibitions should be free to show whatever they wanted to – and that, as a token of their independence, they would refrain from submitting work to the Salon. Nevertheless, this precept was honoured more often in the breach than in the observance – and even Monet, to whom it had been an article of faith, changed his mind in 1880, thereby earning the contempt of Degas and his followers ◆ (p.47). That the dominant role of the Salon should have at first united the Impressionists and then been a cause of disunity ▲ (p.127) is an example of the pressures that provoked them to rebel against the conventions of the Parisian art world of their time.

Myth and Reality

Personally unrebellious, shirking those eccentricities of appearance and attitude that the myth of Bohemia has imposed on the concept of the artist, the Impressionists were not strikingly different from their fellow citizens. Sometimes they were devious, especially towards Durand-Ruel and their patrons; sometimes disloyal to each other; sometimes parsimonious, but more often generous. They were all passionately devoted to their art, though usually less so to their wives or mistresses; and whilst they had periods of creative elation, they were also prey to depression.

They did not see themselves through the eyes of posterity, and to understand them as people as well as artists it is necessary to reconstruct as far as possible the triumphs and tribulations of their daily lives as well as the history of their creative achievements.

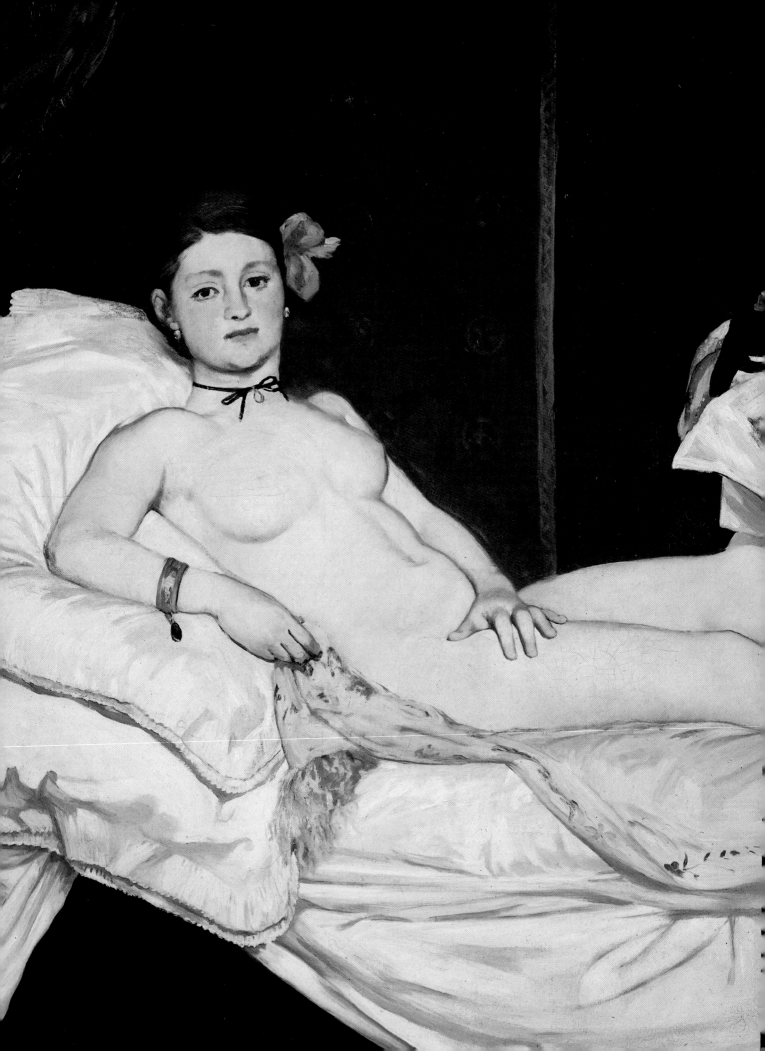

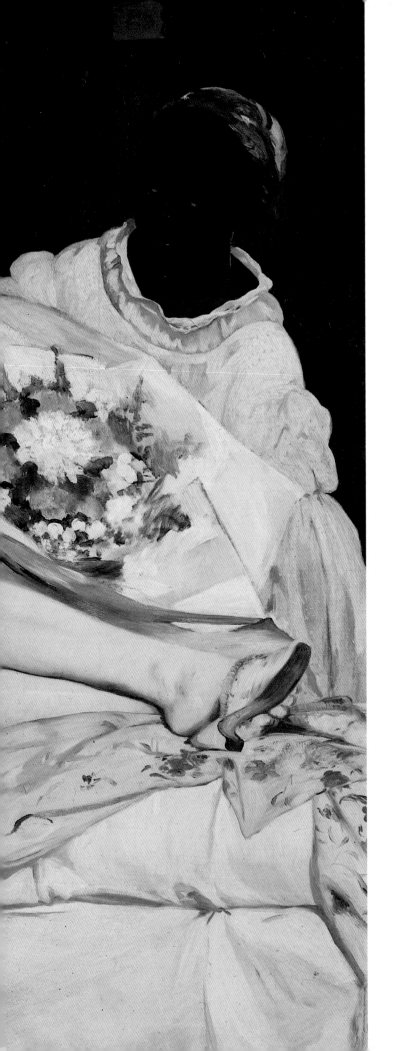

THE DAWN OF
A NEW STYLE
1863–1873

MANET **Olympia** (detail) 1863

1863

Art in Revolt

Furious at their rejection from the Salon, hundreds of French artists complain to the authorities. As a result, the Emperor orders an exhibition of rejected works, the Salon des Refusés. It is dominated by Manet's 'Déjeuner sur l'herbe', showing a naked woman picnicking in the open with two fully clothed men – to young artists a triumph of Realism, to conservatives a shameless piece of pornography.

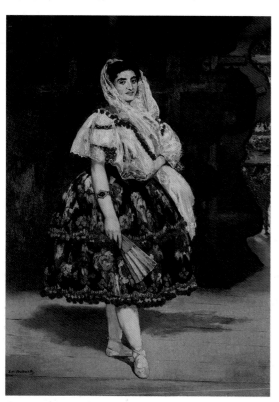

MANET
Lola de Valence
1862

Lola de Valence, star of Mariano Camprubi's ballet, which visited France in 1862–3, seemed to symbolize the spirit of Spain at a time when Spanish themes were in vogue. This was one of a series of paintings by Manet that included *The Spanish Singer*.

JANUARY

15th The Government promulgates new regulations for the Salon whereby no artist can submit more than three works. Those who have won first-class or second-class medals in previous Salons do not have to submit their entries to the jury.

FEBRUARY

20th Lucien ▲ (p.212), the eldest son of Pissarro and Julie Vellay (Pissarro's mother's maid), is born in Paris ◆ (pp.146–7).

MARCH

1st Manet has a one-man exhibition at Louis Martinet's gallery in the boulevard des Italiens. The fourteen works on show include *Lola de Valence* (left), *Music in the Tuileries Gardens* (opposite), *The Old Musician* and *Boy with a Sword*.
7th 'Lola de Valence', a song by Zacharie Astruc about the popular Spanish dancer, is published with a cover by Manet (above right).

APRIL

12th The Salon jury announces its decisions. Of approximately 5000 works submitted, 2217 are accepted. There are 983 exhibitors, a marked drop in numbers from 1289 the previous year. Among the artists rejected is Manet, who had submitted three works – including his recently painted *Déjeuner sur l'herbe* (p.27). Fantin-Latour, Legros, Renoir and Whistler all have work hung.
24th An Imperial decree is published in *Le Moniteur universel* stating that 'Numerous complaints have reached the Emperor on the subject of works of art which have been refused by the [Salon] jury... His Majesty, wishing to let the public know the legitimacy of these

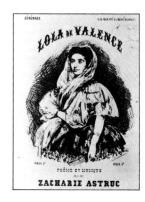

In March 1863 a serenade appeared entitled *Lola de Valence*, dedicated to the Queen of Spain, with words and music by Manet's friend Zacharie Astruc. On the cover of the song sheet was a lithograph of the dancer by Manet.

MANET
Music in the Tuileries Gardens
1862

The gardens of the Tuileries Palace (burned down during the Commune of 1871) were opened to the public by Napoleon III and soon became a popular meeting place. This lively portrait of Second Empire society (many of the figures are thought to have been based on photographs) is an example of Manet's concern with contemporary life. The artist himself can be seen standing in a dandyish pose on the extreme left; among the crowd are Baudelaire, Offenbach, Zacharie Astruc, Théophile Gautier and Fantin-Latour.

complaints, has decided that the rejected works are to be exhibited in another part of the Palais de l'Industrie. This exhibition will be voluntary, and artists who do not wish to participate will need only to inform the administration, which will hasten to return their works to them.'

MAY

1st Opening of the Salon. To avoid favouritism, the pictures are arranged in alphabetical order of the artists' names. Portraits and battle scenes predominate, with a generous scattering of nudes. Corot, Millet, Puvis de Chavannes and Théodore Rousseau are among the more progressive artists included in the exhibition.

17th The Salon des Refusés opens in a separate part of the Palais de l'Industrie from the main Salon. The catalogue lists only 781 exhibits, although there are actually many more. Among those exhibiting are Bracquemond, Cézanne, Manet and Pissarro. Whistler's *The White Girl* (p.26), rejected by the Royal Academy in London in 1862, is the success of the exhibition. Manet's *Déjeuner sur l'herbe* causes a sensation ▲ (p.27), establishing him as the leading dissident of the art world.

23rd Monet and Bazille paint *en plein air* in Chailly. Pissarro moves to Varenne-St-Hilaire.

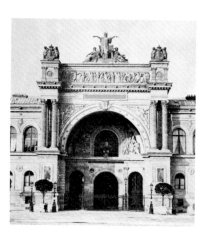

The ornate entrance to the Palais de l'Industrie in the Champs-Élysées, where the annual exhibition of the Salon was held. Completed in 1853, it was built as a permanent exhibition site.

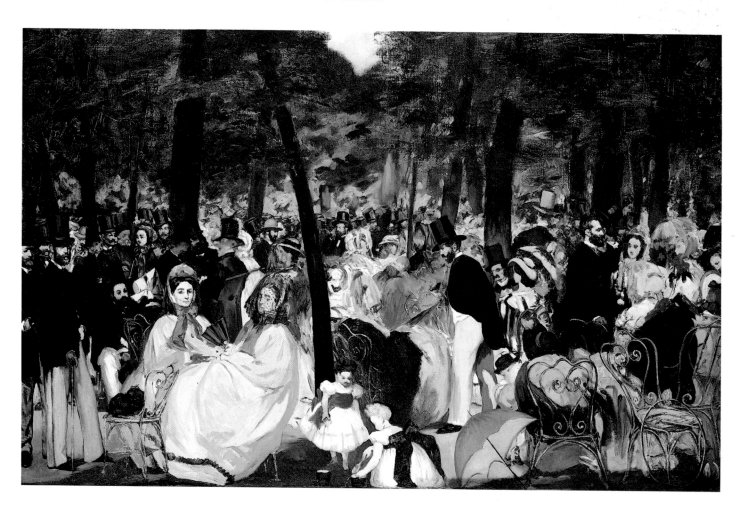

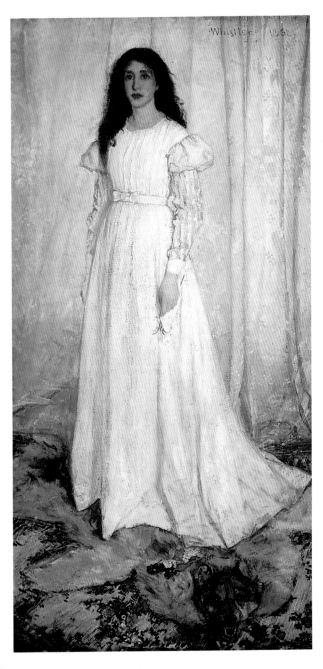

JUNE

23rd Degas visits his cousins the Mussons in Bourg-en-Bresse, where they have settled after leaving America because of the Civil War.
Berthe Morisot goes painting on the Oise with her sister Edma, who is learning to paint.

AUGUST

16th Renoir comes ninth out of twelve candidates in the composition examination at the École des Beaux-Arts.

OCTOBER

28th Manet marries the Dutch pianist Suzanne Leenhoff, with whom he has been having an affair since 1850. Despite their marriage, their son Léon, born in 1852, retains his mother's maiden name.

NOVEMBER

3rd Cézanne applies for permission to study at the Louvre.
13th An Imperial decree is issued making radical changes to the École des Beaux-Arts. Control of the school is to be taken away from the Académie des Beaux-Arts (part of the Institut de France) and vested in the government, which is to appoint the professors, lecturers and administrators. It also stipulates that students must be French nationals between the ages of 15 and 30, and foreigners can only be admitted on an exceptional basis.

WHISTLER
Symphony in White: No. I The White Girl
1862

When this portrait of Whistler's mistress Joanna Hifferman (known as Jo) was exhibited at the Salon des Refusés in 1863, it attracted a great deal of attention and was greeted with enthusiasm by the avant-garde.'

MANET
Déjeuner sur l'herbe
1863

The inspiration for this painting (originally entitled *Le Bain*) came from two sources: Marcantonio Raimondi's engraving (*c.*1500) of Raphael's *The Judgement of Paris* and Titian's *Le Concert Champêtre*, of which Manet owned a copy. The man looking out from the painting is based on one of Manet's brothers (or possibly both), while his companion is the sculptor Ferdinand Leenhoff, brother of Suzanne Leenhoff, whom Manet married in October. The nude sitting with them is Victorine Meurent – who also posed for *Olympia* (p.36).

OTHER EVENTS

- Abraham Lincoln makes his Gettysburg address
- Thiers forms party opposed to Napoleon III
- Prince William of Denmark becomes King of Greece
- French capture Mexico City and proclaim Archduke Maximilian of Austria Emperor
- Commercial treaty signed between France and Italy
- Crédit Lyonnais founded
- First underground railway opens in London
- First aerial photographs of Paris taken by Nadar
- Lenoir drives a motor car on a public highway for the first time (the 10km journey takes 3 hours)
- Publication of Renan's *Vie de Jésus*, which treats Jesus as a 'real' person
- Baudelaire writes a study of Constantin Guys, whose witty drawings and watercolours vividly record contemporary Parisian life

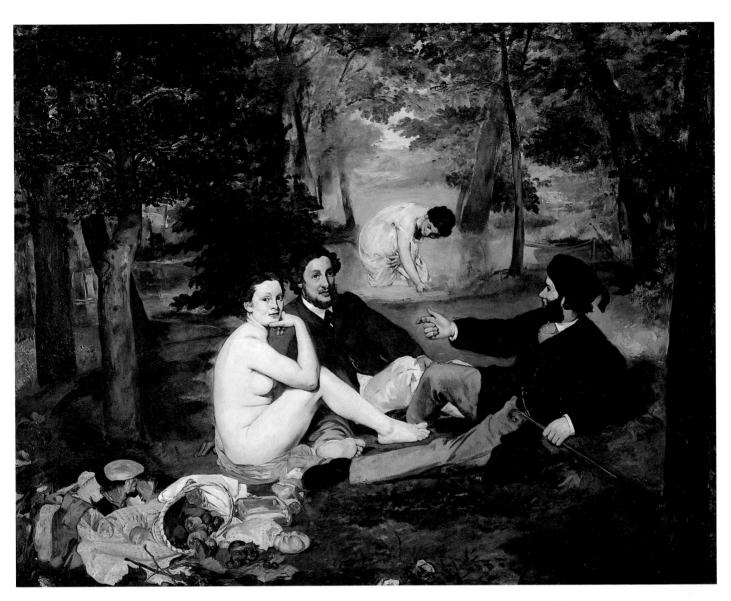

 CRITICAL REACTIONS TO MANET'S 'DÉJEUNER SUR L'HERBE'

I ought not to omit a remarkable picture of the Realist school, a translation of a thought of Giorgione into modern French. Yes, there they are, under the trees, the principal lady entirely undressed, sitting calmly in the well-known attitude of Giorgione's Venetian woman; another female in a chemise coming out of a little stream that runs hard by; and two Frenchmen in wide-awakes [broad-brimmed hats] *sitting on the very green grass with a stupid look of bliss.*

PHILIP HAMERTON, *Fine Arts Quarterly Review*, June 1863

Unfortunately the nude hasn't a good figure and one can't think of anything uglier than the man stretched out beside her, who hasn't even thought of taking off…his horrid padded cap. It is the contrast of a creature so inappropriate in a pastoral scene with this naked bather that is so shocking.

THÉOPHILE THORÉ, *Salons*, 1863

I see garments without feeling the anatomical structure that supports them and explains their movements. I see boneless fingers and heads without skulls. I see side-whiskers made of two strips of black cloth that could have been glued to the cheeks. What else do I see? The artist's lack of conviction and sincerity.

JULES CASTAGNARY, reprinted in *Salons*, 1892

A commonplace woman of the demi-monde, as naked as possible, shamelessly lolls between two overdressed fops, who look like schoolboys on a holiday doing something naughty to play at being grown-up. I search in vain for any meaning to this unbecoming riddle.

LOUIS ÉTIENNE, *Le Jury et les exposants*, 1863

1864

A More Tolerant Salon

FANTIN-LATOUR
Homage to Delacroix
1864

When Delacroix died, on August 13th, 1863, Fantin-Latour invited a number of writers and artists to pose for this group portrait as a memorial to him. They are, from left to right: (back row) Louis Cordier, Alphonse Legros, Whistler, Manet, Bracquemond and Albert de Balleroy; (front row) Duranty, Fantin-Latour, Champfleury and Baudelaire.

As a result of complaints about the Salon of 1863, the number of works rejected by the jury drops by 40 per cent. Manet, Morisot, Pissarro and Renoir exhibit; but Monet and Bazille make no submissions, though both are productive, working together in Honfleur.

JANUARY

1st Renoir begins his military training – incumbent on all French citizens unable to pay for a substitute.

7th Manet poses for Fantin-Latour's *Homage to Delacroix* (exhibited at the Salon in May).

FEBRUARY

4th Louis Martinet's gallery hosts the first exhibition of the Société Nationale des Beaux-Arts, an organization created by Martinet to boost the credibility of mixed exhibitions.

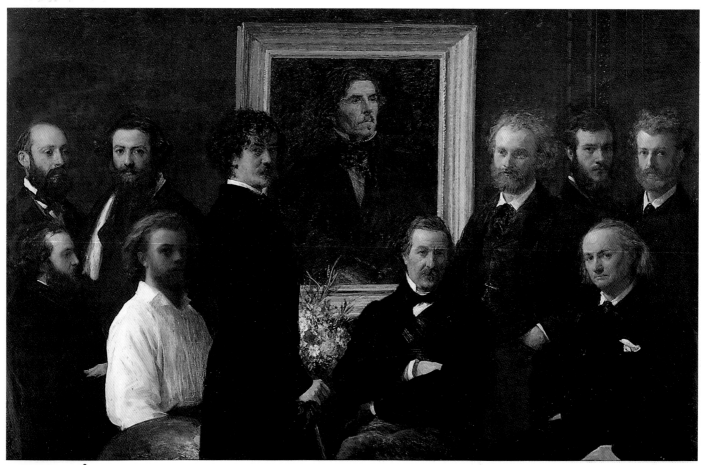

28

27th Manet asks for a ten-day extension for his submissions to the Salon.

MARCH

6th Degas visits Ingres' studio to see an exhibition of his drawings – which are described in the publicity as 'done in the style of the Old Masters'.

7th Renoir finishes his military training.

12th Bazille goes to Honfleur with Monet and visits the latter's parents at the nearby village of Ste-Adresse. Bazille finds them 'charming', and they invite him to spend August with them.

Pissarro paints on the banks of the Marne.

APRIL

5th Renoir, described as a pupil of Charles Gleyre, comes tenth out of 106 candidates in a sculpture and drawing examination at the École des Beaux-Arts.

7th Cézanne obtains permission to copy Poussin's *Shepherds in Arcadia* at the Louvre.

12th Bazille fails his medical exams and decides to become a full-time artist.

22nd René Degas, the painter's youngest brother, writes from Paris to his cousins in America: 'Edgar does an enormous amount of work without seeming to do so. He has not only talents, but genius. Will he ever express it?'

MAY

Charles Gleyre is overwhelmed by financial difficulties. Renoir, Monet, Bazille and Sisley leave his studio shortly before it closes.

3rd Opening of the Salon. This year the jury is much more tolerant, the proportion of rejections having dropped to 30 per cent from 70 per cent in 1863. Works exhibited include *Dead Christ and Angels* and *Episode from a Bullfight* by Manet; *Banks of the Marne* (p.30) and *The Road to Cachalas* by Pissarro, who describes himself as 'a pupil of Corot'; and *A Souvenir of the Banks of the Oise* and *Old Roads at Auvers* by Morisot. Renoir has only one work, *La Esmeralda*, accepted (which he subsequently destroys). Meissonier's *Napoleon III at the Battle of Solferino* is one of the big successes of the exhibition.

Study for a portrait of Manet by Degas (black chalk, *c*.1864). Each witty and sharp-tongued, Manet and Degas maintained a life-long love-hate relationship.

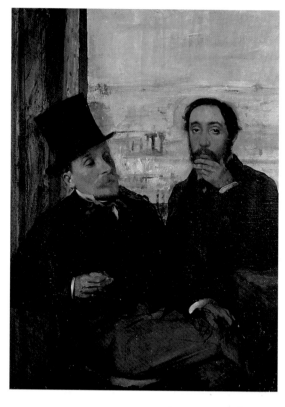

DEGAS
Portrait of the Artist with Évariste de Valernes
c.1864 (unfinished)

This double portrait shows Degas with his friend Évariste de Valernes, an unsuccessful painter of noble origin who subsisted mainly by copying famous paintings. Degas' last self-portrait, it was painted in his studio in the rue Laval. The poses are reminiscent of those used by popular photographers of the time, and X-rays have revealed that originally Degas, like de Valernes, was wearing a top hat.

**PISSARRO
Banks of the Marne**
1864

Exhibited at the Salon of 1864, this view of the banks of the Marne in winter shows the extent to which Pissarro, despite all his stylistic experiments, remained under the lingering influence of Corot, whom he still acknowledged as his master. The Ile de France had been Corot's favourite landscape subject, and Pissarro was preoccupied with the same efforts to depict the play of light on water.

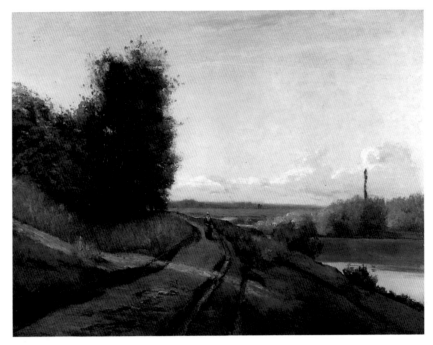

25th Manet departs for a holiday in Boulogne, where he sketches the Unionist corvette *Kearsage*, which is in port there.

JUNE
2nd Bazille, Monet, Renoir and Sisley paint in the forest of Fontainebleau. Renoir meets Diaz de la Peña, whose influence encourages him to lighten his palette.
19th Manet paints the encounter off the French coast between the *Kearsage* and the Confederate warship *Alabama*.
20th Pissarro visits his friend the landscape painter Ludovic Piette at La Roche-Guyon.
27th Manet exhibits *The Battle of the 'Kearsage' and the 'Alabama'* (opposite) at Cadart's gallery in the rue de Richelieu.

JULY
9th Monet departs for Honfleur.
13th Monet writes to Bazille urging him to come to Honfleur ▲ (p.33).

SEPTEMBER
Monet is joined by Bazille. The two artists work together, painting coast scenes in the Honfleur and Le Havre area. They also paint still lifes of flowers.
The Morisots move to 40 rue Villejust (now rue Paul-Valéry), where M. Morisot builds a studio for his daughters in the garden.

NOVEMBER
5th Manet moves into an apartment at 34 boulevard des Batignolles, near his favourite café, the Café de Bade.

DECEMBER
Jules and Edmond de Goncourt visit Manet's studio in search of material for the character of Coriolis in their novel *Manette Salomon*.

MANET
The Battle of the 'Kearsage' and the 'Alabama '
1864

On June 19th, 1864, a corvette of the United States Navy, the *Kearsage*, attacked and sank a confederate raider, the *Alabama*, off Cherbourg. Manet did not witness the encounter, but he had sketched and painted the *Kearsage* while it was in port at Boulogne.

Anxious to produce a painting that would appeal to the Salon jury, he used his own sketches from Boulogne together with newspaper photographs and drawings in order to create what one contemporary critic termed 'a picture of war and aggression'.

Eventually exhibited at the Salon of 1872, it was sold by Durand-Ruel to the American collector John G. Johnson in 1888 for $1500.

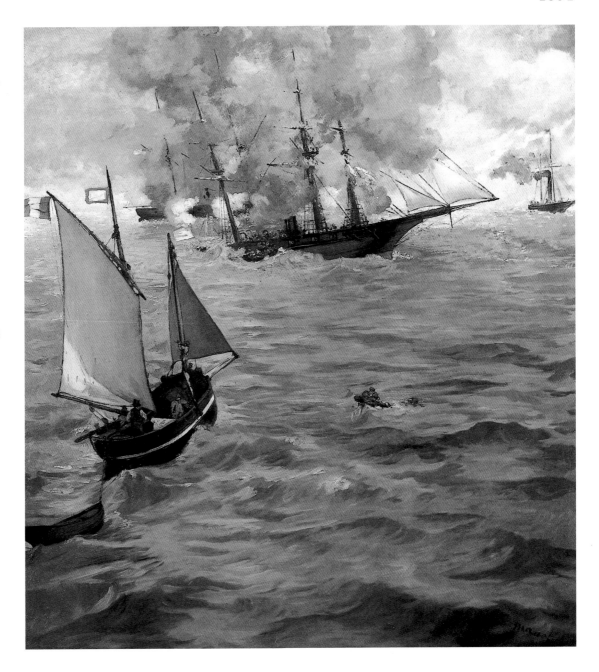

OTHER EVENTS

- Abraham Lincoln re-elected President of USA
- Archduke Maximilian of Austria is crowned Emperor of Mexico
- Austria and Prussia invade Denmark, which cedes Lauenburg and Schleswig-Holstein
- British, French and American ships attack Japan
- Red Cross founded in Geneva
- Karl Marx forms the International Working Men's Association
- Trade unions legalized in France
- Regular steamship service established between Le Havre and New York
- The Lenoir engineering company in Paris receives its first order for a motor car, from Tsar Alexander II
- Tolstoy begins *War and Peace*
- Publication of the Goncourts' *Renée Mauperin* and Dickens' *Our Mutual Friend*
- First performance of Offenbach's *La Belle Hélène*

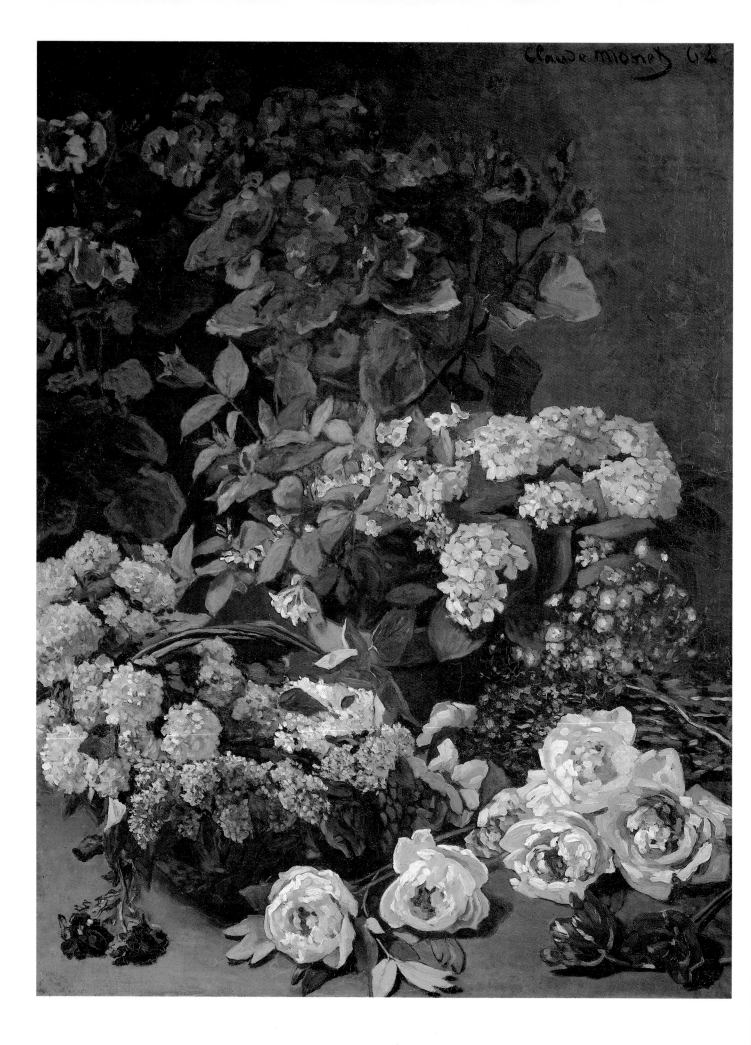

▲ MONET'S LETTERS FROM HONFLEUR

There is something rather moving about the camaraderie of the young artists, later to be known as the Impressionists, who had studied under Charles Gleyre – and it was especially strong between Monet and Bazille. Monet's letters from Honfleur to his friend in Paris give an indication of the spirit that existed between them:

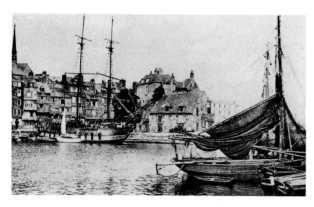

Photograph of the harbour at Honfleur in the 1860s – the time when Monet most frequently painted there.

MONET
Spring Flowers
c.1864

In his letter of August 26th to Bazille, Monet enthused about the flowers in the Honfleur area. The influence of Boudin and Jongkind, who worked with him for a while in 1864, is evident in the rich impasto of this painting.

July 13th

What on earth can you be doing in Paris in such marvellous weather, for I suppose it must be just as fine down there? It's simply fantastic here, my friend, and each day I find something even more beautiful than the day before. It's enough to drive one crazy. Damn it man, come on the sixteenth. Get packing and come here for a fortnight. You'd be far better off; it can't be all that easy to work in Paris.

Today I have exactly a month left to work in Honfleur, and what is more my studies are almost done; I've even got some others back on the go. On the whole, I'm quite content with my stay here, although my sketches are far from being what I would like. It really is appallingly difficult to do something which is complete in every respect, and I think most people are content with just approximations.

Well, my dear friend, I intend to battle on, scrape off and start again, since one can do something if one can see and understand it, and when I look at nature, I feel as if I'll be able to paint it all, note it all down – and then you can forget it once you're working.

All this proves you must think of nothing else. It's on the strength of observation and reflection that one finds a way. So we must dig and delve unceasingly.

August 26th

I had just spent a day at Ste-Adresse when your letter arrived. It gave me great pleasure, please write nice long ones like that more often. I hope you're working hard, it is important that you devote yourself to it wholeheartedly and seriously now that your family is reconciled to your giving up medicine. I'm still at St-Siméon; it's such a pleasant place and I'm working hard, although what I'm doing is far from being what I should like. We are now quite a crowd here in Honfleur, several painters I did not know – and very bad ones at that – but we form a very pleasant little group of our own. Jongkind and Boudin are here, and we get on extremely well and stick together. Ribot is coming too; he's planning to paint a fishing boat with figures 'en plein air'. I'd be interested to see him do it. I'm sorry you're not here, since there's a good deal to be learnt from such company, and the landscape is growing more beautiful. It's turning yellow and becoming more varied, really lovely in fact, and I think I'm going to be in Honfleur for some time yet.

I must tell you that I'm sending my flower picture to the Rouen exhibition, there are some really lovely flowers about at this time. Why don't you do some yourself, since they're an excellent thing to paint?

The popularity of Monet's *The Lighthouse of Honfleur* (hung at the Salon of 1865) is indicated by the fact that this wood engraving of it appeared in the illustrated annual *L'autographe au Salon*.

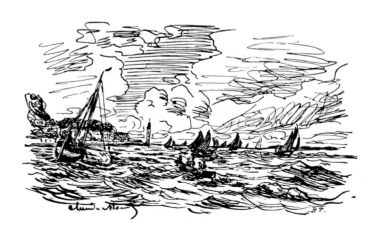

1865

'Olympia' – a Sensation

Manet – the 'father' of Impressionism – causes a sensation with a painting accepted by the the Salon. As with 'Déjeuner sur l'herbe' of 1863, the subject (a recumbent Venus) is inspired by a classical precedent, but it has been reinterpreted in a contemporary manner. Manet's enthusiastic champion, Émile Zola, is one of the few critics to raise his voice in defence of this thoroughly modern nude.

JANUARY
Manet, in a fit of despondency, destroys several of his sketches.

15th Degas goes to stay with his mother's relatives in Bourg-en-Bresse.

21st Bazille invites Monet, who is hard up, to share a studio at 6 rue de Furstenberg, facing the church of St-Germain-des-Prés.

FEBRUARY
3rd Manet submits nine paintings to the dealer Louis Martinet's Société des Beaux-Arts, but only two are accepted.

MARCH
Pissarro takes a job as a bank messenger because he is in such desperate financial straits.

Monet meets and starts living with a nineteen-year-old girl from Lyons named Camille Doncieux.

APRIL
Monet invites Bazille to join him at an inn in Chailly, near Barbizon, so they can paint together. Shortly after his friend's arrival, Monet injures his leg and is confined to bed.

Cézanne meets Pissarro while studying at the Académie Suisse, an art school where there is no formal teaching.

1st The Royal Academy in London rejects two paintings that have been submitted by Manet.

MAY
7th Opening of the Salon. The exhibition includes *Jesus Mocked by the Soldiers* and *Olympia* ▲ (p.36) by Manet; *War Scene from the Middle Ages* by Degas; *Summer Evening* and a portrait of Sisley's father by Renoir; three landscapes by Pissarro; and two works by Morisot. Also included are two of Monet's landscapes, *The Lighthouse at Honfleur* and

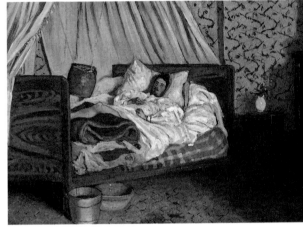

**BAZILLE
Monet in Bed after his Accident**
1866

The intimacy of this portrait of Monet – recovering in bed from the accident to his leg which he suffered shortly after his arrival at the inn in Chailly – gives an idea of Bazille's affection for his friend.

A life-drawing by Cézanne from the period when he was an art student at the Académie Suisse.

The Headland of La Hève at Low Tide, which receive a favourable mention in the *Gazette des Beaux-Arts* and elsewhere – to the fury of Manet, who finds his name has been confused with Monet's by some of the critics.
18th Pissarro's first daughter, Jeanne-Rachel, is born.

JUNE

1st Manet exhibits three still lifes – *Peonies in a Vase*, *Fruit on a Table* and *Still Life with Fish* – at Cadart's gallery in the rue Richelieu.
15th The dealer Jean Durand-Ruel dies, and his son, Paul, takes over the management of the business in the rue de la Paix (*see* pp.14–15). Renoir meets Lise Tréhot, who becomes his model and mistress ◆ (p.50).

AUGUST

Degas copies Whistler's *The White Girl* (p.26) from a drawing sent by Whistler to Fantin-Latour.
5th Manet sets off on a tour of Spain, planned by Zacharie Astruc.

SEPTEMBER

Gauguin enters the Merchant Marine as an apprentice pilot and makes his first trip on the *Luzitano*, from Le Havre to Rio de Janeiro.
14th Baudelaire, now living in Brussels to escape creditors, offers his portrait by Courbet to Manet, who is looking after the poet's interests in Paris. Manet declines and suggests other potential buyers.

OCTOBER

26th Degas copies a Sebastiano del Piombo drawing in the Louvre.
28th Manet has a slight attack of cholera.

MONET
Study for Déjeuner sur l'herbe
1865

In 1865 Monet decided to paint a large picture on the theme Manet had tackled in his *Déjeuner sur l'herbe* (p.27). The location he chose for it was a wood near Marlotte – where he was painting with Bazille, who served as a model for at least two of the male figures. It was Monet's most ambitious *plein air* project to date, but only two fragments of the finished painting have survived, together with this preparatory study.

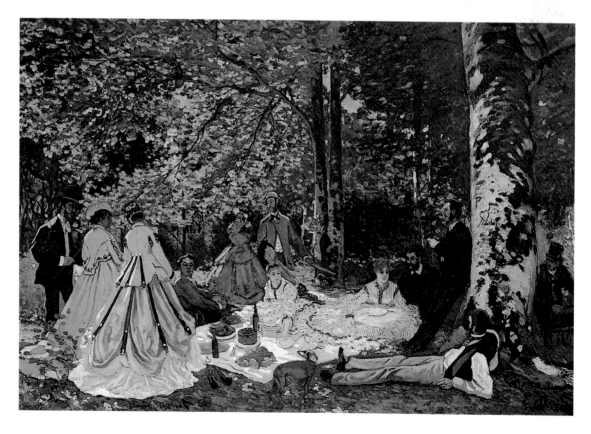

1865

OTHER EVENTS

- Abraham Lincoln assassinated
- End of American Civil War
- Slavery abolished in America
- Japan resumes trade with West
- Paris hosts first international telephone congress
- Gregor Mendel proposes his laws of heredity
- Publication of Jules Verne's *De la terre à la lune*, Lewis Carroll's *Alice's Adventures in Wonderland* and the Goncourts' *Germinie Lacerteux*
- Wagner completes *Tristan and Isolde*

CRITICAL REACTIONS TO MANET'S 'OLYMPIA'

The sensation provoked by *Olympia* at the Salon of 1865 was even greater than that which had greeted *Déjeuner sur l'herbe* ▲ (p.27) – few critics showing the perspicacity of Zola, who in 1867 published the following apostrophe to Manet:

For you a picture is but an opportunity for analysis. You wanted a nude, and you took Olympia, the first to come along; you wanted bright, luminous patches, and the bouquet provided them; you wanted black patches, and you added a black woman and a black cat. What does all this mean? You hardly know, nor do I. But I know that you succeeded admirably in creating a work of painting, of great painting, and in translating into a special language the verities of light and shade, the realities of persons and things.

ÉMILE ZOLA, *L'Artiste*, January 1st, 1867

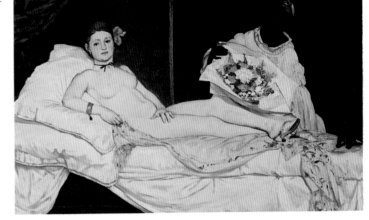

MANET
Olympia
1863

More common were sentiments such as the following:

What's this yellow-bellied odalisque, this vile model picked up goodness knows where and representing Olympia?

JULES CLARETIE, *L'Artiste*, May, 1865

The crowd, as at the morgue, throngs in front of the gamy 'Olympia' and the horrible 'Ecce Homo' of M. Manet.

PAUL DE SAINT-VICTOR, *La Presse*, May 28th, 1865

Criticism of Manet's *Olympia* was directed as much against the 'ugliness' of the model as against its stylistic novelty. It is easy to understand the shock provoked by this painting when it is compared with the pictures by academic painters that were habitually hung in the Salon, with their anonymous faces, contrived poses and total insulation from contemporary reality. (Detail on pp.22–3)

'Olympia' can be understood from no point of view, even if you take it for what it is, a puny model stretched out on a sheet. The colour of the flesh is dirty, the modelling non-existent. The shadows are indicated by comparatively large smears of blacking. What's to be said for the negress, who brings a bunch of flowers wrapped in some paper, or for the black cat that leaves its dirty pawmarks on the bed? We would still forgive the ugliness were it truthful, carefully studied, heightened by some effect of colour. The least beautiful woman has bones, muscles, skin, heightened by some sort of colour. Here is nothing, we are sorry to say, but the desire to attract attention at any price.

THÉOPHILE GAUTIER, *Le Moniteur universel*, June 24th, 1865

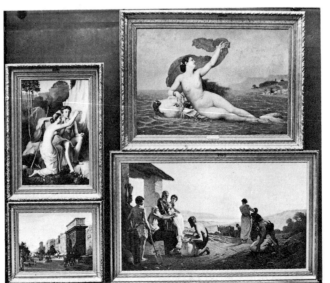

Works by academic painters purchased by the State at the Salon of 1865.

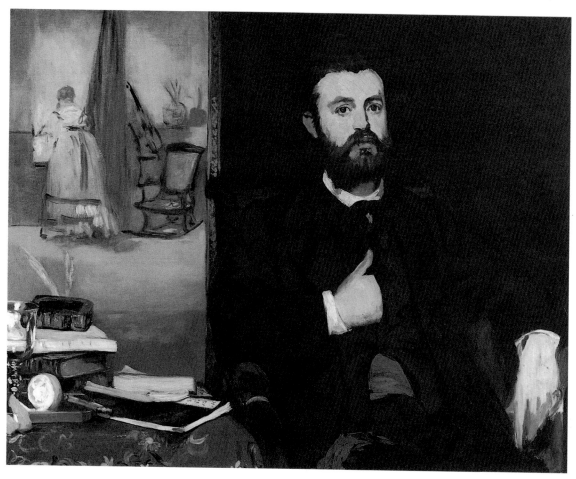

MANET Zacharie Astruc 1866

ZACHARIE ASTRUC
Writer and painter

Zacharie Astruc (1833–1907) was the writer, critic, painter and sculptor whose verses were reproduced in the Salon catalogue entry for Manet's *Olympia* (opposite). They give some indication of his meagre poetic gifts:

Quand, lasse de songer, Olympia s'éveille,
Le printemps entre au bras du doux messager noir,
C'est l'esclave à la nuit amoureuse pareille,
Qui veut fêter le jour, délicieux à voir,
L'auguste jeune fille en qui la flamme veille.

When, tired of dreams, Olympia wakes up,
Spring enters on the gentle black messenger's arm.
It is the slave, akin to the amorous night,
Who wishes to greet the day, delicious to see,
The august young woman in whom the flame
    keeps watch.

Astruc's most important creative work is the statue of *The Mask Peddler* in the Luxembourg Gardens. His greatest achievement in the context of Impressionism, however, lies in the contribution he made to Manet's early career.

The two first met in 1854 or 1855, through Fantin-Latour, and became close friends – by which time Astruc was already eulogizing 'the new school' in his writings, paying particular attention to Manet. He figures in the latter's *Music in the Tuileries Gardens* (p.25) and in Fantin-Latour's *A Studio in the Batignolles Quarter* (p.62), where he is shown turning towards Manet. In 1866 he introduced Monet to Manet, and in 1867 was largely responsible for the preface to the catalogue of the one-man exhibition that Manet staged in a specially built pavilion near the entrance to the Universal Exhibition ▲ (p.45). Astruc exhibited at the first Impressionist exhibition in 1874, though the nature of his contribution is not recorded.

1866

A Defender Appears

Émile Zola — a childhood friend of Cézanne — becomes increasingly identified with the future Impressionists, recognizing in their preference for scenes of contemporary life 'Realist' tendencies complementary to his own literary aims. By publicly lending the artists his support, however, he incurs ridicule and hostility from his readers.

RENOIR
Cabaret of Mère Antony
1866

Mère Antony's inn be-came known through *Scènes de la vie de Bohème* by Henri Murger. Included here are Le Coeur, Sisley and Mère Antony (at the back, with a headscarf).

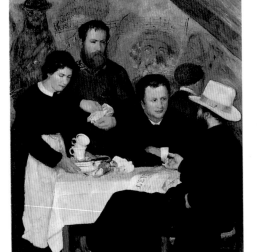

JANUARY

Anxious to escape from the idyllic forest and riverside landscapes favoured by most of his contemporaries, Pissarro moves to Pontoise, a small village near Auvers-sur-Oise, which Berthe Morisot may have recommended to him. (In the seventeen years he was to live there, Pissarro produced at least three hundred oil paintings of the area as well as countless drawings, watercolours and gouaches.)

3rd Renoir shows three works at an exhibition of the Société des Amis des Beaux-Arts in Pau.

FEBRUARY

Renoir, Sisley and Jules Le Coeur ◆ (p.50), a rich architect and amateur painter, walk through the Forest of Fontainebleau to Marlotte and stay at Mère Antony's inn, where Renoir paints them. Pissarro has a disagreement with Corot, who disapproves of new tendencies in his work attributable to the influence of Manet and Courbet. As a result, Pissarro stops describing himself as 'a pupil of Corot' in his Salon submissions.

MARCH

Renoir stays with Sisley at Marlotte, where his friend Jules Le Coeur has taken a house.

APRIL

Guillemet takes Zola to Manet's studio to see paintings rejected by the Salon jury. Zola persuades the editor of the left-wing paper *L'Événement* to let him write a series of articles, signed 'Claude', reviewing the Salon and the state of French art.

MAY

L'Événement starts to publish Zola's articles, but his attacks on the jury and his defence of the future Impressionists, especially Manet, provoke such hostile protests from readers that the series is curtailed ▲ (p.41).

MANET
The Fifer
1866

The boy-soldier who modelled for this painting was a fife player in the light infantry troop of the Imperial Guard; he was brought to pose for Manet by Bazille's uncle, Commandant Lejosne. The style shows the influence of Velázquez, and also of Japanese prints in its sim-plicity and the intensity of the black. No doubt it was these qualities, together with the 'flatness' of the picture, that influenced the Salon jury to reject it, although Zola praised it highly in *L'Événement*.

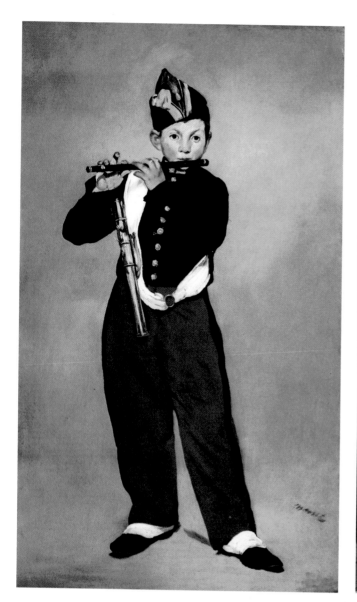

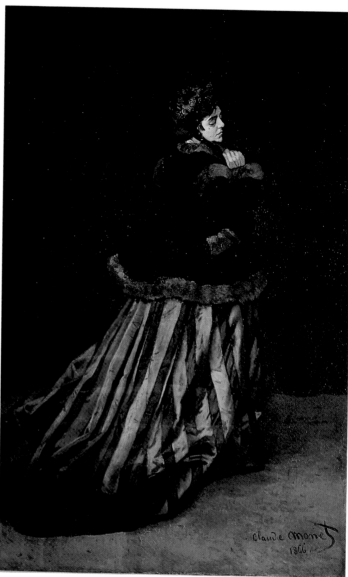

1st Manet exhibits *Reading* (a portrait of his wife, Suzanne, listening to their son Léon reading to her) at the exhibition of the Société des Amis des Beaux-Arts in Bordeaux.

3rd Opening of the Salon. Manet's submissions, *The Fifer* (above left) and *The Artist*, are rejected – as are all of Cézanne's, despite the protests of Daubigny, who is on the jury. Works accepted include Morisot's *La Bermondière* and *A Norman Hearth*; Sisley's *Women Going to the Woods* and *Village Street in Marlotte* (p.40); and Bazille's *Still Life with Fish*. Monet's *Camille: Woman in the Green Dress* (above right), is not only accepted but is highly praised, and the writer Arsène Houssaye buys it for 800 francs. Renoir submits three works, of which one – a mere sketch – is accepted, whereupon he withdraws it as being too insignificant. Both Renoir and Cézanne demand another Salon des Refusés. Pissarro's *Banks of the Marne* (p.30) is hung, as is Degas' *A Steeplechase*. Courbet sells works to the value of more than 150,000 francs.

6th Manet meets Cézanne and compliments him on his still lifes.

MONET
Camille: Woman in the Green Dress
1866

Painted in four days, expressly for the Salon of 1866, this portrait of Camille Doncieux, Monet's mistress (whom he was to marry four years later, in 1870), is intentionally traditionalist in its approach and handling.

1866

9th Manet writes to Zola suggesting a meeting – 'I am at the Café de Bade every day from 5.30 till 7.00.'

20th Zola publishes a pamphlet entitled *Mon Salon* containing his articles on the Salon and the state of French art that were to have appeared in *L'Événement* ▲ (opposite).

JUNE

Berthe Morisot holidays in Pont-Aven, in Brittany.

14th Zola goes to stay with Cézanne at Bennecourt, near Rouen. During his stay he writes a short story, *Une Farce, ou Bohème en villégiature*, based on the experience.

JULY

Bazille works on *The Artist's Family on a Terrace near Montpellier* (p.44) in his studio, having already made preliminary studies for the painting at his family home.

Monet paints in Ville d'Avray (the village near St-Cloud where Corot spent much of his life).

AUGUST

Renoir and Sisley stay with the Le Coeur family at Berck on the Channel coast.

SEPTEMBER

Manet and his family go to live with Manet's mother at 49 rue de St-Pétersbourg.

OCTOBER

Mary Cassatt arrives in Paris and studies with the academic painter Charles Chaplin.

4th Guillemet moves to Aix-en-Provence and works with Cézanne.

23rd Cézanne writes to Pissarro: 'I am in the bosom of my family; the most rotten creatures in the world, its members boring beyond measure.'

SISLEY
Village Street in Marlotte
1866

This is one of two views Sisley painted of the village of Marlotte when working there with Renoir, Bazille and Le Coeur. The bold brushwork suggests the influence of Pissarro on Sisley at this time, while the presence of the man chopping wood provides a touch of Realism reminiscent of Courbet.

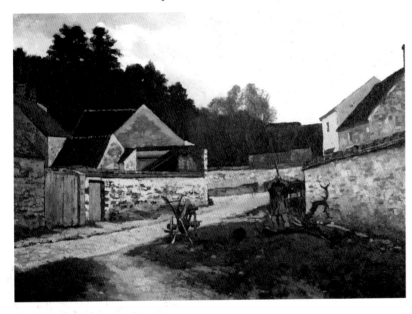

OTHER EVENTS

- French troops start to leave Mexico
- Prussia defeats Austria at Sadowa
- Boulevard St-Germain completed
- Loomis invents radio telegraphy,

Siemens the dynamo and Nobel dynamite
- Underwater cable laid between Ireland and Newfoundland
- Daudet's *Lettres de mon moulin*, Dostoevsky's *Crime and Punishment*,

Victor Hugo's *Les Travailleurs de la mer* and Verlaine's first book of poems, *Poèmes saturniens* published
- Offenbach's *La Vie parisienne* and Smetana's *The Bartered Bride* first performed

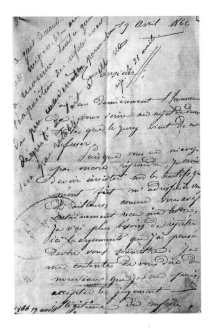

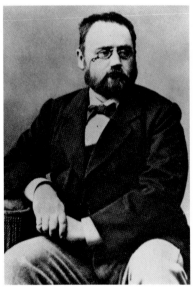

On April 19th Émile Zola (above) helped Cézanne (right) to compose a letter to Comte de Nieuwerkerke, the Superintendent of Fine Arts, complaining that he had received no response to his protest at being rejected by the Salon jury and requesting another Salon des Refusés. Nieuwerkerke's negative reply is scrawled diagonally across Cézanne's letter (top of page).

▲ ZOLA DEFENDS THE IMPRESSIONISTS

The radical paper *L'Événement* printed only six of Zola's projected sixteen or eighteen articles on the Salon and the state of French art. As a result, Zola published the series in pamphlet form under his own name, prefaced with a moving letter to his school friend Cézanne:

It gives me profound pleasure, my friend, to write to you directly. You can't imagine how much I have suffered during this quarrel I have had with the faceless crowd. I have felt myself so misunderstood, so surrounded by hatred, that the pen often fell from my fingers in discouragement. Today, however, I can allow myself the warm pleasure of one of those intimate chats we have been holding between ourselves for ten years now.

For ten years we have been talking together about the arts and literature. We have lived together — do you remember? — and often dawn would find us still arguing, exploring the past, questioning the present, trying to discern the truth and discover for ourselves an infallible, complete religion. We have ploughed through so many hopeless masses of ideas, we have examined and rejected every system, and after such arduous labour we arrived at the conclusion that apart from one's own strong and individual life there was nothing but lies and foolishness.

Happy are those who have such memories!... You are my entire youth; you are part of all my joys, all my suffering. In their fraternal closeness, our minds have developed side by side. Today, as we are setting out in life, we have faith in ourselves, because we have come to know our own hearts and our own flesh.

We were living in our own shadow. Cut off, not very sociable; we were content with our thoughts. We felt ourselves marooned in the midst of a frivolous and complacent crowd...

Do you realize that we were unwitting revolutionaries? I have just managed to say out loud what I have been whispering for ten years. No doubt the sound of the dispute has reached your ears, and you will have seen the reception our cherished thoughts were given. Ah, the poor boys who lived so wholesomely in Provence, under the generous sun, in whom apparently such malevolence and madness were raging...

So, the battle is over and I have been beaten as far as the public is concerned. There is applause and gloating on all sides.

I was loath to deprive the crowd of its amusement, and so I am publishing 'Mon Salon'. In two weeks the clamour will have died down, the most partisan will be left with only a vague memory of my articles. The articles will no longer be before the eyes of the mockers; the fleeting pages of 'L'Événement' will have gone with the wind, and things I did not say will be imputed to me; arrant stupidities I never wrote will be imputed to me. I don't want that to happen, and it is for that reason that I am collecting the articles I submitted to 'L'Événement' under the pen-name Claude. I want 'Mon Salon' to remain intact, I want it to be what the public itself expected...

It gives me pleasure to express my ideas for a second time. I know that in a few years the whole world will come to believe that I was right. I have no fear that they will later be thrown back in my face.

ÉMILE ZOLA, *Mon Salon*, May 20th, 1866

1867

Manet's Personal Exhibition

MANET
View of the Universal Exhibition
1867

Manet painted this panoramic view of the Universal Exhibition from a point in the rue Franklin near the Trocadéro. The balloon from which Nadar took photographs of the city can be seen in the top right-hand corner. On the left are the Pont de l'Alma and the Pont d'Iéna, leading into the exhibition grounds.

Capitalizing on the vast number of people expected to visit the Universal Exhibition, Manet and Courbet each erect a pavilion in the Place de l'Alma, near one of the entrances, in order to display their own work. Despite widespread publicity and the amount of money lavished on the pavilions, both exhibitions are no more than a partial success and neither receive much critical acclaim.

JANUARY

Bazille and Renoir rent a studio together at 20 rue Visconti, near St-Germain-des-Prés.

Sisley takes an apartment in the Batignolles quarter.

1st Zola publishes an enthusiastic article about Manet in *L'Artiste*.

3rd Manet asks his mother for money from his inheritance so he can stage a one-man show near the Champ-de-Mars, where the Universal Exhibition is to be held. She subsequently advances him 28,305 francs to cover the cost of building a temporary gallery.

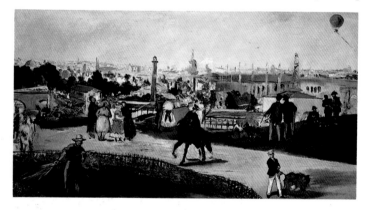

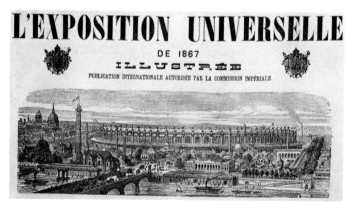

Cover of one of the many illustrated publications produced to promote the Universal Exhibition.

FEBRUARY

12th Ingres retrospective at the École des Beaux-Arts – of special interest to Degas, who regards Ingres as one of the greatest exponents of the classical tradition.

17th Manet sits for Fantin-Latour.

MARCH

5th Renoir's *Diana* (opposite above), Bazille's *The Artist's Family on a Terrace near Montpellier* (p.44) and works by Cézanne, Pissarro and Sisley are rejected by the Salon jury.

30th The rejected artists forward a petition to the Minister of Fine Arts demanding another Salon des Refusés.

Although Renoir had originally intended this painting to be 'nothing more than a study of a nude', he thought that by adding a bow and the carcass of a deer it would become less 'improper'. It was painted specifically for the Salon of 1867 – but strangely, in view of its academic nature, it was rejected by the jury.

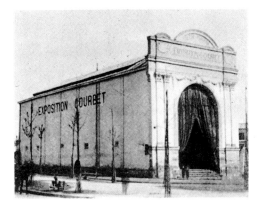

Courbet's 'Pavilion of Realism'. Like Manet's pavilion, it was caricatured in *Le Journal amusant* (p.45).

RENOIR
Bazille at his Easel
1867

This portrait of Bazille intent on painting was probably done in the studio Renoir shared with Monet, Sisley and Bazille (a snow scene by Monet is visible on the wall). A similar portrait of Renoir at his easel was produced by Bazille.

In a letter to his parents, Bazille mentions that he is thinking of trying to organize an independent exhibition.

APRIL
Berthe Morisot exhibits at Cadart's gallery.
2nd Opening of the Salon. Fantin-Latour's *Portrait of Édouard Manet* (p.45) and two paintings by Degas – each entitled *Family Portrait* – are hung, but Monet's *Women in the Garden* is rejected. In view of Monet's poverty and the fact that his mistress, Camille Doncieux, is pregnant, Bazille buys the painting for 2500 francs payable in instalments of 50 francs a month.
8th Courbet's 'Pavilion of Realism', devoted to his own work, opens in the Place de l'Alma near the Universal Exhibition. It receives plenty of publicity, but little critical acclaim.

MAY
3rd Opening of the Universal Exhibition. Some 11 million people flock to see it – but only 98,000 visit the fine-art section, which includes no Impressionist works.
22nd Manet's one-man show ▲ (p.45) opens in a specially built pavilion near the Pont de l'Alma, facing one of the entrances of the Universal Exhibition. He has about fifty works on display, but the exhibition is not a popular success.
30th Manet and Zola reprint Zola's article from *L'Artiste* (*see* January 1st) in pamphlet form, to sell at Manet's exhibition. It includes a portrait of Manet by Bracquemond and an etching of *Olympia* (p.36).

JUNE
3rd Sisley paints in Honfleur.
7th Sisley's son Pierre is born to his mistress, Marie-Adélaïde-Eugénie Lescouezec.
29th *Le Journal amusant* devotes two pages of caricatures to Manet's exhibition (p.45).
30th Morisot departs for Lorient, a Breton port that is one of her favourite painting sites.

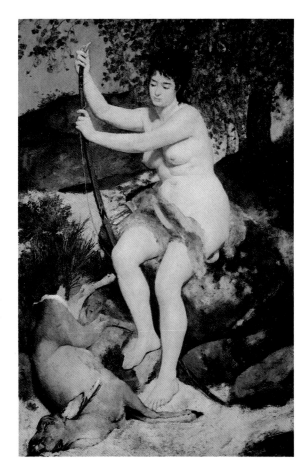

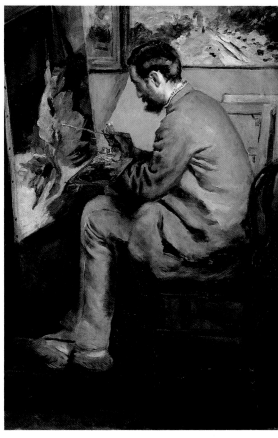

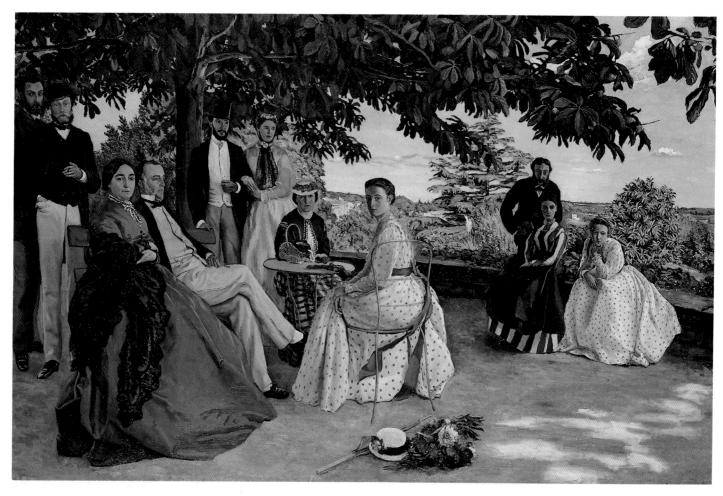

BAZILLE
The Artist's Family on a Terrace near Montpellier
1867

Bazille's family posed for this charming portrait on the terrace of the family home outside Montpellier, where they owned extensive vineyards. Bazille himself is on the extreme left.

AUGUST

15th Manet departs for a holiday in Trouville with his friend Antonin Proust (p.124), a journalist, aspiring politician and amateur painter.
25th Monet's son Jean is born to Camille Doncieux in Paris; Monet, who is in a state of great impoverishment, is staying with his parents in Le Havre – where Sisley is painting, too.

SEPTEMBER

Monet joins Bazille and Renoir in their studio at 20 rue Visconti.
Manet starts work on a series of politically emotive paintings depicting the execution of the Emperor Maximilian of Mexico ◆ (pp.56–9).
2nd Manet attends Baudelaire's funeral.

OTHER EVENTS

- Emperor Maximilian of Mexico executed by Republican troops
- Garibaldi marches on Rome
- United States purchases Alaska
- Café-concerts proliferate in Paris after relaxation of theatre laws
- Census reveals population of Paris has risen by 800,000 since 1850
- Publication of Baudelaire's *Curiosités esthétiques*, Zola's *Thérèse Raquin*, the Goncourts' *Manette Salomon* (a novel about the Paris art world) and Karl Marx's *Das Kapital*
- Ibsen completes *Peer Gynt*
- Strauss composes *Blue Danube Waltz*
- Verdi's *Don Carlos* first performed

▲ MANET'S APOLOGIA FOR HIS EXHIBITION

In the preface to his catalogue, written with the help of Zacharie Astruc ● (p.37), Manet explained why he had found it necessary to stage an exhibition of his work:

Official recognition, encouragement and prizes are, in fact, regarded as proofs of talent; the public has been informed, in advance, what to admire, what to avoid, according as to whether the works are accepted or rejected. On the other hand, the artist is told that it is the public's spontaneous reaction to his works which makes them so unwelcome to the various selection committees. In these circumstances the artist is advised to be patient and wait. But wait for what? Until there are no selection committees? He would be much better off if he could make direct contact with the public, and find out its reactions. Today the artist is not saying 'come and see some perfect paintings' but 'come and see some sincere ones'.

It is sincerity which gives to works of art a character which seems to convert them into acts of protest, when all the artist is trying to do is to express his own impressions.

Monsieur Manet has never wished to protest. On the contrary, the protest, which he never expected, has been directed against himself; this is because there is a traditional way of teaching form, techniques and appreciation, and because those who have been brought up to believe in those principles will admit no others, a fact which makes them childishly intolerant. Any works which do not conform to those formulae they regard as worthless. They not only arouse criticism, but provoke hostility, even active hostility. To be able to exhibit is the all important thing, the sine qua non for the artist, because what happens is that, after looking at a thing for a length of time, what at first seemed unfamiliar, or even shocking, becomes familiar. Gradually it comes to be understood and accepted. Time itself imperceptibly refines and softens the apparent hardness of a picture.

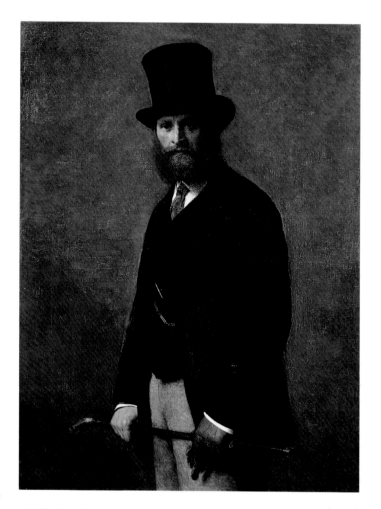

FANTIN-LATOUR Portrait of Édouard Manet 1867

By exhibiting, an artist finds friends and allies in his search for recognition. Monsieur Manet has always recognized talent when he has seen it; he has no intention of overthrowing old methods of painting, or creating new ones. He has merely tried to be himself, and nobody else.
ÉDOUARD MANET, 'Reasons for Holding a Private Exhibition', 1867

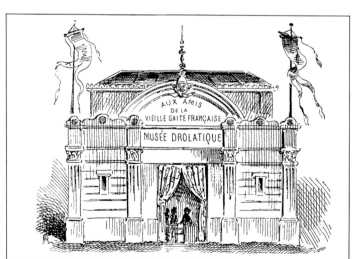

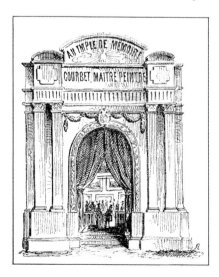

The pavilions erected by Manet and Courbet close to the Universal Exhibition attracted a good deal of satirical attention. These two architectural caricatures by Georges Randon appeared in *Le Journal amusant*. Courbet's pavilion (left) bears the ironical inscriptions 'To the Temple of Memory' and 'Courbet, Master Painter', while Manet's (far left) is labelled 'To the Friends of the Old French Vaudeville' and 'Comic Museum'.

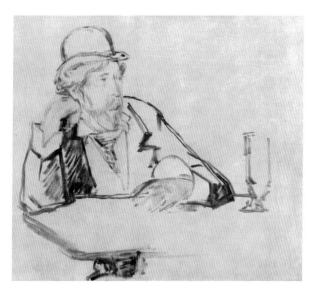

MANET
George Moore at the Café
1878 or 1879

Situated at the Nouvelles-Athènes this portrait of the Irish writer was roughed out in light brushwork without any preliminary drawing. If intended as a study for a more finished painting, the project must have been abandoned at an early stage.

 IMPRESSIONIST CAFÉS

George Moore – the raffish Irish novelist and haunter of French artistic circles – once said: 'He who would know something of my life, must know something about the academy of fine arts. Not the official stupidity you read of in the daily papers, but the real French academy, the café.'

Impressionism grew and flourished in cafés, of which there were at least 24,000 in the Paris area. Indeed, establishments such as the Volpini, the Voltaire, the Dôme, the Coupole, the Brasserie Lip and the Deux Magots played a central role in the cultural life of the period. By their very nature the cafés attracted those who were alienated by the anonymity of the modern industrial city, and their attractiveness was enhanced during and after the Second Empire by the wide pavements of the new boulevards created by Baron Haussmann's comprehensive replanning of Paris.

At first Manet frequented the Café de Bade at 23 boulevard des Italiens, but in 1864 he moved into an apartment at 34 boulevard des Batignolles, in the area where Baudelaire, Bazille, Caillebotte, Alphonse Daudet, Fantin-Latour, and later Cézanne, Mallarmé ◆ (pp.220–1), Pissarro and Renoir all lived. By 1866 he had started using the Café Guerbois, at 11 rue des Batignolles, where he met his friends most evenings (Thursday being the most popular). In addition to the artists, the circle included writers such as Zola ● (p.53), Duranty, Duret and Armand Silvestre, who in his autobiographical *Au Pays des souvenirs*, written in 1892, provided a fascinating account of the Guerbois' golden years. The group of painters who frequented the café were dubbed by the critics 'L'École des Batignolles' – and if Impressionism could be said to have a birthplace,

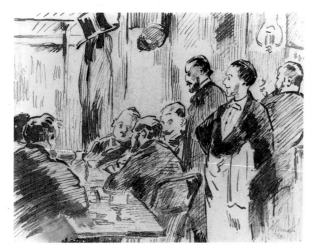

This pen-and-ink drawing made by Manet in 1869 is thought to show the interior of the Café Guerbois.

the Café Guerbois was it. As Monet later recalled, 'Nothing could have been more stimulating than the regular discussions which we used to have there, with their constant clashes of opinion. They kept our wits sharpened, and supplied us with a stock of enthusiasm which lasted us for weeks, and kept us going until the final

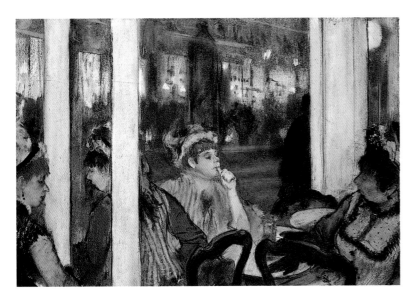

DEGAS
Women on a Café Terrace, Evening
1877

In this vignette of café night-life, Degas gives particular emphasis to the expression of combined boredom and professional allurement that masks the women's faces.

realization of an idea was accomplished. From them we emerged with a stronger determination and with our thoughts clearer and more sharply defined.'

By 1877, however, the Café Guerbois had begun to lose its popularity to the Nouvelle-Athènes in the Place Pigalle. The Nouvelle-Athènes had a distinguished pedigree. Under the Empire it had been frequented by the leading figures of the opposition to Napoleon III – men such as Clemenceau, Courbet, Gambetta, Nadar, Daudet and Castagnary. Two significant icons of Impressionism – Degas' *The Absinthe Drinker* ◆ (pp.192–3), showing the actress Ellen Andrée with Marcellin Desboutin (who had been one of the first habitués), and Manet's *George Moore at the Café* (opposite) – were painted at the Nouvelle-Athènes.

Among those who frequented the café were Renoir, Monet, Pissarro and occasionally Cézanne; the writers Villiers de l'Isle Adam, Ary Renan and Zola's friend Paul Alexis; the musicians Chabrier and Cabaner; and Manet's favourite model, Victorine Meurent, who posed for *Olympia* (p.36) and *Déjeuner sur l'herbe* (p.27). The Nouvelle-Athènes also witnessed the schism developing amongst the Impressionists – stimulated by Degas, who was often to be found there, supported by his 'gang', which consisted of Forain, Raffaëlli, Zandomeneghi and, whenever he was in Paris, the Florentine critic Diego Martelli ▲ (p.121). Indeed, Caillebotte complained that Degas was guilty of introducing 'disunity into our midst, and spends all his time haranguing people in the Nouvelle-Athènes.'

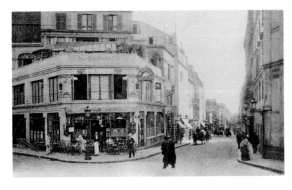

Photograph of the Nouvelle-Athènes, which replaced the Café Guerbois as the Impressionists' favourite meeting place around 1877.

By the mid 1880s the Impressionists were beginning to spend more time outside Paris – Monet in Giverny, Pissarro in Éragny, Cézanne in Aix-en-Provence, Renoir in Essoyes and elsewhere. As a result, the casual meetings in cafés were supplanted by more organized dinners, held either at the restaurant in the boulevard Voltaire belonging to Eugène Murer – where the owner offered his friends free hospitality on Wednesday evenings – or at the Café Riche in the boulevard des Italiens.

mid 80's disperse outside Paris

1868

The Realist Impulse

Most of the artists have works accepted by the Salon this year. Their submissions vary tremendously in technique and subject matter, being connected only by a shared concern with contemporary life. Renoir's 'Lise with a Parasol' – described by one critic as 'the fat woman daubed in white' – attracts attention because of the freshness of the image and the directness of Renoir's brushwork.

RENOIR
The Engaged Couple
c.1868

The couple portrayed here were thought to be Sisley and his mistress Marie-Adélaide-Eugénie Lescouezec, by whom he had a son in June 1867. More recent opinion, however, is inclined towards the idea that the woman is Renoir's favourite model Lise Tréhot ◆ (p.50).

This engraving of the Salon of 1868 shows how closely the exhibits were crowded together. Large paintings were generally hung above smaller ones.

JANUARY
Bazille and Renoir move to a studio at 9 rue de la Paix (renamed rue de la Condamine later in the year) – near the Guerbois, a café popular with progressive artists and writers ◆ (p.46–7).

FEBRUARY
Zola sits for Manet.
Cézanne submits an application for permission to copy paintings in the Louvre.
Gauguin enlists in the French navy and joins the cruiser *Jérôme Napoléon*.

MARCH
Renoir is commissioned to decorate Prince Georges Bibesco's house at 22 boulevard de la Tour-Maubourg through Charles Le Coeur (brother of his friend Jules Le Coeur), who had been the architect. He paints two ceilings after the style of Tiepolo and Fragonard.
22nd Degas enrols as a copyist at the Louvre for the last time.

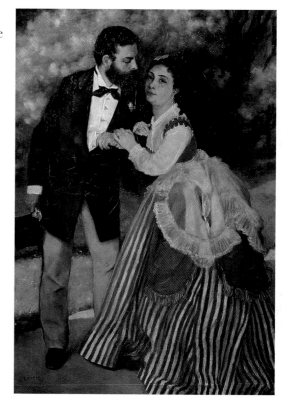

APRIL
Sisley takes a studio in the same building as Bazille and Renoir.
10th Renoir paints *The Engaged Couple* (above) during a visit to Chailly.

MAY
1st Opening of the Salon. Among the works hung are Manet's *Portrait of Émile Zola* (p.53) and *Young Woman with a Parrot*; Renoir's *Lise with a Parasol*, which is greatly praised by the critics ▲ (pp.51–2); Bazille's

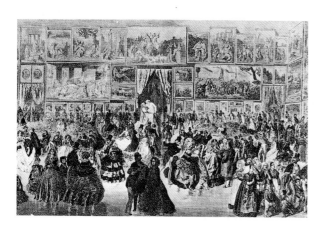

Flower Piece and *Portrait of the Family*, another version of *The Artist's Family on a Terrace near Montpellier* (p.44), which had been rejected the previous year; *Ships Coming Out of the Harbour at Le Havre* by Monet, whose other works have been rejected; *Côte du Jallais* and *The Hermitage at Pontoise* by Pissarro; *Chestnut Trees at St-Cloud* by Sisley; *Ros-bas, Finistère* by Morisot; and *Portrait of Mlle Eugénie Fiocre in the Ballet 'La Source'* by Degas.

10th Cézanne goes to Aix-en-Provence, where he remains for the rest of the year.

JUNE

29th Monet describes his desperate financial situation in a letter to Bazille, and implies that he has tried to drown himself.

JULY

Berthe Morisot and her sister are introduced to Manet by Fantin-Latour while they are copying a work by Rubens in the Louvre.

15th Manet wins a silver medal for *The Dead Man* at an exhibition in Le Havre.

AUGUST

Renoir's parents move to the neighbourhood of Louveciennes, but he remains at Ville d'Avray. Manet makes a two-day trip to London, where he hopes to exhibit.

SEPTEMBER

Berthe Morisot, Fanny Claus and Guillemet pose on the balcony of Manet's studio in the rue Guyot for *The Balcony* (p.60) – which will be exhibited at the Salon in 1869.

1st Zola decides to dedicate his novel *Madeleine Férat* to Manet.

OCTOBER

Monet receives a silver medal from the Amis de l'Art in Le Havre and secures a new patron, Louis-Joachim Gaudibert, a local manufacturer and amateur painter.

17th Publication of Manet's lithographic poster (p.50) for *Les Chats* by Champfleury – the pseudonym used by Jules Husson – a defender of Realism and close friend of Courbet who figures in Manet's *Music in the Tuileries Gardens* (p.25) and Fantin-Latour's *Homage to Delacroix* (p.28). The book includes an illustration by Manet.

30th Manet is introduced to the radical politician Léon Gambetta at the Café de Londres.

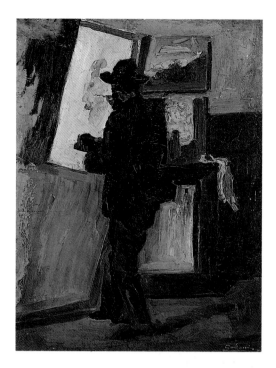

GUILLAUMIN
Portrait of Pissarro Painting a Blind
c.1868

Although it was lack of money that forced Guillaumin and Pissarro to take up painting blinds, the occupation was not so demeaning as it may seem. In fact it was quite common for artists to supplement their earnings by doing this kind of work, and it could require considerable skill. Renoir, for instance, had at one time worked for a M. Gilbert who sold 'blinds of all sorts', including 'religious blinds, perfect imitations of stained glass for churches… monumental and artistic blinds'. Such tradesmen often gave artists commissions to execute at home.

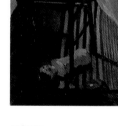

MONET
The Luncheon
1868

When Monet produced this painting depicting a comfortable bourgeois interior he was enjoying a respite from poverty thanks to his new patron, Louis-Joachim Gaudibert. Seated at the table are Monet's mistress, Camille Doncieux, and their son Jean.

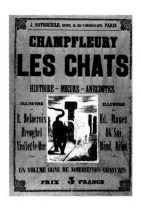

Poster, with a lithograph by Manet, for Champfleury's book of cat stories.

NOVEMBER

Guillaumin and Pissarro endeavour to eke out a living by painting blinds. Guillaumin paints a portrait of Pissarro at work (p.49). Monet is happily living at Étretat (a fishing village not far from Le Havre) with his mistress, Camille Doncieux, and their son Jean. Manet asks Monet whether he would like to become a member of the circle of artists and writers who meet at the Café Guerbois ◆ (pp.46–7). Monet invites Renoir and Sisley to join the group.

DECEMBER

Manet shows *The Spanish Singer* and *Boy with a Sword* at an exhibition of the Société Artistique des Bouches-du-Rhône in the hope of selling them, but no sale results.

OTHER EVENTS

- Regulations governing public meetings eased in France
- Bakunin founds the International Alliance of Social Democracy

- Meiji dynasty restored in Japan
- Bibliothèque Nationale, designed by Labrouste, opens in Paris
- Publication of Dostoevsky's *The Idiot* and Wilkie Collins' detective story *The Moonstone*

- Brahms completes his *German Requiem*; Tchaikovsky composes his Symphony No.1
- First performance of Wagner's *Die Meistersinger von Nurnberg*
- Rossini dies

RENOIR AND LISE TRÉHOT

One of Renoir's closest friends after leaving the École des Beaux-Arts was Jules Le Coeur, an architect and amateur painter, whose brother Charles secured a commission for Renoir to decorate the house of Prince Georges Bibesco. In 1863 Jules, who was nine years older than Renoir, decided to give up architecture and devote himself entirely to painting. Two years later he took a house and studio, where Renoir often painted, at Marlotte in the Forest of Fontainebleau.

Around this time Le Coeur, whose wife had died in 1863, embarked on a love affair with Clémence Tréhot, by whom he had a daughter. Clémence's father had been postmaster of Ecquevilly, a small country town, and moved to Paris with his family when the job was abolished. Renoir became acquainted with Clémence and her seventeen-year-old sister Lise in 1865, and for eight years

the Tréhot sisters and the Le Coeurs were to play an important role in his life – Lise becoming his favourite model and probably his mistress. It was a time of great productivity for Renoir, and Lise posed for nearly all his most important works of the period. She appears in *Lise with a Parasol* (opposite), *Girl with a Bird* and *Lise Holding a Bunch of Wild Flowers*, all painted in 1867; *Lise Sewing* and *The Gypsy Girl* (both 1868); *Bather with a Griffon*, *A Woman of Algeria* (pp.64–5) and *Lise with a White Shawl* (all 1870); and *Parisian Women in Algerian Dress* (1872).

In the year Renoir painted that last picture Lise married a young architect, Georges Brière de l'Isle, and her marriage brought to an end a most fruitful relationship. Lise kept the paintings that Renoir had given her, but destroyed all their correspondence. She outlived him by five years, dying in 1924.

RENOIR
Lise with a Parasol
1867

This romantic portrait, which gave Renoir his first success at the Salon, was also one of the first he painted of Lise Tréhot. Zola described it as a successful exploration of the 'modern' – Lise, he felt, was 'one of our wives, or rather our mistresses'. The composition and atmosphere owe something to Manet, and something to Whistler's *The White Girl* (p.26).

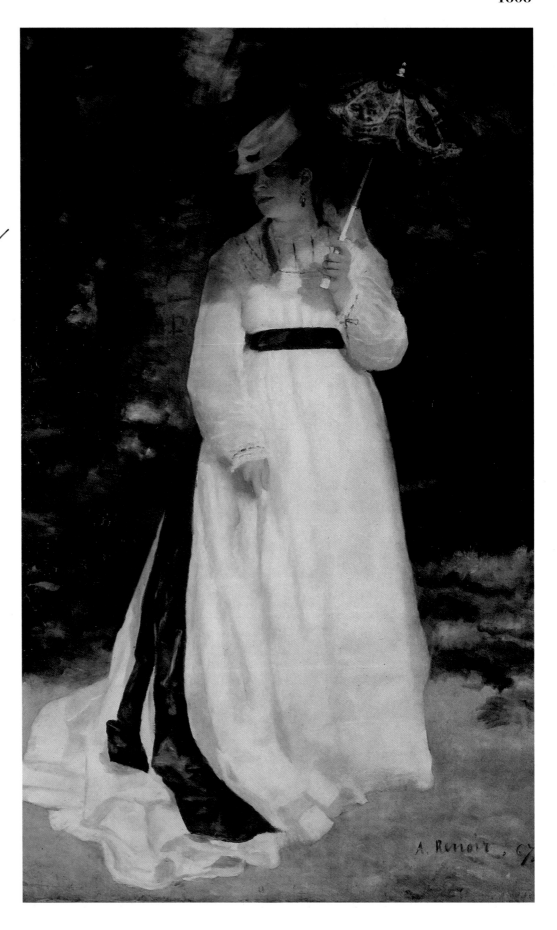

CRITICAL REACTIONS TO RENOIR'S 'LISE WITH A PARASOL'

The other painting I wish to speak of is that which M. Henri [sic] Renoir has called 'Lise', and which represents a young woman in a white dress, sheltering beneath a parasol. This 'Lise' seems to me the sister of the 'Camille' of M. Monet. She is shown facing us, coming out of the trees, her supple body balanced, cooling herself from the boiling afternoon heat. She is one of our wives, or rather our mistresses, painted with great frankness and an appropriate investigation of the modern world.
ÉMILE ZOLA, *L'Événement*, March 24th, 1868

I discovered in the furthest salon, the one known as the 'Room of the Outcasts', the figure of a fat woman daubed in white, labelled simply 'Lise', whose author M. R. (I trust he will allow me to designate him only by his initials) was clearly no longer even inspired by the great example of M. Courbet, but by the curious models of M. Manet. And this is how the demise of the Realist school, as it moves from imitation to imitation, becomes more and more inevitable. So be it!
FERDINAND DE LASTERIE, *L'Opinion nationale*, June 20th, 1868

M. Manet is already a master apparently, since he has some imitators, amongst whom must be included M. Renoir, who has painted, under the title of 'Lise', a woman of natural grandeur walking in the park. This painting captures the attention of connoisseurs, as much by the strangeness of its effect as by the justness of its tone. This is what, in the language of the Realists, is called 'a fine touch of colour'.
MARIUS CHAUMELIN, *La Presse*, June 23rd, 1868

The 'Lise' of M. Renoir completes an odd trinity that started with the very strange, expressive and notorious 'Olympia'. In the wake of Manet, Monet was soon to create his 'Camille', the young girl in the green dress putting on her gloves. Here now is 'Lise', the most demure of them all. Here we have the charming Parisian girl in the Bois, alert, mocking and laughing, playing the 'grande dame', somewhat gauchely savouring the shade of the wood for all the diversions that may be had there: the dancing, the open-air café, the fashionable restaurant, the amusing dining room fashioned from a distorted tree.

Lise's hair is adorned with a dainty straw hat. She wears a white dress, drawn in at the waist with a black sash. A parasol shades her face. She stops amidst the forest trees in a ray of sunlight, as if waiting for a friend. It is an original image. The painting has great charm, beautifully rendered effects, a delicate range of tones, a general impression that is unified, and clear and well-conceived lighting. The art that has gone into this painting seems simple, but in fact it is very unusual and very interesting. Given a subject whose charm is its light, it could hardly have been executed with greater clarity. The sunlit whites are delicious. Wherever the eye wanders, it is enchanted by the most delicate of nuances and a very distinctive lightness of touch.

All praise to a joyful canvas made by a painter with a future, an observer who is as responsive to the picturesque as he is careful of reality. This painting deserves to be singled out. By an inconceivable error, which I would prefer to think of as ignorance, she has suffered the fate of the rejected work [although hung, the painting did not win a prize]. *At the Salon, with its array of marketable objects, such work stands by its art, its taste and its exceptional character, which command our attention and our study. It was obvious to all the painters, but not to the jury.*
ZACHARIE ASTRUC, *L'Étendard*, June 27th, 1868

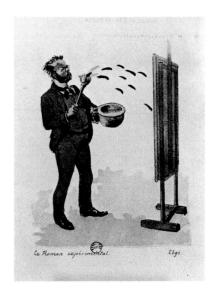

Caricature of Émile Zola by Le Bourgeois entitled 'The Experimental Novel', showing the novelist and art critic in the act of spattering a canvas with excrement.

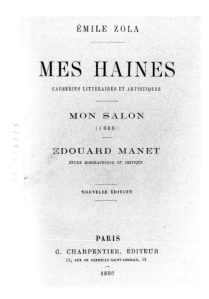

The title page of *Mes Haines (My Hates)*, the collection of 'literary and artistic discourses' by Zola published in 1880, which included the series of articles rejected by *L'Événement* in 1866 ▲ (p.41).

ÉMILE ZOLA
Novelist and critic

Defender of lost or unpopular causes ranging from Impressionism to Captain Dreyfus, novelist and journalist of distinction, Émile Zola (1840–1902) was born in the town of Aix-en-Provence, where he went to school with Cézanne. He came to Paris in the early 1860s and, after unsuccessful attempts to become a playwright, obtained a job with the publishing house of Hachette, then became the literary editor of the radical weekly *L'Événement*.

Thanks to his friendship with Cézanne, Zola was able to keep abreast of current art controversies. In 1863 he visited the Salon des Refusés, and in 1866 wrote an enthusiastic defence of Manet in *L'Événement*, complaining bitterly about the

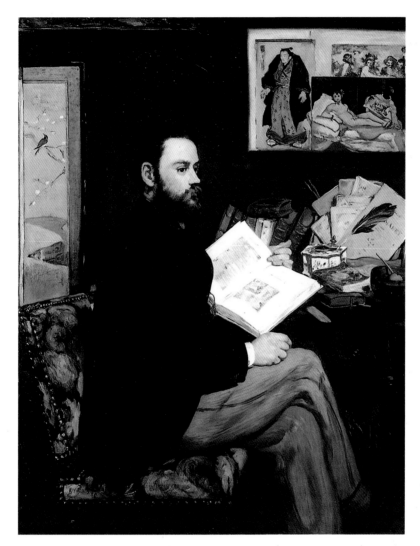

MANET Portrait of Émile Zola 1868

artist's rejection from the Salon of that year. This article was published as a pamphlet – with additions, some suggested by the painter – which was on sale at Manet's personal exhibition ▲ (p.41). In February 1868 Manet painted his well-known portrait of the writer, and for the next decade Zola was to be an inveterate defender of the group of artists who frequented the Café Guerbois ◆ (pp.46–7). In 1880 he published a selection of his art criticism – with the aggressive title *Mes Haines (My Hates)*.

Zola's visual sensibilities were very largely moulded by his preoccupations as a Realist writer – applying to the description of human life a kind of scientific rigour based on material circumstances and facts, which he accumulated

with dedicated enthusiasm. After the war of 1870 and the failure of the Commune, he embarked on *Rougon-Macquart: histoire naturelle et sociale d'une famille sous le second Empire*, a massive cyclical work running to some twenty volumes, completed in 1893, which brought him fame and wealth. Because a concern with contemporary life was part of the Impressionists' approach, Zola regarded them as the visual equivalent of the literary Realists – indeed, in his reviews he frequently referred to the Impressionists as Realists and tended to overemphasize their credentials as exponents of this doctrine.

By 1879, when he was acting as Paris correspondent for the Russian magazine *Viestnik Europi (Le Messager de l'Europe)* ▲ (p.114), Zola's enthusiasm for the Impressionists had begun to wane. 'The tragedy', he wrote in his review of the 1880 Salon, 'is that there is not one artist of the group who has forcibly and definitively expressed the formula which all of them share and which is scattered through all their individual works.'

From that moment the relationship between Zola and the Impressionists steadily deteriorated, until finally in 1886 it reached breaking point when he published *L'Oeuvre*, a novel about the Parisian art world in which the principal character – a frustrated, unsuccessful, embittered and creatively impotent artist – was clearly recognizable as a combination of Cézanne and Manet.

1869

Manet Falls Foul of the Censor

Manet is fully aware that his decision to paint the execution of Emperor Maximilian – a controversial episode from recent political history – is unlikely to win the approval of the authorities. He therefore is not surprised when the Salon refuses to exhibit it. At the same time, however, he craves official recognition and doesn't withdraw 'The Balcony' from the exhibition.

JANUARY

Manet's painting of *The Execution of the Emperor Maximilian* (p.59) is not accepted at the Salon for political reasons ◆ (pp.56–9), and his lithograph of the same subject (p.58) is banned by the censor.
29th Sisley's second child, Jeanne-Adèle, is born.

FEBRUARY

The Belgian art dealer Arthur Stevens introduces Eva Gonzalès to Manet, who takes her on as his only pupil.
The Ministry of Fine Arts decrees that artists who have had pictures hung in the Salon at any time are now entitled to vote for two-thirds of the jury.
4th *La Tribune française* publishes an article by Zola virulently attacking the censorship of Manet's lithograph of the execution of Emperor Maximilian.
9th Degas visits Brussels and is offered a contract by Arthur Stevens.

MARCH

1st Durand-Ruel founds the *Revue internationale de l'art et de la curiosité.*

APRIL

Pissarro paints in Louveciennes.
Cézanne is living in Paris. He meets nineteen-year-old Hortense Fiquet, who becomes his mistress.

MAY

1st Opening of the Salon. Monet and Cézanne have all their submissions

MANET
Portrait of Eva Gonzalès
1870

The daughter of a well-known novelist, Eva Gonzalès was a talented but unenterprising painter, who became Manet's only pupil. Berthe Morisot related that Manet repainted the head of this portrait forty times. Both in pose and treatment, the work has an air of eighteenth-century artifice.

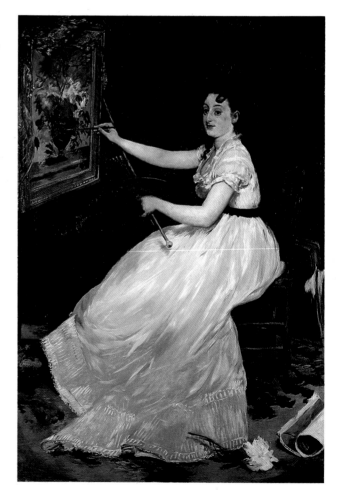

MONET
La Grenouillère
1869

La Grenouillère was a popular bathing place on Croissy Island, a short walk from Bougival. An entrepreneur named Seurin had moored two converted barges there, which provided dining and dancing facilities. A footbridge connected the island with a small circular islet, called the Camembert because of its shape.

Monet produced two views of the footbridge and one of the islet itself (right).

RENOIR
La Grenouillère
1869

The paintings of La Grenouillère by Renoir and Monet mark a significant stage in the evolution of both artists in their efforts to capture an impression of the natural scene. Liberated from academic convention by the fact that these are in a sense 'sketches', the free, seemingly erratic brush-strokes reproduce perfectly the sparkle of the water, the light on the trees and the movement of the boats.

Whereas Renoir focuses upon the islet, so placing emphasis on the figures, Monet adopts a more distant viewpoint that allows him to highlight the texture of the water, a subject that endlessly intrigued him.

Renoir painted four versions of *La Grenouillère* – one of the islet (right), two of the river bank, and one of the footbridge connecting Croissy Island to the islet.

rejected. Degas' *Portrait of Mme G.* (Joséphine Gaujelin) is hung (p.61), but not his portrait of Mme Camus. Among the other works accepted are Bazille's *View of the Village* (p.61), though he has a nude rejected; Manet's *The Balcony* (p.60) and *Lunch in the Studio* (p.56); Pissarro's *The Hermitage at Pontoise*; and Renoir's *Study in Summer* (a study of Lise, sometimes known as *La Bohèmienne*). Morisot does not submit.

JUNE
Monet writes to the writer and critic Arsène Houssaye asking if he would like to buy some of his paintings 'before they are taken by the bailiffs.' Renoir, in straitened circumstances, stays with his parents at their home at Voisins-Louveciennes. He travels almost daily to visit Monet, who is living at St-Michel near Bougival. Both artists paint La Grenouillère (The Froggery).

Manet and his family holiday at Boulogne – where they are visited by Degas, who has been working in pastels at Étretat and Villers-sur-Mer.

30th Van Gogh, aged 16, becomes an employee of the Goupil art gallery in The Hague.

SEPTEMBER
Paintings by Renoir, priced 100 francs each, are on display in Charpentier's art shop at 8 boulevard Montmartre – the same address is used by Pissarro in his submissions to the Salon.

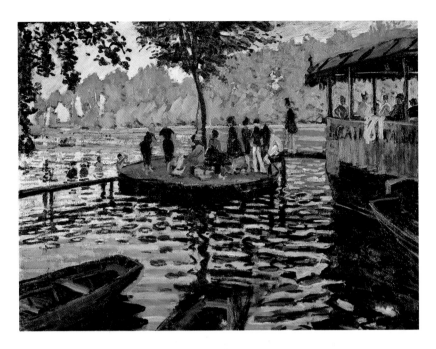

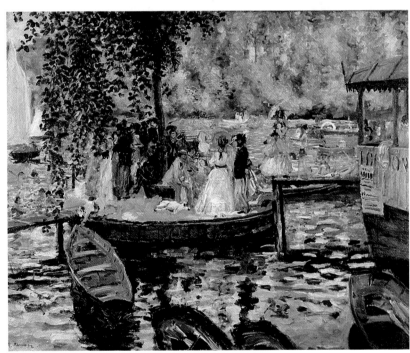

MANET
Lunch in the Studio
1868

This scene in the artist's studio, in which the figures have no interaction, remains one of Manet's most enigmatic works. This might in part be due to the fact that the boy depicted is Léon Leenhoff, who, although passed off as the brother of Manet's wife Suzanne, was almost certainly their son – born eleven years before their marriage. The female figure is clearly a maid, and in the background is Auguste Rousselin, a painter and pupil of Couture. The painting was exhibited at the Salon of 1869.

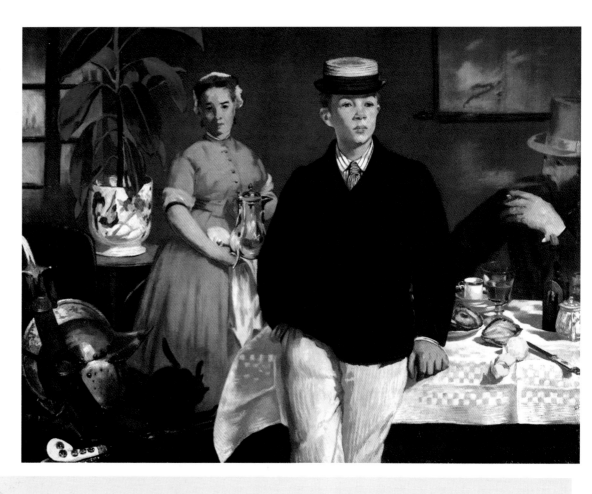

OTHER EVENTS

- France signs a secret treaty with Austria and Italy against Prussia
- Liberal politician Émile Ollivier becomes Prime Minister of France
- Suez Canal opens
- Inauguration of the first Vatican Council
- International Exhibition in Munich
- Du Hauron patents method for printing colour photographs
- Publication of Flaubert's *L'Education sentimentale* and Verlaine's *Fêtes galantes*

 MANET AND MAXIMILIAN

Manet's resolution to paint the execution of the Emperor Maximilian clearly reveals the tensions that existed between two sides of his character – the rebellious and the ambitious. The event which it depicts was the tragic sequel to the inept machinations of Napoleon III. For political and economic reasons, the Emperor had been determined to install the Archduke Maximilian, brother of the Austrian Emperor Franz-Josef, as Emperor of Mexico (hitherto a republic), which had been 'pacified' by a French expeditionary force between 1861 and 1863. When Mexico City fell to the French, the Republicans took to the hills and a pro-French puppet government invited Maximilian to become Emperor. He accepted, but only on condition that the French retained an army of 24,000

BAZILLE
Manet Sketching
1869

In this drawing of Manet, Bazille captures much of his friend's personality, so eloquently described by the critic and playwright Armand Silvestre: 'This revolutionary – the word is not too strong – had the manners of a perfect gentleman. With his gaudy trousers, short jackets, a flat-brimmed hat set on the back of his head, and always with his impeccable suede gloves, Manet had nothing of the bohemian in him, and was in no way bohemian. He had the ways of a dandy.'

The new emperor arrived in Mexico in June 1864, but within a year relations between Maximilian and France had deteriorated. The Republicans – led by Benito Juárez and surreptitiously aided by America – began to advance from the North, and in March 1867 Napoleon recalled his troops to France. Deprived of their backing, two months later Maximilian surrendered to Juárez; and on June 19th the Emperor and two of his generals were executed by firing squad.

The news reached Paris on the prize-giving day of the Universal Exhibition. Within a week or so, photographs of the event were on sale – some authentic, some fake and some doctored – and there was widespread revulsion throughout France, much of the blame being attributed to Napoleon III. As a result, the death of Maximilian was transformed into a symbol of anti-Bonaparte feeling – a factor that must have influenced Manet's decision to make the execution the subject of a painting on which he worked for more than a year, producing a lithograph as well as three versions in oil.

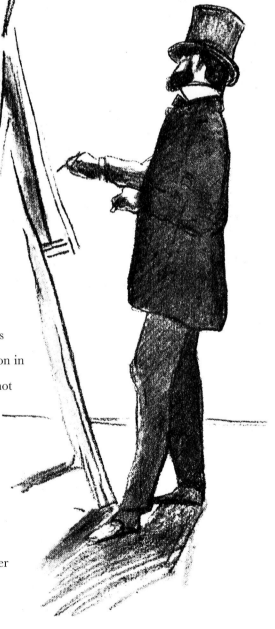

There can be no doubt that in choosing this subject Manet was aware of its political implications. He was a staunch Republican, and Berthe Morisot's mother referred to him only half jokingly as 'that Communist'. Later, in the early 1870s, he was to show sympathy for the Communards and was the only one of the Impressionists to record any aspect of that tragic episode. More significantly, the authorities considered the picture subversive. On February 7th, 1869, the *Gazette des Beaux-Arts* reported: 'M. Édouard Manet has painted the tragic episode that brought our intervention in Mexico to a close. The death of Maximilian has still not been accepted as history, since M. Manet has been unofficially informed that his picture, which is in fact excellent, would be rejected at the next Salon if he insisted on presenting it. This is strange, but what is even stranger is that when M. Manet executed a sketch of the picture on a lithographic stone and the printer Lemercier presented it for registration, an order was immediately given that the image should not be authorized for sale, even though it bears no title.'

MANET
The Execution of the
Emperor Maximilian
1867

Manet produced three oil paintings and a lithograph of the execution of the Emperor. Although the key compositional elements did not vary significantly in these works, they became successively anti-Napoleonic in their treatment of the theme. In this, the first version, the firing squad's uniform is blatantly Mexican (observe their wide-bottomed trousers and the hat of the man to the right of the squad), and the figure of the Emperor as victim is indistinct.

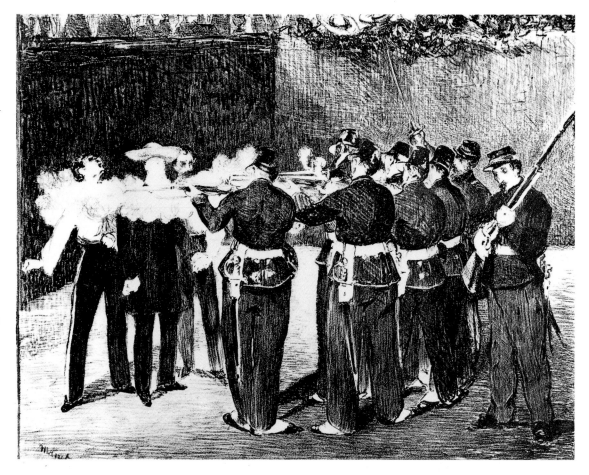

MANET
The Execution of the
Emperor Maximilian
1868

Only three fragments of Manet's second oil painting have survived, but it is thought to have been the basis for this lithograph. Maximilian and his two Mexican generals are shown linking hands as they face the firing squad, who are now wearing what appear to be French uniforms. A wall has also been introduced, behind which can be seen the crosses and tombstones of a cemetery.

The government censor refused to allow this lithograph to be sold, despite its having no title – thus prompting Zola to write an impassioned attack on censorship in *La Tribune française* on February 4th.

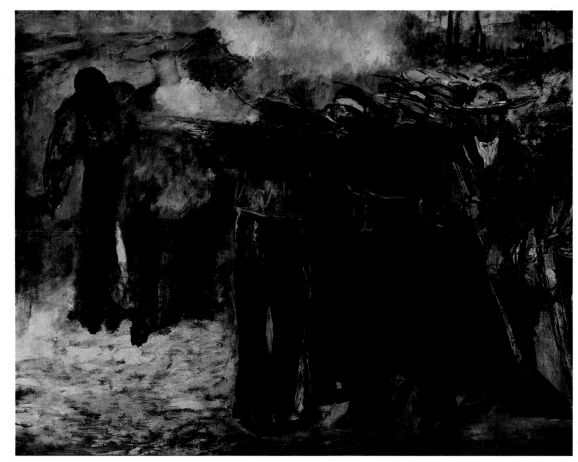

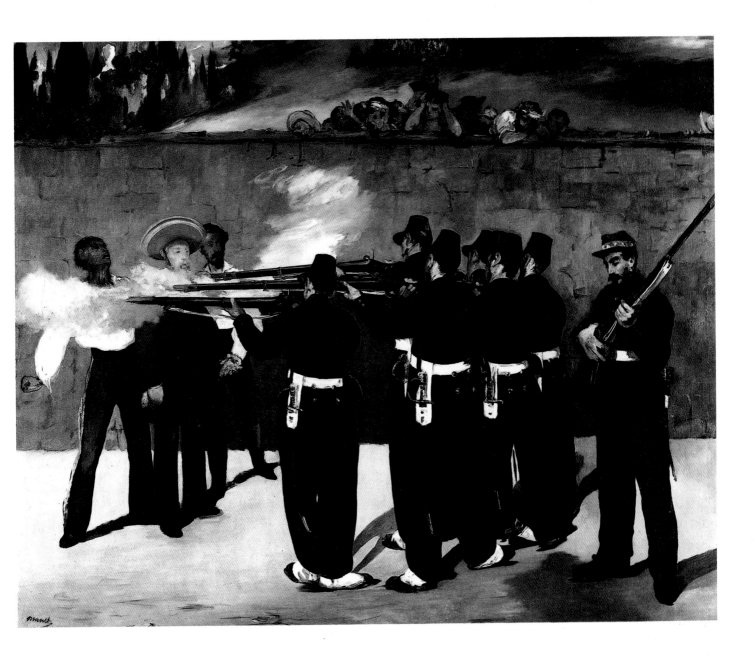

MANET
The Execution of the
Emperor Maximilian
1868–9

In this, the final version of the painting, Manet's political intention is even more clear. The Emperor stands 'Christ-like' between the two generals, his sombrero tipped backward to form a 'halo', whilst the Mexican peasants behind the cemetery wall look on in horror. Finally, the soldiers' uniform with its kepi, white leather belt and tapered trousers, is French.

Manet had in fact emphasized his political intention. In the first version the firing squad was dressed in Mexican costume. In later versions they are wearing what are virtually French Army uniforms. He even persuaded his friend Commandant Lejosne to 'lend' him a platoon of soldiers to serve as models.

But Manet was not solely motivated by political concerns. He had always wanted to paint a large historical painting of the kind that would normally have appealed to the Salon jury. Moreover, he was the only Impressionist who consistently submitted works to the Salon, and this craving for official recognition was possibly one of the reasons why he never 'compromised' himself by exhibiting at any of the Impressionist exhibitions. In the preface to the catalogue of his one-man exhibition in 1867 Manet had explicitly stated that he 'never wished to protest', the clear inference being that he wanted to avoid alienating the official art world. Indeed, some years later he tried to secure a commission to decorate the Hôtel de Ville when it was being rebuilt after the Commune. He also longed for the Legion of Honour – and when he eventually received it, complained that it had arrived too late.

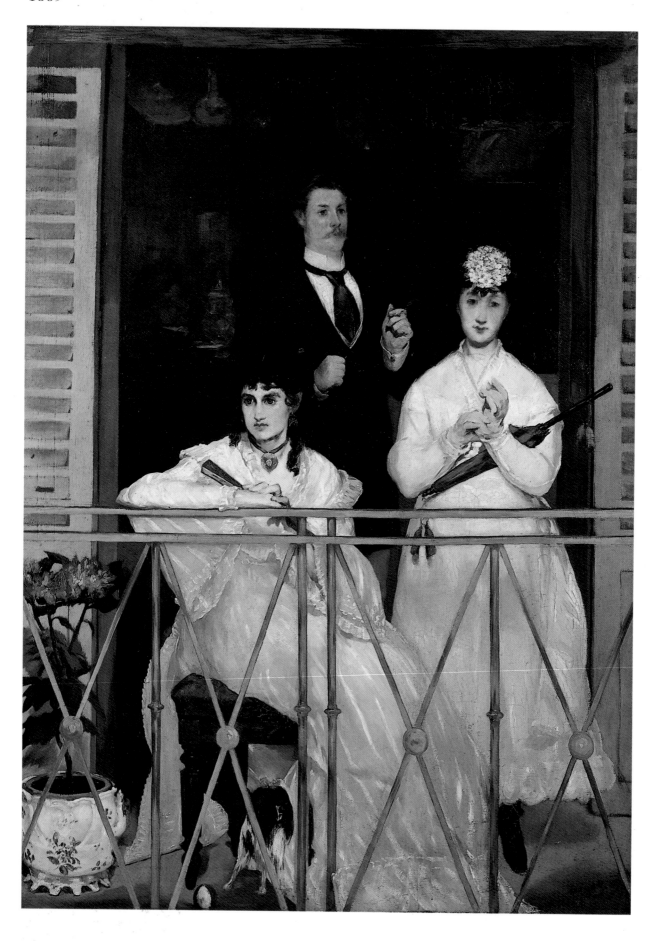

MANET
The Balcony
1868–9

Loosely based on Goya's *Majas on the Balcony*, this painting was shown at the Salon of 1869, where it attracted a good deal of contumely, such as the caricature by Bertall which first appeared in *Le Journal amusant* on May 15th, 1869 (right). The figures are: Berthe Morisot (seated); Antoine Guillemet, an academic painter of landscapes; and Fanny Claus, a young violinist. Barely visible in the background, bearing a ewer, is the figure of Léon Leenhoff, Manet's putative son.

DEGAS
Portrait of Mme G.
1868–9

Joséphine Gaujelin was a ballet-dancer at the Opéra (where the archives record her name, correctly spelt, as Joséphine Gozelin). She also features in the centre of Degas' *The Dance Class* of 1871.

BAZILLE
View of the Village
1868

Berthe Morisot was not alone in appreciating this painting at the Salon of 1869. Shortly after the exhibition opened, Bazille wrote to his parents: 'I have received compliments from M. Puvis de Chavannes, which flattered me a lot.'

▲ THE SALON OF 1869

Berthe Morisot did not enter any work for the 1869 Salon, but described her reactions to the exhibition in a letter to her mother:

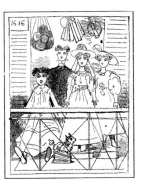

I need hardly tell you that the first thing I did was to go to Room M [where Manet's The Balcony, which featured her portrait was hanging]. There I found Manet with his hat on, standing in bright sunshine, and looking dazed. He begged me to go and look at the painting, as he did not dare move a step.

I have never seen a face as expressive as his; he was laughing at one moment, and looking worried at the next, assuring everybody that his picture was no good, and then adding in the same breath that it was bound to be a success. I think he has a very charming temperament, which I greatly like.

His works give the impression of a wild, or even an unripe fruit. I do not dislike them, though I prefer his portrait of Zola (p.53).

I myself look more strange than ugly. It seems that people are using the phrase 'femme fatale' about the painting…

Degas has a very pretty painting [Portrait of Mme G.] of a very ugly woman in black, with a hat and a cashmere shawl falling from her shoulders. The background is that of a very light interior, showing a corner of a mantelpiece in half-tones. It is very subtle and distinguished. Antonin Proust's entries look very well, despite the fact that they are badly hung. Corot is very poetic, as usual. I think that he has spoiled the sketch we saw at home by working too much on it in his studio.

The tall Bazille has painted something that is very good [View of the Village]. It is a little girl in a light dress, seated in the shade of a tree, with a glimpse of the village in the background. There is much light and sun in it. He has tried to do what we have often attempted – a figure in the outdoor light – and he seems to have been successful.

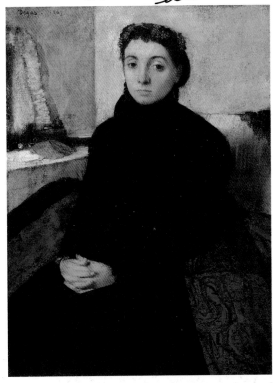

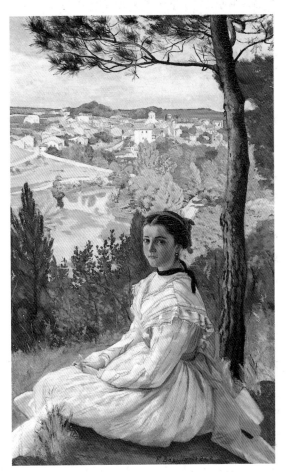

red on face & hat all reflection of sash.

1870

Soldiers and Exiles

BAZILLE
The Artist's Studio
1870

Bazille was sharing a studio with Renoir at 9 rue de la Condamine when he painted this work. Shown are: Edmond Maître, at the piano; Manet, looking at the easel; Monet, behind him, smoking a pipe; Zola, on the stairs; and Renoir, sitting on a table. Manet later added the tall figure of Bazille. (Detail on pp.254–5.)

Political events – the outbreak of the Franco-Prussian war, the proclamation of the Third Republic and the Siege of Paris – greatly affect the lives of the artists. Manet, Degas and Renoir enlist; Bazille is killed in action, aged 29; and Monet and Pissarro flee to England, where they meet the Parisian dealer Paul Durand-Ruel.

JANUARY

Fantin-Latour paints *A Studio in the Batignolles Quarter* (below right) depicting most of the Batignolles group whose meetings at the Café Guerbois ◆ (pp.46–7) contributed to the birth of Impressionism. It was exhibited at the Salon in April.

Durand-Ruel establishes himself in an inferior gallery in the rue Lafayette. He later describes the move as 'the greatest mistake I ever made'.

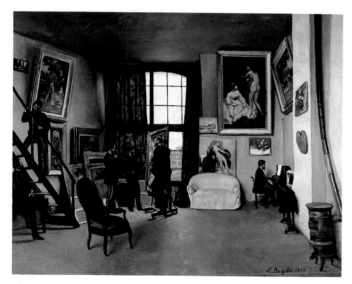

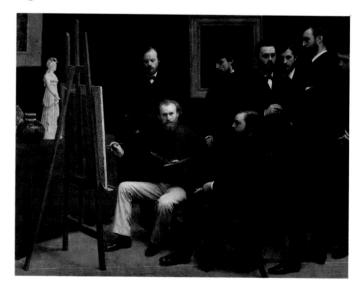

FEBRUARY

Monet and Renoir work, in shared poverty, at Bougival.
18th Manet exhibits *The Philosopher* and watercolours at the Cercle de l'Union Artistique in the Place Vendôme.
23rd Manet has a duel with Edmond Duranty at the Café Guerbois over an insulting remark made by the critic. Duranty is injured, but they make it up almost immediately.

MARCH

Manet virtually repaints Morisot's portrait of her mother and sister (p.66), which she is planning to send to the Salon. She is furious, and very reluctant to exhibit the painting, but eventually relents.

FANTIN-LATOUR
A Studio in the Batignolles Quarter
1870

The portraits in this work were painted during individual sittings in Manet's studio, and are of: (from the left) Scholderer, Manet, Renoir, Astruc (seated), Zola, Maître, Bazille and Monet.

MONET
On the Beach, Trouville
1870

Monet was working in Trouville when the Franco-Prussian war broke out. A number of the paintings from this period reveal the extent to which, both in subject matter and treatment, he was moving towards the ideals of Impressionsim. Notable in this sketch is the way he juxtaposes light and dark tones to emphasize the value of each. The figure on the left is that of his wife, Camille.

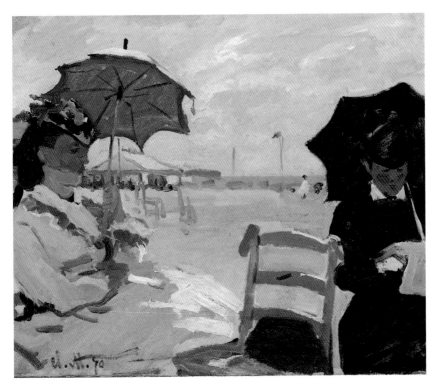

Bazille paints a picture of his friends in his studio – to which Manet later adds a portrait of the artist (opposite).

20th A number of progressive artists put forward a list for the Salon jury as an alternative to the one drawn up by the conservative majority. Manet and Millet are included in the alternative list of candidates, but are not selected for the jury.

APRIL

Renoir and Bazille share rooms at 8 rue des Beaux-Arts.

Monet works in Trouville and Le Havre.

3rd Opening of the Salon. Among the works hung are Bazille's *Summer Scene*; Degas' *Madame Camus in Red*; Manet's *The Music Lesson* and *Portrait of Eva Gonzalès* (p.54); Morisot's *The Mother and Sister of the Artist* (p.66) and *Young Woman at a Window*; Pissarro's *Autumn*, plus another landscape by him; Renoir's *Bather with a Griffon* and *A Woman of Algeria* (pp.64–5); and two views of the Canal St-Martin by Sisley.

12th Degas has a letter published in *Paris-Journal* calling for a better hanging of the Salon. He suggests there should be only two rows of pictures, with a space of about 30cm (12in) between each picture; oil paintings and drawings should not be separated; and each exhibitor should have the right to withdraw his work after a certain period.

MONET
The Hôtel des Roches-Noires
1870

The Hôtel des Roches-Noires – so called because of the seaweed-covered rocks in the area – was the most sumptuous in Trouville, with 150 rooms, indoor bathing facilities and a concert hall. To emphasize its cosmopolitan flavour, Monet painted the American, French and British flags fluttering in front of it.

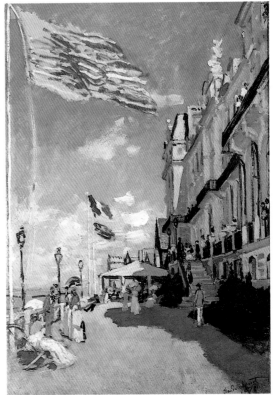

MAY

18th Cézanne is a witness at Zola's wedding.

JUNE

28th Monet marries Camille Doncieux in Paris.

JULY

Manet stays at St-Germain-en-Laye with his friend the Italian painter Giuseppe de Nittis.

AUGUST

10th Following France's declaration of war against Prussia, Renoir is called up and posted to Bordeaux with the 10th Cavalry Division. Bazille enlists in the 1st Zouave Regiment.

SEPTEMBER

The siege of Paris begins. Degas enlists in the National Guard and is posted with the artillery, although he is 'virtually blind in one eye'.
Manet's sends his family to Oloron-Ste-Marie in the Pyrenees, shuts up his studio, and sends thirteen of his paintings to Duret.
Mary Cassatt returns to the USA.
Monet moves to London, staying first at 11 Arundel Street, Piccadilly, then at 1 Bath Place, Kensington.
Cézanne takes refuge from conscription in L'Estaque, where he is visited by Zola.
Durand-Ruel moves to London with an extensive collection of pictures, some committed to him for safe-keeping. He takes a house for his family in Brompton Crescent and rents the unfortunately named 'German Gallery' at 168 New Bond Street.
Pissarro and his family go to stay with his friend Ludovic Piette in Brittany.
Sisley, according to one account stays in Louveciennes, according to another in Bougival. He also spends some time in Paris – where his father dies, leaving him nothing.

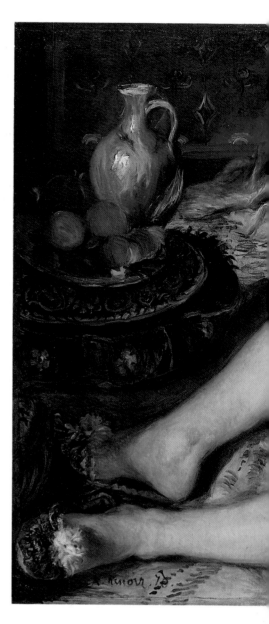

OCTOBER

Degas is posted to the fortifications of Paris, north of the Bois de Vincennes, where his commanding officer is Henri Rouart, a friend from school days who is an industrialist and amateur painter. (Rouart would later become an ardent patron of the Impressionists.)

NOVEMBER

Daubigny introduces Monet to Durand-Ruel in London.
Pissarro's daughter, born in October, dies.
11th Manet enlists as a lieutenant in the National Guard.
28th Bazille is killed, aged 29, in a minor skirmish at Beaune-la-Rolonde in Burgundy.

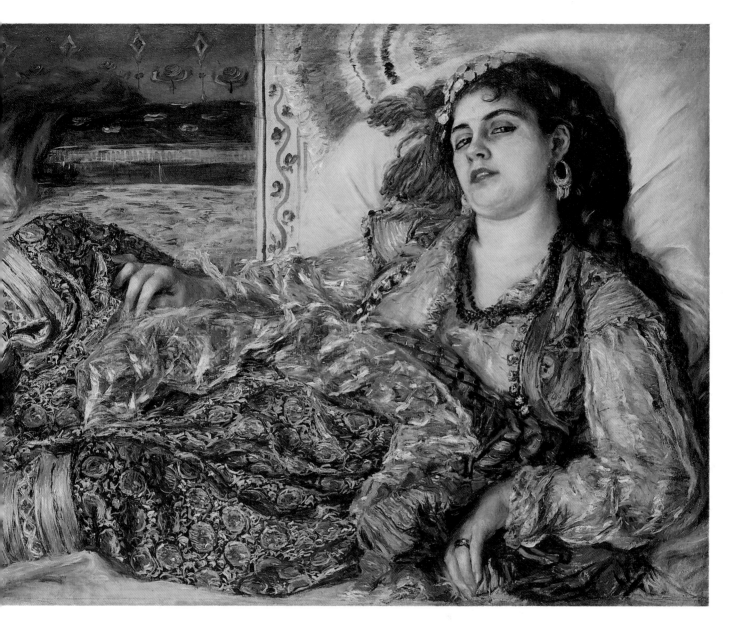

DECEMBER

Pissarro and his family move to London, living at 2 Chatham Terrace, Palace Road, Norwood ▲ (p.71). He meets Durand-Ruel.

7th Manet is transferred to staff headquarters, where he is in company with Meissonier and other painters.

10th Zola leaves Paris for Marseilles. He then goes to Bordeaux, where the government is situated, and is employed as secretary to a politician. Durand-Ruel's gallery in New Bond Street holds the first exhibition of the Society of French Artists (devised by Durand-Ruel largely for public relations purposes), under the patronage of Corot, Courbet, Millet, Diaz de la Peña, Daubigny and Dupré. The 144 works on show are mostly by earlier Romantic painters and members of the Barbizon School, but there are also two views of Sydenham and Norwood by Pissarro (which Durand-Ruel buys) and Monet's *Entrance to Trouville Harbour*, which the artist had brought with him from France.

RENOIR
A Woman of Algeria
1870

Inspired by Delacroix, who visited Algiers and painted a large number of pictures with Algerian motifs, Renoir produced a few paintings in an 'Orientalist' style, although not travelling to Algeria himself until 1881. When exhibited at the Salon of 1870, the work received favourable notice from the critics. The model was Lise Tréhot ◆ (p.50), this being one of the last paintings in which she posed for Renoir.

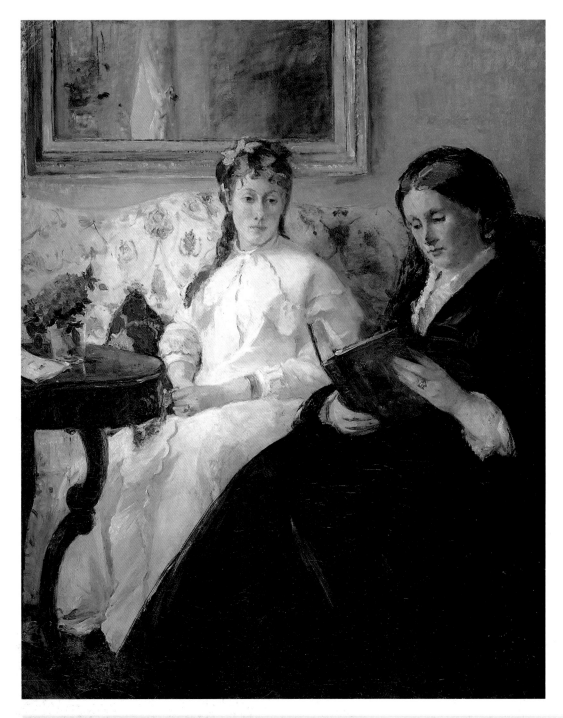

MORISOT
The Mother and Sister of the Artist
1870

Painted for the Salon of 1870 and retouched by Manet against Morisot's wishes (*see* March), this portrait shows Mme Morisot reading to her daughter, Edma. The latter had recently married Adolphe Pontillon, a naval officer, and had come home to have her first child. Edma's pregnancy is not highlighted, but her reflective air and accented resemblance to her mother suggest that Morisot regarded the work as an intimate family document.

OTHER EVENTS

- France lured into invading Prussia
- Paris besieged
- Napoleon III abdicates after French defeat at Sedan; Third Republic proclaimed in France
- The French withdraw from Rome, which becomes the capital of Italy
- Compulsory education introduced in England
- Doctrine of papal infallibility promulgated by Vatican Council
- Lister invents antiseptic spray
- First train journey across the American continent
- Schliemann begins excavations at Hissarlik, in Turkey, which he believes to be the site of Troy
- Jules de Goncourt, Dumas *père* and Dickens die

MANET'S LETTERS FROM THE SIEGE OF PARIS

During the siege of Paris Manet wrote regularly to his wife, Suzanne, at Oloron-Ste-Marie, the letters being delivered by the famous balloon post that kept the capital in touch with the rest of the country.

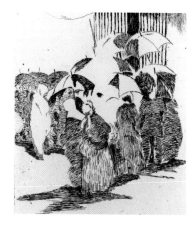

An etching by Manet (1870–1) of a queue outside a butcher's shop.

September 30th

It's a long time since I heard from you. Some of my letters should have reached you by the balloons that left Paris. I think there's one leaving tomorrow or the day after. The Prussians seem to be regretting their decision to besiege Paris. They must have thought it easier than it is. It's true that we can't have milk with our coffee any more; the butchers are only open three days a week, people queue up outside from four in the morning, and there's nothing left for the latecomers. We eat meat only once a day, and I believe all sensible Parisians must be doing the same.

I've seen the Morisot ladies recently, who are probably going to leave Passy, which is likely to be bombarded. Paris nowadays is a huge camp. From five in the morning until evening, the Militia and the National Guards who are not on duty do drill, and are turning into real soldiers. Otherwise life is very boring in the evenings – all the café-restaurants are closed after ten, and one just has to go to bed.

October 23rd

The weather is terrible today, my dear Suzanne. It's impossible to set foot outside, particularly since my foot is only just getting better and I can only wear very light shoes. You must have seen from the papers that the Paris army made a concerted attack on the enemy positions on Friday. The fighting went on all day and I believe the Prussians sustained great losses… We're having enough of being boxed in here without any outside contacts. A smallpox outbreak is spreading, and at the moment we're down to 75 grams of meat per person, while milk is only available to the children and the sick.

November 23rd

Marie's big cat has been killed, and we suspect somebody in the house; it was for a meal, of course, and Marie was in tears! She's taking very good care of us. One doesn't feel like seeing anyone, it's always the same conversations; the evenings go very slowly; the Café Guerbois is my only distraction, and that's become pretty monotonous.

I think of you all the time and have filled the bedroom with your portraits. Tell mother not to worry and to make the most of the good weather. We're having torrential rain here and I'm revelling in your woollen socks, which come in very handy because we're up to our ankles in mud on the fortifications.

To Eva Gonzalès:

November 19th

For the past two months I've had no news from my poor Suzanne, who must be very anxious, though I write to her frequently. We're all soldiers here. Degas and I are in the artillery as volunteer gunners. I'm looking forward to having you paint my portrait in my huge gunner's greatcoat when you're back. Tissot covered himself in glory in the action at La Gonchère. My brothers and Guillemet are in the National Guard battle units, and are waiting to go into action. My paintbox and easel are stuffed into my knapsack, so there's no excuse for wasting my time, and I am going to take advantage of the facilities available. A lot of cowards have left here, including our friend Zola, Fantin, etc. I don't think they'll be very well received when they return. We're beginning to feel the pinch here; horse meat is a delicacy, donkey is exorbitantly expensive; there are butchers' shops for dogs, cats and rats. Paris is deathly sad. When will it all end?

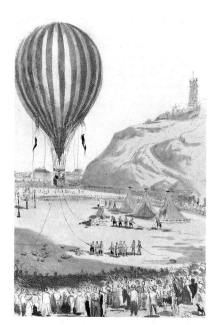

The dispatch of the balloon which carried post out of Paris to unoccupied France.

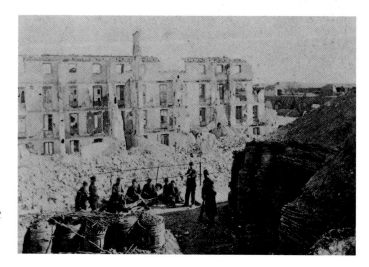

A view of the fort of Montrouge during the siege of Paris.

1871

The 'Terror' of the Commune

MANET
The Barricade
1871

Manet had intended to paint a large work in protest against the suppression of the Commune, but he only produced a drawing and two lithographs (*see* p.10).

The Franco-Prussian War is followed by the proclamation of the Commune in Paris. Courbet's first action as President of the Art Commission is to organize the demolition of the Napoleonic column in Place Vendôme, but after seventy-two days the Commune is suppressed and Courbet imprisoned. In London, Durand-Ruel exhibits the works of Monet and Pissarro, and forges a lasting and significant link with the future Impressionist artists.

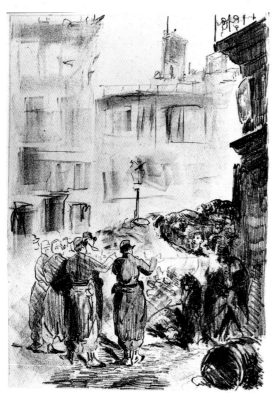

The Communard, Gustave Lemaire, was among those who received an invitation (above right) to watch the destruction of the column in Place Vendôme. Courbet, who ordered the demolition, was the subject of many caricatures, including this one of him using the Napoleonic column as a walking stick (below right).

JANUARY

4th Renoir is posted to Libourne, where he contracts dysentery. He convalesces with his uncle in Bordeaux.

21st In a letter to Pissarro, Durand-Ruel apologizes for not meeting him when he came to his London gallery and adds:

'Your friend Monet has asked me for your address. He did not know that you were in England.'

FEBRUARY

A Paris National Guard is formed in protest at the armistice between France and Prussia. Anti-government demonstrations take place across the capital.

12th Manet joins his family at Oloron-Sainte-Marie in the Pyrenees. Nine days later they travel to Bordeaux, where they meet Zola.

MARCH

Renoir is stationed at Vic-en-Bigorre, near Tarbes for two months, where he spends much of his time riding and teaching a young girl to paint.

Monet paints views of Hyde Park, the Pool of London and the Thames at Westminster (opposite).

The Royal Academy rejects works by Pissarro and Monet. Sisley moves to Louveciennes.

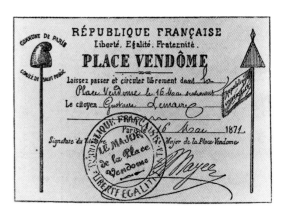

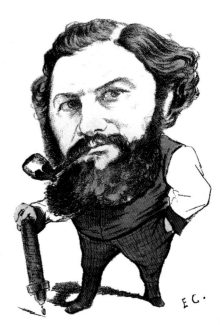

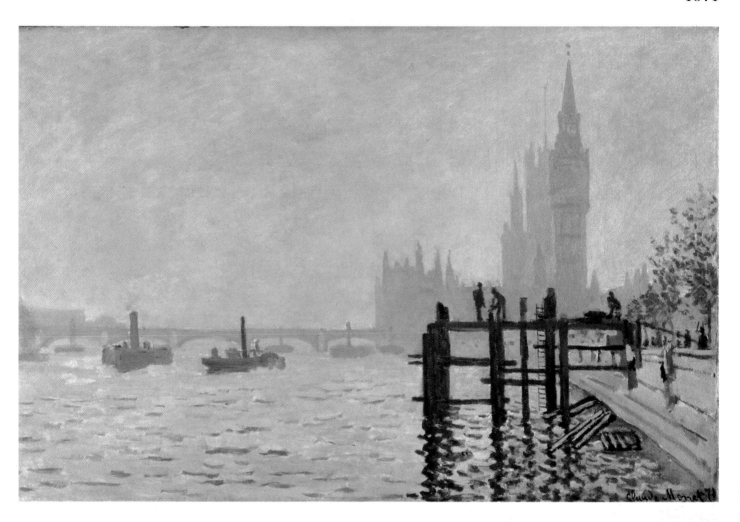

Degas visits his friends the Valpinçons at Ménil-Hubert.

18th The second exhibition of Durand-Ruel's Society of French Artists opens at his gallery in London. A total of 139 paintings are shown, including two each by Monet and Pissarro.

28th Proclamation of the Commune in Paris. Courbet is made President of the Art Commission. Under his leadership, the French Academy in Rome, the École des Beaux-Arts and the awarding of prizes at the Salon are abolished.

APRIL

The Commune sets up a federation of artists, consisting of fifteen painters (including Manet) and ten sculptors.

Durand-Ruel opens a gallery in the Place des Martyrs in Brussels.

Manet goes to stay at Le Pouliguen in Brittany for a month.

Berthe Morisot and her parents move to St-Germain-en-Laye.

Renoir returns to Paris and rents a room in the rue du Dragon. He secures a pass from Raoul Rigaud, the Commune's Prefect of Police, enabling him to go sketching outside the walls.

23rd Gauguin is demobilized from the navy. Through the good offices of his guardian, Gustave Arosa – whose daughter teaches him to paint – he obtains a job with Bertin, a firm of stockbrokers in the rue Lafitte.

**MONET
The Thames and Westminster**
1871

The subject of this painting was one to which Monet would revert frequently over the next twenty years. This early version is unusual, however, as its viewpoint is at ground level on the Embankment – most of the other versions were painted from a room in the Savoy Hotel ◆ (p.229).

MAY

12th Through the intervention of Durand-Ruel, Monet's *Repose* and *Camille: Woman in the Green Dress* (p.39) as well as Pissarro's *Lower Norwood, London: Snow Effect* (opposite) and *Penge Station, Upper Norwood* are exhibited at the International Exhibition of Fine Art in Kensington. They are ignored by the critics.

16th Courbet presides over the demolition of the column to Napoleon in Place Vendôme.

28th The Communards are suppressed by the government.

JUNE

14th Pissarro marries Julie Vellay, his mother's servant (with whom he has been living since 1860), at the Registry Office in Croydon.

20th Durand-Ruel buys two paintings from Pissarro for 200 francs each. The painter returns to France to find his home despoiled by the Prussians, and most of his work either stolen or destroyed.

JULY

Manet goes to Versailles, where the government is now located, to try to persuade Léon Gambetta to sit for him – but his journey is in vain.

AUGUST

Manet holidays in Boulogne.
Renoir visits Bougival and Marlotte.
Berthe Morisot visits Cherbourg.

SEPTEMBER

Renoir rents a room at 34 rue Notre-Dame-des-Champs.
Monet goes to Holland – probably with Daubigny, who buys a picture from him. He paints mainly at Zaandam, near Amsterdam.

OCTOBER

Degas visits London, where he stays at the Hotel Conté in Golden Square. He goes to see the third exhibition of the Society of French Artists at Durand-Ruel's gallery in New Bond Street.
Monet and his family settle at Argenteuil.

NOVEMBER

22nd Pissarro's third son, Georges, is born in Louveciennes.

PISSARRO
Lower Norwood, London: Snow Effect
1870

Pissarro and his family arrived in London in 1870 and settled in the pleasant suburb of Upper Norwood at 2 Chatham Terrace, Palace Road (now 65 Palace Road). This work, one of the earliest Pissarro painted of the neighbourhood, is probably the same as that entitled *Snow Effect*, which was exhibited at Durand-Ruel's gallery in London during December 1870 and the International Exhibition of Fine Art, Kensington, in May of the following year.

OTHER EVENTS

- Wilhelm I, King of Prussia, is declared Emperor of Germany in the Hall of Mirrors at Versailles
- Paris surrenders to the Prussians
- France signs the Peace of Frankfurt, ceding the greater part of Alsace-Lorraine to Prussia
- Thiers elected President of France
- British Act of Parliament legalizes labour unions
- Mont Cenis Tunnel, linking Italy and France, is completed
- First ascent of Mont Blanc by a woman climber
- Zola starts writing the first of his *Rougon-Macquart* novels
- Publication of Charles Darwin's *The Descent of Man*, Lewis Carroll's *Through the Looking Glass* and George Eliot's *Middlemarch*
- First performance of Verdi's *Aida* at the Opera House in Cairo

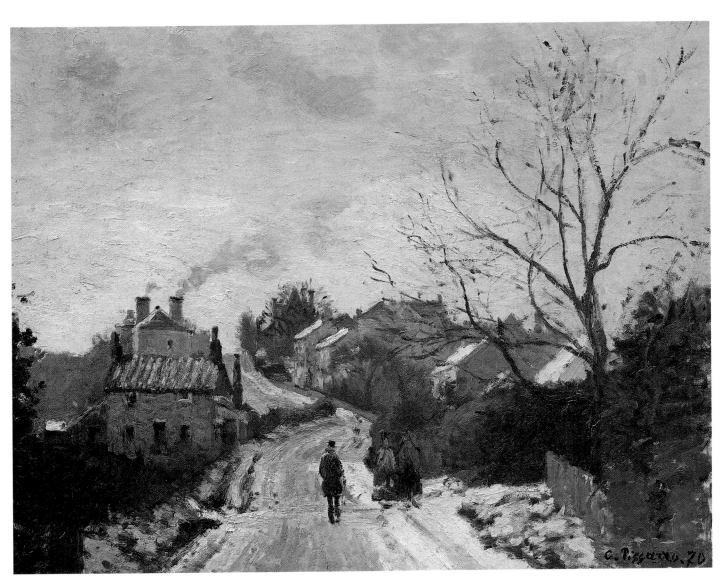

PISSARRO'S REACTIONS TO LIFE IN LONDON

Pissarro's initial disillusionment with life in England, especially the London art world, is evident from a letter to the art critic Théodore Duret (who was, in fact, an enthusiastic Anglophile):

I am here for only a short time. I count on returning to France as soon as possible. Yes, my dear Duret, I shan't stay here, and it is only abroad that one feels how beautiful, great and hospitable France is. What a difference here! One attracts only contempt, indifference, even rudeness; amongst colleagues there is the most egotistical jealousy and resentment. Here there is no art; everything is a question of business. As far as my private affairs are concerned, I've done nothing, except with Durand-Ruel who has bought two small paintings from me. My painting doesn't catch on at all, a fate that pursues me more or less everywhere.

LETTER TO THÉODORE DURET, June 1871

Nevertheless, both he and Monet enjoyed the change of landscape and familiarized themselves with British art:

Monet and I were very enthusiastic about the London landscapes. Monet worked in the parks, while I, living in Lower Norwood, at that time a charming suburb, studied the effect of fog, snow and springtime. We worked from nature. We also visited the museums. The watercolours and painting of Turner and Constable, the canvases of Old Crome, have certainly had an influence on us. We admired Gainsborough, Reynolds, Lawrence etc., but we were mostly struck by the landscape painters, who shared more in our aim with regard to 'plein-air' painting, light and fugitive effects. Watts, Rossetti strongly interested us among the modern men. Turner and Constable, while they taught us something, showed in their works that they had no understanding of the analysis of shadow, which in Turner's case is, in effect, a mere absence of light. As far as tone division is concerned, Turner proved the value of this as a method … although he did not apply it correctly and naturally.

LETTER TO WYNFORD DEWHURST, November 1902

1872

The Rise of Durand-Ruel

Not consigned?

SISLEY
The Square at Argenteuil
1872

This is one of four works that Sisley painted while staying with Monet. The artist uses perspective to lead the eye into the composition, in the background of which appears the tower of the church of Notre-Dame.

<u>*Buying*</u> *in bulk gives the dealer Durand-Ruel the opportunity to purchase works by Degas, Manet, Renoir and Sisley relatively cheaply. This year he also mounts the first exhibitions of Impressionist work to be held in London, though these are not a commercial success.*

JANUARY

Sisley stays with Monet at Argenteuil.

Durand-Ruel buys three works from Degas, his first purchase of the artist's work. He also buys twenty-four paintings from Manet for 35,000 francs.

4th Cézanne has an illegitimate son, Paul, by Hortense Fiquet and conceals the fact from his father ▲ (p.111).

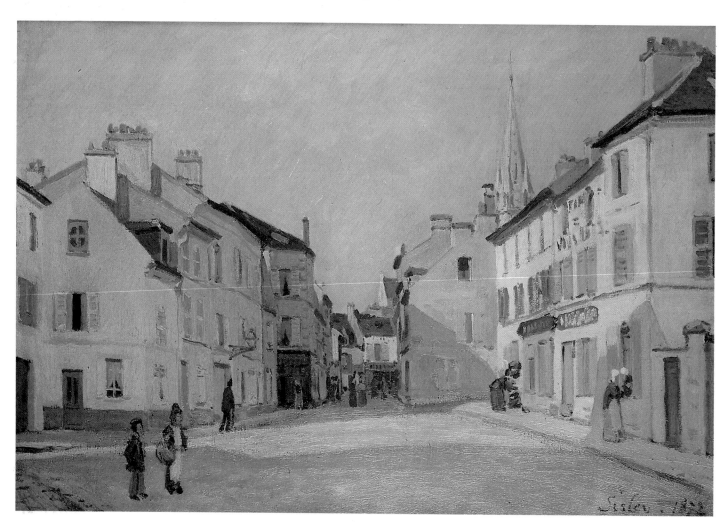

MARCH

12th Durand-Ruel buys his first painting by Sisley. Two days later he also buys his first painting by Renoir, *The Pont des Arts*, for 200 francs.

APRIL

12th Renoir's former model Lise Tréhot marries the architect George Brière de l'Isle ◆ (p.50).

29th The singer and collector Jean-Baptiste Faure ● (p.81) sells forty-two Impressionist paintings at auction. Prices are very low, Manet's *Pulcinello* attracting the highest bid at 2000 francs. Many of the paintings are withdrawn, since they fail to reach their reserves.

MAY

1st Opening of the Salon. Renoir's *Parisian Women in Algerian Dress* is rejected. Manet's *The Battle of the 'Kearsage' and the 'Alabama'* (p.31), on loan from Durand-Ruel (who had bought it in January for 3000 francs), is hung. Berthe Morisot and Mary Cassatt each have two works accepted. Degas, Monet, Pissarro and Sisley do not submit.

JUNE

4th The fourth exhibition of Durand-Ruel's Society of French Artists opens in London, including work by Degas, Monet, Pissarro and Sisley.

18th Cézanne, Manet, Pissarro, Renoir, Sisley and others sign a petition demanding another Salon des Refusés.

25th During one of his regular visits to Holland, Manet visits the Frans Hals Museum in Haarlem, where he is greatly impressed by the Vermeers.

JULY

Berthe Morisot visits Spain, then stays with her married sister Edma (pp.66 and 89) in Maurecourt.

AUGUST

Sisley working in Villeneuve-la-Garonne. Pissarro moves to the rue de l'Hermitage in Pontoise, where he is joined by Cézanne.

OCTOBER

12th Degas and his brother set sail for America on the *Scotia*. They arrive in New York on October 24th, then go on to New Orleans.

NOVEMBER

2nd The fifth exhibition of Durand-Ruel's Society of French Artists opens in London. It includes work by Degas, Manet, Pissarro, Renoir and Sisley.

19th In a letter to Tissot from New Orleans, Degas relates the pleasures of family life and the problems of painting family portraits ▲ (p.75).

MANET
Berthe Morisot
1884

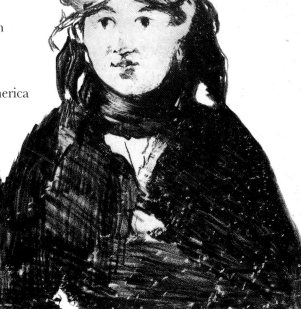

In 1872 Manet painted a portrait of Morisot which was highly praised by Mallarmé. Subsequently he produced two lithographs and an etching of her. In this lithograph Manet has emphasized the tonal contrast between Morisot's skin and clothes.

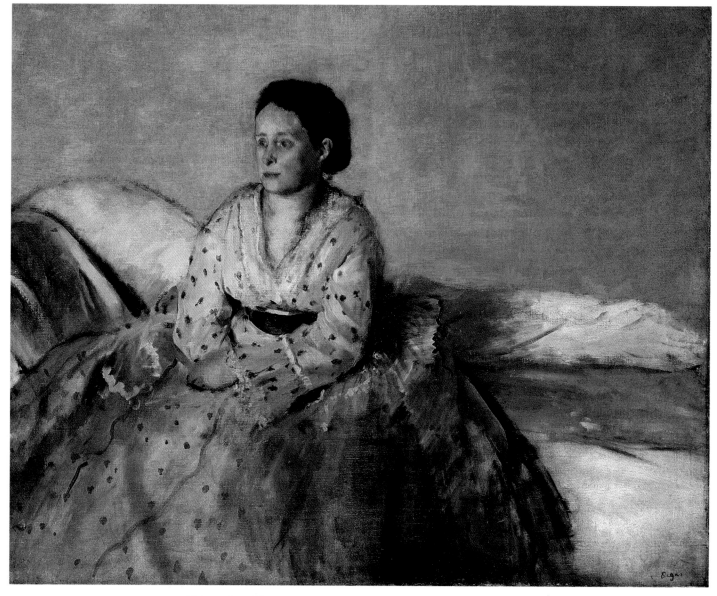

26th Sisley gives Pissarro one of his pictures.
He also suggests organizing a dinner for Durand-Ruel (there is, however, no record of the dinner taking place).

DECEMBER
The Seine bursts its banks. Sisley paints his first series of 'flood paintings' at Marly (p.94).

OTHER EVENTS

- Three-Emperors League formed in Berlin; an alliance between Russia, Germany and Austria-Hungary
- Civil war breaks out in Spain
- Grant re-elected President of USA
- Universal conscription introduced in France
- Business boom; France pays off debt to Germany
- Publication of Samuel Butler's *Erewhon* and Daudet's *Aventures prodigeuses de Tartarin de Tarascon*
- Bizet's *L'Arlésienne Suite* first performed
- Foundation stone of Wagnerian opera house laid in Bayreuth

DEGAS
Madame René de Gas
1872–3

DEGAS WRITES FROM AMERICA

DE GAS BROTHERS, New Orleans

What do you say to the heading? It is the firm's note paper. Here one speaks of nothing but cotton and exchange. Why do you not speak to me of other things? You do not write to me. What impression did my dance picture [exhibited by Durand-Ruel in London] *make on you and the others? Were you able to help in selling it? And the one of the family at the races, what is happening to that? Oh, how far from everything one is.*

DEGAS
Madame René de Gas
1872–3

Degas painted several portraits of his family while staying in New Orleans. His brother René had married his cousin, the young, blind widow Estelle Balfour. When this work was painted she was heavily pregnant with her fourth child, Jeanne, to whom Degas became godfather.

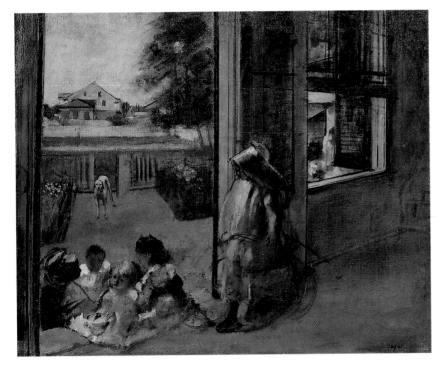

DEGAS
Children on a Doorstep (New Orleans)
1872

Degas began this work three weeks after his arrival in New Orleans, and in a letter to Tissot ▲ (right) mentioned the difficulties he found in persuading the children to pose. The painting went virtually unnoticed when shown at the second Impressionist exhibition ■ (p.96).

Excellent journey. New York has some charming spots. We spent scarcely two days there. What a degree of civilization! Steamers coming from Europe arrive like omnibuses at a station. We pass carriages, even trains on the water. It's like England in her best mood.

After four days on the train, we arrived in New Orleans. You cannot imagine a wagon-lit 'sliping car' [sic]. *A real dormitory. Behind curtains one can undress down to one's vest, if one wants to, and then climb into a proper, well-made bed. Everything is done simply and, except for some details of taste, one says to oneself. 'It's true, just what I needed.'*

Villas with columns in different styles, painted white, in gardens of magnolias, orange trees, banana trees, negroes in old clothes like the junk from La Jardinière

[a junk shop in Paris] *or Marseilles, rosy white children in black arms, charabancs or omnibuses drawn by mules, the tall funnels of the steamboats towering at the end of the main street, that is a bit of local colour, with a brilliant light at which my eyes complain.*

Everything is beautiful in this world of the people, but one Paris laundry girl with bare arms is worth it all for such a confirmed Parisian as I am. The right way is to concentrate, and one can only do that by seeing little. I am doing some family portraits, but the big thing will be when I come back.

René [the artist's brother] *has superb children, an excellent wife* (opposite), *she scarcely seems blind, though her case is almost hopeless, and he has a good position in business. He is happy, and it is his country, even more perhaps than France.*

You with your fantastic energy would be able to extract money from this crowd of stockbrokers and cotton dealers. I shall make no attempt to earn money here.

I hope this letter crosses one from you. Did you get my photographs? Here I have acquired the taste for money, and once back I shall know how to earn some, I promise you.

If you see Millais, tell him I'm very sorry to have missed him, and tell him how much I appreciate him. Remember me to young Deschamps, to Legros, to Whistler, who has really struck a truly personal note in that finely balanced power of expression, a mysterious mingling of land and water.

I have not yet written to Manet, and naturally, he has not sent me a line. The arrival of the mail in the morning really excites me. Nothing is more difficult than doing family portraits. To make a cousin sit for you when she is nursing a brat of two months is quite hard work. To get young children to pose on the steps is another job of work which doubles the fatigues of the first. It is the art of giving pleasure, and one must look the part.

A good family! It really is a good thing to be married, to have fine children, to be free of the necessity of always being gallant. I must say it's time one thought about it.

Good-bye. Write to me. I shall not leave the country before the middle of January.

LETTER TO TISSOT, November 19th, 1872

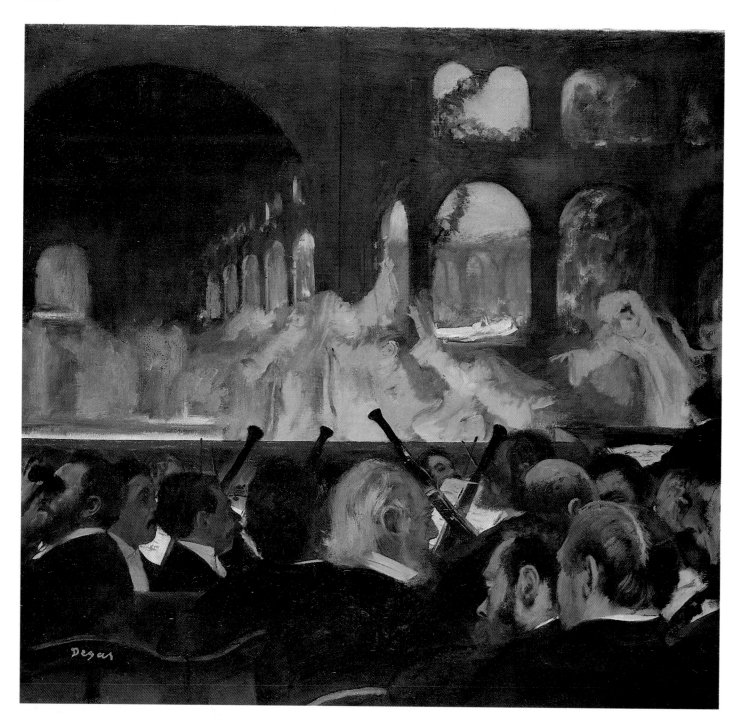

 THE IMPRESSIONIST MARKET IN BRITAIN

In the early 1870s, thanks to Durand-Ruel, whose gallery showed works by Monet and Pissarro and later by Degas, Renoir and Sisley, Londoners had an opportunity to see Impressionist works before Impressionism was recognizable as a movement. But at first Durand-Ruel appears to have made no sales to British buyers – who seem to have felt little sympathy for the Impressionists' paintings, despite the fact that these owed a great deal to the landscape traditions of Turner and Constable. Nor were

DEGAS
The Ballet from 'Robert le Diable'
1876

This, the second version of *Robert le Diable*, was commissioned by Faure ● (p.81) in 1874. The subject, the most famous scene from an opera by Giacomo Meyerbeer, was close to the singer's heart as the composer was Faure's mentor and friend. Those portrayed include: Désiré Dihau, musician (third from the left); Albert Hecht, collector and close friend of Degas (far left with opera glasses); and Ludovic Lepic, painter and engraver (the bearded figure in profile, second from the right).

collectors willing to offer much for them, even though they were prepared to pay huge sums for paintings by living British artists (Alma-Tadema's *Roman Picture Gallery*, for example, fetched £10,000 and Holman-Hunt's *The Shadow of the Cross* sold for £11,000).

Probably the first British collector to purchase works by the Impressionists was Henry Hill of Marine Parade, Brighton, to whom Durand-Ruel sold 'five or six very fine pictures' by Degas before he closed his New Bond Street Gallery in 1875. After Hill's death these paintings were auctioned at Christie's in 1889 and 1892 ('pour rien', as Durand-Ruel ruefully remarked), which constituted the first appearance of the Impressionists in the London salerooms ◆ (p.190).

In 1881 the Greek-born stockbroker Constantine Alexander Ionides bought Degas' *The Ballet from 'Robert le Diable'* (opposite), which had been commissioned by Faure ● (p.81) and is now in the Victoria & Albert Museum in London. But in the following years only a few individuals ventured to buy these 'dangerous' new paintings, and even then only on a small scale.

Sickert bought four or five works by Degas at the Hill sale, but had to sell them on his divorce; Arthur Kay, who had studied art in Paris, bought one of Monet's *Haystacks* in 1892 for £200; and in the same year an otherwise unknown Mr Burke of London bought two pictures by Pissarro, followed by two Sisleys in 1893 and a Degas in 1898.

The writer George Moore (p.46) assembled a small collection of relatively minor works by Manet, Monet and Berthe Morisot, and also persuaded his friend Lord Grimthorpe to buy several Impressionist works. Grimthorpe's collection was sold at Christie's on May 12th, 1906, achieving the following amounts: Degas' *Dancer with a Tambourine*, 35 guineas; Sisley's *View on the Seine*, 160 guineas; Monet's *The Hospice Lighthouse*, 195 guineas; Manet's *Young Girl with a White Cravat*, 245 guineas; and a pastel by Manet, *Lady with a Fan*, 17 guineas. It is interesting to note that only twelve years later, when the pictures of another of Moore's friends, Sir William Eden, were sold at the same auction rooms, Degas' pastel *The Dancer* fetched 2000 guineas and *The Laundresses* 2300 guineas.

Up to the time of Durand-Ruel's magnificent exhibition at the Grafton Galleries in 1905 (*see* p.232), British collectors had bought only fifty Impressionist paintings – whereas their American counterparts had amassed about 200. Sales at the exhibition itself were disappointing: of the 312 paintings on show, Durand-Ruel only sold about ten. However, one of the buyers was Mr (later Sir) Hugh Lane, who was anxious to acquire a collection of modern French pictures in order to found a gallery of modern art in Dublin; and either then or shortly afterwards he bought a remarkable group of Impressionist paintings, including Manet's *Music in the Tuileries Gardens* (p.25) and *Portrait of Eva Gonzalès* (p.54), Monet's *Vétheuil*, Renoir's *Umbrellas* and Pissarro's *Spring in Louveciennes*. When Lane perished in the sinking of the *Lusitania* in 1915, his pictures were on loan to the National Gallery in London but had been relegated to the cellars. There they remained until 1917, when they became the subject of prolonged litigation between the national galleries of England and Ireland due to the ambiguous wording of Lane's will.

1873

Gathering of the Future Impressionists

MANET
Repose: A Portrait of
Berthe Morisot
1870

Exhibited at the Salon of 1873, this was the second portrait by Manet of Berthe Morisot, painted when she was thirty. Its loose, sketchy style aroused considerable criticism, mixed with some praise for its 'modernity'. Morisot later told her daughter that she was in considerable discomfort while sitting for the portrait as her left leg was drawn up underneath her, and Manet would not let her alter its position.

Despite the fact that an increasing number of the future Impressionists are still working outside Paris, there is a growing sense of common purpose among the artists, which culminates in the formation of the Société Anonyme des Artistes, the primary aim of which is to mount group exhibitions free from selection by a jury.

JANUARY

Théodore Duret buys Renoir's *Study in Summer* for 400 francs from a dealer, and then *Lise with a Parasol* (p.51) from the artist for 1200 francs.

FEBRUARY

Cézanne stays with Dr Gachet at his new house in Auvers-sur-Oise.

MARCH

Inspired by Gachet, who is an enthusiastic engraver, Pissarro decides to takes up etching again.
The sixth exhibition of Durand-Ruel's Society of French Artists opens in London, including work by Degas, Manet, Monet, Pissarro and Sisley.

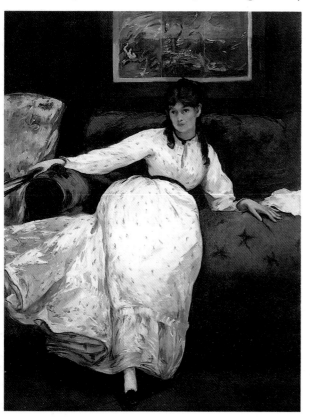

APRIL

Morisot paints at Fécamp in Normandy. Durand-Ruel buys several paintings from Monet and pays Degas 1000 francs for unspecified works.

MAY

Opening of the Salon. Renoir's *Riding in the Bois de Boulogne* (opposite left) is rejected. Manet exhibits *Repose: A Portrait of Berthe Morisot* (left) and *Le Bon Bock*, which is enthusiastically received. Other works hung include a pastel by Berthe Morisot and a painting by Mary Cassatt. Monet, Pissarro and Sisley do not submit.
15th The Exposition Artistique des Oeuvres Refusés (organized, like the Salon des Refusés of 1863, on the initiative of the artists themselves) opens in a disused drill hall. It arouses a great deal of interest, and Renoir's *Riding in the Bois de Boulogne* (opposite left) is well received.

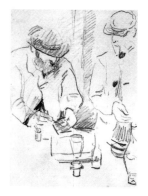

CÉZANNE
The Artist Engraving
beside Dr Gachet
1873

Dr Gachet moved to Auvers-sur-Oise in 1872. He converted the attic of his house into a studio, where the following year he, Cézanne, Pissarro and Armand Guillaumin produced engravings.

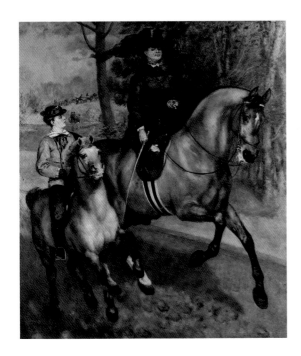

RENOIR
Riding in the Bois de Boulogne
1873

Intended for the Salon of 1873, this painting was, to Renoir's chagrin, rejected by the jury. In size – it was the largest picture he had ever painted – and in subject matter, it seemed suitable for that institution, and its rejection was one of the factors that inclined Renoir towards the idea of an independent exhibition.

DEGAS
The Dancing Examination
1873–5

This, the first large-scale painting by Degas of a group of dancers, was one of six works commissioned by the singer Faure ● (p.81). It is noticeable that the dancers are paying little attention to the *maître de ballet*, the renowned Jules Perrot, and it is now thought that his figure was added at a later date.

JUNE

Monet is introduced to Caillebotte. He builds a studio boat at Argenteuil, where Renoir visits him. Courbet – who had been imprisoned for presiding over the demolition of the column to Napoleon in the Place Vendôme (p.68) during the Commune – is released from jail because of ill health. Shortly afterwards he flees to Switzerland.
14th Van Gogh joins the London branch of Goupil's gallery. Sisley paints in Louveciennes and Pontoise.

JULY

Manet and his family spend the summer in Étaples, a fishing village near Boulogne.

SEPTEMBER

Renoir rents a studio at 35 rue St-Georges, in Montmartre.

OCTOBER

14th Manet makes sketches of the trial of Marshal Bazaine, court-martialled for surrendering to the Prussians at Metz in 1870. Bazaine receives a twenty-year sentence.
28th Faure ● (p.81) commissions *The Dancing Examination* (right) from Degas, reputedly for 5000 francs.

NOVEMBER

18th Manet sells five paintings to Faure at prices ranging from 2500 to 6000 francs.

DECEMBER

Cézanne meets Père Tanguy ● (p.194), the dealer and supplier of artist's materials, who starts to sell his work and gives him valuable encouragement.
16th Degas buys Pissarro's *Market Gardens at Osny* from Durand-Ruel.
27th A group of artists, including all the future Impressionists, meets in Renoir's studio to ratify the constitution of the Société Anonyme des Artistes – an association set up to promote sales through group exhibitions ■ (p.86).

MANET
Bazaine before the Council of War
1873

Manet made this drawing while attending the trial of Marshal Bazaine at Versailles.

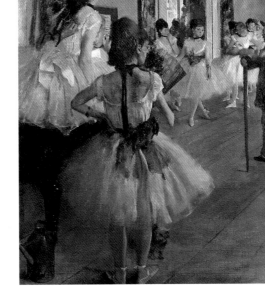

DURAND-RUEL'S CATALOGUE

In 1873 Durand-Ruel brought out a lavish catalogue in the form of a three-volume album of engravings reproducing 300 works of art that he currently had in stock. In his preface the critic Armand Silvestre attempted to analyse the appeal of the Impressionists:

At first sight one is hard put to distinguish between the works of Monet, those of Sisley, and the style of the last of them, Pissarro. After a little study, however, one comes to realize that M. Monet is the most skilful and the most daring, M. Sisley the most harmonious, and the most timid, M. Pissarro the most direct and the most naïve. These nuances are not, however, our only concern. What is certain is that the painting of these three landscapists bears no relation at all to that of the other [non-Impressionist] masters whose works we have been considering, and that we can trace its ancestry to a point which is distant and indirect, except for a closer temporal relation to the works of M. Manet. It is a form of painting that states its premises with conviction and with a power that imposes on us the duty of recognizing and defining what one may call its indeterminate direction.

What immediately strikes one when looking at a painting of this kind is the immediate caress which the eye receives; above all else it is harmonious, and what really distinguishes it is the simplicity of the means whereby it achieves this harmony. In fact one very quickly discovers that its secret is based on a fine and exact observation of the relation of one tone to another. In reality it is the scale of tones, reconstructed after the great colourists of the century, a sort of analytical process, which does not change the palette into a kind of banal percussion instrument, as one might first be tempted to believe. The

meaning of these relationships in their precise accuracy, is a very special gift, and one which constitutes the real genius of a painter. The art of landscape runs no risk of vulgarity from this sort of study…

It is M. Monet who, by the choice of the subjects themselves, betrays his preoccupations most clearly. He loves to juxtapose on the lightly ruffled surface of the water the multicoloured reflections of the setting sun, of brightly coloured boats, of changing clouds. Metallic tones given off by the smoothness of the waves which splash over small even surfaces are recorded in his works, and the image of the shore is mutable – the houses are broken up as they are in a jigsaw puzzle. This effect, which is absolutely true to experience, and may have been borrowed from the Japanese school, strongly attracts the young painters, who surrender to it absolutely.

The rustic interiors of M. Pissarro are considerably more complex than one might have expected. Do the painters cancel each other out? Certainly not, since nobody knows who will insert, in its proper place, that stone which each of them contributes to the great edifice of art. This uncertainty gives to art its real unity. Each one has his part to play.

What could help to secure the eventual success of these young painters is the fact that their pictures are done in a singularly bright tonal range. A blond light pervades them, and everything is gaiety, clarity, spring festivals, golden evenings, or apple trees in blossom – once again an inspiration from Japan. Their canvases, uncluttered, medium in size, are open in the surface they decorate; they are windows opening on the joyous countryside, on rivers full of pleasure-boats stretching into the distance, on a sky which shines with light mists, on the outdoor life, panoramic and charming.

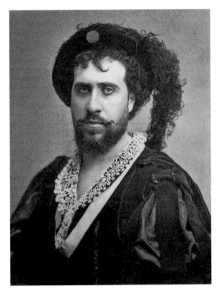

Photograph of Faure in the role of Hamlet.

JEAN-BAPTISTE FAURE
Collector and singer

Faure (1830–1914) was one of the most popular baritones of his day. A friend of Durand-Ruel, they spent 1870 to 1871 together in London, where Faure's singing was very well received, and lived in Brompton Road. An admirer of the Impressionists, in 1873 he bought a group of Manets at prices ranging from 2500 to 6000 francs; he also became friendly with Degas and purchased eleven paintings from him.

A year later the singer bought back six paintings, with which Degas was dissatisfied, from Durand-Ruel for 8000 francs. Faure handed them over to the artist, together with 1500 francs, on the understanding that Degas would give him four paintings on which he was currently working. The artist finished two of these in 1876, but did not deliver the other two until 1887 – and then only as a consequence of legal action. The dispute soured their friendship. Faure stopped buying the artist's work, and three years later sold all the pictures by Degas that he had collected.

On his retirement from the stage in 1880, Faure commissioned Manet to paint a portrait of him as Hamlet

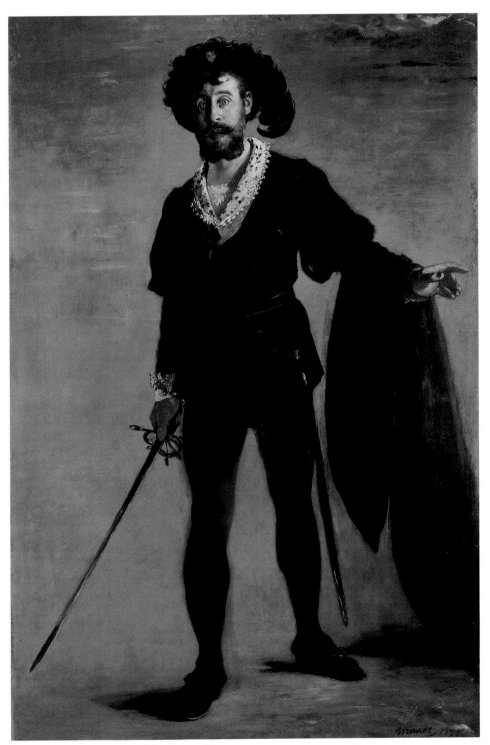

MANET   Faure in the Role of Hamlet   1876

in Ambroise Thomas's opera of that name. During one period his collection included sixty-eight works by Manet, twenty-three by Monet, thirty by Sisley, and a smaller number of Renoirs and Pissarros. In April 1878 he sent forty-two of his pictures for sale at the Hôtel Drouot
◆ (p.102), but withdrew most of them when they failed to reach their reserve prices.

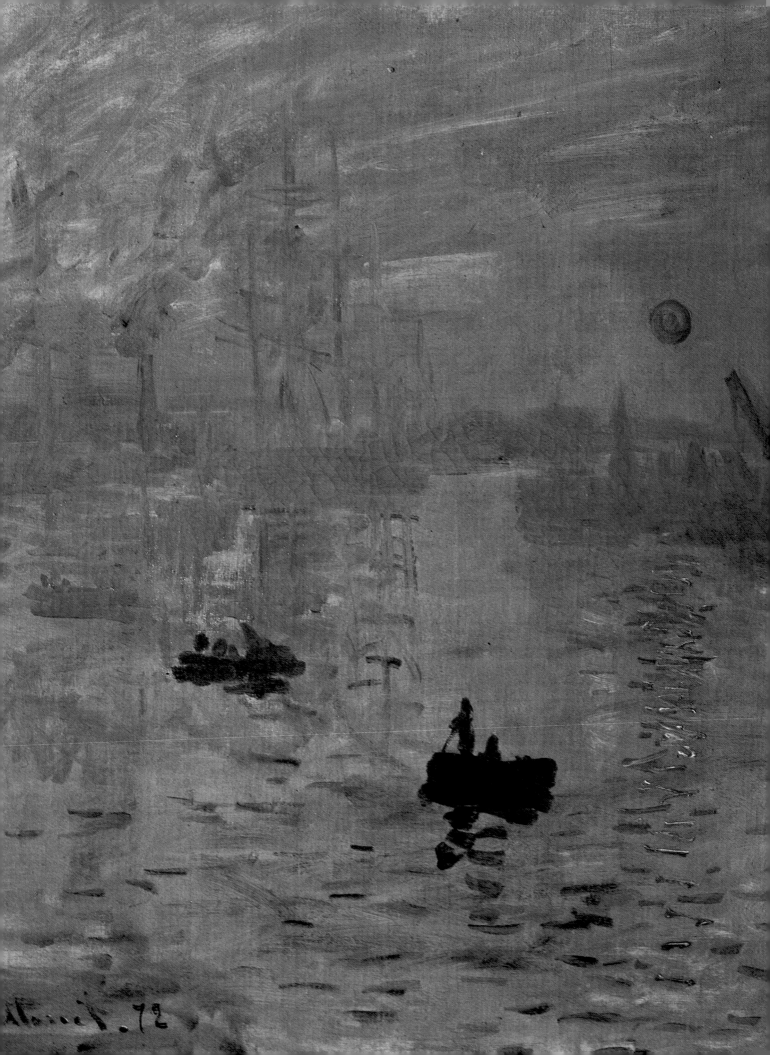

THE EXHIBITION YEARS
1874–1886

MONET **Impression: Sunrise** (detail) 1872–3

1874

The Birth of Impressionism
THE FIRST IMPRESSIONIST EXHIBITION

Exhibitors at the first Impressionist exhibition are offered the freedom to show whatever they choose, without the interference of a jury – but the group of painters who have formed the Société Anonyme des Artistes are saddled with the sobriquet 'Impressionists' by a facetious critic.

JANUARY

24th Berthe Morisot's father dies.

FEBRUARY

12th Edmond de Goncourt describes Degas in his *Journal* as 'a bizarre painter – a strange fellow, neurotic, sickly, with bad eyesight – he's always frightened of going blind – so far the most likely person I've met who can catch the essence of modern life in describing it.'

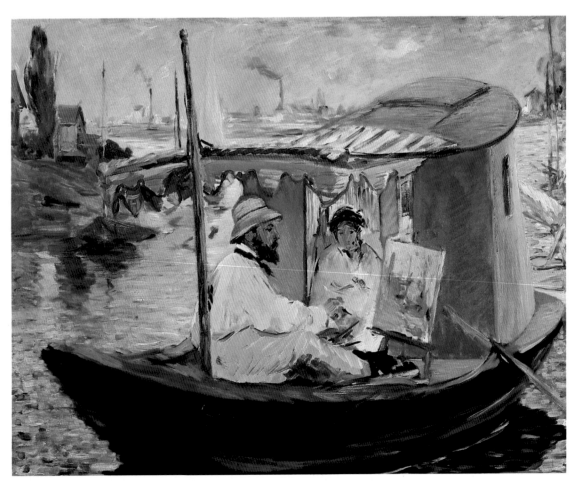

MANET
Monet Working on his Boat in Argenteuil
1874

In the summer of 1874 Manet visited his family home in Gennevilliers, near Argenteuil, where Monet was renting a house. One of the first fruits of the excursion was this painting of Monet and his wife in his studio boat (which had been constructed in imitation of the one used by Daubigny). Despite being essentially a sketch, it shows the increasing confidence with which Manet was starting to use Impressionist techniques. Little hint is given of the condition of the river at the time, which according to a contemporary official report, was choked with 'an accumulation of filth, putrefying dead cats and dogs and slime'.

15th Manet publishes *Boy with Dog* and *Civil War* (p.10).
16th Degas persuades Faure to buy back from Durand-Ruel six paintings with which he is dissatisfied ● (p.81).
23rd Degas' father dies in Naples.

MARCH

Dr Gachet urges Pissarro to organize a benefit auction of works by various artists to help Daumier, who has become virtually blind.

APRIL

12th Opening of the Salon. Manet's *The Railroad* (p.153) and *Pulcinello*, are accepted; but his *Masked Ball at the Opera* (p.167) and *The Swallows* are rejected, provoking a remonstrative article by Mallarmé in *La Renaissance littéraire et artistique*. Mary Cassatt's *Ida* is admired by Degas.
15th The first exhibition of the Société Anonyme des Artistes opens at 35 boulevard des Capucines ■ (p.86).
25th Reviewing the exhibition, the critic Louis Leroy refers to the artists as 'the Impressionists'.

MAY

Sisley stays in London and paints at Hampton Court and Molesey.

JUNE

Durand-Ruel's Society of French Artists puts on an exhibition that includes works by Manet, Monet, Pissarro and Sisley.

AUGUST

Manet spends the summer at his family home in Gennevilliers, whilst Monet rents a house across the Seine at Argenteuil. Renoir often visits them, and the three artists paint each other and their families.
Pissarro stays with the landscape painter Ludovic Piette in Normandy.

OCTOBER

Van Gogh is transferred from London to Goupil's Paris headquarters.

DECEMBER

3rd Van Gogh returns to London.
17th At a meeting in Renoir's studio, it is decided to wind up the Société Anonyme des Artistes because of lack of funds.
22nd Berthe Morisot marries Manet's brother Eugène.
Renoir's father dies.

MANET
Boy with Dog
1868–74

One of two lithographs Manet published in February, *Boy with Dog* is a faithful, even restrained, rendering of the painting of the same title that dates from 1861.

OTHER EVENTS

• Monarchy restored in Spain
• Disraeli new Prime Minister of UK
• Factory inspectors introduced and child labour banned in France

• Foundation stone of the basilica of Sacré-Coeur laid
• Industrial production of bromide plates makes photography cheaper
• National inventory of works of art initiated in France

• Publication of Flaubert's *La Tentation de Sainte Antoine* and Verlaine's *Romances sans paroles*
• Mussorgsky's *Boris Godunov*, Johann Strauss' *Die Fledermaus* and Verdi's Requiem first performed

THE FIRST IMPRESSIONIST EXHIBITION

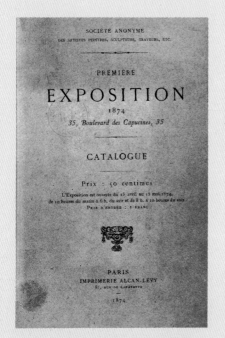

Cover of the catalogue
of the first Impressionist
exhibition.

MONET
Boulevard des Capucines
1874

Painted shortly before
the opening of the first
Impressionist exhibition,
this urban view, Monet's
most ambitious to date, was
highly criticized. Leroy's
imaginary academician,
M. Vincent ▲ (p.88), was
particularly outraged by
Monet's depiction of the
people, whom he described
as looking like 'black
tongue-lickings'.

The first exhibition of the Société
Anonyme des Artistes (Peintres,
Sculpteurs, Graveurs etc.) was held at
35 boulevard des Capucines, in what
had until recently been the studios of
Nadar, the photographer. A flight of
stairs led directly from the street to
the rooms, the walls of which were
covered in red – a colour favoured by
Nadar. Admission cost 1 franc, and
the catalogue (edited by Renoir's
brother Edmond) 50 centimes. The
exhibition, which ran from April 15th
till May 15th, was open not only
during the daytime but, as a gesture
to the working classes, from 8.00 to 10.00 in the
evenings. Despite the significance of the event for
the history of art, the primary purpose of the
organizers was not so much to promote a new style
of painting as to escape the constraints of the Salon
and to give the artists an opportunity to show their
work freely, without the interference of a jury or
any State involvement.

The society had
been constituted as
a 'société anonyme'
(a limited liability
company) open to
anyone prepared to
pay 60 francs a year.
Each artist was
entitled to have two
pictures hung –
though this rule was
not adhered to. All
members had equal
rights and could
participate in the

election of the committee of fifteen members.
Originally the Impressionists intended to publish a
journal, but this ambition was not realized until
1877 (p.100). To cover expenses, a commission of
10 per cent was levied on sales. Exhibits were to be
grouped in alphabetical order of artists' names,
according to size, and hung no more than two
rows deep. The hanging was in the hands of a
committee chaired by Renoir, who did most of the
work himself as other members failed to turn up.

There were 165 works in the exhibition,
including five oil paintings and seven pastels by
Monet; four oils, two pastels and three watercolours by Morisot; six oil paintings and one pastel
by Renoir; ten works by Degas; five by Pissarro;
three by Cézanne; and three by Guillaumin. Some
of the pictures were on loan, including Cézanne's
Modern Olympia, Morisot's *Hide and Seek* (owned by
Manet) and two Sisley landscapes that had been
bought by Durand-Ruel. Works exhibited that are
well known today included Degas' *At the Races in the
Country* (p.89), Monet's *Impression: Sunrise* (p.88) and

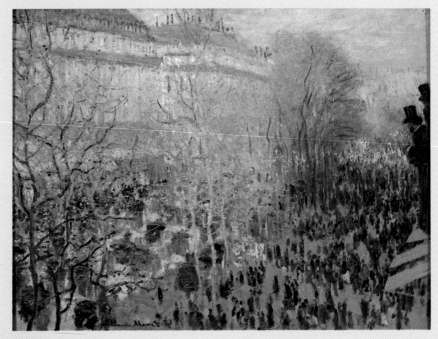

his *Boulevard des Capucines* (opposite), Morisot's *The Cradle* (p.89), Pissarro's *The Orchard* (painted in 1872) and Renoir's *La Loge* (right).

The majority of the participants were not connected with the so-called Batignolles group and had been recruited by one or other of the sixteen founding members, Degas being especially active in this respect. Most of these 'outsiders' were regular exhibitors at the Salon. Some of the subscribers to the society did not participate.

There were 175 visitors on the first day of the exhibition and 54 on the last, the total attendance being around 3500. Nor was the exhibition disastrous from a selling point of view, although some exhibitors had pitched their prices too high – Pissarro wanted 1000 francs for *The Orchard* and Monet asked the same for *Impression: Sunrise* (p.88), neither of which sold. Admittedly Sisley sold a landscape for 1000 francs, but that may well have been the result of a manoeuvre by Durand-Ruel. The sum that accrued to the society from the 10 per cent commission on sales amounted to 360 francs, which implies that 3600 francs worth of pictures were sold. It is known that Monet received a total of 200 francs, Renoir 180 francs and

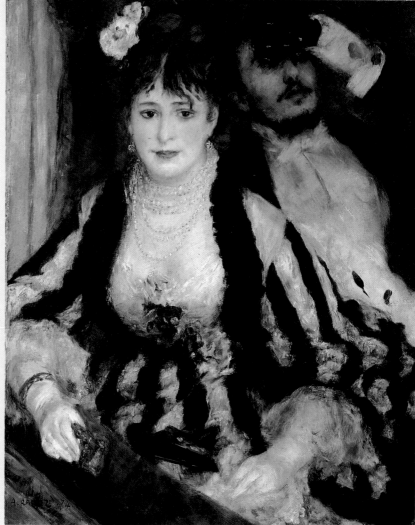

Pissarro 130 francs, while Cézanne got 300 francs for his *House of the Hanged Man* (p.88). Although Renoir failed to achieve the 500 francs he wanted for *La Loge* (above), later he managed to sell it for 450 francs to Père Martin, a small-time dealer and loyal supporter of the group. Neither Morisot nor Boudin sold anything, nor did Degas (most of his works, however, were lent).

The accounts showed that the expenses of the exhibition came to 9272 francs and the receipts 10,221 francs, leaving 949 francs profit, to which were notionally added 2360 francs due in unpaid shares. As a commercial venture it was a failure: the amount the members received was not even sufficient to cover their dues, and Cézanne had to ask his father for money to pay what he owed.

RENOIR
La Loge
1874

This painting was one of the few in the first Impressionist exhibition that was not received with hostility by the critics; indeed, many praised it. The sitters were the artist's brother Edmond and a model known as Nini.

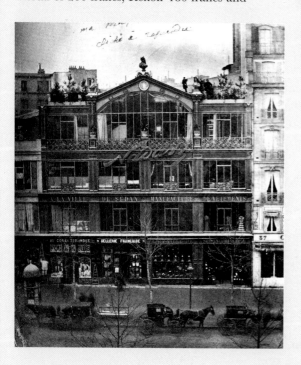

Contemporary photograph of Nadar's studio in the boulevard des Capucines, venue of the first Impressionist exhibition.

▲ CRITICAL REACTIONS TO THE FIRST IMPRESSIONIST EXHIBITION

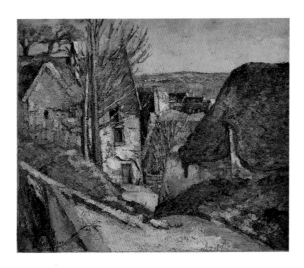

CÉZANNE
House of the Hanged Man
1873

Painted while he was staying with Dr Gachet in Auvers-sur-Oise, this was one of three works shown by Cézanne at the first Impressionist exhibition. It was purchased by Count Armand Doria, an avid collector of Impressionist paintings, for 300 francs.

The exhibition received wide coverage in the press, and many of the reviewers reacted favourably. Nevertheless, there was no shortage of hostile reviews. The most notorious of these was Louis Leroy's piece headed 'The Exhibition of the Impressionists', published in the satirical magazine *Le Charivari*, which was responsible for the name 'Impressionist' catching on. In his review (part of which is reproduced below) Leroy described a visit to the exhibition with an imaginary companion, M. Vincent – a distinguished academician who ceaselessly poured scorn on the artists' efforts, deriding the 'impressions' that they were striving to achieve. As a final gibe, Leroy pictured M. Vincent standing in front of a fictitious attendant, yelling exasperatedly: 'Is he ugly enough? From the front he has two eyes, a nose and a mouth. The Impressionists wouldn't have sacrificed to detail in this way!'

At the sight of this astounding landscape [Pissarro's *The Ploughed Field*], *the good man* [M. Vincent] *thought that his spectacles were dirty, and wiping them carefully set them on his nose. 'Good God,' he said, 'What on earth is that?' 'It's a hoar frost on deeply ploughed furrows,' I replied. 'Those things furrows? That stuff frost? They look more like palette scrapings placed uniformly on a dirty canvas. It has neither head nor tail, top nor bottom, front nor back.' 'Perhaps, but the impression is there.' 'Well, it's a damned funny impression.'*

…A little later he stopped in front of Monet's 'Impression: Sunrise'. His countenance was turning a deep red. A catastrophe seemed to me imminent, and it was reserved for M. Monet to contribute the last straw. 'Ah, there he is; there he is!' he shouted in front of No. 98, 'I recognize him; Papa Vincent's favourite! What does the canvas depict? Look at the catalogue, "Impression: Sunrise". I was certain of it! I was just telling myself that since I was impressed there had to be some impression in it … and what freedom; what ease of workmanship! Wallpaper in its embryonic state is more finished than that seascape.'

LOUIS LEROY, Le Charivari, April 25th

M. Manet is among those who maintain that in painting one can, and ought to be, satisfied with the impression. We have seen an exhibition by these impressionalists on the boulevard des Capucines, at Nadar's. M. Monet, a more uncompromising Manet, Pissarro, Mlle Morisot etc. appear to have declared war on beauty.

JULES CLARETIE, L'Indépendant, April 20th

MONET
Impression: Sunrise
1872–3

The painting which aroused the ire of M. Vincent and gave its name to the group was originally entitled *Sunrise at Le Havre*. According to Edmond Renoir it was he who suggested to Monet that the title should be altered. It is thought that the work in fact portrays a sunset, not a sunrise. (Detail on pp. 82–3.)

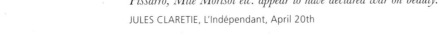

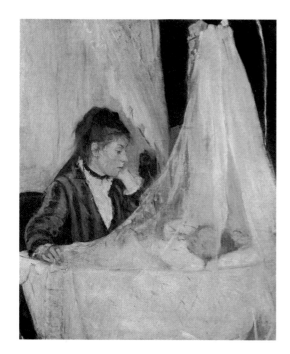

MORISOT
The Cradle
1872

One of the few successes of the first Impressionist exhibition, *The Cradle* appealed as much by virtue of its subject matter as by its style. What is essentially a portrait of Morisot's sister, Edma Pontillon, looking at her newly-born second child, can also be seen as being somewhat in the tradition of nineteenth-century sentimental painting.

Berthe Morisot has wit to the tips of her fingers, especially at her fingertips. What fine artistic feeling! You cannot find more graceful images handled more deliberately and delicately than 'The Cradle' and 'Hide and Seek'. I would add that here the execution is in complete accord with the idea to be expressed.
JULES CASTAGNARY, Le Siècle, April 29th

What pleases us is the initiative taken by these artists, who without recriminations, protests or polemics, opened a room and said to the crowds: 'We see like this, we understand art in this way. Come on in, look, and buy if you like.'
ÉDOUARD DRUMONT, Le Petit Journal, April 19th

The means by which they search for their impressions will infinitely serve contemporary art. It is the range of painting's means that they have restored. And don't believe that this makes the palette a banal percussion instrument, as one might initially think. You need special eyes to be sensitive to the subtlety of their tonal relations, which constitutes their honour and their merit.
ARMAND SILVESTRE, L'Opinion nationale, April 22nd

Looking at the first rough works — and rough is the right word — you simply shrug your shoulders; seeing the next lot, you burst out laughing; but with the last ones you finally get angry. And you are sorry you did not give the franc you paid to get in to some poor beggar.
UNSIGNED REVIEW, La Patrie, April 21st

DEGAS
At the Races in the Country
1869

While he was staying with his friends the Valpinçons at Ménil-Hubert, Degas painted the racecourse at nearby Argentan. Paul Valpinçon is depicted driving the tilbury, with his wife, recently-born son and a nurse seated behind him. The critic Ernest Chesneau praised the work when it was shown at the first Impressionist exhibition.

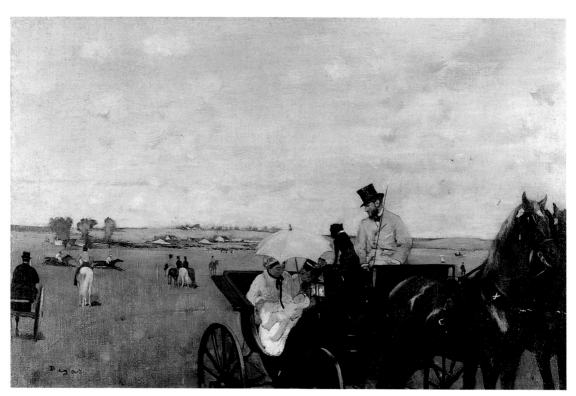

1875

An Unfortunate Experiment

Renoir convinces Monet, Morisot and Sisley that the best way to raise money quickly is to hold an auction of works at the Hôtel Drouot. This attracts far greater numbers than anticipated, but most turn out to taunt rather than to purchase.

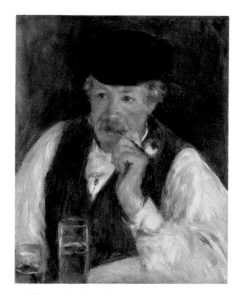

RENOIR
M. Fournaise
1875

Alphonse Fornaise was the proprietor of a restaurant on an island in the Seine at Chatou, which was to provide the background for Renoir's famous *Luncheon of the Boating Party* (p.132). This portrait bears a slight resemblance to Manet's *Le Bon Bock* (1873), though this may be due in part to the beer glasses on the table.

JANUARY

Renoir is commissioned to paint a portrait of a lady with her two daughters, for which he is paid the sum of 1200 francs. He uses the money to rent a studio at 38 rue Cortot in Montmartre.
Pissarro visits Monfoucault, where he makes a will.

FEBRUARY

Père Tanguy ● (p.194) starts exhibiting and selling works by Cézanne at 50 francs each. During the course of the year he sells four – including one to Victor Chocquet ▲ (p.224), a senior official in the Customs Service who is a keen collector.
Pissarro returns to Pontoise from Brittany.
28th Degas goes to Italy for a three-month stay.

MARCH

24th At the suggestion of Renoir, the Impressionists hold an auction of their works at the Hôtel Drouot ◆ (p.102), with Durand-Ruel acting as their adviser and Charles Pillet, his assistant, as auctioneer (the catalogue includes a preface by the critic Philippe Burty). Rowdy scenes occur during the proceedings, stirred up by a hostile audience, and the event is almost a total failure – the most successful of the participants being Morisot, whose oil paintings fetch around 250 francs each. The 73 works offered for sale realize only 11,496 francs. Many of Renoir's works do not even reach 100 francs, and he is forced to buy several himself to avoid them going too cheaply (including *La Source*, which Durand-Ruel would eventually sell in 1905 to Prince de Wagram for 70,000 francs). Sisley's paintings – including some done recently in England – sell for an average of 122 francs, while Monet's fetch around 233 francs each. As a result of the exhibition, Chocquet commissions Renoir to paint portraits of himself and his wife.

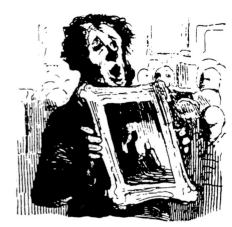

A woodcut by Daumier (1861) depicting a sale at the Hôtel Drouot.

APRIL

3rd Opening of the Salon. Renoir has had all his submissions rejected. Manet exhibits *The Seine at Argenteuil* (one of his first truly Impressionist pictures, painted in 1874 while in close contact with Monet). In contrast to *Le Bon Bock* (which was such a success in 1873), it is greeted with howls of derision – *Le Figaro* dismissing it as 'marmalade from Argenteuil spread on an indigo river. The master returns as a twentieth-year student.'

MAY

23rd Van Gogh returns to Paris from London to work at Goupil's gallery, and immerses himself in a study of the Bible.

Mallarmé's translation of Edgar Allan Poe's poem *The Raven*, illustrated by Manet, is published. Dante Gabriel Rossetti describes it as 'a huge folio of lithographed sketches by a French idiot named Manet, who must be the greatest and most conceited ass who ever lived.'

JUNE

Cézanne – who is living near the Quai d'Anjou in Paris – paints with Guillaumin, frequently choosing identical views.
28th In a letter to Manet from Argenteuil, Monet begs for 20 francs as he does not have 'a penny left since the day before yesterday'.

JULY

Renoir visits Père Fournaise, the owner of a popular restaurant on the Ile de Chatou on the Seine, and paints portraits of the restaurateur (opposite) and his daughter Alphonsine.

AUGUST

In association with the entrepreneur and painter Alfred Meyer, Pissarro starts *L'Union* – a new organization intended to replace the Société Anonyme des Artistes (which had been dissolved in December 1874). Berthe Morisot visits England, where she paints views of London and the Isle of Wight.

The publication of Mallarmé's prose translation of Edgar Allan Poe's *The Raven*, illustrated by Manet, was not a success. Although Swinburne praised it for being 'perfectly translated twice over, thanks to the collaboration of two great artists', the majority of critics believed with Rossetti that 'A copy should be bought for every hypochon-driacal ward in lunatic asylums.' Above is a detail from the poster by Manet.

GUILLAUMIN
The Seine at Bercy
1873–5

Guillaumin's view of this industrialized part of the banks of the Seine (below left) was virtually copied by Cézanne some three years later (below right). In 1875 Guillaumin and Cézanne were living next door to each other by the Quai d'Anjou, near to the site of this painting.

CÉZANNE
The Seine at Bercy
1876–8

This copy after Guillaumin was painted while Cézanne was experimenting with a square brushstroke. In *Studies in Impressionism* (1985) Rewald comments that it is almost as if Cézanne was seeing what would be the likely effect of this technique on a typical Impressionist painting.

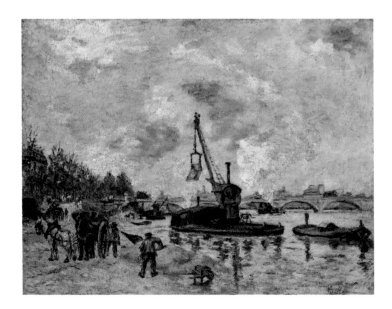
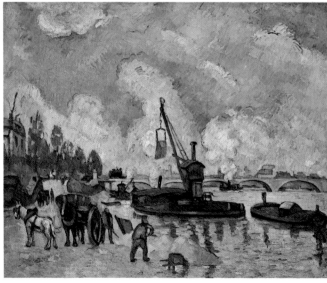

SEPTEMBER

The eighth exhibition of Durand-Ruel's Society of French Artists opens in London, including work by Degas, Monet, Pissarro, Renoir and Sisley.

OCTOBER

3rd Manet and his wife Suzanne depart for a holiday in Venice ▲ (below), together with Tissot. (Although Manet is reported to have made numerous sketches, only two paintings – both of the Grand Canal – appear to have survived.)

DECEMBER

Durand-Ruel closes his London gallery.

MANET
The Grand Canal, Venice
1875 *P.C.*

Charles Toché referred to this work in his account of the artist in Venice: 'Through the row of gigantic twisted posts, one saw the domes of the incomparable Salute, dear to Guardi. "I shall put in a gondola," cried Manet.'

OTHER EVENTS

- Britain buys shares in Suez Canal from Khedive of Egypt
- Bosnia and Herzegovina throw off Turkish rule
- Religious orders abolished in Germany
- Theosophical Society founded by Mme Blavatsky in New York
- Captain Matthew Webb becomes the first person to swim across the English Channel
- New York photographer Thomas Adams invents chewing gum
- Electric dental drill patented by George F. Green of Michigan
- Publication of Mary Baker Eddy's *Science and Health*
- Bizet's *Carmen* and Tchaikovsky's Piano Concerto No.1 first performed
- Bizet, Hans Christian Andersen and Charles Kingsley die

 MANET IN VENICE

Seated in Florian's one evening during his stay in Venice, Manet met a young French painter, Charles Toché, whom he allegedly greeted with the words 'I can see you're a Frenchman. God, how boring it is here.' Toché later recalled their painting excursions together in great – and possibly partly fictitious – detail to Ambroise Vollard, who recorded them in his *Recollections of a Picture Dealer* (1936). The following is Toché's account of Manet's response to a regatta at Mestre:

When faced with such a distractingly complicated scene, I must first of all choose a typical incident and define my picture as if I could already see it framed. In this case the most striking features are the masts with their fluttering multi-coloured banners, the red-white-and-green Italian flag, the dark swaying line of boats crowded with spectators, and the gondolas like black-and-white arrows shooting away from the horizon; then at the top of the picture, the watery horizon, the marked target and the islands in the distant haze.

I would try first to work out logically the different values, in their nearer or more distant relationships, according to spatial and aerial perspective.

The lagoon mirrors the sky, and at the same time acts as a great stage for the boats and their passengers, the masts, the banners etc. It has its own particular colour, the nuances it borrows from the sky, the clouds, from crowds, from objects reflected in the water. There can be no sharp definition, no linear structure in something that is all movement; only tonal values, which, if correctly observed will constitute its true volume, its essential underlying design.

The gondolas, and other boats, with their generally dark colours and reflections, provide a base on which to set my watery stage. The figures, seated or in action, dressed in dark colours, or brilliantly vivid materials, with their parasols, handkerchiefs, and hats, appear as crenellated forms of differing tonal values, providing the necessary 'repoussoir' [contrast in the foreground] and defining the specific character of the areas of water and gondolas that I can see through them.

Crowds, rowers, flags and masts must be sketched in with a mosaic of coloured tones, in an attempt to convey the fleeting quality of gestures, the fluttering flags, the swaying masts.

On the horizon, right at the top, are the islands. There should be no more than a suggestion of the most distant places, veiled in the subtlest, most accurately observed tints.

Finally the sky should cover and envelop the whole scene, like an immense, shining canopy, whose light plays over all the figures and objects.

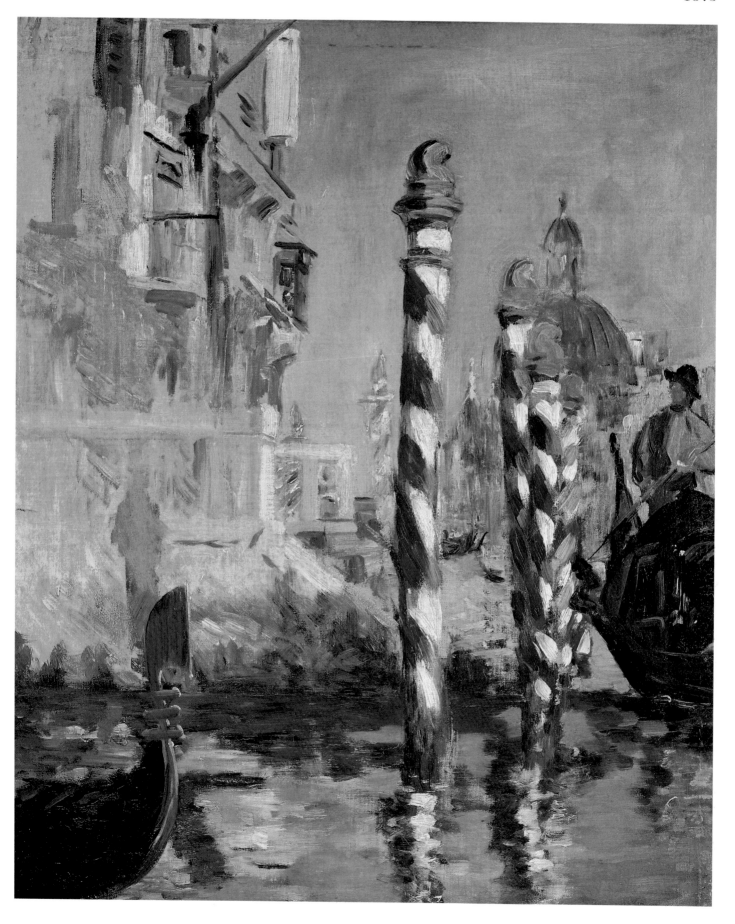

1876

Gaining Ground

THE SECOND IMPRESSIONIST EXHIBITION

All the major Impressionist artists save for Manet are included in the second Impressionist exhibition, and an important newcomer is introduced – Gustave Caillebotte. His work steals the show and helps to make the second exhibition far more of a popular success than the first.

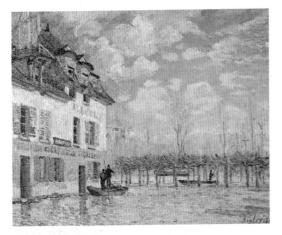

SISLEY
Flood at Port-Marly
1876

Of the eight landscapes that Sisley showed at the second Impressionist exhibition, three, including this work, depicted a flooded wine merchant's shop, as seen from the rue de Paris. Adolphe Tavernier, a critic, bought this version, and on the sale of his collection in 1900 it was acquired by Count Isaac de Camondo for 43,000 francs, who gave it to the Louvre in 1908.

FEBRUARY

4th Cézanne takes his patron Victor Chocquet ▲ (p.224) to meet Monet at Argenteuil.

MARCH

Manet has two paintings, *The Artist* and *Le Linge*, rejected by the Salon and exhibits them, with others, at his studio.
Van Gogh is dismissed from Goupil's gallery.
Sisley goes to live at Marly.

APRIL

In London the dealer Émile Deschamps exhibits works by Degas, Manet, Morisot and Sisley.
Manet's *In a Canoe* is bitterly attacked by a reviewer in *The Times*, who feels the mode of execution is as unpleasant as the subject ('a singularly offensive couple'). The British collector Henry Hill visits the exhibition and buys four Degas dance pictures ◆ (pp.76–7).
Van Gogh obtains a position as an assistant teacher in England at a school in Ramsgate (he subsequently moves to the Jones Methodist School in Isleworth, where he is also a lay preacher).
1st Opening of the second Impressionist exhibition ■ (p.96) at Durand-Ruel's gallery in rue Le Peletier.
3rd The Salon opens. Eva Gonzalès as 'a student of Manet' is accepted, but Manet himself is rejected, as is Cézanne.
Gauguin starts buying works by Cézanne, Manet, Monet and Pissarro – largely as a result of meeting Pissarro, who helps him with his painting.

MAY

Duranty publishes *La Nouvelle peinture* – the first book devoted to Impressionism, though the word is never used. (The subtitle of the book is *À propos du groupe des artistes qui expose dans les galeries Durand-Ruel.*)
13th Henry James praises the Impressionists in the *New York Tribune*. Strindberg, as a young visitor to Paris, sees the Impressionist exhibition and (as he later wrote to Gauguin) is greatly excited by it.

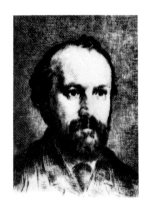

DESBOUTIN
Portrait of Edmond
Duranty
c.1876

An active member of the Café Guerbois circle ◆ (pp.46-7), Marcellin Desboutin was a talented engraver and a mediocre painter, who was the subject of Manet's *The Artist* (1875) and the male figure in Degas' *The Absinthe Drinker* ◆ (pp.192-3) of the following year. Edmond Duranty was one of the main critical exponents of Realism in art and literature and the author of *La Nouvelle peinture* (1876), written in defence of the Impressionists.

JUNE

Degas goes to Naples to discuss the debts of his family's firm.

Monet's *Impression: Sunrise* – the work that prompted Leroy to coin the term Impressionism ▲ (p.88) – sells at the Hôtel Drouot for 210 francs.

JULY

Renoir starts to frequent the Moulin de la Galette (p.105), an open-air dancing establishment in Montmartre frequented by shop assistants.

Cézanne paints at L'Estaque near Marseilles.

Manet spends two weeks with the Hoschedé family ◆ (pp.146-7) in Montgeron. After his departure Monet comes to stay with the family and paints decorative panels in the house, as well as several landscapes.

AUGUST

31st Degas assumes a major part of the responsibility for the debts incurred by the family firm.

Monet settles at 26 rue d'Edimbourg, near the Gare St-Lazare.

SEPTEMBER

Renoir stays at Champrosay with Alphonse Daudet, the Realist novelist and playwright.

Degas' *The Absinthe Drinker* is exhibited in the winter exhibition at Brighton Museum under the title *A Sketch in a French Café* ◆ (pp.192-3).

23rd Mallarmé writes an article on 'The Impressionists and Édouard Manet' for the *Art Monthly Review* ▲ (p.99).

OCTOBER

Georges Charpentier (the publisher of Daudet, Flaubert, the Goncourts, Maupassant and Zola) commissions Renoir to decorate his Paris home in the rue de Grenelle.

Pissarro starts to paint decorative tiles while staying with his friend Ludovic Piette at Montfoucault in Normandy.

NOVEMBER

3rd Caillebotte draws up a will providing money for an Impressionist exhibition to be held after his death and bequeathing his collection of Impressionist paintings to the State on condition that they should first be exhibited in a museum devoted to contemporary art and eventually in the Louvre ◆ (pp.197–8).

MANET
Visitors in the Studio
c.1872–76

In April 1876 Manet held an exhibition in his studio at 4 rue de St-Pétersbourg. This sketch probably dates from that period. The exhibition was very popular – it was rumoured that up to 4000 visitors attended.

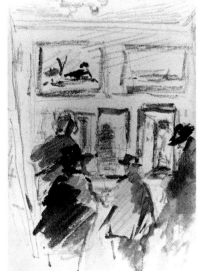

OTHER EVENTS

- Republicans win French elections
- Battle of Little Bighorn
- Serbia and Montenegro declare war on Turkey
- The First International is dissolved, following wrangling between Marxist and Anarchist factions
- Alexander Graham Bell invents the telephone
- Mallarmé writes *L'Après-midi d'un faune*
- Publication of Mark Twain's *The Adventures of Tom Sawyer*
- Brahms composes First Symphony
- First performance of Wagner's *The Ring of the Nibelung*
- George Sand dies

THE SECOND IMPRESSIONIST EXHIBITION

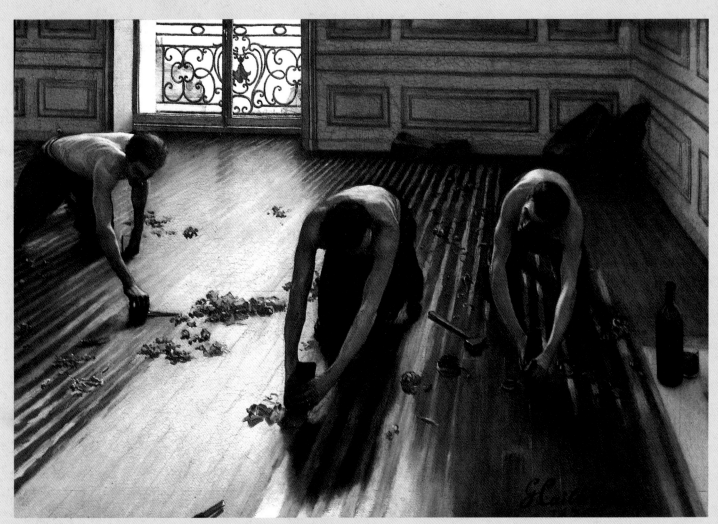

CAILLEBOTTE
The Floor Strippers
1875

Critics such as Edmond Duranty (opposite) saw the sense of contemporary realism, which was often to be found in Impressionist works, as one of their greatest virtues. This quality was strikingly present in Caillebotte's remarkable picture of three men renovating the floor of his new apartment. The work did not appear in the exhibition catalogue (right).

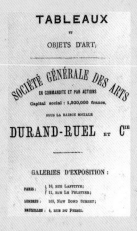

TABLEAUX
ET
OBJETS D'ART

SOCIÉTÉ GÉNÉRALE DES ARTS
EN COMMANDITE ET PAR ACTIONS
Capital social : 1,500,000 francs,
SOUS LA RAISON SOCIALE

DURAND-RUEL ET Cⁱᵉ

GALERIES D'EXPOSITION :

PARIS : { 16, RUE LAFFITTE;
         { 11, RUE LE PELETIER;
LONDRES : 168, NEW BOND STREET;
BRUXELLES : 4, RUE DU PERSIL.

The second Impressionist exhibition – entitled simply 'La Deuxième Exposition de Peinture par…' – was held at Durand-Ruel's gallery, 11 rue Le Peletier, from April 11th to May 9th. Some of the exhibitors had no connection with the Impressionists, but there was one important newcomer, Gustave Caillebotte, whose *The Floor Strippers* was one of the sensations of the show. Caillebotte had been introduced to the group by Monet and Renoir. He was extremely wealthy and supported most of the subsequent Impressionist exhibitions. Another notable supporter of the Impressionists, remarkable for his enthusiasm, was Renoir's new friend Victor Chocquet ◆ (p.224), who played an active part in promoting the exhibition and visited it every day, eagerly expounding the beauties of the paintings to anyone who would listen.

There were 252 works shown, including twenty-four by Degas, eighteen by Monet, seventeen by

**RENOIR
Nude in the Sunlight
1875**

This work had a mixed reception when shown at the second Impressionist exhibition. Warmly praised by some critics, it aroused the venomous contempt of Albert Wolff, critic for *Le Figaro*, which damned it in the eyes of the contemporary public. Altogether a striking composition, the backgound emphasizes the remarkable rendering of the effect of dappled sunlight filtering through the foliage, with the light dissolving the outline of the girl's face. The model was Anna Leboeuf, who died at the age of 23.

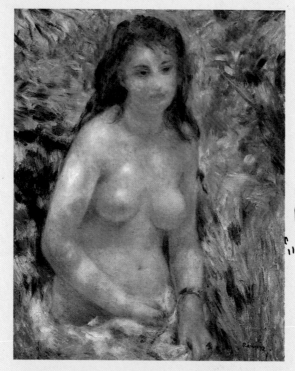

Morisot, thirteen by Pissarro, fifteen by Renoir and eight by Sisley. Caillebotte apparently exhibited eight paintings, though they are not mentioned in the catalogue. There were also two works by Bazille, included as a memorial to the artist, who had been killed in November 1870 in a minor skirmish during the Franco-Prussian war. Monet's name and Sisley's were printed incorrectly in the catalogue as 'Monnet' and 'Sysley'.

DEGAS
Portraits in an Office
1873

With its instantaneous veracity, this painting clearly reflects the influence of the camera. Set in a cotton market in New Orleans, Degas originally intended to send the work to Agnew, the Manchester art dealer, as he thought a 'wealthy spinner' might buy it. However, the planned negotiations with Agnew did not take place, and the work was eventually bought in 1878 by the Museum of Pau for 5000 francs.

Arranged by artists, the paintings which were 'easiest' to appreciate were hung in the front rooms and the more 'difficult' ones in the rooms at the back. Degas broke new ground by including photographs of paintings for sale that were not on show. The pictures that attracted most comment were Degas' *Portraits in an Office* (right) and Monet's *The Japanese Girl* (p.98) – a huge portrait of a young woman dressed in a

kimono. Although Monet later dismissed this painting as 'rubbish', it sold for the comparatively high price of 2000 francs.

The second Impressionist exhibition attracted wider review coverage than the first, and on the whole critical comment was slightly more favourable. Inevitably there were the usual vicious attacks from critics such as Albert Wolff, who described Renoir's *Nude in the Sunlight* (left) as a 'mass of flesh in the process of decomposition, with green and violet spots which denote the state of complete putrefaction of a corpse.' Nevertheless, complimentary reviews appeared in left-wing papers such as *Le Rappel*, *La République française* and *La Presse*. The English magazine *The Academy* carried a favourable review by Philippe Burty; and the *New York Tribune* published an appreciative, although ill-informed, article by the writer Henry James, which compared the Impressionists with the Pre-Raphaelites.

Although attendance figures do not seem to have been very high, the group was able to pay Durand-Ruel 3000 francs for renting the gallery. They were also able to repay the exhibitors the 1500 francs each had advanced, and in addition distributed a dividend of 3 francs.

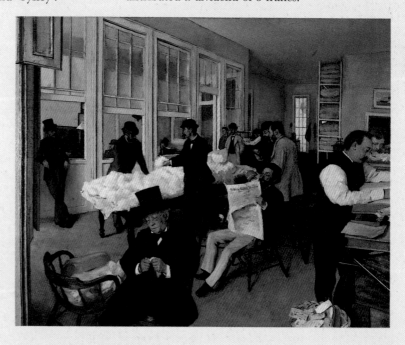

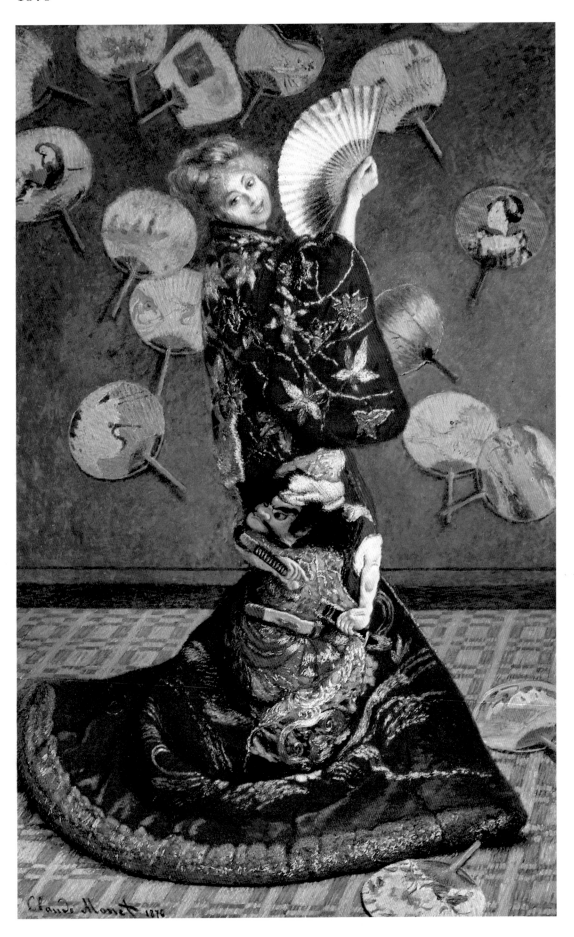

Claude Monet 1876

MONET
The Japanese Girl
1875–6

Throughout his life Monet was fascinated by all things Japanese, and at the time when this work was painted the style was particularly in demand. Intent on making a good impression at the Salon, the artist combined all the features that he thought might commend it to a fashionable audience. His wife Camille, in a blond wig, looks out provocatively at the spectator in a pose similar to those adopted by Japanese courtesans in popular prints. *The Japanese Girl* is imbued with a general sense of sexual innuendo, of the kind admired by devotees of Salon art.

MANET
Portrait of Stéphane Mallarmé
1876

When Manet painted this portrait, Mallarmé was 34, ten years his junior. The poet looked up to the painter, not only as a hero of the avant-garde, but also as a one-time friend of Baudelaire, whose works had so much influenced him. This work was painted in Manet's studio – the Japanese-style hanging behind him is the same as that in *Nana* (p.101).

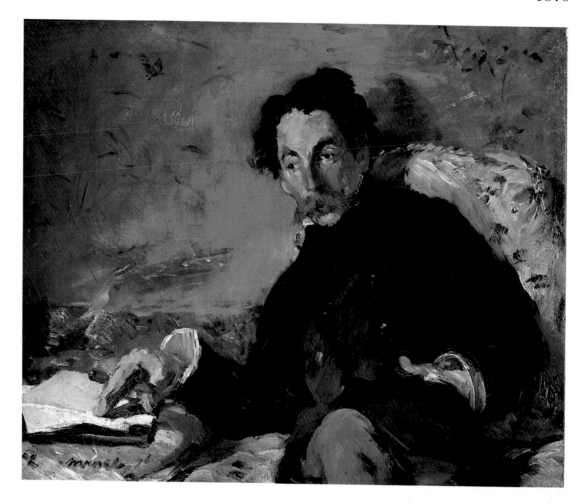

Below: Frontispiece by Manet to Mallarmé's *L'Après-midi d'un faune*, 1876.

 ## MALLARMÉ ON IMPRESSIONISM

The poet Stéphane Mallarmé (1842–98) became an active defender of the Impressionists. His apartment on the rue de Rome in the Batignolles Quarter acted as a lively centre of Parisian cultural life, and he enjoyed a close relationship with Degas, Manet and Renoir. This extract is from an article written in English for the *Art Monthly Review* in London:

The search after truth, peculiar to modern artists, which enables them to see nature, and reproduce her, such as she appears to pure and just eyes, must lead them to adopt air almost exclusively as their medium, or at all events to work in it freely and without restraint; there should at least be in

the revival of such a medium, if nothing more, an incentive to a new manner of painting. This is the result of our reasoning, and the end I wish to establish. As no artist has on his palette a transparent and neutral colour answering to open air, the desired effect can only be obtained by lightness or heaviness of touch, or by the regulation of tone. Now Manet

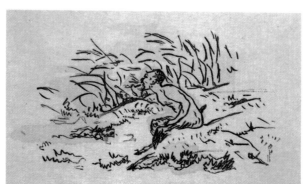

and his school use simple colour, fresh, or lightly laid on, and their results seem to have been attained at the first stroke, so that the ever-present light blends with and vivifies all things. As to the details of the picture, nothing should be absolutely fixed in order that we may feel that the bright gleam which lights the picture, or the diaphanous shadow which veils it are only seen in passing, and just when the spectator beholds the represented, which being composed of a harmony of reflected and ever-changing lights, cannot be supposed always to look the same, but palpitates with movement, light, and life.

STÉPHANE MALLARMÉ,
'The Impressionists and Édouard Manet',
Art Monthly Review and Photographic
Portfolio, September 30th, 1876

1877

Financial Disaster

THE THIRD IMPRESSIONIST EXHIBITION

Three years after the first exhibition, 1877 brings no improvement in the Impressionists' financial position, and Degas, Monet, Pissarro and Sisley are particularly afflicted. The third exhibition is not a great financial success and begins to sow the <u>seeds of disunity</u>.

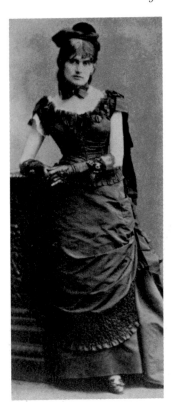

A photograph of Berthe Morisot, taken around 1877 when she was still in mourning after the death of her mother in 1876.

JANUARY

<u>Degas pays 20,000 francs</u> to the Bank of Antwerp to cover debts <u>incurred by his brother René</u> in managing the family bank. Caillebotte invites Degas, Manet, Monet, Pissarro, Renoir and Sisley to dinner at his apartment in order to discuss plans for the third Impressionist exhibition (*see* p.105).

FEBRUARY

15th L'Union – set up by Pissarro and Alfred Meyer (a minor painter and part-time dealer) as an alternative group to the Impressionists – holds an exhibition at the Grand Hôtel in the boulevard des Capucines. It is a complete failure, Cézanne, Guillaumin and Pissarro having decided to leave the group shortly before the opening of the exhibition.

MARCH

Berthe Morisot rents an apartment for painting in Paris, near L'Étoile, in order to free herself from the family environment.
19th Manet asks Albert Wolff, the art critic of *Le Figaro*, to support a sale of paintings that the Impressionists are planning to hold at the Hôtel Drouot ◆ (p.102) by writing a favourable preview.

APRIL

Gauguin moves to 74 rue des Fourneaux. Influenced by his landlord, the sculptor Bouillot, he begins to sculpt and produces a bust of his wife Mette ■ (p.119).
<u>Cézanne stays with Pissarro at Pontoise.</u>
4th The third Impressionist exhibition ■ (p.104) opens in an apartment at 6 rue Le Peletier, near Durand-Ruel's gallery.
6th Publication of the first issue of *L'Impressionniste, journal d'art* – a weekly journal edited by 22-year-old Georges Rivière, a friend of Renoir's who features in his painting *Dancing at the Moulin de la Galette* (p.105). (The journal appeared regularly throughout the exhibition. Renoir, who had actively supported the idea from the first, was one of the contributors.)

The front page of the first edition of the journal *L'Impressionniste*, which appeared weekly and ran to four issues during the third Impressionist exhibition. The first issue contained a letter to the editor of *Le Figaro*, attacking the paper's art critic Albert Wolff for his venomous opposition to the movement.

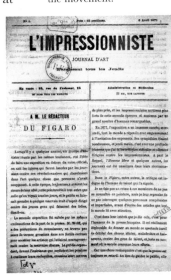

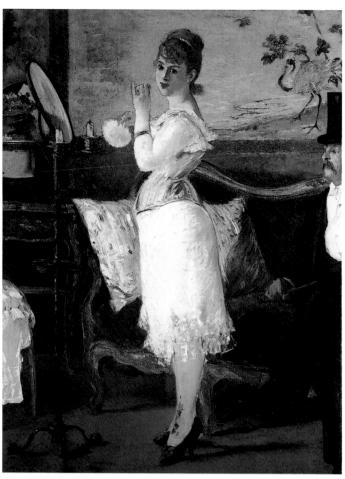

MANET
Nana
1877

The title suggests that this painting was an illustration for Zola's novel of the same name, but this had in fact yet to be written. The character Nana does, however, appear towards the end of Zola's *L'Assommoir* of 1877: 'Since the morning, she had spent hours in her chemise before the bit of looking glass hanging above the bureau.' This is a young, fresh Nana, at the beginning of her career and the model for the painting was Henriette Hauser, a young actress who was the mistress of the Prince of Orange.

MAY

1st Opening of the Salon. Manet's *Faure in the Role of Hamlet* (p.81) is accepted, but the jury rejects his *Nana* (left) on the grounds of impropriety – as its subject is the prostitute in Zola's novel *L'Assommoir*, which is currently the talk of Paris. The painting is also criticized for its loose technique and garish colours. All Mary Cassatt's submissions are rejected.
10th Manet's *Nana* (left) is exhibited in the window of Giroux's, a fashionable millinery shop in the boulevard des Capucines.
19th Van Gogh begins to study for the ministry in Amsterdam.
21st Degas, deeply depressed, writes to the wife of Giuseppe de Nittis: 'To live alone without a family is too hard. I never thought that I would suffer so much. Here I am, getting old, and almost penniless. I have organized my life in this world very badly.'
28th The sale at the Hôtel Drouot ◆ (p.102), organized by Renoir, is financially disappointing. Renoir's fifteen paintings fetch a total of 2005 francs; Pissarro's go for 50 to 260 francs each, and Sisley's for 105 to 165 francs. Caillebotte is more successful, selling one painting for 635 francs. The forty-five canvases altogether command little more than 7610 francs.

AUGUST

Degas visits the Valpinçon family at Ménil-Hubert.

OCTOBER

15th Renoir meets Léon Gambetta, the successful left-wing politician, who is now Minister of Public Instruction, and asks him for a job as curator of a provincial museum.
25th Degas moves into a new apartment at 50 rue Lepic, off the boulevard Clichy.

NOVEMBER

The *pâtissier* Eugène Murer, a new patron of the Impressionists, opens a restaurant at 95 boulevard Voltaire and offers to holds dinners there for his painter friends on Wednesday evenings.

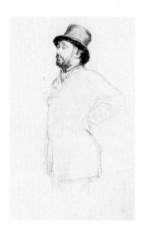

DESBOUTIN
Portrait of Degas
c.1876

Desboutin adroitly captures Degas' figure in this etching, which shows him standing imperiously, elbows thrust behind him, hands on hips.

DEGAS
The Star
1876–7

One of a series of pastelized monotypes that Degas started in 1876, *The Star* was the only work Degas sold at the third Impressionist exhibition. It was bought by Caillebotte.

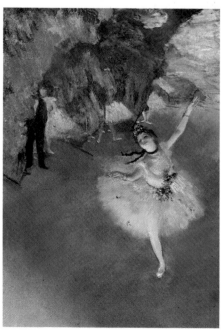

OTHER EVENTS

- Russia declares war on Turkey and invades Romania
- France occupies the Congo
- Britain annexes the Transvaal
- President MacMahon dissolves the French parliament and dismisses the Prime Minister
- Queen Victoria proclaimed Empress of India
- Rutherford B. Hayes inaugurated as President of USA
- Porfirio Diaz becomes President of Mexico
- Edison invents the phonograph
- The Grosvenor Gallery (centre of the Aesthetic movement in the 1880s) opens in London
- First performance of Ludovic Halévy's play *La Cigale*, based on the Impressionists' experiences
- Publication of Zola's *L'Assommoir* and Henry James's *The American*
- Saint-Saëns completes *Samson and Delilah*
- Courbet dies in Switzerland

THE HÔTEL DROUOT

Named after one of Napoleon's marshals, whose home it had been, the Hôtel Drouot was the state-controlled auction house often used by artists, not only as a saleroom but as a gallery where they could exhibit their work. For art buyers and dealers, it provided a good guide to the kind of prices works of art were currently fetching. It was also the place where an artist's unsold works were auctioned following his death. When Manet died in 1883, 159 of his works were sold at the Hôtel Drouot for 116,637 francs (*see* p.138).

On two occasions, in 1875 and again in 1877, groups of Impressionists – first Monet, Morisot, Renoir and Sisley, then Caillebotte, Monet, Pissarro and Sisley – attempted to circumvent the dealers by offering their work directly to the public. But at the first of the two sales the public jeered and heckled the auctioneer to such an extent that the police had to be summoned, and both events proved to be financially disappointing. Although dealers such as Paul Durand-Ruel and Georges Petit were capable of inflating prices artificially at such auctions, generally the prices at the Hôtel Drouot reflected prevailing market conditions.

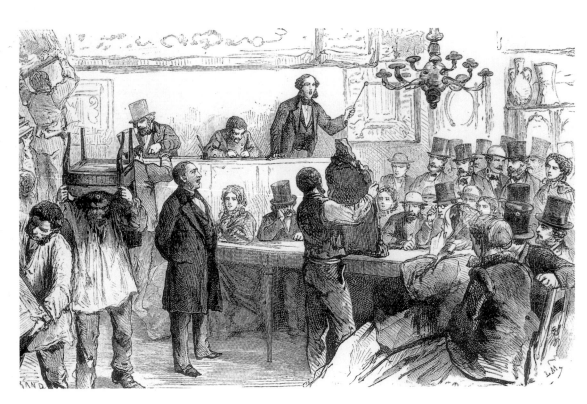

CAILLEBOTTE
The Pont de l'Europe
1876

The Pont de l'Europe was one of the major engineering achievements of Baron Haussamann's redevelopment of Paris. It spanned the station and engine-sheds of St-Lazare and was the focal point of the Quartier de l'Europe (so called because many of the streets took their names from European cities). The figure of the top-hatted man walking towards us is based on Caillebotte himself.

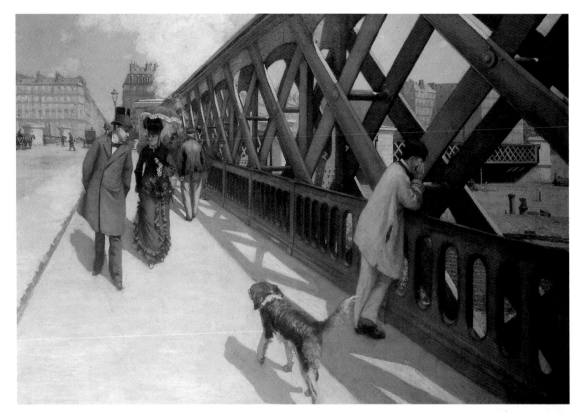

CAILLEBOTTE
Street in Paris,
A Rainy Day
1877

Caillebotte painted this monumental work when he was 29 years old. One of the most remarkable essays in urban Realism produced during the nineteenth century, it gives an insight into the extraordinary effect that the development of this district must have had on the artist – when Caillebotte was born the area was a relatively unsettled hill outside the city limits. Instead of the bustling crowds seen in so many Impressionist street scenes, such as Monet's *Boulevard des Capucines* (p.86), this painting shows a vast expanse peopled by isolated pedestrians ▲ (p.106).

Opposite: An engraving by Mouchot showing an auction at the Hôtel Drouot.

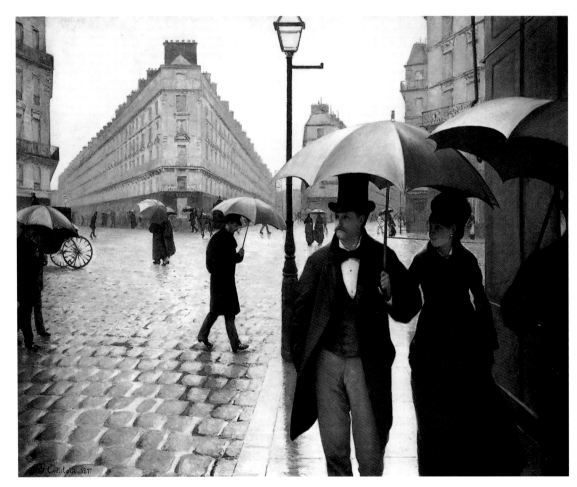

THE THIRD IMPRESSIONIST EXHIBITION

Entitled simply 'Exposition de peinture par…', the third Impressionist exhibition was held at 6 rue Le Peletier from April 4th to 30th. Only eighteen artists participated, compared with thirty in 1874 and nineteen in 1876. Altogether 241 works were on show, including six by Caillebotte, sixteen by Cézanne, twenty-five by Degas, including *The Star* (p.101), thirty by Monet (mostly painted during the previous year), twenty-eight by Pissarro's friend Ludovic Piette, twenty-two by Pissarro, twenty-one by Renoir and seventeen by Sisley. Many of the works were on loan. Of the Monets, for instance, eleven were lent by Ernest Hoschedé ◆ (pp.146–7), one by Manet and ten by other collectors; and of the Sisleys, three were lent by Hoschedé, three by Georges de Bellio (a Romanian doctor who was a keen collector of Impressionist paintings), two by the publisher Charpentier, one by Duret and one (*The Bridge at Argenteuil*) by Manet.

The exhibition was held in a five-room apartment almost opposite Durand-Ruel's gallery, the rent being paid by Caillebotte, who was to be reimbursed out of the admission charges. Extensive advance publicity had been organized – including widely displayed posters, once again paid for by Caillebotte. It was estimated that there were 8000 visitors; and many of them were harangued by Victor Chocquet ▲ (p.224) – who was in attendance every day, energetically expatiating on the little-appreciated merits of Cézanne. Coverage by the press was extensive, some fifty reviews appearing in an impressive variety of newspapers and journals ▲ (p.106).

The largest room contained works by Caillebotte, Monet, Pissarro and Sisley. Degas was the only artist to have a room devoted entirely to his own work. In addition to seven paintings of the Gare St-Lazare (the first of Monet's series), Monet exhibited *The White Turkeys* (p.195) – a large painting lent by Hoschedé, for whose house at Montgeron (which can be seen in the background) it was intended, as part of the decorative scheme. Other significant works included Caillebotte's *Street in Paris, A Rainy Day* (p.103), which he had finished the previous month, and his *The Pont de l'Europe* (p.103), painted in 1876. Renoir's masterpiece *Dancing at the Moulin de la Galette* (opposite), also

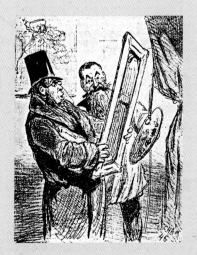
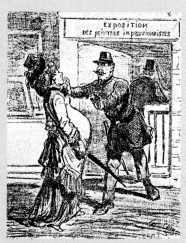

These two caricatures by Cham ridiculing the third Impressionist exhibition appeared in the magazine *Le Charivari*. In the first, the critic is saying 'But these are the colours of a corpse', to which the painter replies 'Unfortunately I can't get the smell.' In the second, the gendarme is advising the pregnant lady 'Madame, it would be unwise to go in.'

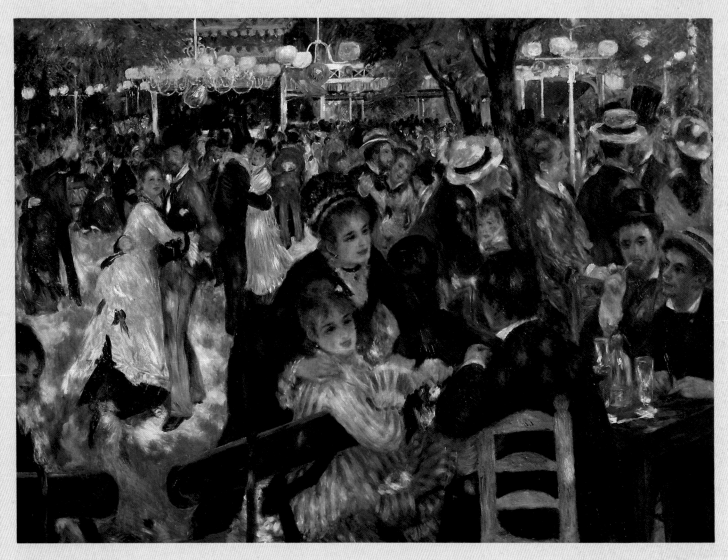

RENOIR
**Dancing at the Moulin
de la Galette**
1876

One of several mills in Montmartre, the Moulin de la Galette ('galette' meaning a small pancake) was close to the rue Cortot, where Renoir had taken a studio specifically to paint this scene. Many of the figures in the painting are recognizable as the artist's friends and acquaintances. Well received at the third Impressionist exhibition ▲ (p.106), it was bought by Caillebotte, who included it in the background of his *Self-Portrait at the Easel*.

painted in 1876, which was given the place of honour in the third room, dominated critical comment on the exhibition.

The hanging – carried out by a committee consisting of Caillebotte, Pissarro and Renoir – had been the subject of considerable thought and discussion. Indeed, unlike the previous shows, the third exhibition was very carefully planned and arranged. Most of the works had been chosen with an artistic audience in mind, and there was even a balanced selection of subjects, rural and urban landscapes, genre scenes, portraits and still lifes being fairly evenly represented.

At Caillebotte's dinner party in January a policy had evidently emerged of making the exhibition not merely an opportunity to display the artists' work, but also to establish the Impressionists as a coherent and clearly recognizable stylistic force. Ironically, however, it succeeded in fostering latent rivalries among them and promoted yearnings for individual recognition rather than for closer association. It is significant that at the next exhibition, two years later, Cézanne, Morisot, Renoir and Sisley did not participate.

See next page

CRITICAL REACTIONS TO THE THIRD IMPRESSIONIST EXHIBITION

MONET
The Gare St-Lazare
1877

Monet obtained official permission to paint the engine-sheds at the Gare St-Lazare. In this view he managed to catch perfectly the light, airy atmosphere created by Eugène Flachat, who in 1837 designed the station as the terminus of the first railway built in France.

RENOIR Dancing at the Moulin de la Galette

Renoir exhibits a large canvas showing a dance at the Moulin de la Galette in Montmartre (p.105). The painter has very accurately presented the boisterous and slightly disorderly scene at this open-air café with dancing, perhaps the last such café remaining in Paris. People are dancing in the little garden next to the mill. A great, brutal light falls from the sky through the green, transparent foliage, gilding blonde hair and pink cheeks, and tossing sparks onto the ribbons of the young girls. This light illumines the painting right to the background with a joyful glow which is even reflected on the shadows. In the midst of all this light, a crowd of dancers twists and turns in the many postures of a frantic choreography. It is like the shimmer of a rainbow.

C. FLOR O'SQUARR, *Le Courrier de France*, April 6th

CAILLEBOTTE Street in Paris, A Rainy Day

This painting (p.103) shows the intersection made by the rue de Turin and the rue de Moscou, seen on a rainy day. Again this is very well drawn, only Caillebotte has neglected to provide any rain. That day the rain seems to have left no impression on him at all.

L'Événement, April 6th

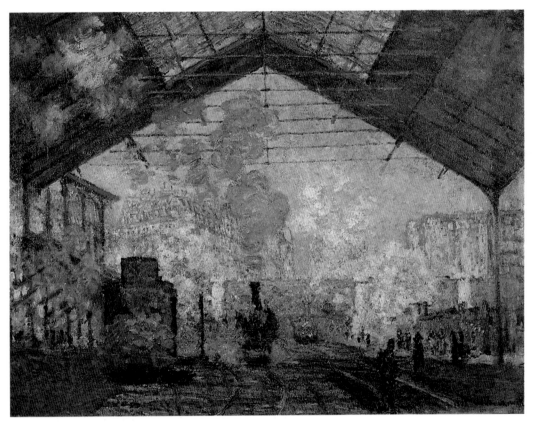

MONET The Gare St-Lazare

Monet loves this station and he has presented it several times before, with less success. This time it is really wonderful. His brush has expressed not only the movement, colour and activity, but the clamour; it is unbelievable. Yet this station is full of din – grindings, whistles – that you can make out through the confusion of clouds of grey and blue smoke. It is a pictorial symphony.

'JACQUES', *L'Homme libre*, April 11th

DEGAS Portrait

It is hard to understand exactly why Degas categorized himself as an Impressionist. He has a distinct personality and stands apart from the group of so-called innovators. Moreover, Degas does not seek to hide the sources of his talent, and even gives us an autobiographical sketch. Presented on an easel and under a carefully chosen ray of light is a portrait of a woman that evidently was not painted for the good of the cause, as it is dated 1867. The work is serious, with some Italian reminiscences. Its individual character has clearly been sought for; the modelling is simple and broad. We shall not ask ourselves how the Florentine of ten years ago has become today's Impressionist. Proximity does not create kinship. Degas may be exhibiting near Pissarro, Sisley, Cézanne and Claude Monet, but he does not belong to the family. He is an observer; a historian perhaps.

PAUL MANTZ, *Le Temps*, April 22nd

◆ IMPRESSIONIST TECHNIQUE

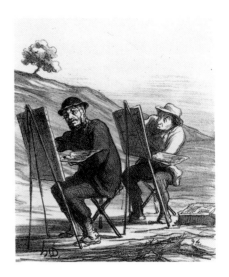

A lithograph by Daumier published in the satirical magazine *Le Charivari* in 1865. The caption reads 'Landscape Painters: the First copies Nature, the Second copies the First.'

It cannot be sufficiently stressed that the Impressionists did not possess a strictly defined set of technical rules, nor did they share the same attitudes towards considerations such as composition, brushwork and colour manipulation. There is, for instance, little to link the style and technique of Monet with that of Degas, little even to link an early Manet such as *Olympia* (p.36) with a later work such as *Argenteuil*.

There are, however, certain technical attitudes which are generally assumed to be typical of the Impressionist movement. The most frequently quoted of these is *plein-air* painting, which is based on the desire to capture the immediate impact of a visual expression by painting a picture out of doors, consistently in the same light. This technique was not quite as innovative as is sometimes claimed. Powered to a certain extent by the essentially Romantic concept of 'Nature', which had been evolving since the late eighteenth century, it was practised extensively not only by Turner and the painters of the Barbizon school but also by academic teachers such as Delaroche and Couture, who took their students on open-air painting excursions. Dr Gachet noted how it was practised by Cézanne; and Monet, its most vocal exponent, would have ten or fifteen paintings of the same site going simultaneously, each one marked on the back with its date and time.

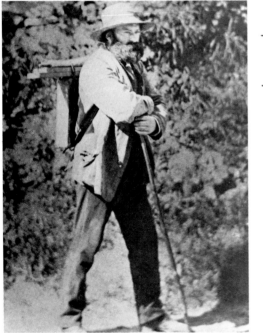

Cézanne setting out on an open-air painting expedition in Auvers, *c.*1874.

However, many of Monet's claims to absolute dependence on *plein-airisme* must be treated with caution. Many of his works were finished in the studio, and there is some evidence to suggest the he occasionally relied on the camera to record certain effects for subsequent reference.

The second technical characteristic of the Impressionists was in their approach to colour. This can be attributed in part to the discoveries of the chemist Eugène Chevreul (1786–1889), predominantly those principles which concerned mixed and successive contrasts. Chevreul demonstrated that if two strips of the same colour but of different shades are placed side by side, then the part of the lighter strip nearest to the darker strip will appear lighter than it is. He also showed that every colour tends to tint its neighbours with its own complementary colour (p.13).

1878

Multiple Disappointments

Not only does Manet have to abandon his plans to stage a one-man show outside the Universal Exhibition, but also the Faure and Hoschedé Impressionist sales at the Hôtel Drouot are spectacular failures, with the paintings either selling for derisory sums or having to be bought in.

JANUARY

Manet decides to hold a one-man exhibition of 100 works near the forthcoming Universal Exhibition (but nothing comes of his plans). Anxious to help Monet, who is in deep financial trouble, Manet sends him 1000 francs 'against merchandise'. This allows Monet to move from Argenteuil to Vétheuil – also on the Seine, but further away from Paris. He doesn't have enough money to pay the removal men.
Degas' *Portraits in an Office* (p.97) is exhibited by The Société des Amis des Arts de Pau, who later purchase the painting.

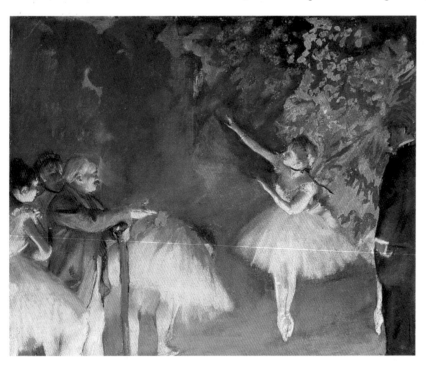

FEBRUARY

Mary Cassatt's friend Louisine Waldron-Elder – later married to the collector Henry Havemeyer ● (p.233) – lends Degas' *Ballet Rehearsal* (1876–7) to the American Watercolour Society of New York for their annual exhibition. This is the first time Degas' work has been exhibited in the USA.

MARCH

Claude and Camille Monet's second son, Michel, is born.

4th Cézanne acknowledges receipt of artist's materials to the value of 2174 francs from Père Tanguy ● (p.192). (Cézanne, who is facing financial disaster, fails to pay for these items, and Tanguy has to send him a reminder in August 1885.)
15th Caillebotte, Degas, Renoir and others meet at Caillebotte's studio

DEGAS
Ballet Rehearsal
1876–7

Painted in pastel and gouache over monotype, this is one of a number of works by Degas which feature Jules Perrot, a leading choreographer of the nineteenth century. Perrot was *maître de ballet* at Covent Garden from 1842 to 1848, then moved to the St Petersburg Opera, before taking the same post at the Paris Opéra.

to discuss plans for a fourth Impressionist exhibition. (Cézanne, Monet, Renoir and Zola also hold a meeting, at the Café Riche, at about the same time.)

19th The museum in Pau buys Degas' *Portraits in an Office* (p.97) for 2000 francs – the first of his works to be hung in a public collection.

20th Cézanne's father discovers the existence of Paul – the artist's illegitimate son, now aged 6, who is living with his mother, Hortense Fiquet, in Marseilles – and halves Cézanne's allowance. To help them survive, Zola starts sending Hortense monthly payments of 60 francs ▲ (p.111).

APRIL

The Italian art critic and painter Diego Martelli ▲ (p.121) arrives in Paris for a thirteen-month visit. He becomes friendly with several of the Impressionists – including Degas (who later paints his portrait) and Pissarro.

3rd Opening of the Salon. Exhibits include Renoir's *The Cup of Chocolate*.

29th Faure ● (p.81) offers a group of Impressionist paintings from his collection for sale at the Hôtel Drouot ◆ (p.102), expecting to make a profit. The proceeds do not even cover his expenses, and he has to buy many of the paintings himself because the bidding is so low.

MAY

Théodore Duret's *Les Peintres impressionnistes* (left) is published, explaining the significance of the movement and giving biographical details about its leading exponents. It is illustrated with a drawing by Renoir after *Lise with a Parasol* (p.51).

JUNE

Pissarro starts to paint fans. He rents a room in Montmartre where he can exhibit his paintings.

An illustrated edition of Zola's *L'Assommoir* (*see* p.101) is published. It includes engravings after drawings by Butin, Castelli, Gill, Goeneutte and Renoir (right).

5th Manet and his family move from 49 to 39 rue de St-Pétersbourg. He takes a studio at No.4.

6th The department-store owner Ernest Hoschedé ◆ (pp.146–7) is made bankrupt, and his entire collection of Impressionist art is auctioned at the Hôtel Drouot. The sale is a spectacular failure: three Renoirs go for a total of 157 francs; Sisley's paintings sell for an average price of 112 francs; Monet's for 150 francs; and Manet's for 583 francs (less than Durand-Ruel had paid for them originally). Mary Cassatt buys a Monet and a Morisot at the auction.

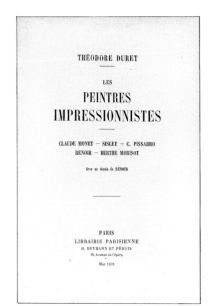

THÉODORE DURET

LES

PEINTRES
IMPRESSIONNISTES

CLAUDE MONET – SISLEY – C. PISSARRO
RENOIR – BERTHE MORISOT

Avec un dessin de RENOIR

PARIS
LIBRAIRIE PARISIENNE
H. HEYMANN ET PÉROIS
38, Avenue de l'Opéra
Mai 1878

The cover of Duret's study of the lives and work of Monet, Sisley, Pissarro, Renoir and Morisot.

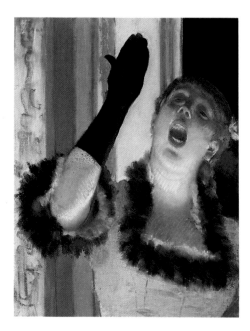

DEGAS
Singer with a Glove
1878

Between 1876 and 1878 Degas produced a series of monotypes of the café-concerts held at the Alcazar-d'Été and the Café des Ambassadeurs, some of which he reworked in pastel. *Singer with a Glove* is a pastel and distemper depiction of one of the most popular singers of the period, Emma Valadon (known professionally as 'Thérésa'), who also appears in Degas' *The Song of the Dog* (*c*.1876–7) and *The Singer in Green* (*c*.1884).

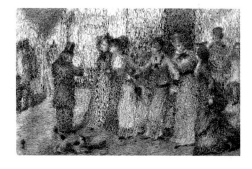

Renoir's illustration for a special edition of Zola's *L'Assommoir*. The original brush drawing was too faint for reproduction, so Renoir traced it over in pen and ink.

**RENOIR
Mme Charpentier
and her Children**
1878

This family portrait was painted at the sitters' home. According to the artist's brother Edmond, 'None of the furniture was moved from its usual place and nothing was pre-arranged to emphasize one part of the painting rather than another.' The result bears little resemblance to the majority of society portraits of the period.

JULY

Madame Hoschedé and her children join the Monets at Vétheuil. Monet's wife, Camille, is ill.
15th Durand-Ruel holds a prestige exhibition of 360 painters of the Barbizon school. Victor Hugo is Honorary President of the exhibition.

SEPTEMBER

The politician Antonin Proust asks Manet to paint his portrait, which he eventually does, two years later (p.124).
14th Pissarro's second son, Rodo, is born.
Seurat gains admission to the École des Beaux-Arts.

OCTOBER

Mme Charpentier, wife of the publisher, commissions Renoir to paint a portrait of herself and her two children, Georgette and Paul, in the 'Japanese salon' of their house in the Place St-Germain-l'Auxerrois.

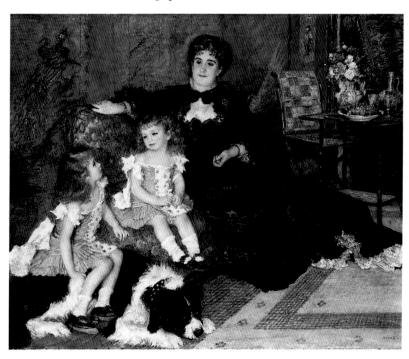

NOVEMBER

14th A daughter, Julie, is born to Berthe Morisot and her husband, Manet's brother Eugène.

DECEMBER

4th Degas, in common with other artists, is intrigued by an illustrated article in *La Nature*, giving an account of Eadweard Muybridge's investigation of animal movement, carried out by taking photographic sequences of horses in motion ◆ (p.160).

OTHER EVENTS

- Greece declares war on Turkey
- Bulgaria, Romania, Serbia and Montenegro become independent
- Pope Leo XIII succeeds Pius IX
- Population of USA overtakes that of any European country except Russia

- Microphone invented in USA
- London has electric street lighting
- Universal Exhibition opens in Paris (coinciding with first Fête Nationale since 1870); the art section does not include any Impressionist works
- New method of teaching drawing, based on mathematical principles, introduced in French schools

- Zola buys a house at Médan thanks to the success of *L'Assommoir*
- Ruskin ridicules Whistler's *Nocturnes*; the artist thereupon sues the critic for libel
- Publication of Hardy's *The Return of the Native*
- Brahms composes his Violin Concerto

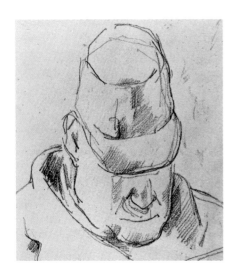

A pencil sketch by Cézanne of his father (*c.*1877–80).

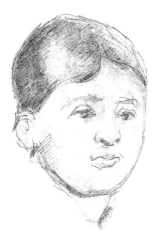

A pencil sketch (*c.*1878–81) by Cézanne of Hortense Fiquet, whom he met in 1869 and married in April 1886.

CÉZANNE
The Artist's Son Paul
1877–9

For the first six years of his life, Paul and his mother Hortense Fiquet travelled surreptitiously around France, following Cézanne. As the boy reached school age, around 1878, this became more difficult. Hortense settled in Marseilles with Paul, where Cézanne's father learned of their existence.

▲ CÉZANNE'S FAMILY PROBLEMS

From the start, Cézanne didn't want his parents to find out about his liaison with Hortense Fiquet – an artist's model he met in Paris in 1869 – and it was only in March 1878 that his father learned of the existence of their illegitimate son, Paul, then 6 years old. The banker, who was seen as a pillar of the community in Aix-en-Provence, immediately halved Cézanne's allowance, leaving him without means to support his mistress and child. In despair, Cézanne confided in Zola, who responded by sending money to Hortense. These extracts from Cézanne's letters to Zola show his financial predicament:

March 23rd

I am on the verge of having to provide entirely for myself, if indeed I am capable of it. The situation between my father and myself is becoming extremely tense, and I risk losing my entire allowance. A letter M. Chocquet wrote to me in which he mentioned 'Madame Cézanne and baby Paul' completely revealed my situation to my father, who for that matter was already on the alert and full of suspicions, and had nothing better to do than to unseal and read the letter addressed to me.

March 28th

It's more than probable that I shall only get 100 francs from my father, even though he promised me 200 when I was in Paris. So I will have to rely on your kindness, especially as the child has been ill for two weeks with a mucous infection. I'm doing everything I can to prevent my father obtaining definite proof. You will pardon me making the following remark – but the paper you use for writing and your envelopes must be very thick; I had to pay 25 centimes at the Post Office because there weren't

enough stamps on it, and all your letter contained was a double sheet. When you write to me, could you please use only one sheet folded in half?

April 4th

Please send 60 francs to Hortense at the following address: Madame Cézanne, 183 rue de Rome, Marseilles. I slipped away Tuesday a week ago to see the child. He's better, but I had to return to Aix on foot, since the train marked on my timetable was an error, and I had to show up in time for dinner – I was an hour late.

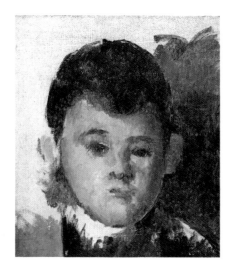

May

Since you have offered to come to my assistance once again, I ask that you send 60 francs to Hortense at the same address.

June 1st

Here is my monthly solicitation again. I hope it doesn't bother you too much and that it doesn't seem too importunate. I'm asking you to be so kind as to send 60 francs to Hortense.

September 14th

Here is the latest blow to befall me. Hortense's father wrote to his daughter addressing his letter to Madame Cézanne. My landlord immediately forwarded the letter to the Jas de Bouffan. My father opened it and read it; you can imagine the results. I made violent denials, and since, very fortunately, Hortense's name didn't occur in the letter, I swore it was addressed to some other woman.

Nota bene. Papa gave me 300 francs this month. Unheard of! I think he's been flirting with a charming young maid we have in Aix. Mama and I are still in L'Estaque.

November 4th

The reason for my letter is as follows. Hortense is in Paris on urgent business; I beg you to send her 100 francs, if you can advance me that much. I'm in a real mess, but I expect to get out of it.

1879

Publication of 'La Vie moderne'
THE FOURTH IMPRESSIONIST EXHIBITION

A surge of confidence among the group is reflected in the founding of 'La Vie moderne', a periodical dedicated to the promotion of Impressionism, the premises of which also house an art gallery. Renoir plays a major part in its conception.

JANUARY

Degas begins to make regular visits to the Cirque Fernando (right), a popular circus near the Place Pigalle (later frequented and painted by Toulouse-Lautrec).

FEBRUARY

3rd Sisley exhibits three works at the Société des Amis des Arts de Pau. None are sold.
23rd One of Renoir's favourite models, Alma Henriette Leboeuf, known as Anna (p.97), dies at the age of 23.
Eva Gonzalès (p.54) marries the engraver Henri Guérard.

MARCH

Cézanne returns to Paris, then moves to Melun.

APRIL

1st Manet moves into his last studio at 77 rue d'Amsterdam.
10th Encouraged by his wife, Marguerite (p.110), the publisher Georges Charpentier – a friend and patron of Renoir – launches a magazine entitled *La Vie moderne* (left), which aims to promote the work of the Impressionists. An announcement in the first issue states that the magazine has an art gallery on its premises with direct access to the street, which is 'intended to transfer the atmosphere of an artist's studio to the boulevard; a hall which will be open to everybody, where the collector can come when he pleases, thus avoiding possible friction and having no fear of imposing himself.'
Manet unsuccessfully submits a plan for the decoration of the council chamber in the new Hôtel de Ville.
Opening of the fourth Impressionist exhibition, at 28 avenue de l'Opéra ■ (p.115).
20th Sisley moves to 164 Grande-rue in Sèvres, helped by the sale of six paintings to Charpentier for 400 francs.

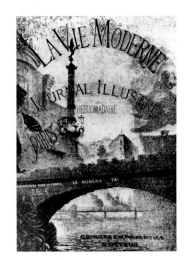

The cover of the first issue of *La Vie moderne*, published by Georges Charpentier.

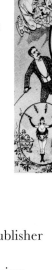

A poster for the Cirque Fernando in Montmartre, which Degas started to frequent in 1879.

MAY

Mary Cassatt exhibits at the Society of American Artists in New York.

3rd Opening of the Salon. Manet and Eva Gonzalès both have work accepted, but Cézanne and Sisley are rejected. Renoir's *Madame Charpentier and her Children* (p.110) is hung prominently. The portrait elicits warm applause from the critics, and even the most conservative reviewers express satisfaction at Renoir's return to the Salon.

JUNE

12th Renoir suggests to Charpentier that he should stage an exhibition of forty paintings by Sisley – some of which 'would be bound to sell.'

19th An article by Edmond Renoir on his brother's paintings appears in *La Vie moderne* (*see* opposite). (Edmond had been involved with the magazine from the start and would become its editor.)

Zola criticizes certain aspects of Impressionism in *Viestnik Europi*, a Russian periodical to which he is contributing regular articles and reviews ▲ (p.114).

JULY

5th An exhibition of Impressionist drawings opens at the gallery of *La Vie moderne*, and attracts around 2000 visitors a day.

26th *Le Figaro* reprints Zola's article from *Viestnik Europi* under the headline 'M. Zola has broken with Manet' ▲ (p.114).

27th An exhibition of paintings by Monet, Pissarro and Sisley opens at the offices of the left-wing paper *L'Événement.*

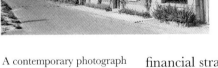

A contemporary photograph of Monet's house in Vétheuil, by Pierre Baudin.

AUGUST

7th Monet, who has been living and working in Vétheuil, is in desperate financial straits. He writes to one of his patrons, the Romanian doctor Georges de Bellio, asking for money to help support his wife who is sick.

SEPTEMBER

5th Monet's wife, Camille, has a slow and painful death. Her husband is appalled by the detachment with which he has been able to paint her in her last hours (right).

DECEMBER

Manet's *The Execution of the Emperor Maximilian* ◆ (pp.56–9) has a mixed reception when shown in New York and Boston for several weeks.

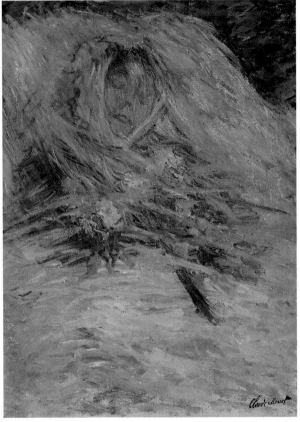

MONET
Camille Monet on her Deathbed
1879

Monet remarked to Clemenceau on this macabre work: 'I caught myself... searching for the succession, the arrangement of coloured gradations that death was imposing on her motionless face.'

1879

OTHER EVENTS

- MacMahon resigns, Grévy becomes President of France
- French Chamber of Deputies returns to Paris from Versailles
- Amnesty proclaimed for Communards in exile or prison
- Prince Imperial, son of Napoleon III, killed in action
- Panama Canal Company organized under Ferdinand de Lesseps
- Installation of London's first public telephone exchange
- Publication of Robert Louis Stevenson's *Travels with a Donkey* and Henry James's *Daisy Miller*
- First production of Ibsen's *A Doll's House*
- First performance of Tchaikovsky's *Eugen Onegin*

ZOLA IMPUGNS THE IMPRESSIONISTS

All the Impressionists are poor technicians. In the arts, as well as in literature, form alone sustains new ideas and new methods. In order to assert himself as a man of talent, an artist must bring out what is in him, otherwise he is but a pioneer. The Impressionists, as I see it, are but pioneers. For a moment Manet inspired great hopes, but he appears exhausted by hasty production; he is satisfied with approximations; he doesn't study nature with the passion of true creators. All these artists are too easily contented. They woefully neglect the solidity of works meditated on for a long time. And for this reason it is to be feared that they are merely preparing the path for the great artist of the future expected by the world.

ÉMILE ZOLA, 'M. Zola has broken with Manet',
Le Figaro, July 26th – reprinted from *Viestnik Europi*
(*Le Messager de l'Europe*), St Petersburg, July 1879

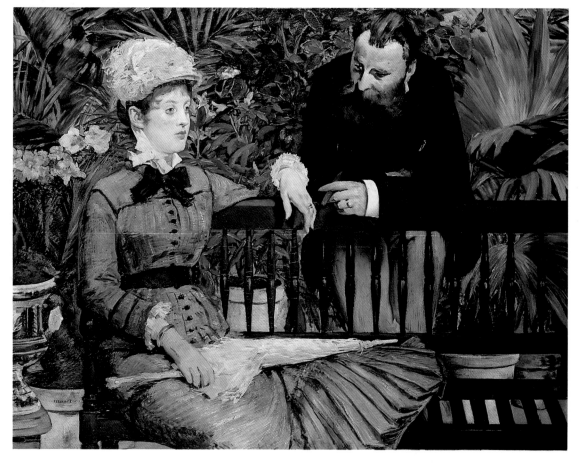

MANET
In the Conservatory
1879

Manet painted this double portrait of M. and Mme Jules Guillemet, owners of a fashionable shop in the prestigious rue du Faubourg, in his studio at 77 rue d'Amsterdam. When the painting was shown at the Salon of 1879, Manet asked the State to purchase it, but was unsuccessful in this request. On January 1st, 1883, however, it was acquired by Faure for 4000 francs.

FOURTH IMPRESSIONIST EXHIBITION

The fourth Impressionist exhibition – entitled '4e Exposition faite par un groupe d'artistes indépendants, realistes et impressionnistes' – was held at 28 avenue de l'Opéra from April 10th to May 11th. Altogether, there were fifteen exhibitors. Gauguin was invited to participate, but failed to submit his entries in time to be included in the catalogue. Pissarro had thirty-eight works on show (including four fans and a view of Norwood); Monet exhibited twenty-nine items (mostly landscapes of Vétheuil); and Degas contributed twenty-nine works in various media (including some fans), of which the most prominent was his oil painting *Miss La La at the Cirque Fernando*.

Monet had not wanted to exhibit, and did not appear at the exhibition. It was Caillebotte who collected his works and hung them; he also lent a number of Monets from his own collection. Cézanne, Renoir and Sisley did not exhibit at all. The imprint of Degas' personality was clearly apparent. In the first place, he insisted that the word 'Impressionist' should not be given undue prominence in the title of the exhibition. Secondly, many of the exhibitors – including Cassatt, Rouart, Zandomeneghi and Forain – were Degas' special protégés.

Attendance was better than at the third exhibition. Admission cost 50 centimes, and on the first day the receipts amounted to 400 francs. At the end of the exhibition Caillebotte reported that there had been 15,400 admissions; all the expenses had been covered, and each member of the group received approximately 440 francs.

One of the visitors was Georges Seurat, then a student at the École des Beaux-Arts, who was so enthused by what he saw that he decided to leave that institution and work on his own.

Critical reception was generally hostile – much of it harping on the theme, not entirely unjustified, that the Impressionists were finished as a group. But not all the notices were bad. Edmond Duranty wrote a favourable review in the *Gazette des Beaux-Arts*, in which he praised Monet and Pissarro as well as Degas and his circle; and in Italy, *Roma Artistica* published a long laudatory article.

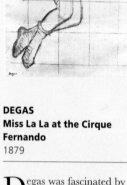

DEGAS
Miss La La at the Cirque Fernando
1879

Degas was fascinated by this acrobat, a mulatto woman known as 'Miss La La', who during her act was pulled up to the dome of the theatre by a rope, which she hung from by her teeth. The above drawing is one of a series of four studies that Degas produced in black chalk and watercolour between January 19th and 25th, 1879, as preparation for the finished painting (right).

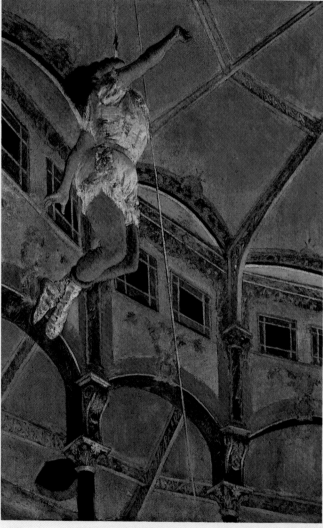

1880

Growing Dissent

THE FIFTH IMPRESSIONIST EXHIBITION

The artists cannot agree about a title for their exhibition and Cézanne, Monet, Renoir and Sisley ultimately refuse to participate. The show is therefore very unbalanced and – badly lit, poorly hung and unsuitably housed – has poor attendance figures and even worse reviews.

JANUARY

Manet's health begins to deteriorate.

Renoir breaks his right arm, and has to paint left-handed.

19th Sisley moves to Moret-sur-Loing, near Fontainebleau, at the confluence of the Seine and the Loing.

24th *Le Gaulois* announces plans to publish a portfolio entitled *Le Jour et la Nuit* containing prints by Bracquemond, Caillebotte, Cassatt, Degas, Forain, Pissarro, Raffaëlli and Rouart, which is to be issued at irregular intervals priced between 5 and 20 francs. (Cassatt's mother would later blame Degas for the portfolio's failure to appear.)

MARCH

Durand-Ruel obtains the backing of M. Feder, the director of the Union Génerale bank, and resumes buying works of art on a large scale.

3rd *La Vie moderne* stages an exhibition of decorated ostrich eggs, including several painted by Manet, Pissarro and Renoir.

APRIL

1st The fifth Impressionist exhibition opens at 10 rue des Pyramides ■ (p.119).

8th An exhibition of pastels entitled 'Recent Works by M. Manet' opens at the gallery belonging to *La Vie moderne*.

9th The critic Edmond Duranty (p.75) dies. Degas arranges a sale of works of art for the benefit of Duranty's mistress, Pauline Bourgeois. Cézanne comes to Paris. He visits Zola at Médan.

MAY

Monet rents a studio at 20 rue de Vintimille. Diego Martelli's lecture on Impressionism given to the Circolo Filologico of Livorno in 1879 is published in pamphlet form in Pisa ▲ (p.121).

The poster for the fifth Impressionist exhibition.

Pages from the catalogue of Manet's exhibition at the gallery of *La Vie moderne* in April, with reproductions of two lithographs by the artist that have since been lost.

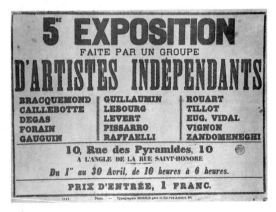

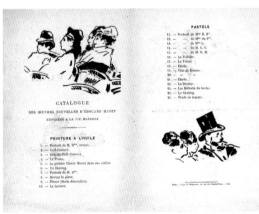

MANET
Chez le père Lathuille
1879

Père Lathuille owned a famous restaurant in the Batignolles area which had been founded at the beginning of the century. This scene is set in its terrace garden. The ardent young man dressed in an artist's smock is Louis Gauthier-Lathuille, the proprietor's son. The actress Ellen Andrée first posed for the woman, but was succeeded by Judith French, a cousin of the composer Offenbach.

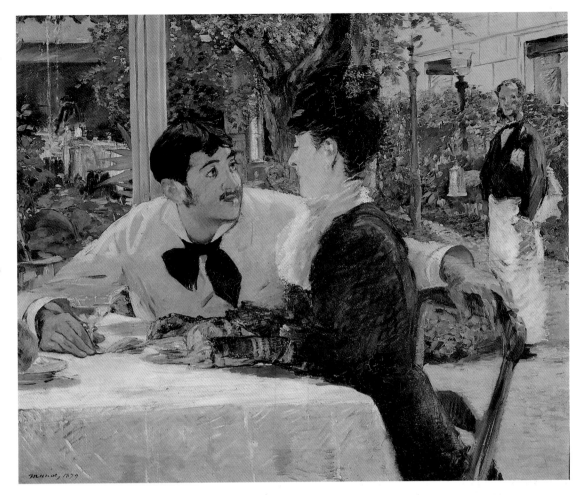

2nd Opening of the Salon. Manet's *Chez le père Lathuille* and his portrait of Antonin Proust (p.124) are hung. Renoir has two submissions accepted. Eva Gonzalès' entries are praised by critics. Monet makes his last appearance at the Salon; he has one work accepted and one rejected.
10th Monet and Renoir write to the Minister of Fine Arts objecting to the way the pictures are hung at the Salon. Cézanne sends Zola a copy of their letter, asking him to publicize it.
23rd The *Gazette des tribuneaux* publishes a scheme to reform the Salon devised by Renoir and sent to the paper by the restaurateur Eugène Murer. It entails four stylistic categories, each of four hundred artists.

JUNE

Monet has an exhibition at the gallery of *La Vie moderne*. Not a single painting is sold, but afterwards Marguerite Charpentier buys *Floating Ice on the Seine* (p.118) for 1500 francs (the exhibition price was 2000 francs). Renoir spends several weeks at Wargemont, near Dieppe, staying at the country house of his friend the diplomat and banker Paul Berard (p.231). Mme Cahen d'Anvers and M. Turquet, the former Under-Secretary for Fine Arts, commission Renoir to paint their portraits. He works on these in Paris during July.
Murer demands that Sisley repay 1200 francs, which he had lent the artist, and threatens to send in debt collectors if he fails to do so.

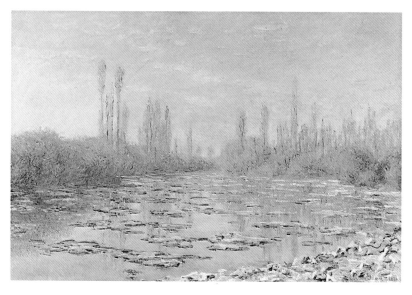

MONET
Floating Ice on the Seine
1880

During the very cold winter of 1879–80 the Seine froze over, then early in January a sudden thaw sent massive blocks of ice down the river. Monet produced several paintings of this dramatic natural phenomenon. Despite the artist's constant protestations about painting in the open air, however, this version was clearly painted in the studio – a smaller canvas exists showing the ice blocks in an identical position. Mme Charpentier bought *Floating Ice on the Seine* for 1500 francs, payable in three instalments, as a present for her husband.

18th–22nd Four articles by Zola appear in *Le Voltaire*. In them he airs the complaints made by Renoir and Monet about the hanging of the Salon – but goes on to call the Impressionists mere 'forerunners', stating that 'no artist of this group has achieved powerfully the new formula which, scattered through their works, they all offer.'

JULY

Manet rents a house at Bellevue, just outside Paris, where he starts to have hydrotherapy treatment for his circulatory problems.
Berthe Morisot spends the summer in Bougival.
Renoir stays at Chatou, near Argenteuil, where he begins work on *Luncheon of the Boating Party* (p.132); he meets 21-year-old Aline Charigot (his future wife), who appears in the painting.
14th Murer gives a banquet to celebrate Bastille day.
Van Gogh writes to his brother, Theo, explaining why he has decided to become an artist.

SEPTEMBER

Monet paints at Petit-Dalles, on the Normandy coast.
Durand-Ruel sends 233 paintings, most of them by Impressionists, to an exhibition in Oran in Algeria.

OCTOBER

Degas starts looking for a new dealer to replace Durand-Ruel.
Seurat moves to Paris and studies Old Masters in the Louvre.

DECEMBER

Pissarro has a tear duct infection (the first sign of future eye trouble).
Durand-Ruel buys several works by Sisley and a pastel by Degas.

OTHER EVENTS

- First Boer War commences following Transvaal's declaration of independence
- Gladstone succeeds Disraeli as British Prime Minister
- Garfield elected President of USA
- France annexes Tahiti
- Lefuel completes rebuilding and extension of the Louvre
- Guimet collection of Oriental art moved from Lyon to Paris
- Edison devises practical electric lights
- Half-tone printing developed
- Publication of Zola's *Nana*, Dostoevsky's *The Brothers Karamazov* and Maupassant's *Boule de Suif*
- Gilbert and Sullivan complete *The Pirates of Penzance*
- Flaubert and Offenbach die

THE FIFTH IMPRESSIONIST EXHIBITION

The fifth Impressionist exhibition was held at 10 rue des Pyramides from April 1st to 30th. From the start, Degas and Caillebotte disagreed about the title of the exhibition. Consequently, the exhibitors were described as 'A Group of Independent Artists' on the posters (which was Degas' formula), but on the catalogue the title appeared as '5e Exposition de peinture par…'

The premises, on the corner of the rue des Pyramides and the rue St-Honoré, were in process of being rebuilt. As a result, there was constant noise and vibration – a fact commented on by the critics, who also noted that the exhibition was badly lit and badly hung. Attendance was poor, and it was generally agreed that this was not primarily an Impressionist exhibition. There were, for instance, thirty-five works by Raffaëlli – one of Degas' protégés, who was a kind of academic Realist. On the other hand, Degas himself failed to send in all the works he announced in the catalogue (including a wax statue of a 14-year-old dancer (p.126) and the *Young Spartans Exercising*, which he had painted in 1860); and four of the leading Impressionists – Cézanne, Monet, Renoir and Sisley – did not participate at all.

As well as nine oil paintings, Pissarro exhibited five groups of etchings mounted on yellow paper in purple frames. There were six paintings by Gauguin (most of them executed at Pontoise under Pissarro's influence) and also a highly finished, almost academic, marble bust of his Danish wife, Mette, sculpted in 1877 (right). Marie Bracquemond was represented by three works and Félix Bracquemond by two, including a portrait of Edmond de Goncourt in charcoal on canvas that attracted a great deal of attention. Guillaumin contributed twenty-one paintings, which were described by one critic as 'inexplicable barrages of

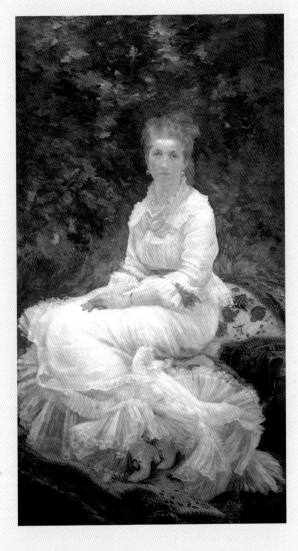

colour'. There were also sixteen works by Mary Cassatt, eighteen by Caillebotte and fifteen by Berthe Morisot.

This time it was not only critics opposed to Impressionism as a matter of principle who wrote unfavourable reviews. Indeed, most damning of all was a piece by Armand Silvestre in the columns of George Charpentier's pro-Impressionist periodical *La Vie moderne*, who complained that there was 'no trace of the vision that gave the little school the recognition it deserved in the art of recent years' and suggested that some of the pictures on view were not even worthy of the Salon.

BRACQUEMOND
Young Woman in White
1880

In many ways a more complex painter than her husband Félix (whose forte was engraving), Marie Braquemond was interested in open-air painting, which she once said had 'produced not only a new, but also a very useful way of looking at things.' This portrait is of her sister Louise Quiveron – one of her favourite models.

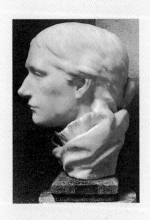

Bust by Gauguin of his wife Mette (1877).

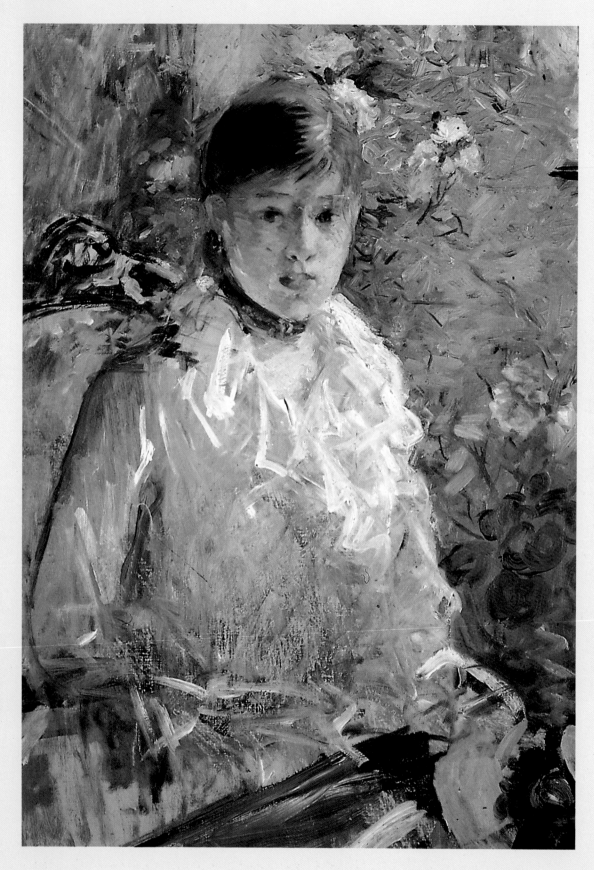

MORISOT
Summer
1878

One of a pair of paintings (the other representing winter) that Morisot showed at the Impressionist exhibition of 1880. The thematic title suggests a departure from the artist's previous emphasis on specific subjects, and the radiance of the sitter is clearly an allegory for the season.

DEGAS
Portrait of Diego Martelli
1879

This is one of Degas' most striking portraits, painted from a viewpoint above the sitter's head. The artist made numerous preliminary sketches for this work, including one dated April 3rd, 1879 – hardly a week before the opening of the fourth Impressionist exhibition, at which this canvas was first shown.

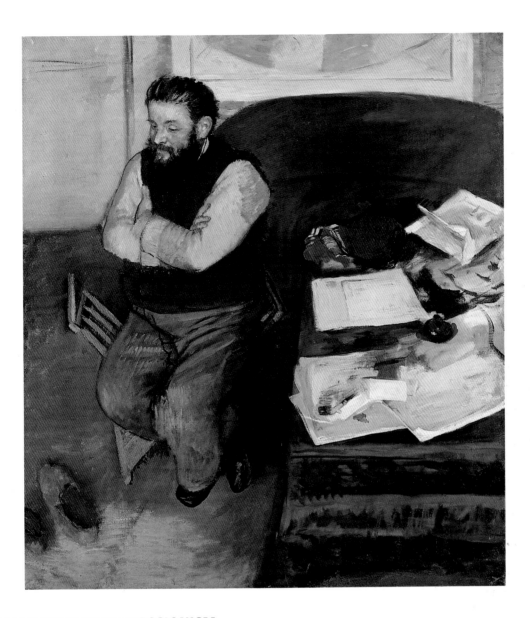

 AN ITALIAN VIEW OF IMPRESSIONISM

In 1879 Diego Martelli, the Italian painter and art critic, gave a lecture on Impressionism to the Circolo Filologico of Livorno, which was published in pamphlet form in 1880. In the following extract, he explains how a greater understanding of the workings of the human eye was the basis of the Impressionists' approach:

Impressionism is not only a revolution in the field of thought, it is also a revolution in the physiological understanding of the human eye. It is a new theory which depends upon a different mode of perceiving the sensation of light and of expressing impressions. The Impressionists did not construct their theories first and then adapt their paintings to them after the fact, but on the contrary, as is always the case with real discoveries, the paintings were born out of the unconscious discoveries of

the artist's eye, which, when considered later on, gave rise to the reasoning of the philosophers.

Until now drawing has generally been believed to be the firmest, most certain and positive part of art. To colour was conceded the unpredictable magic of the realm of the imagination. Today we can no longer reason in this manner, for analysis has shown us that the real impression made upon the eye by objects is an impression of colour, and that we do not see the contours of forms, but only the colours of these forms.

Even if we accept this train of thought, however, drawing need not be renounced, for the revolutions of science, which take place not for secondary ends but with a view to the highest aims, do not destroy that which is good. Drawing therefore is simply conceived by the Impressionists in another way, and takes on a different meaning and function.

1881

Degas Steals the Show

THE SIXTH IMPRESSIONIST EXHIBITION

*The Realist tendencies of the previous year are confirmed in the
composition of the sixth Impressionist show, dominated by Degas.
Caillebotte believes Degas to be responsible for dividing the group, and
joins those boycotting the exhibition.*

JANUARY

Durand-Ruel starts buying from Renoir.
Sisley has an exhibition at the gallery belonging to *La Vie moderne*
(the periodical founded by Charpentier in 1879).

FEBRUARY

Durand-Ruel buys a number of paintings from Pissarro for 12,000
francs, thus temporarily alleviating his financial difficulties.

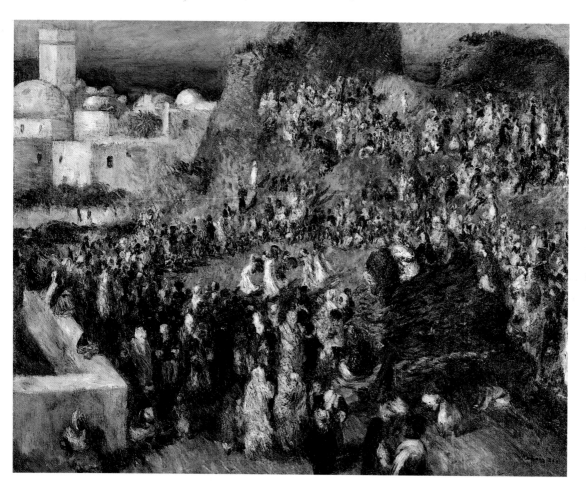

RENOIR
Arab Festival
1881

The most ambitious
figure painting Renoir
brought back from his
first Algerian trip in 1881,
its subject matter has
caused controversy – some
commentators asserting that
the crowds are involved in a
religious service, others that
they are watching jugglers.
The work was first shown
at Durand-Ruel's gallery in
1888, and was subsequently
sold to Monet in 1900.

MARCH

The Ministry of Fine Arts relinquishes control over the Salon to a body of artists named the Société des Artistes Français. Under a new constitution any artist whose work has been accepted by the Salon will be entitled to vote for the jury.

7th Renoir departs for a brief visit to Algiers and writes to Duret: 'I am set on seeing London this year'. (He later abandons his plans.)

APRIL

Van Gogh leaves Brussels to stay with his family at Etten.

2nd The sixth Impressionist exhibition ▪ (p.125) opens.

20th Renoir rents a studio at 18 rue Norvins. Later he meets Whistler while visiting Chatou.

MAY

1st Opening of the Salon. Manet and Renoir each have two works accepted, and Manet is awarded a second-class medal for his portrait of the veteran Communard Henri Rochefort (above).

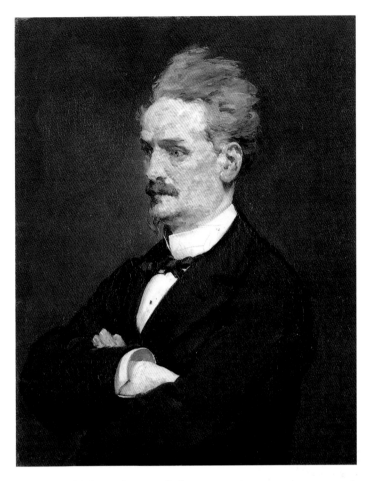

MANET
Portrait of Henri Rochefort
1881

An active Communard, Henri Rochefort was exiled to New Caledonia in 1873. The following year he escaped and, as a result of the Amnesty Act, was able to return to Paris on July 21st, 1880, where he was greeted as a public hero. Marcellin Desboutin (p.95) introduced Rochefort to Manet, who was anxious to paint his portrait. Unfortunately, the sitter disliked the result and rejected it. Manet sold the work to Faure ● (p.81) in 1882, as one of five works for which he was paid a total sum of 11,000 francs.

7th Cézanne and Pissarro paint in Pontoise, where they are joined by Gauguin.

18th Durand-Ruel pays Degas 5000 francs for *The Dance Lesson* (p.127), which he immediately sells to Mary Cassatt's brother for 6000 francs.

JULY

Manet spends the summer in Versailles as an invalid, due to his chronic circulatory problems. Berthe Morisot holidays in Bougival.

Renoir stays with his patrons the Berards ● (p.231) at Wargemont and visits the painter Jacques-Émile Blanche in Dieppe.

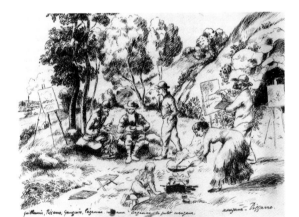

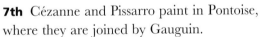

An Impressionist Picnic (c.1881) by Pissarro's son Georges, showing: Guillaumin, Camille Pissarro, Gauguin, Cézanne, Mme Cézanne and Georges' son Manzana.

AUGUST

2nd Pissarro's daughter, Jeanne, is born.

OCTOBER

15th Cézanne returns to Aix-en-Provence from Pontoise.

28th Renoir leaves for a three-month tour of Italy. He is accompanied, at least for part of the time, by his mistress Aline Charigot.

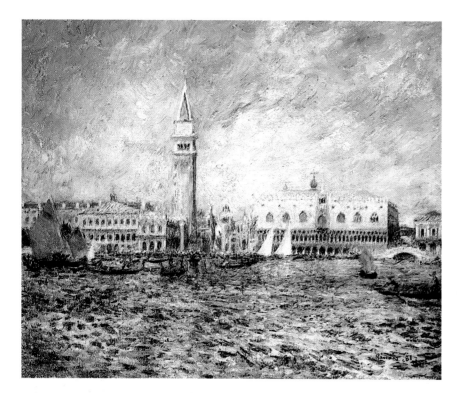

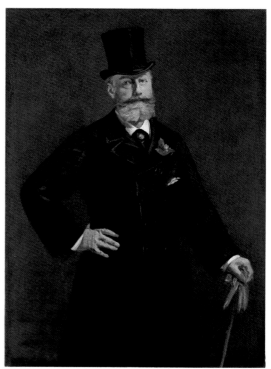

RENOIR
The Doge's Palace, Venice
1881

On his tour of Italy in 1881, Renoir made his first major stop in Venice, and was delighted by the city. His Venetian canvases focus on the famous sites – he painted the Piazza San Marco and the Grand Canal as well as this view. Most of the works, as he confessed to Durand-Ruel, were not finished in Venice but completed on his return to Paris.

NOVEMBER

6th Berthe Morisot departs for Nice, where she remains for the winter.
12th Manet's friend Antonin Proust (above right) becomes Minister of Fine Arts in Gambetta's government.
26th Eadweard Muybridge gives a demonstration of his photographic recording of the movement of horses in Meissonier's studio (*see* p.110).

DECEMBER

8th Degas is introduced to Jacques-Émile Blanche at a sale of Courbet's works. (The two artists become friends, and Degas frequently stays with Blanche in Dieppe.)
10th Monet moves to Poissy with Madame Hoschedé and her children.
15th Degas writes to Pissarro saying that he is resigning from the Impressionist group 'because I cannot continue to serve as a prop to M. Raffaëlli and company.'
30th Manet is made a Chevalier of the Legion of Honour. His state of health deteriorates.

MANET
Portrait of Antonin Proust
1880

Manet first portrayed his lifelong friend Antonin Proust in the mid 1850s, and twice attempted to paint him in 1877. He obviously found the subject difficult – Proust related that Manet used seven or eight canvases before he was happy with the result. The portrait was submitted to the Salon of 1880, where, although generally well-received, it was criticized both by Zola and Joris-Karl Huysmans.

OTHER EVENTS

- President Garfield of USA and Tsar Alexander II assassinated
- First Boer War ends with British recognition of independent Transvaal Republic
- Gambetta becomes Prime Minister of France
- Invention of process engraving
- Electric tramway built in Berlin
- Discovery of typhoid bacillus
- Pasteur tests anthrax vaccine on sheep
- 'Chat Noir' cabaret opens in Paris
- Publication of Verlaine's *Sagesse*, Flaubert's *Bouvard et Pécuchet* and Henry James's *Portrait of a Lady*
- First production of Ibsen's *Ghosts*
- Offenbach's *Tales of Hoffmann* first performed
- Dostoevsky dies

THE SIXTH IMPRESSIONIST EXHIBITION

The sixth Impressionist exhibition ran from April 2nd to May 1st, and was simply titled '6e Exposition de peinture par …' The premises were the same as for the first exhibition ■ (pp.86–7) – Nadar's old studios at 35 boulevard des Capucines – but it was shown in five smaller rooms at the back of the building that were badly lit, low ceilinged and cluttered with furniture.

Degas exhibited six paintings and a sculpture, which was not in position until April 14th. There were seven paintings and two sculptures by Gauguin; seven works (both paintings and pastels) by Morisot; and eleven by Cassatt. Pissarro contributed twenty-seven works, including a number of pastels in gold frames that were tinted with various shades of green and yellow, with the edges painted in complementary colours. The other exhibitors – all protégés of Degas – were Raffaëlli, Rouart, Tillot, Vidal, Vignon and Zandomeneghi.

This was definitely a Degas exhibition, with a heavy emphasis on Realism as one of the alternative hallmarks of the new movement – complementing, or competing with, the stylistic concerns of painters such as Cézanne, Monet, Renoir and Sisley, none of whom participated. Even Pissarro – though normally more concerned with the considerations that preoccupied the abstainers – was predominantly represented by works of a Realist kind, many of them featuring either rural labourers or the market gardens that had sprung up around Paris to satisfy the needs of the ever-growing population.

In addition to the emphasis on Realism, the exhibition was notable for the almost universal approval given to works by Cassatt and Morisot; and also for the presence of three-dimensional work by Degas and Gauguin. Both Degas' wax figure of the 14-year-old Belgian dancer Marie van Goethem (p.126) and Gauguin's woodcarving *Dame*

en promenade were remarkable for the almost brutal quality of their appearance, and also for their use of colour – in the clothes of the dancer and in the wood of the walking figure, which was stained red.

In terms of attendance numbers and review coverage the sixth exhibition was not a success. More significantly, it emphasized the schism that had taken place in the movement.

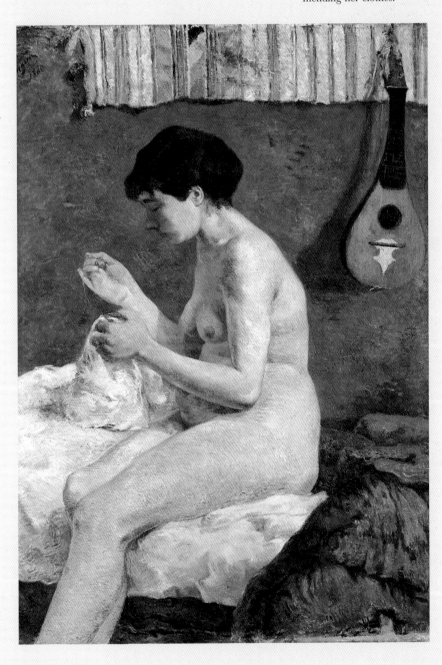

GAUGUIN
Nude
1880

This work was admired by Huysmans, who wrote: 'Here is a girl of our time, who doesn't pose for an audience, who is neither lascivious nor affected, who is simply concerned with mending her clothes.'

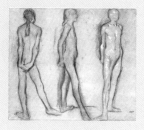

In preparation for his sculpture of *The Little Dancer of 14 Years* (right), Degas made a number of drawings in a variety of media in his notebooks. The one above (*c.*1878–80) turns the figure to explore the stance, and is drawn in charcoal, heightened with white.

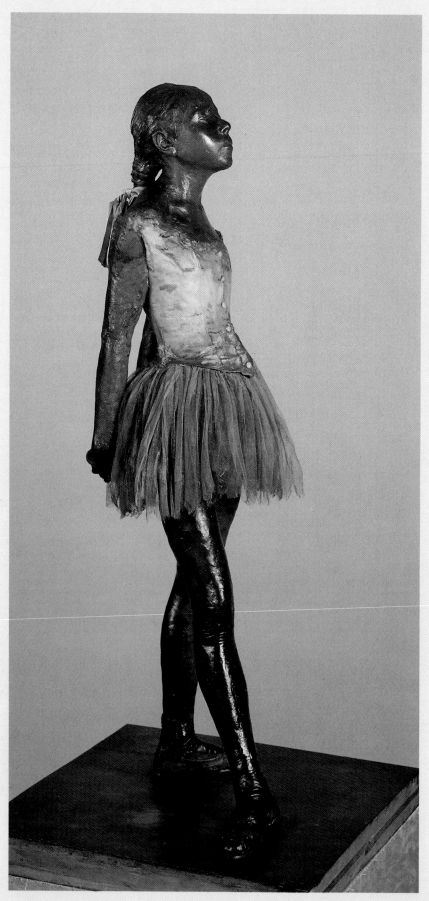

DEGAS
The Little Dancer of 14 Years
1879–81

Made in translucent wax, the figure wears a wig, which was probably bought from the model's landlady (a Mme Cusset, who specialized in the sale of wigs for dolls). The dancing shoes, gauze tutu, stockings and silk faille bodice are all real, as is the green ribbon which binds the hair. The model was Marie van Goethem, a dancer at the Opéra, who spent much of her time at the Brasserie des Martyrs, a well-known haunt of painters and sculptors.

Although Degas listed *The Little Dancer of 14 Years* in the catalogue of the fifth Impressionist exhibition, he withdrew it (the reason for which is unknown). The figure eventually appeared at the sixth Impressionist exhibition, where it was shown in a glass case.

DISUNITY IN OUR MIDST

The dissensions that existed amongst the Impressionists are strikingly illustrated by a letter Caillebotte wrote to Pissarro in January 1881, which was found among the latter's papers after his death:

What is to become of our exhibitions? This is my well-considered opinion: we ought to continue, and continue only in an artistic direction, the sole direction – in the final sense – that is of interest to all of us. I ask, therefore, that a show should be composed of all those who have contributed anything of real interest – that is you, Monet, Renoir, Sisley, Mme Morisot, Mlle Cassatt, Cézanne, Guillaumin; if you wish, Gauguin, perhaps Cordey [a disciple of Renoir], and myself. That's all, since Degas refuses a show on such a basis. I should rather like to know whether the public is interested in our individual disputes. It's very naive of us to squabble over such things. Degas introduced disunity into our midst. It is unfortunate for him that he has such an unsatisfactory character. He spends his time haranguing at the Nouvelle-Athènes or in society. He would do much better to paint a little more. That he is a hundred times right in what he says, that he talks with infinite wit and good sense about painting, no one doubts (and isn't that the outstanding part of his reputation?). No, he has gone sour. He doesn't hold the prominent place that he ought to according to his talent and, although he will never admit it, he bears the whole world a grudge…

He has almost a persecution complex. Doesn't he want to convince people that Renoir has Machiavellian ideas?… One could put together a whole volume of what he has said against Manet, Monet and you…

I ask you: isn't it our duty to support each other and to forgive each other's weaknesses rather than to tear each other down? To cap it all, the very one who has talked so much and wanted to do so much has always been the one who has contributed the least…All this depresses me deeply. If there had been only one subject of discussion among us, that of art, we would always have been in agreement. The person who shifted the question to another level is Degas, and we would be very stupid to suffer from his follies. He has tremendous talent, it is true. I'm the first to proclaim myself his great admirer. But let's stop there. As a human being he has gone so far as to say to me, speaking of Renoir and Monet, 'Do you invite these people to your house?' You see, though he has great talent, he doesn't have a great character.

DEGAS
The Dance Class
c.1878–81

An X-ray analysis of this work shows that Degas made frequent changes to the position of the dancers. Once satisfied, however, that these were correct, the artist painted several variations on the theme. This canvas was commissioned by Mary Cassatt for her brother Alexander, and the family's correspondence reveals their frustration with the delay in the painting's delivery.

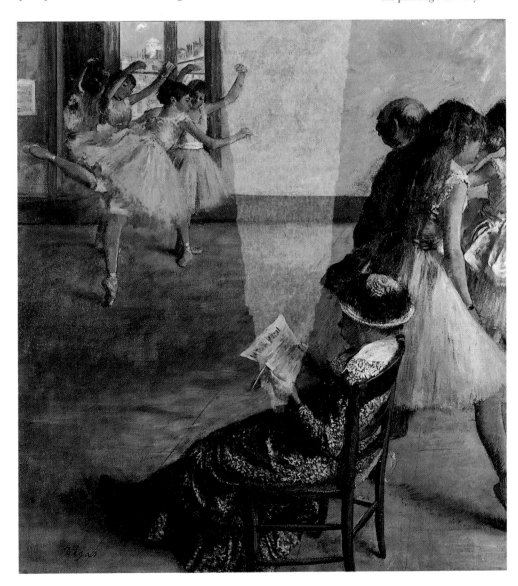

1882

Cassatt Sides with Degas
THE SEVENTH IMPRESSIONIST EXHIBITION

RENOIR
Rocky Crags at L'Estaque
1882

While visiting L'Estaque, Renoir was impressed by Cézanne's highly constructed compositions. The influence can be seen here, notably in the parallel diagonal strokes to the left.

This year, in an attempt to restore a semblance of unity to the group, Durand-Ruel takes the artists in hand and organizes their exhibition. His motives are partly commercial, as it proves an excellent shop-window for a wide range of his stock

JANUARY

14th Renoir visits Wagner, who is composing the opera *Parsifal* in Palermo, and paints his portrait (right) in 35 minutes. They discuss the 'iniquities' of Jewish composers.

25th Degas sells twelve studies of dancers and two pastels to Durand-Ruel for 2450 francs.
Following continuous squabbles about the next Impressionist exhibition, Durand-Ruel decides to organize it himself. He plans to include works by Renoir and Monet, mostly from his own stock.

FEBRUARY

1st Feder's Union Générale bank fails – placing Durand-Ruel in a difficult financial position, since he has to repay extensive loans obtained from the bank.
23rd Renoir stays at the Hôtel des Bains in L'Estaque, where he paints with Cézanne. During his stay in L'Estaque, he catches pneumonia. Cézanne and Cézanne's mother look after him while he is ill.

MARCH

1st The seventh Impressionist exhibition opens in the Salons du Panorama at 251 rue St-Honoré ▪ (pp.131–2).

RENOIR
Portrait of Richard Wagner
1882

After painting this portrait of the composer in Palermo, Renoir reported to a friend: 'Wagner was in a jolly mood, but I was very nervous and I regret that I am not Ingres.'

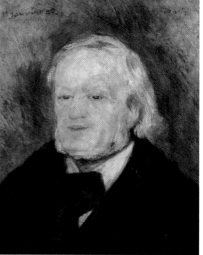

CÉZANNE
Rocks at L'Estaque
1882

The landscape at L'Estaque was central to Cézanne's development as an artist. In a letter to Pissarro he wrote: '... it seems as though the objects are silhouetted, not only in black and white, but in blue, red, brown and violet.' Increasingly in his work he focused upon abstract elements of form and colour.

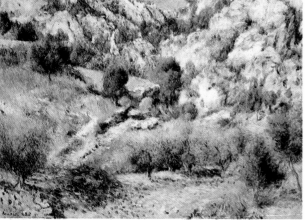

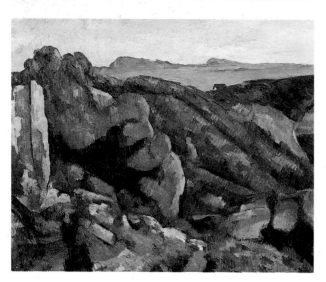

9th A retrospective exhibition of works by Courbet opens at the École des Beaux-Arts.

13th Durand-Ruel pays Degas 400 francs for the pastel *Sur la scène*. (A month later he sells it to Pissarro for 800 francs.)

14th On his doctor's advice, Renoir goes to Algiers. (He plans to stay there for a fortnight but remains for six weeks.)

APRIL

Georges Petit – the owner of a fashionable gallery in the rue de Sèze who is becoming increasingly interested in the Impressionists – founds the Expositions Internationales de Peinture in collaboration with the society painter Giuseppe de Nittis. Their aim is to invite twelve painters to exhibit each year, three of whom would be French.

Cézanne visits Zola and Chocquet, whose wife has inherited a fortune. Monet paints on the Channel coast.

MAY

3rd Opening of the Salon. Manet exhibits *Bar at the Folies-Bergère* and *Jeanne*. Works by Cézanne and Renoir are also accepted.

MANET
Bar at the Folies-Bergère
1881–2

This work, Manet's last masterpiece, was painted in the artist's studio, though the subject was one of the most renowned Parisian venues for café-concerts. The woman, named Suzon, was not a professional model, but a barmaid at the Folies-Bergère. The man talking to her, whose reflection can be seen in the mirror, was the painter Gaston Latouche. Manet took the subject from a passage in Zola's novel *Le Ventre de Paris*, of which he owned an autographed copy.

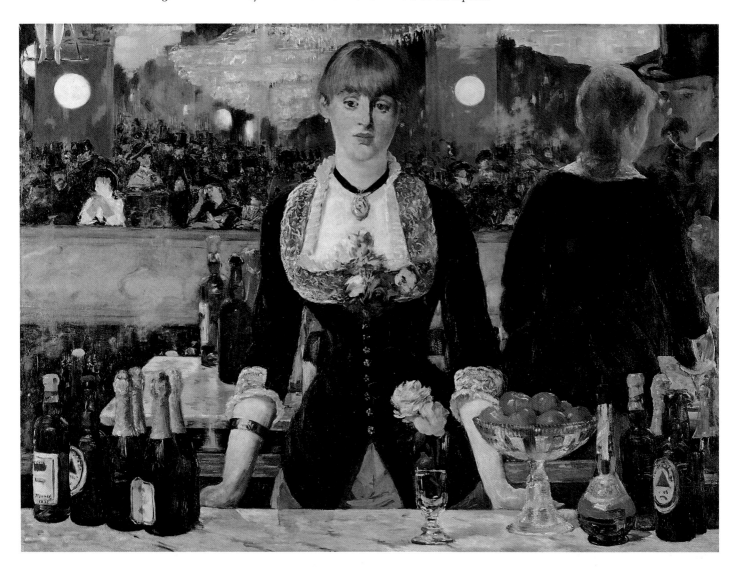

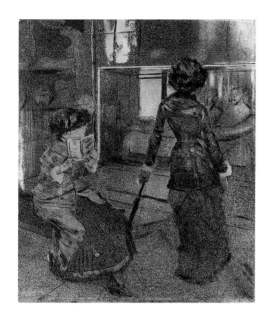

DEGAS
Mary Cassatt at the Louvre
1879–80

Degas was experimenting with a recently introduced technique known as 'electric crayon' when he produced this etching. The result was an extraordinary variety of surfaces, most noticeably the marbling of the pilasters, the oak parquet floor, the frames of the pictures and the textures of the dresses of Cassatt and her sister Lydia.

5th Durand-Ruel holds an exhibition at White's Gallery, 13 King Street, London, which includes works by Cassatt, Degas, Monet, Renoir and Sisley, as well as Delacroix and Millet. The exhibition is favourably reviewed in the *Evening Standard*.

JULY

Manet rents a house at Rueil from the playwright Eugène Labiche and paints there, though unwell.

AUGUST

Pissarro visits Burgundy.
Degas visits Étretat.
Morisot goes to Bougival, where she stays till the end of the year.

SEPTEMBER

Cézanne paints at the Jas de Bouffan, an estate rented by his father, near Aix-en-Provence.
Degas visits Veyrier in Switzerland.
Van Gogh studies with the academic painter van Rappard in The Hague.

OCTOBER

1st Durand-Ruel sends works by Monet, Pissarro, Renoir and Sisley to an exhibition of the Société des Amis des Arts de Touraine in Tours.

NOVEMBER

4th Monet and Sisley have a discussion about the future of the group exhibitions, as Durand-Ruel has been suggesting a series of one-man shows instead. Monet favours two annual exhibitions, one devoted to landscape painters and the other to figure painters. Sisley supports Durand-Ruel's plan.
12th Mary Cassatt's sister Lydia dies – the two sisters feature in Degas' *At the Louvre* (1879) and his subsequent etching *Mary Cassatt at the Louvre*.
27th Cézanne asks Zola's advice about drawing up a will.

DECEMBER

Pissarro moves to Osny, near Pontoise.

OTHER EVENTS

- Triple Alliance formed between Germany, Austria and Italy
- British troops occupy Egypt
- Ferdinand de Lesseps commences construction of the Panama Canal
- The architect Francisco del Villar starts work on the church of the Sagrada Familia in Barcelona
- First family planning clinic opened in Amsterdam
- First performance of Ibsen's *An Enemy of the People*
- Publication of Robert Louis Stevenson's *Treasure Island* and Sardou's *Fédora*
- Wagner's *Parsifal* and Tchaikovsky's *1812 Overture* first performed
- Darwin, Emerson, Gambetta, Longfellow and Rossetti die

THE SEVENTH IMPRESSIONIST EXHIBITION

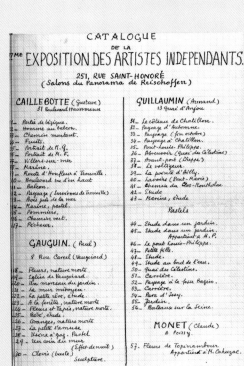

The front page of the hand-written, mimeographed catalogue produced for the seventh Impressionist exhibition.

DEGAS
Henri Rouart in front of his Factory
c.1877

Degas once said that the Rouarts were his only 'family' in France. This is one of several portraits he painted of Henri, Degas' old school friend, all of which showed the industrialist's left profile. Rouart's factory, depicted in the background, manufactured equipment for the military.

The seventh Impressionist exhibition – entitled the '7e Exposition des artistes indépendants' – was held in the Salons du Panorama de Reichshoffen, at 251 rue St-Honoré. It was in some respects a strange choice of venue: the main attraction of the building was a panorama of one of the most crushing defeats suffered by the French army during the Franco-Prussian war, and the upper sections of the exhibition rooms were adorned with tapestries – limiting usable wall space to such an extent that several of the exhibits had to be displayed on easels. Nevertheless, the building – designed by Charles Garnier, architect of the new Opéra – had come to be accepted as a suitable space for art exhibitions, and bodies such as The French Society of Landscape Painters and the Society of Animal Painters had already shown there.

Although the exhibition was in effect a shop window for Durand-Ruel, who partly filled the rooms with works from stock, the rent of 6000 francs was paid by Degas' friend Henri Rouart, a wealthy engineer and amateur painter who had participated in most of the previous exhibitions (this time, however, he did not submit any work). Unlike the catalogues of the previous shows, the one for the present exhibition was an amateurish-looking production, handwritten and reproduced by a copying process. Presumably because of the nature of the premises, the closing time was eleven o'clock in the evening. On the first day

receipts amounted to 950 francs, suggesting that approximately 1900 people came to see the exhibition; on subsequent days the attendance figure was around 350.

There were about 210 exhibits (not all of which were listed), including thirty-five by Monet, thirty-four by Pissarro, twenty-five by Renoir and twelve by Morisot. Prices ranged from 500 to 2500 francs – the higher price range, fixed by Durand-Ruel, embracing Monet and Sisley. The hanging seems to have been mainly the work of Caillebotte, and a party was held on the night before the opening so friends could view the final stages. As to framing, there was a diversity of styles: Gauguin favoured white frames, Pissarro coloured and gilded ones, and Morisot grey with gold ornaments.

Partly thanks to the active cooperation of Durand-Ruel and the fact that Degas' influence had largely been eliminated, this was the most 'Impressionist' of the exhibitions held to date.

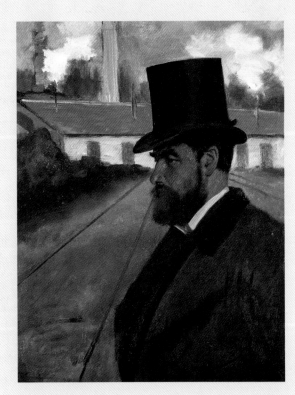

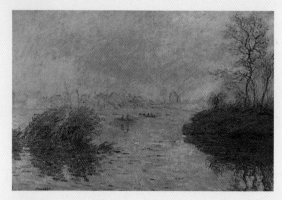

MONET
Sunset on the Seine,
Winter Effect
1880

Painted in Monet's studio from sketches, this work was exhibited at the gallery of *La Vie moderne* in 1880.

As Pissarro put it in a letter to the collector Georges de Bellio, the participants did not have 'any too obvious blemishes to deplore'. The critics generally recognized this and reacted favourably, especially to Renoir's exhibits – although Philippe Burty suggested that Renoir (who was still recuperating from pneumonia in L'Estaque at the time when the exhibition was assembled) might have made a rather different selection.

Some reviews, however, were less than flattering. Caillebotte's paintings came in for a good deal of unfriendly comment, one critic describing them as 'hilarious'; and Monet was pilloried by a reviewer in the appropriately named *Le Soleil* who wondered why *Sunset on the Seine, Winter Effect* (left) made him think of 'a slice of tomato stuck onto the sky, casting a violet light on the water and river banks.' Huysmans was unexpectedly acid about the girls in Renoir's *Luncheon of the Boating Party* (below), and at the same time ambiguously flattering to the English demi-monde: 'They do not', he complained, 'exude the aroma of Parisians; they are Spring-like trollops fresh off the boat from London.'

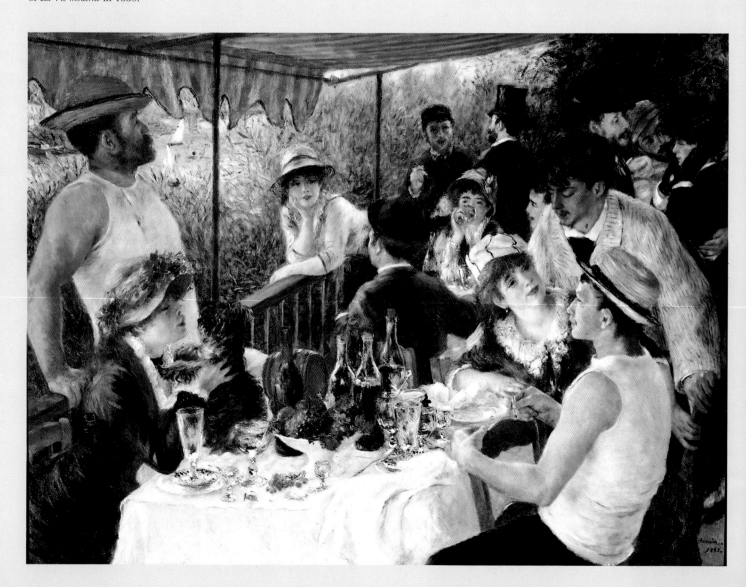

▲ BEHIND THE SCENES

At the time when the seventh Impressionist exhibition was being hung, Berthe Morisot was in Nice with her baby, Julie. Her husband (Manet's brother Eugène), who had returned to Paris, therefore supervised the hanging of her work. In his letters to her, written at the beginning of March, Eugène described the preparations for the exhibition:

March 1st

As soon as I got back to Paris I went directly to the Salle des Panorames. I found all the scintillating group of Impressionists hanging pictures in an enormous hall. Everybody was delighted to see me, especially as I had come for the purpose of arranging your works… It is sure

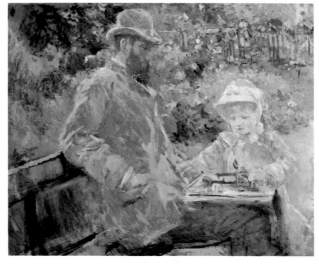

to be a success. Sisley is most fully represented, and has made great strides. He has a painting – a pond or a canal surrounded by trees – which is a real masterpiece. Pissarro is more uneven, but he has two or three figures of peasant women in landscapes that are far superior to those of Millet in drawing and colour. Monet has some weak things side by side with some very good ones, particularly winter landscapes – ice drifting on a river – which are quite beautiful.

Renoir's painting of boatmen looks very good. The views of Venice are awful – real failures. A scene with palm trees very good. Two very pretty figures of women. Gauguin and Vignon very poor. Caillebotte has some very boring figures done in blue ink, and some excellent small landscapes in pastel.

This morning only your portrait of Marie was in place. It was not well lit, nor was it at the right angle. Nivard has promised your frames in two days. Vignon has lent me a white frame in which your painting of the beach at Nice looks very nice. I have ordered frames for the other pictures.

I hope that you will send something within a week; don't forget to tell me the size of your canvas. Your 'Blanchisseuse' is very much improved, as well as all of your Nice pictures that are framed. My portrait is very good, it is beautifully drawn and the colour is excellent.

March 4th

I have ordered a white frame for your portrait of Marie on the porch. Don't be upset because the papers don't mention you. The problem is that you are not to be seen at the exhibition, whilst all your colleagues make great efforts to be around…

March 6th

You will have twelve pictures, including my portrait. Only nine are listed in the catalogue that I am sending you…The Impressionists are doing well, especially Renoir and Sisley. Durand-Ruel gets 2000 francs for a Sisley. Édouard [Manet] says one must ask high prices.

March 7th

Your pictures were put up this morning; all are in grey frames with gold ornaments. 'Marie' has been reframed, taken from the position where it did not look well, and placed on an easel in the main gallery. It is now in the best possible light. 'Bibi and Pasie' [Berthe's baby and her nurse] is placed below 'Marie'; its white and gold frame improves it enormously. Facing it, on an easel, are the 'Villa Arnulfi' on top and 'La Blanchisseuse' in the middle, with 'Bibi et son tonneau' underneath. My portrait is in the entrance hall in the somewhat unfavourable position previously occupied by 'Marie'.

Édouard, who came to the exhibition this morning, says that your pictures are among the best, and he has changed his opinion about the effect of my portrait. Duret, who has returned from London, congratulated me on your paintings. I have no doubt about your future success. I have asked 500 francs each for your smaller pictures, 1000 for 'La Blanchisseuse' and 'Bibi and Pasie', and 1200 for 'Marie'.

MORISOT
Eugène Manet and his Daughter at Bougival
1881

Between 1881 and 1884 Berthe Morisot and her husband Eugène Manet had a holiday home at 4 rue de la Princesse in Bougival on the Seine. There the artist painted several pictures of her daughter Julie, including this small canvas, showing the child playing under the eye of her father.

RENOIR
Luncheon of the Boating Party
1880–1

This work may have been a response to Zola's plea for the Impressionists to paint more ambitious pictures of modern life. The site is the upstairs terrrace of the Restaurant Fournaise (p.90). Among those shown are Alphonse Fournaise Jnr (the proprietor's son), standing on the extreme left. In front of him is Aline Charigot, who later became Renoir's wife.

1883

The One-Man Shows

The feuds and struggles surrounding the most recent group exhibitions have led Durand-Ruel to believe that one-man shows might be more successful. Degas – always at loggerheads with his fellow artists – won't participate, but Monet, Pissarro, Renoir and Sisley have shows in quick succession at the dealer's Paris gallery.

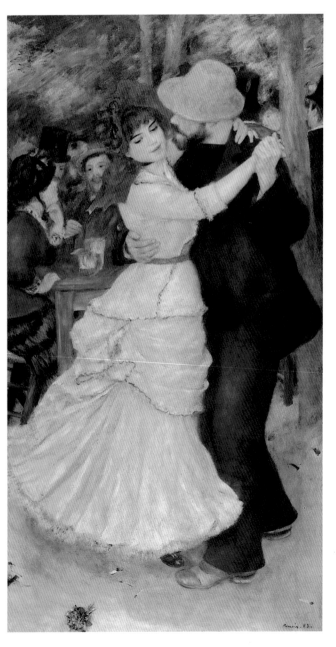

JANUARY

Degas refuses to join Durand-Ruel's scheme for a series of one-man exhibitions by each of the Impressionists – to be held on the mezzanine floor of 9 boulevard de la Madeleine. Gauguin resigns from his job with a bank, and declares 'From now on I paint every day.'

FEBRUARY

14th Durand-Ruel buys *A Gentleman-Amateurs' Horse Race: Before the Start* (painted in 1862 and retouched in 1882) from Degas for 5200 francs.

MARCH

1st Monet has a one-man show at Durand-Ruel's gallery in the boulevard de la Madeleine. (At the majority of Durand-Ruel's one-man exhibitions, there are around seventy pictures on view.)

APRIL

1st Renoir has a one-man show at Durand-Ruel's gallery. In his introduction to the catalogue, Théodore Duret writes: 'I regard M. Claude Monet as the Impressionist group's most typical landscape painter, and M. Renoir as its most typical figure painter.'
15th Durand-Ruel puts on an exhibition by the 'Society of

RENOIR
Dance at Bougival
1882–3

In 1882 Renoir painted three pictures of dancing couples, each located in a different place – the city, the country and at Bougival. At the time very specific social nuances were attributed to the various places of entertainment in Paris. Bougival exemplified a venue frequented by 'decent' couples who were neither oversophisticated nor unduly concerned with sexual encounters. The woman was Suzanne Valadon, who also posed for Renoir and was the mother of Maurice Utrillo.

Impressionists' at Dowdeswell's Galleries, 133 New Bond Street, London. Exhibitors include Boudin, Cassatt, Degas, Manet, Morisot, Pissarro and Sisley. Degas' *A Gentleman-Amateurs' Horse Race: Before the Start* is priced at £400, Manet's *The Pont de l'Europe* at £400 and Renoir's *Dance at Bougival* (opposite) at £600.

20th Manet's left leg is amputated because of a circulatory disease.

30th Manet dies at the age of 51.

MAY

Monet settles in Giverny with Mme Hoschedé ◆ (pp.146–7).

1st Cézanne goes to L'Estaque, where he stays till November.

3rd Opening of the Salon. Renoir exhibits *Madame Clapisson (Lady with a Fan)*. Whistler's *The Artist's Mother* is enthusiastically received. Pissarro has a one-man show at Durand-Ruel's gallery.

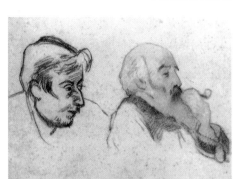

Manet is buried at Passy. His funeral is attended by, among others, Duret, Monet, Antonin Proust and Zola.

5th Eva Gonzalès dies, aged 34, after childbirth.

9th Pissarro recommends Huysmans' recently published *L'Art moderne* ▲ (p.136) to his son Lucien.

JUNE

1st Sisley has a one-man show at Durand-Ruel's gallery.

3rd The first exhibition of work by the Impressionists to be seen in Germany opens at the Gurlitt Galleries in Berlin, creating a sensation.

7th Gauguin, accompanied by his family, spends three weeks with Pissarro at Osny.

AUGUST

While visiting the Valpinçons at Ménil-Hubert, Degas produces preparatory studies for a portrait of Hortense, the family's eldest daughter.

Renoir visits Caillebotte at Petit-Gennevilliers and paints a portrait of Caillebotte's mistress, Charlotte Berthier.

Sisley decides to move from Moret-sur-Loing to Les Sablons, a neighbouring district.

SEPTEMBER

3rd The first important group of Impressionist works to be seen in the USA is on show at the American Exhibition of Foreign Products, Arts and Manufacture, held in the Mechanics' Building in Boston. Durand-Ruel has sent two Manets, three Monets, six Pissarros, three Renoirs and three Sisleys to Boston for the exhibition, and the catalogue has a drawing of Manet's *The Entombment of Christ* on the front cover. The pictures, however, fail to sell and are not even mentioned by the press.

6th Renoir sets off on a six-week visit to Jersey and Guernsey, accompanied by his mistress, Aline Charigot, and the artist Paul Lhote.

A drawing produced in 1883 when Gauguin and Pissarro were working together at Osny, near Pontoise. Pissarro's sketch of Gauguin is on the left, Gauguin's of Pissarro on the right. The artists' early relationship had been that of teacher and pupil, but by 1893 Gauguin was beginning to distance himself from the older man.

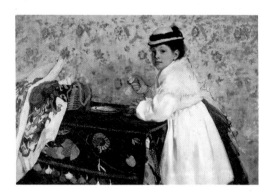

DEGAS
Hortense Valpinçon as a Child
1871–2

Degas was captivated by Hortense Valpinçon and painted this portrait of her as a child in 1871. He attempted to paint her again while visiting the family in 1883, but only produced a series of drawings and pastels, most of which have disappeared.

OCTOBER

Formation in Brussels of Les Vingt, a group of progressive artists led by the lawyer, journalist and critic Octave Maus ◆ (pp.214–5).
Berthe Morisot and her husband (Manet's brother Eugène) start preparing for the posthumous sale of Manet's works.
Renoir moves to 18 rue Houdon, off the boulevard Clichy.
Gauguin visits Pissarro, who is staying in Rouen.

DECEMBER

3rd An 'art loan' exhibition, arranged to raise funds for the purchase of a pedestal for the Statue of Liberty, opens at the American Academy of Design, New York. William Merritt Chase ◆ (p.253) and Carrol Beckwith, who are the selectors, contribute works by Degas, Manet and other Impressionists. These, together with works of a related kind which are lent by other American collectors, form the focal point of the show. The exhibition marks the start of more-widespread American interest in Impressionist art ▲ (p.167).

8th Monet and Renoir tour the Mediterranean coast from Marseilles to Genoa, visiting Cézanne in Aix-en-Provence on their way back.

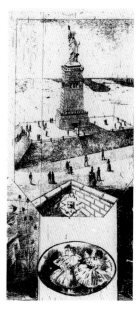

Engraving of the opening of the 'art loan' exhibition in New York, from *The Graphic*.

OTHER EVENTS

- Paul Kruger becomes President of the Transvaal
- Britain decides to evacuate Sudan
- Édouard Delamare-Deboutteville builds the first petrol-engined car
- First skyscraper built in Chicago
- The Orient Express makes its first run from Paris to Istanbul
- Metropolitan Opera House opens in New York
- Gaudi takes over as architect of the Sagrada Familia in Barcelona
- Publication of Maupassant's *Une Vie*, Zola's *Au bonheur des dames* and Nietzsche's *Thus Spake Zarathustra*
- Marx, Wagner and Turgenev die

 HUYSMANS ON THE IMPRESSIONISTS

L'ART
MODERNE
PAR
J.-K. HUYSMANS

PARIS
G. CHARPENTIER, ÉDITEUR
13, RUE DE GRENELLE-SAINT-GERMAIN, 13
1883
Tous droits réservés.

Title page of Huysman's *L'Art moderne*, 1883.

The publication in 1883 of Joris-Karl Huysmans' *L'Art moderne* (a collection of art criticism mostly about the Salons and the Impressionists) marked the emergence before a larger audience of a writer who was to have considerable influence upon public taste – an influence reinforced by his reputation as a novelist. Huysmans' attitudes were literary rather than visual, and his support for the Impressionists was founded on the Realist beliefs that had informed his earlier writings rather than on an awareness of the artistic innovations of the Impressionist movement. In 1889 *L'Art moderne* was followed by *Certains* ▲ (pp.172–3), a second collection of writings on art.

On Pissarro

M. Pissarro may now be classed among the number of remarkable and audacious painters we possess. If he can preserve his perceptive, delicate and nimble eye, we shall certainly have in him the most original landscapist of our time.

On Gauguin's 'Study of a Nude'
(painted in 1880 and exhibited at the sixth
Impressionist exhibition)

I do not hesitate to assert that among contemporary artists who have painted nudes, none – and I do not except Courbet from these artists – has produced such a vivid note of realism as Gauguin in his nude (p.125). Here is a girl of our time, a girl who doesn't pose for an

CAILLEBOTTE
View Across a Balcony
1880

Huysmans described this picture as epitomizing bourgeois life in late nineteenth-century Paris. The figures have no contact with each other and exude a sense of boredom, unrelieved by their material wealth. The painting was admired by Signac, who ten years later produced a work using the same subject – *The Parisian Sunday*.

audience, who is neither lascivious nor affected, who is simply concerned with mending her clothes.

Oh, the nude woman! Who else has shown her as she is – real, without premeditated arrangements, without adulteration of her features?

On Berthe Morisot

These lifeless sketches reek of a heady, mundane elegance, and perhaps it is right to use the word hysterical to characterize these surprising improvisations.

On Degas' 'The Dancing Examination' (c.1880)

A dancer bends over retying a lace, and another has her head on her chest, her hooked nose protruding from her mop of red hair. Near them are a friend in street clothes, vulgar, her cheeks covered in freckles, her shock of hair stuffed under a hat bristling with red feathers, and a woman, somebody's mother, with the puffy face of an old concierge, wearing a shawl – the sort of person who chats during the intervals. What truthfulness!

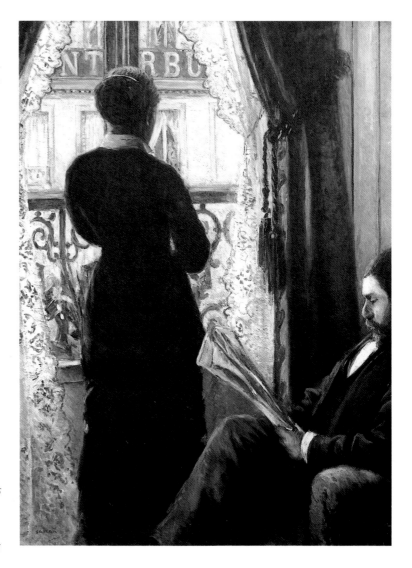

What sense of life! See how realistic these figures are, how accurately the light bathes the scene. Look at the expressions on these faces, the boredom of painful mechanical effort, the scrutiny of the mother whose desires are fulfilled whenever the body of her daughter begins its laborious efforts, the indifference of the friends to the familiar fatigue. All these things are noted with analytical insight, at once subtle and cruel.

On Caillebotte's 'View Across a Balcony'
(painted in 1880 and exhibited at the fifth Impressionist exhibition)

A woman standing at a window turns her back to us, and a man sitting in an armchair, seen in profile, reads the newspaper near her – that's all, but what is truly magnificent is the frankness, the life of this scene.

The woman, who looks at the street, palpitates, moves. One sees her lower back move under the marvellous dark-

blue velvet that covers it. If you touch her with your finger, she will yawn, turn round, exchange an empty word with her husband, who appears to be only vaguely interested in the article he is reading.

It is a moment of contemporary life, frozen in time. The couple is bored, as so often happens in life. The odour of a well-to-do middle-class household emanates from this interior. Caillebotte is the painter of the bourgeoisie of finance and business in their hours of relaxation, able to provide for their own needs, without being very rich, living near the rue Lafayette, or near the boulevard Haussmann.

As for the execution of this canvas, it is simple, sober – I would say almost classical. There are neither fluttering brush strokes, nor fireworks, nor intentions merely indicated, nor weaknesses of any kind.

1884

The Manet Sale

The Impressionists attend the sale of the contents of Manet's studio, but find that the paintings have been overpriced by Durand-Ruel. Before long Durand-Ruel himself is threatened with bankruptcy, in response to which Monet and Renoir suggest that he reduces the prices of their paintings.

MONET
Bordighera
1884

Despite his financial worries, Monet was entranced by his visit to the Mediterranean coast in 1884 and produced a large number of works there, many of the same site. At Bordighera he was particularly attracted by the trees, which in this work frame the old town and the sea.

JANUARY

1st Gauguin and his family move to Rouen, where Pissarro is staying.

3rd Renoir has two paintings on show at an exhibition held by the Cercle Artistique de la Seine. Cassatt and Sisley also take part.

5th A Manet retrospective opens at the École des Beaux-Arts. The exhibition comprises 179 works, including pastels, lithographs, drawings and 116 paintings. The catalogue has a preface by Zola.

19th Monet goes to paint in Bordighera in Italy, near the frontier with France.

26th Monet writes to Alice Hoschedé ◆ (pp.146–7) from Bordighera, saying that he has produced five paintings in a day.

FEBRUARY

Eugène Manet gives his brother's *Departure of the Folkestone Boat* to Degas as a memento.

4th–5th The contents of Manet's studio are sold at the Hôtel Drouot ◆ (p.102). They fetch more than expected, 159 pictures going for a total of 116,637 francs. Degas buys three drawings for 141 francs; Caillebotte pays 3000 francs for *The Balcony* (p.60); Duret 3500 francs for *Chez le Père Lathuille* (p.117); and Rouart 4400 francs for *The Music Lesson*. Three paintings – *Olympia* (p.36), *Christ Insulted by the Soldiers* and *The Old Musician* – are withdrawn without a bid, largely because Durand-Ruel, who is acting as valuer, has priced them at around 10,000 francs each.

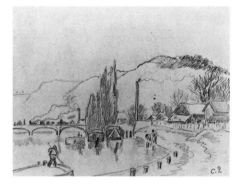

PISSARRO
The Côte Ste-Catherine, Rouen
1884

This pencil drawing is a preparatory study (in reverse) for a print of the same title, executed in etching and drypoint with aquatint. The hill in the background is the Côte Ste-Catherine, which is situated to the north-east of Rouen, overlooking the city.

MARCH

Diego Martelli ▲ (p.121), the well-known Italian art critic, who is a close friend of Degas, publishes a laudatory article about Manet in the periodical *Fieramosca*.

25th Durand-Ruel buys five paintings from Sisley for 1700 francs.

APRIL

Durand-Ruel holds an exhibition of twenty-four Impressionist paintings at the Dudley Gallery in London.

4th Pissarro moves to Éragny-sur-Epte.

6th Monet moves from Bordighera to Menton for two weeks.

MAY

In a letter to Durand-Ruel, Renoir describes his plans for a 'Société des Irregularistes' ▲ (p.141). He starts work on a *Grammar of Art*, which he mentions as part of the society's intended programme, and asks Lionel Nunès (a relative of Pissarro) to do some research for the book. Durand-Ruel faces the possibility of bankruptcy. Renoir and Monet suggest that he might reduce the prices of their paintings.

2nd Opening of the Salon. Seurat's portrait of Edmond Aman-Jean (a painter who shared a studio with him) is accepted.

14th The newly formed Groupe des Artistes Indépendants holds an exhibition in a temporary post-office building on the site of the ' Tuileries. On show are works by 402 artists rejected by the Salon, including Seurat's *Bathing at Asnières*. The police have to be summoned to quell fights between members of the executive committee, several of whom are arrested for assault.

SEURAT
Bathing at Asnières
1883–4

Monumental figures and stylized shadows, simplified contours and a distinct overall rhythm made this a key work in the revolt against Impressionism. At the same time, however, the landscape background, with the bridge and smoking factory chimneys, is still Impressionistic in feeling.

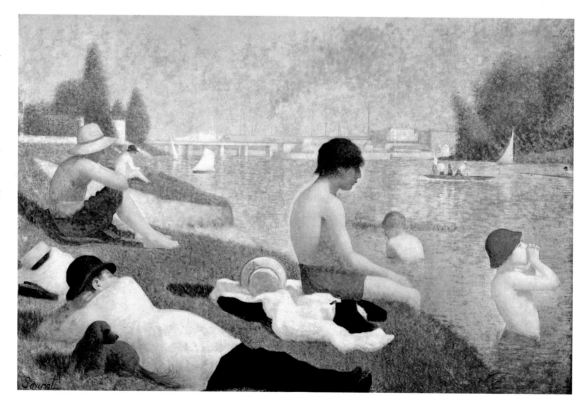

JUNE

Encouraged by Pissarro, Paul Signac, a young painter who is a friend of Seurat (and, like Seurat, a future exponent of Pointillism), buys one of Cézanne's landscapes from Père Tanguy ● (p.192).

Murer puts on an exhibition at his Hôtel du Dauphin et de l'Espagne in Rouen of Impressionist paintings from his own collection. On view are nine works by Pissarro, four by Sisley, one by Cézanne, one by Gauguin and several by Guillaumin.

9th The affairs of the Groupe des Artistes Indépendants have become so muddled and the feuding among the committee so bitter that a meeting is called, chaired by the artist and writer Odilon Redon, to discuss the group's future.

11th A new body, the Société des Artistes Indépendants, is legally constituted to replace the Groupe des Artistes Indépendants, with the aim of 'suppressing' juries and enabling artists 'freely to present their works for the judgment of public opinion.' (It would survive and become one of the constituent elements of the French art world.)

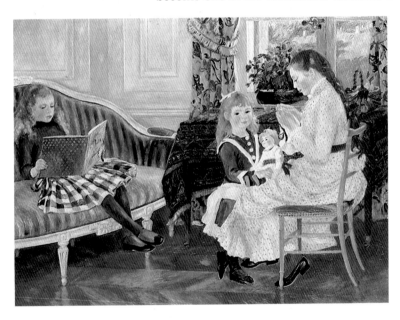

RENOIR
Children's Afternoon at Wargemont
1884

The children in this work are the daughters of Paul Berard: 14-year-old Marthe (seated on the right), Marguerite, aged 10 (on the couch), and 4-year-old Lucie (standing). Renoir's new 'classical' style ◆ (pp.158–60) is evident in the clearly defined faces and the clean modelling of the forms.

AUGUST

Renoir stays at the Berards' house near Dieppe ● (p.231), where he paints *Children's Afternoon at Wargemont* in the more classical style he is developing ◆ (pp.158–60). Degas visits the Valpinçons at Ménil-Hubert and works on a life-size bust of their daughter Hortense (it disintegrates due to lack of care). He stays till November. Monet paints at Étretat.

21st The painter Giuseppe de Nittis dies.

NOVEMBER

Gauguin and his family move to Copenhagen.

DECEMBER

2nd The Société des Artistes Indépendants holds its first exhibition, which includes works by Seurat, Signac and Gauguin's former banking colleague Émile Schuffenecker.

8th Octave Mirbeau, the critic and novelist, publishes a laudatory article on Renoir in *La France*.

12th Monet suggests that the Impressionists should hold monthly meetings over dinner.

14th Two of Degas' horse-racing pictures – *A Gentleman-Amateurs' Horse Race: Before the Start* and *Start* (an unknown work) – are included in an exhibition entitled 'Sport in Art' organized by the dealer Georges Petit.

OTHER EVENTS

- The Mahdi besieges General Gordon in Khartoum
- Fourteen nations meet in Berlin to discuss the future of Africa
- Grover Cleveland elected President of the USA
- French divorce laws liberalized
- Members of French royal family excluded from presidency
- Automatic machine gun invented
- Fabian Society formed in London
- Fénéon's *Revue indépendante* launched
- Publication of Huysmans' *A Rebours* and Mark Twain's *Huckleberry Finn*
- Massenet's *Manon* and Bruckner's Seventh Symphony first performed

THE SOCIETY OF IRREGULARISTS

In May Renoir wrote to Durand-Ruel saying that he was on the verge of calling the 'first assembly of a new society that I wish to found' and enclosing the following outline of its aims. Renoir's interest in 'irregularism' reflects his own youthful apprenticeship as a painter of porcelain, the teachings of Ruskin and the current concern with the decorative arts.

Among all the controversies that questions of art provoke every day, the main point to which we want to draw attention is one that has been constantly overlooked. 'Irregularity' is the theme that we wish to discuss.

Scientists say that nature abhors a vacuum; they could well extend this axiom by adding that nature has a horror of regularity.

Those who study the natural world know that, despite the simplicity of the laws governing their creation, the works of nature ... are infinitely varied. The two eyes of even the most beautiful face are always slightly dissimilar; no nose is ever situated exactly above the middle of the mouth; the sections of an orange, the leaves of a tree, the petals of a flower, are never identical. It even seems that beauty of every kind derives its charm from this diversity ...

One can say without fear of error that all truly artistic creations have been conceived and executed according to the principle of irregularity; in short, to use a neologism that expresses our thought more completely, they have always been the work of an irregularist.

In an age in which our French art, which until the beginning of this century had been so replete with penetrating charm and exquisite fantasy, is starting to perish thanks to aridity, regularity and a mania for false perfection, which nowadays makes the austere puritanism

of the engineer its ideal of perfection, we think it a good thing to react promptly against the fatal doctrines which are threatening it with extinction, and that the duty of all men of taste and sensibility, whatever their reluctance to be aggressive, is immediately to band together in order to rebel and protest.

An association is therefore necessary.

Without wishing to be too specific, the general ideas of the founders of the association are roughly as follows.

Its aim will be to arrange as soon as possible exhibitions in which all artists, painters, decorators, architects, jewellers, textile designers etc. whose aesthetic is based on irregularity will be able to participate.

Among other conditions of admission, the regulations will stipulate specifically that so far as architecture is concerned all ornaments must be made after nature, without any motif, flower, leaf, figure etc. being reproduced precisely; that even the smallest outline must be executed by hand, without any mechanical instrument being used; and that others, such as jewellers, embroiderers, painters on porcelain and the like, must exhibit alongside their finished products the drawings on which they were based.

A complete grammar of art, dealing with the aesthetic principles of the society, describing its goals and demonstrating its utility, will be published by the founding committee with the collaboration of those members who are prepared to offer their cooperation.

Photographs of famous works of art or decorations intended to support the principle of irregularity will be acquired at the expense of the society and installed in a special gallery where they will be accessible to the public.

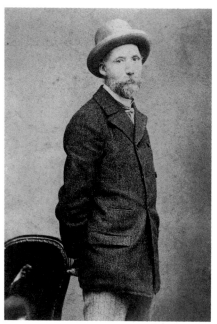

A contemporary photograph of Renoir (*c*.1885).

1885

The Wider World

Despite his recent financial setback, Durand-Ruel is more than ever determined to promote the artists and to sell and exhibit their works abroad. He organizes shows in Brussels and Amsterdam, but meets with reluctance from the artists themselves when the opportunity arises to stage an exhibition in New York.

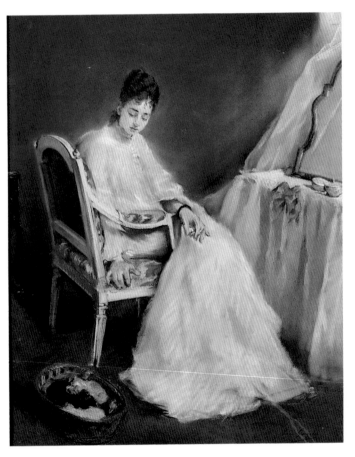

JANUARY

16th Antonin Proust (p.124) and the Manet family organize a banquet at Père Lathuille's restaurant (p.117) to celebrate the anniversary of Manet's retrospective exhibition. Monet writes to Pissarro: 'Everyone thinks it is ridiculous and unnecessary, but everyone will be there and nobody feels able to refuse.' Pissarro does refuse to attend, considering it too 'official'.

22nd Exhibition of works at *La Vie moderne* by Eva Gonzalès (*see* p.112).

FEBRUARY

Duret publishes *Critique de l'avant-garde* ▲ (p.145) – a collection of his reviews and other writings on art.

MARCH

Cézanne suffers from neuralgia.

6th Delacroix exhibition opens at the École des Beaux-Arts.

21st Renoir's first son, Pierre, is born. The address given on the birth certificate is 18 rue Houdon. His godfather is Caillebotte.

28th Theo van Gogh sells a landscape by Monet to the collector Victor Desfossés.

APRIL

Gauguin has a six-day exhibition at the Society of the Friends of Art in Copenhagen, which is not a success.

Pissarro establishes close links with the anarchist movement.

22nd Degas sells three pastels to Durand-Ruel for 2000 francs.

GONZALÈS
Pink Morning
1874

Of the eighty-five works shown at Gonzalès' retrospective exhibition at *La Vie moderne*, twenty-one (including *Pink Morning*) were in pastel. The sitter was probably the artist's sister Jeanne.

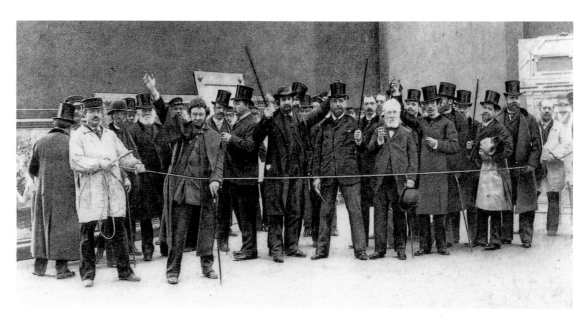

Photograph of a Salon jury (*c*.1885), showing Tattegrain, Cormon, Dantan, Lefèbvre, Tony Robert-Fleury, Maignan and other well-known academic artists.

MAY

4th Monet exhibits ten paintings at Georges Petit's annual Exposition Internationale (*see* p.129).

Opening of the Salon. Out of the 38,515 paintings submitted, 1243 are accepted; of these ninety-eight are by Americans, forty-seven by Belgians, thirty-one by Germans and thirty-four by British artists. The exhibition is seen by approximately 238,000 visitors.

The doors of Durand-Ruel's salon painted with floral decorations by Monet.

18th Degas buys *Oedipus and the Sphinx*, a small painting by Ingres, at a sale of works from the collection of the Comte de Brandière at the Hôtel Drouot ◆ (p.102).

Gauguin bitterly attacks Degas' attitudes ▲ (p.127) in a letter to Pissarro, complaining that 'his conduct is becoming more and more absurd.'

Monet paints floral decorations for the door panels of Durand-Ruel's house at 35 rue de Rome (left).

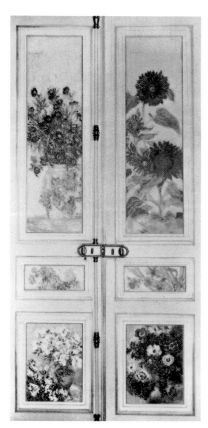

JUNE

Gauguin returns to Paris with his son, Clovis, and lives in the Impasse Frémin.

4th Durand-Ruel holds an exhibition of Impressionist works at the Hôtel du Grand Miroir in Brussels (which has a considerably impact on the new generation of Belgian painters).

7th Monet tries to exchange one of his own paintings for a Degas through Durand-Ruel.

8th Renoir goes to stay at La Roche-Guyon, near Giverny.

15th Cézanne, Hortense Fiquet and their son, Paul, go to stay with Renoir.

JULY

Cézanne paints at Gardanne, in Provence.

3rd The American Art Association invites Durand-Ruel to mount an Impressionist exhibition in New York. He accepts,

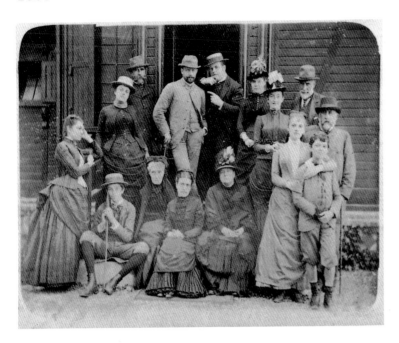

A photograph taken in 1885 in Dieppe showing Degas (extreme right) with Sickert and members of the Halévy and Blanche families.

but the painters are reluctant to participate. (Manet once said that he thought little of 'the land of the Yankees', and added 'In Paris alone is there any taste.' It seems that the other Impressionists agreed.)
12th Durand-Ruel stages an exhibition in Amsterdam of Impressionist paintings.

AUGUST

25th Cézanne tells Zola that he has started frequenting brothels in Aix-en-Provence: 'I pay; it's a dirty word, but I need relaxation, and even at this price I must have it.'
28th Degas visits the Halévys in Dieppe and meets the British painter Walter Sickert, with whom he becomes friendly.
30th Berthe Morisot and her husband visit Holland and Belgium.

SEPTEMBER

Renoir visits Essoyes, his mistress Aline Charigot's home village in southern Champagne (p.147).
Pissarro meets Signac and then Seurat at Guillaumin's studio. He is deeply impressed by the stylistic innovations of their work.

OCTOBER

Monet goes to stay with the singer and collector Jean-Baptiste Faure ●(p.81) at Étretat, where he remains till December.

NOVEMBER

5th Durand-Ruel writes a long letter to *L'Événement* rebutting allegations of forgery made by Goupil.

DECEMBER

Berthe Morisot begins to hold regular soirées for friends that are artists or writers, including Mallarmé ◆ (pp.200–1).

MANET
Portrait of Théodore Duret
1868

Manet and Duret first met by chance in a Madrid restaurant in 1865 and became firm friends. In 1868 Duret (a staunch Republican), together with Zola, Pelletier and Jules Ferry, founded *La Tribune française*, and Manet frequently visited their offices.

OTHER EVENTS

- General Gordon killed when the Mahdi captures Khartoum
- Typhus epidemic in France, originating in Marseilles
- Phylloxera ruins French vineyards
- Daimler patents first motorcycle; Benz produces three-wheeler cars
- Pasteur devises a rabies vaccine
- Galton proves the individuality of fingerprints
- Golf introduced to USA
- Aristide Bruant founds Le Mirliton
- Kropotkin's anarchist review *La Révolte* moves to Paris
- Publication of Zola's *Germinal*, Maupassant's *Bel Ami*, Taine's *Philosophie de l'art* and Rider Haggard's *King Solomon's Mines*
- Victor Hugo dies

▲ DURET ON THE AVANT-GARDE

In February Théodore Duret published *Critique de l'avant-garde*, a collection of his writings on art, which included his reviews of the Salon and some of the introductory pieces that he had written for the catalogues of various exhibitions. In the following extract he describes the uncomprehending response that an innovative artist is likely to receive from the public:

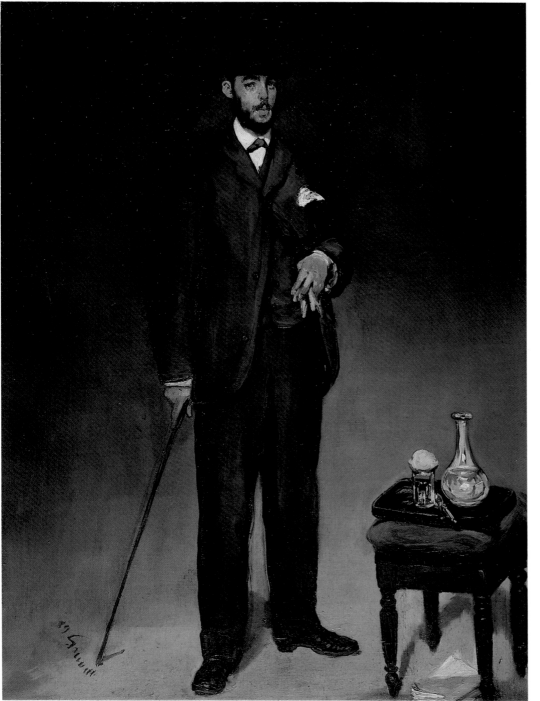

Only yesterday people were poking fun at Courbet, but now they praise him to the skies and burn incense on his altar. But then his work has become a familiar sight; people have got used to him, and thus the endeavours of routine (which scoffs at anything that is new) and of mediocrity (which hates anything that is original) have now been concentrated on the latest arrival, Manet. We shall therefore stop in front of the canvases of M. Manet – but we are not alone. Quite the contrary: we are surrounded by a crowd, and are immediately aware that the good public, which only a little while ago was entranced by even the most insignificant imitations, here mocks our original artist just because of his originality and sense of invention.

'Oh, how poorly he draws!' (This has been said of Delacroix for thirty years.)

'But this is not properly finished! These are mere sketches!' (Only yesterday they were saying that about Corot.)

'Good God! How ugly these people are! What horrible models!' (This is still more or less a valid summary of bourgeois opinion about Millet.)

And thus it is going to be for M. Manet until eventually the public gets used to the combination of qualities and faults, of light and shadow, which make up his personality, and will accept him, going on to deride some other newcomer.

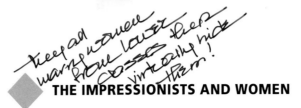

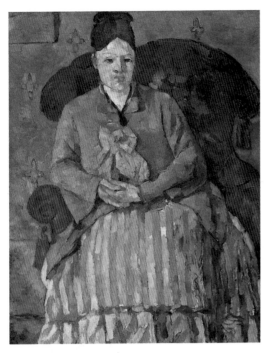

CÉZANNE
Madame Cézanne in a Red Armchair
c.1877

One of Cézanne's most colourful portraits of Hortense Fiquet, this work was painted around the time of his second and last showing with the Impressionists ■ (pp.104–5).

THE IMPRESSIONISTS AND WOMEN

When, in August 1885, Cézanne told Zola about his brothel-visiting activities he was 46 and had been living with the artists' model Hortense Fiquet for sixteen years (they would eventually marry in 1886). Nevertheless, even after their son was born, Cézanne carefully concealed their liaison from his family ▲ (p.111).

The pattern was not an unfamiliar one among the Impressionists. Although Manet married the Dutch pianist Suzanne Leenhoff in 1863, for a considerable time he was chary about introducing her to his friends in Paris and passed off their son Léon (born in 1852) as Suzanne's brother.

Clearly, wives and mistresses from the lower classes or demi-monde were not presentable in polite society. Pissarro, for example, started an affair with his mother's maid, Julie Vellay, in 1860, and their first child was born in 1865. But, although he eventually married Julie in London in 1871, she never participated in his social life.

For the same reason, although Sisley had been living with the florist Marie-Adélaide-Eugénie Lescouezec since 1867, he only married her thirty years later, shortly before her death. The two cases suggest that if Britons went to France for illegitimate experiences, Frenchmen came to Britain to legitimize their liaisons.

Monet's matrimonial life was rather different. In 1878, after his patron Ernest Hoschedé (p.12) was declared bankrupt, Alice Hoschedé and their six children came to live with the Monets. (Ernest subsequently went off to Paris to pursue 'an impecunious bachelor life' and wrote a booklet on the Salon of 1882.) When Monet's wife, Camille, died in 1879, Alice continued living with him, in effect replacing Camille, and remained in that socially ambiguous situation until 1892, when she and Monet were united in marriage following Ernest's death.

Renoir's attitude towards women hardly coincided with the adoration of their beauty expressed in his paintings. According to his son Jean, when somebody mentioned a woman lawyer, he retorted 'I can't see myself getting into bed with a lawyer. I like women best when they don't know how to read, and when they wipe their babies' bottoms themselves.' On another occasion, he told his friend Lestringuez 'What women may gain from education they lose in other fields. I am afraid that the generations to come won't know how to make love well, and that would be most unfortunate for those who haven't painting.'

The last phrase is significant. He once said 'It's with my brush I make love.' He wanted his paintings to evoke the physical sense of the model, to make the spectator want to 'stroke a breast'...

or a back.' Aline Charigot, whom he met in 1880 and married in 1890 (five years after the birth of their first son), was a country girl who had come to Paris to learn dressmaking. Possessed of a voracious appetite, she was buxom in early life, but later grew very fat and finally died four years before her husband from a heart attack. Renoir – who, in contrast to his wife, was slightly built, restive and in many ways unsure of himself – accepted Aline's dominant position in their household, but kept her away from the art world because of her humble origins. Once, watching a boy and a girl quarrelling, Renoir told the writer Georges Rivière that he was sure the girl would win – and Rivière couldn't help noticing that he 'took pleasure in noting the inevitable victory of the woman over the man.' Degas' timidity with women was

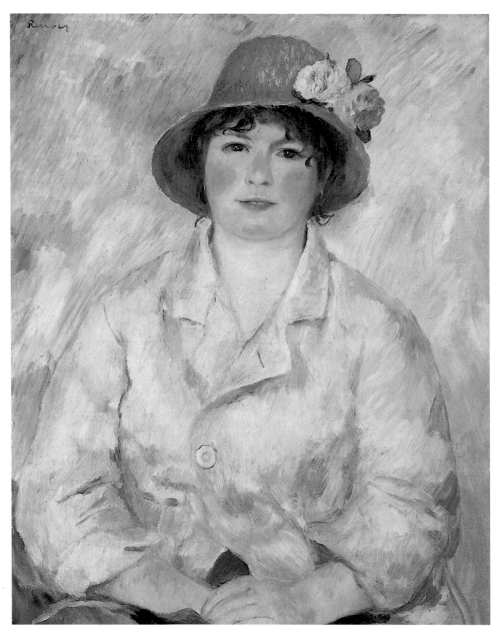

RENOIR
Portrait of Aline Charigot
c.1885

Probably painted at Essoyes after the birth of their first son, Pierre, this is one of the few portraits Renoir painted of his mistress and future wife, although she often posed for his group subjects.

commented on by many of his friends, including Manet. Perhaps as a result of this timidity, two women were to dominate his life. The first was the opera singer Rose Caron (p.174), with whom he was never intimate, but whose performances he attended with unflagging devotion – sometimes going to the opera as frequently as twelve times a month, and travelling as far as Strasbourg to hear her perform. The second was his housekeeper, Zoé Closier, who during the latter years of his life looked after him like an attendant dragon, keeping visitors at bay, bullying him about his domestic affairs, producing meals of gastronomic horror, and combining the roles of nurse and companion. Degas' preoccupation with revealing the intricacies of female toilet, coupled with his remarkably frank and brutal pastels of brothel life, would seem to indicate a desire at worst to humiliate women, at best to strip them of any romantic ideas of untouchable beauty.

1886

The End of an Era

THE EIGHTH IMPRESSIONIST EXHIBITION

Despite problems with customs, the New York Impressionist show goes ahead, opening a month before the eighth and last group exhibition in Paris. Sadly, there is a great deal of acrimony among the artists – not least over the inclusion of the 'Neo-Impressionists' Seurat and Signac.

JANUARY

The New English Art Club is formed in London for artists with Impressionist leanings (founders include Clausen, Sargent and Steer).
1st Morisot visits Renoir and admires his new style ◆ (pp.158–60).
7th Degas visits Naples in connection with family affairs.

FEBRUARY

8th Through Durand-Ruel, Monet, Renoir and Redon send about

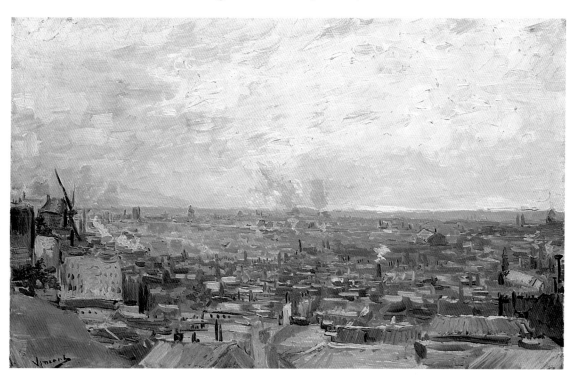

VAN GOGH
View of Montmartre
1886

Painted when he was 33, shortly after his arrival in Paris, this work shows the extent to which van Gogh's contact with the Impressionists, especially Pissarro, lightened his palette and gave his work a sense of space that it had not possessed before.

eight works each to an exhibition staged by the avant-garde organization Les Vingt in Brussels ◆ (pp.214–5). Degas is invited to exhibit, but declines.
Durand-Ruel buys his last painting from Sisley.
20th Van Gogh arrives in Paris and stays with his brother Theo.

MARCH

Pissarro starts to work in Pointillist style. When he tells Degas that Seurat's *Sunday Afternoon on the Island of La Grande Jatte* (p.152) is 'very interesting', Degas replies 'It's certainly very big.'

23rd Durand-Ruel enters forty-three cases at the New York Customs House, containing some three hundred pictures valued at $81,799, which he has sent in preparation for his first exhibition in the USA. Monet paints at Étretat.

APRIL

Gauguin finds work as a billposter at 5 francs an hour. He urgently needs money as his son Clovis is ill.

1st Publication of Zola's novel *L'Oeuvre*, about the Parisian art world. The central character, based mainly on Cézanne and partly on Manet, causes great offence in Impressionist circles ● (p.53).

3rd Cézanne writes his last letter to Zola.

10th Durand-Ruel's exhibition of 'Works in oil and pastel by the Impressionists of Paris' opens at Moore's American Art Galleries, 290 Fifth Avenue, New York. The catalogue (which confuses Monet with Manet) includes an introduction by Duret and extracts from favourable reviews in various French and English papers ▲ (p.153).

14th Pissarro's first Pointillist paintings are displayed at Closet's gallery in the rue de Châteaudun.

15th Monet goes to Holland at the invitation of the Secretary to the French Embassy in The Hague. He spends a fortnight painting in the tulip fields.

17th Degas and Cassatt give each other one of their own works.

28th Cézanne marries Hortense Fiquet in Aix-en-Provence and legitimizes their son Paul ◆ (pp.146–7).

MAY

15th The eighth Impressionist exhibition opens at 1 rue Lafitte ▓ (pp.151–2).

20th Pissarro, Seurat, Gauguin and others hold a dinner to celebrate the exhibition.

JUNE

6th Opening of the fifth International Exhibition at Georges Petit's gallery. It includes works by Monet, Renoir and Rodin.

8th Berthe Morisot and her husband holiday on the Isle of Wight.

16th Mirbeau publishes a laudatory article on Renoir in *Le Gaulois*.

25th Durand-Ruel's New York exhibition moves to the National Academy of Design – with additional pictures, thirteen of them lent by American collectors, including the Havemeyers ● (p.233).

28th Gauguin makes his first visit to Pont-Aven in Brittany.

GAUGUIN
Breton Girl
1886

This study in pastel for his painting *The Four Breton Girls* was executed during Gauguin's first visit to Pont-Aven.

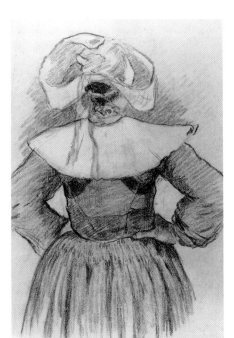

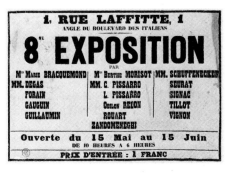

A poster for the eighth Impressionist exhibition.

JULY

8th Durand-Ruel sees the new 'classical-style' Renoirs ◆ (p.158–60) at Georges Petit's gallery and says he doesn't like them at all.

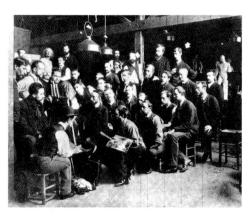

Photograph of Cormon's *atelier*. Toulouse-Lautrec (at the front, extreme left) is among the students.

AUGUST

3rd Opening of the Salon des Indépendants. The exhibition (the second held by the Société des Artistes Indépendants) includes works by Pissarro, Seurat, Signac and Douanier Rousseau.
10th Renoir goes to La Chapelle-St-Briac in Brittany, where he rents a house for two months.

SEPTEMBER

Van Gogh starts studying at the studio of the academic painter Fernand Cormon, where he meets Toulouse-Lautrec (left).

4th Monet goes to stay with Octave Mirbeau in Noirmoutiers. On the way there he paints on Belle-Ile, off the coast of Brittany.

OCTOBER

17th The anarchistic Exposition des Arts Incohérents opens at the Eden Theatre in Montmartre. The participants use pseudonyms, and Toulouse-Lautrec exhibits a painting entitled *Les Batignolles 3¹/₂ BC* satirizing the Impressionists.
23rd Cézanne's father dies, leaving him a large sum of money.
25th Van Gogh admires a 'marvellous Degas' at the branch of Boussod & Valadon managed by his brother Theo.
28th Renoir moves to 35 boulevard Rochechouart.

NOVEMBER

5th Degas and Gauguin are reconciled. The latter distances himself from Pissarro, his former mentor.
25th Gauguin meets Vincent van Gogh at Theo's gallery.

DECEMBER

Gauguin has to go into hospital.
A Whistler exhibition opens at Georges Petit's gallery.
3rd Pissarro, Seurat and Signac exhibit at Martinet's gallery in the boulevard des Italiens.
14th Toulouse-Lautrec invites van Gogh to Aristide Bruant's cabaret, Le Mirliton, to see his work displayed there.

MORISOT
In the Dining Room
1885–6

This evocative painting is set in Morisot's dining room at her home in the rue Villejust. The pose of the maid, seemingly interrupted in the middle of her chores, the open cupboard door and the lively little dog in the corner all contribute to the work's sense of immediacy. Also, the tiered view – from the doorway, through the room to the landscape background outside the window – makes it one of Morisot's most spatially complex paintings.

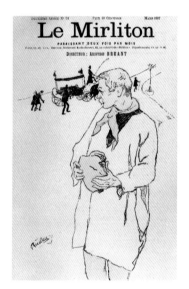

The front cover of the March 1887 edition of the satirical magazine *Le Mirliton*. The illustration is Toulouse-Lautrec's *The Last Farewell*.

OTHER EVENTS

- General Boulanger becomes French Minister of War
- Bonaparte and Orléans families banished from France
- Gladstone introduces Home Rule for Ireland Bill
- Ludwig II of Bavaria drowns himself and is succeeded by Otto I
- Discovery of process for extracting aluminium
- Institut Pasteur founded in Paris
- Canadian Pacific Railway finished
- Publication of Rimbaud's *Les Illuminations* and Robert Louis Stevenson's *Dr Jekyll and Mr Hyde*
- Liszt dies

THE EIGHTH IMPRESSIONIST EXHIBITION

The eighth Impressionist exhibition (described in the catalogue simply as 'Exposition de peinture par…') was held from May 15th to June 15th on the second floor of the Maison Dorée, a well-known restaurant at the corner of the rue Lafitte and the boulevard des Italiens.

Degas wrote to Félix Bracquemond early in May : 'We are opening on the 15th. Everything is being done at once! You know that we uphold the condition not to send anything to the Salon. You do not fulfil this condition, but how about your wife? Monet, Renoir, Caillebotte and Sisley have not answered the call. Expenses are covered through an arrangement which I have no time to explain. In case entrance fees do not cover these expenses, we'll pass the hat round among the exhibitors. The premises are not as large as they should be, but are admirably situated…the Jablochkof Company is proposing to install electric lighting for us.'

There were 246 works on show, and exhibitors included Marie Bracquemond, Cassatt, Degas, Forain, Gauguin, Guillaumin, Morisot, Camille and Lucien Pissarro, Odilon Redon, Rouart, Schuffenecker, Seurat, Signac, Tillot, Vignon and Zandomeneghi. There was also a Comtesse de Rambure, of whom Félix Fénéon acidly remarked 'the catalogue does not dare to mention her works.'

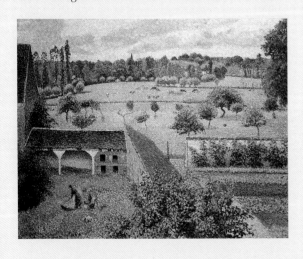

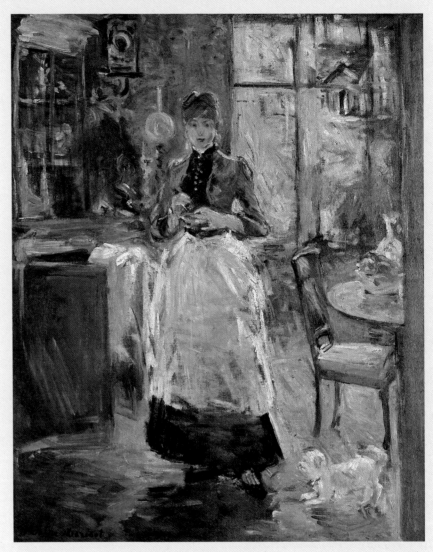

Preliminary discussions had started in October, and had been marked by even more acrimony than usual. When was the exhibition to be held? Were Seurat and Signac to be admitted? (This problem was solved by assigning them a room of their own.) Was Gauguin's friend Schuffenecker, who had participated in the first exhibition of the Indépendants, to be admitted?

From the start, it was clear that this was the end of Impressionism in the sense of the movement that had begun in 1874. The guiding spirits of the exhibition were Degas and Pissarro, who by his own conversion to a somewhat diluted form of

PISSARRO
View from my Window
1886 (reworked 1888)

Pissarro's use of pointillist technique is evident in this painting, both in the broken, 'dotted' brushwork and in his use of complementary colours to depict the light of the sky.

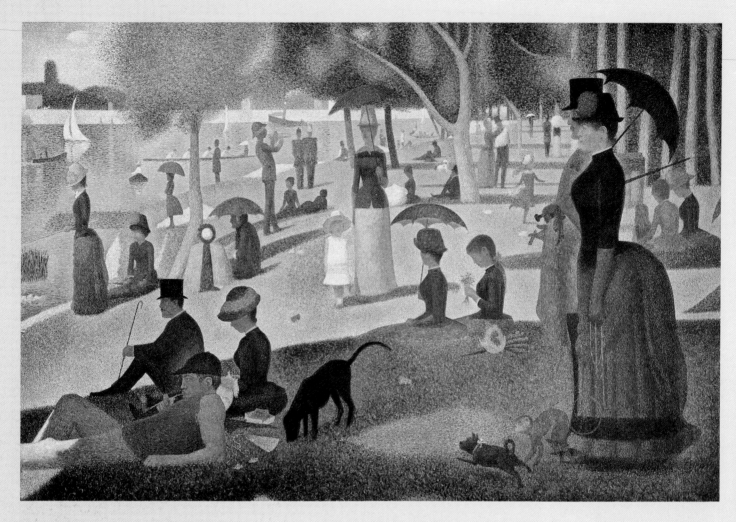

Pointillism, as well as his insistence on admitting Seurat, Signac and Lucien Pissarro, was making the point that there was a viable successor to the original movement.

The critics – indeed, art opinion generally – concentrated on two aspects of the exhibition. The first was Degas' pastels showing women engaged in activities such as washing or dressing. Typically, detailed analysis of their surroundings – cheap furniture and metal bathtubs etc. – was combined with comments on their physical ugliness ('distressing and lamentable poems about flesh', 'frog-like appearances', 'stout women with swollen flesh, who rest their hands on their buttocks'), culminating in the accusation that Degas was 'a ferocious misogynist' who wilfully debased women, reducing them to 'animal and nearly monkey-like functions'.

The other focus of comment was Seurat's *Sunday Afternoon on the Island of La Grande Jatte*, which dominated the exhibition by virtue of its size, its technique and its subject matter. It did not arouse quite so much derision as might have been expected, for it clearly involved a great deal of diligent application – invariably one of the criteria by which the public judged a work of art. A number of reviewers drew attention to the revolutionary qualities apparent in Seurat's representation of all classes of society, including workers, nursemaids and soldiers. But there was also a realization that here was the foundation of a new 'scientific' movement that would dispense with the bravura and individualism of Impressionism. Here, it seemed, was an art which was not fragmentary and did not depend on instinctive and haphazard responses to nature.

SEURAT
Sunday Afternoon on the Island of La Grande Jatte
1886

In this work Seurat perfected his pointillist technique of applying small points of pure pigment over a layer of fine paint. Its hues and tones, produced by an optical rather than a physical mixture of the paints, had an unprecedented freshness, particularly suited to a scene with strong colours and pronounced contrasts of light and shade.

Although Seurat based this work on sketches done *en plein air*, he eliminated non-essentials to produce a monumental canvas, entirely devoid of the spontaneity of Impressionist painting.

▲ AN AMERICAN JUDGEMENT

Durand-Ruel's first American exhibition opened at Moore's American Art Galleries in New York on April 10th, then moved to the National Academy of Design in June. The exhibition included forty-eight works by Monet, forty-two by Pissarro, thirty-eight by Renoir, twenty-three by Degas, seventeen by Manet, fifteen by Sisley, three by Seurat, and several by Caillebotte, Cassatt and Morisot. Among the most important were: Degas' *The Singer in Green* (*c*.1884); Manet's *The Absinthe Drinker* (1858–9), *The Balcony* (p.60) and *The Railroad*; Renoir's *Luncheon of the Boating Party* (p.132) and *Dance at Bougival* (p.134); Morisot's *La Toilette* (*c*.1875); and Seurat's *Bathing at Asnières* (p.139). One of the few favourable reviews of the exhibition appeared in the June issue of *Cosmopolitan*. Written by Luther Hamilton, it was short on the specific and long on the generalized, but it did try to identify the special characteristics of the movement:

The Impressionists believe in the possibility of making closer approximations to many appearances in nature than have been in vogue, and even in the possibility of approximating in the symbolism of painting phases of nature that have not hitherto been attempted.

On these theories, one of them paints, say a man rowing on a lake, aiming to give the impression of the broken reflections produced by his oars, and, perhaps, doing it wonderfully; but between the painter and the observer there must be generally lacking that common understanding before referred to. The approximation may be far closer than in various ambitious portrayals of Niagara Falls with which the observer is familiar. But long experience has taught him that certain woolly appearances do nominally represent Niagara Falls,

while the yellow splashes of paint suggesting the broken reflections he sees in all their nakedness as yellow splashes of paint.

Moreover, the tendency is not even to compare the new approximation with nature, but with other and different pictures, the measure of the nearness being also the measure of the condemnation meted out.

One of the greatest stumbling-blocks in the Impressionist work, as shown here, was the prevalence of violet shadows. In considering this, it must be remembered that there are more violets in the shadows in many parts of France than in this country; also the violet in out-of-doors pictures greatly brightens the effect of the yellow sunshine, and to give any impression of light and brilliancy, in the least suggesting of nature's, is always the painter's most impossible problem. The Impressionists, with their violet shadows, have made by far the closest approximation we have yet had. We can well afford to take the little exaggeration, or even falsity, for the sake of the far larger and more important truth thus attained.

MANET
The Railroad
1872–3

Manet is likely to have been attracted by the Gare St-Lazare when living nearby at 4 rue de St-Pétersbourg. Typically, he did not focus on the industrial aspects of the station, but on a figurative scene.

The woman is Victorine Meurent, who ten years earlier posed for *Olympia* (p.36), and the girl is the daughter of his friend and neighbour Alphonse Hirsch.

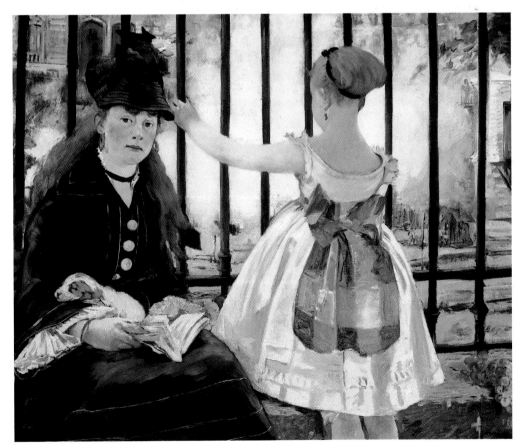

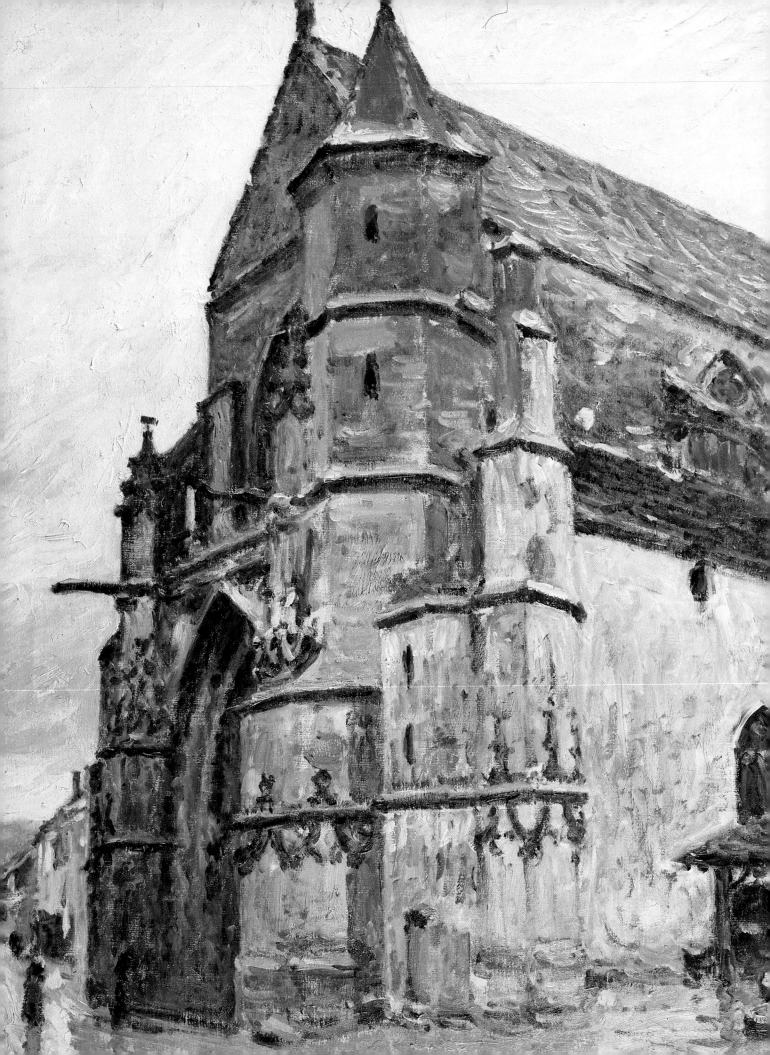

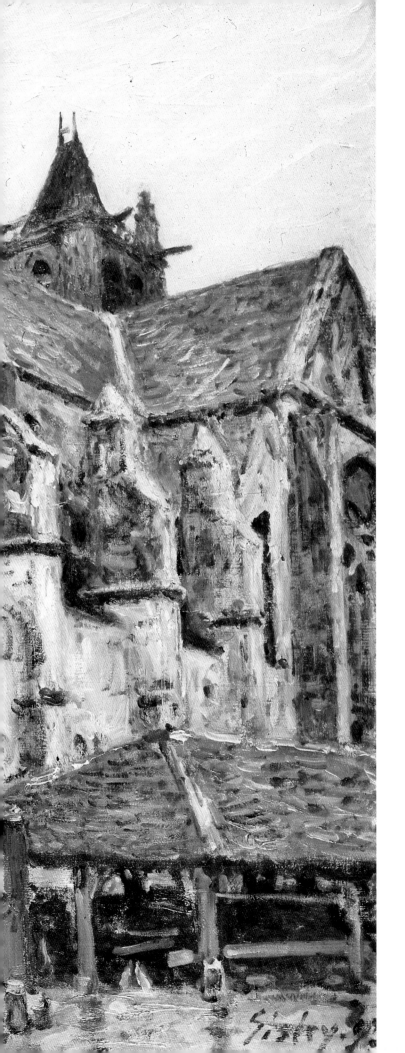

DIVERGENT DESTINIES
1887–1899

SISLEY **The Church at Moret, Rainy Morning** (detail) 1893

1887

Exotic Influences

A number of the younger generation of artists begin to widen their horizons, many looking to Japanese art, which is becoming increasingly popular through exhibitions held in Paris. Gauguin embarks upon a pilgrimage in search of the exotic, travelling as far as the Caribbean.

JANUARY

A 'collection of modern paintings selected during the last summer by Mr Durand-Ruel' is shown at Moore's American Art Galleries in New York.

Degas buys a copy of Eadweard Muybridge's book of photographs entitled *Animal Locomotion* ◆ (p.160).

25th Pissarro, who is in financial difficulties, sells a Degas pastel (given to him by the artist) for 1200 francs.

FEBRUARY

Vincent van Gogh organizes an exhibition of Japanese prints at the Café Tambourin.

The avant-garde organization Les Vingt ◆ (pp.214–5) holds an exhibition in Brussels that includes works by Pissarro, Rodin and Seurat.

A Millet retrospective opens at the École des Beaux-Arts.

APRIL

7th Theo van Gogh begins to buy paintings from Monet for Boussod & Valadon's Montmartre gallery.

10th Gauguin embarks for Panama and Martinique.

MAY

8th The sixth International Exhibition opens at Georges Petit's gallery. Monet, Pissarro, Renoir and Sisley are among the exhibitors.

25th Durand-Ruel's second exhibition sponsored by the American Art Association opens at the National Academy of Design in New York. It includes works by Delacroix and Puvis de Chavannes as well as Monet, Pissarro, Renoir and Sisley.

JULY

22nd Theo van Gogh buys *Woman Seated by a Vase of Flowers* (opposite) from Degas for 4000 francs. (In the course of the next three years he is to buy some twenty-five works from him.)

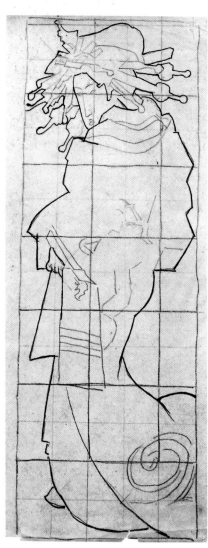

Tracing by van Gogh of a Japanese print, from the cover of *Paris Illustré*, 1887.

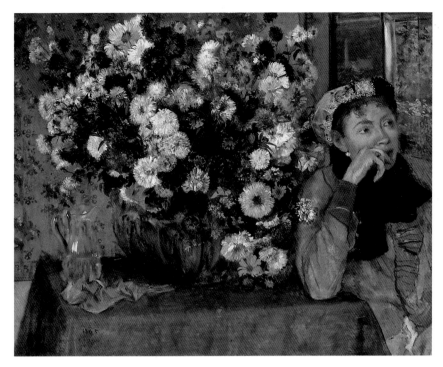

DEGAS
Woman Seated by a Vase of Flowers (Woman with Chrysanthemums)
1858–65

Despite its alternative title, the flowers in this painting include yellow and red sunflowers, gaillardia, marguerites, cornflowers and dahlias, with only a few chrysanthemums. The figure (Mme Valpinçon) was added to what had been solely a still life, and the original date (1858) is still discernible.

AUGUST

Renoir goes to stay at Le Vésinet, near Pontoise.
13th Monet departs for a fortnight in London, where he stays with Whistler.

OCTOBER

A major exhibition of Japanese art opens at the Union Centrale des Arts Décoratifs in Paris. Renoir visits his friend Murer in Auvers-sur-Oise, where they are joined by Pissarro.

NOVEMBER

A Puvis de Chavannes exhibition opens at Durand-Ruel's gallery. Gauguin returns from Martinique and goes to live with Schuffenecker, his former colleague at Bertin's stockbroking company, who is an amateur painter. He works on ceramics with Ernest Chapelet, a ceramist and porcelain painter trained at Sèvres (right).

DECEMBER

Theo van Gogh plans an exhibition of works by Gauguin, Guillaumin and Pissarro, to take place in 1888 at Boussod & Valadon's gallery. Monet exhibits four paintings at the Royal Society of British Artists in London, thanks to Whistler, who is President of the society.
Works by Manet, Camille and Lucien Pissarro, Seurat and Signac are included in an exhibition at the offices of Fénéon's *La Révue indépendante*.

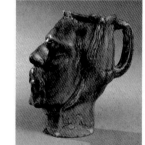

Gauguin's *Vase in the Shape of a Head* is an imaginative exercise in stoneware, executed while he was working with the porcelain painter Ernest Chapelet.

OTHER EVENTS

- Grévy resigns as President of France due to a financial scandal
- Queen Victoria's Golden Jubilee
- First Colonial Conference opens in London
- Construction of Eiffel Tower begins
- Mimeograph duplicating machines introduced by A. B. Dick & Co.

- Monotype typesetting system invented by Tolbert Lanston
- Goodwin invents celluloid film
- Théâtre Libre (which was to become a centre for Symbolist art and drama) founded in Paris
- Ludovic Zamenhof publishes his first Esperanto textbook
- Publication of *A Study in Scarlet* (Conan Doyle's first Sherlock

Holmes story), and Thomas Hardy's *The Woodlanders*
- Paderewski gives his first piano recital
- Debussy completes *Printemps*
- Verdi's *Otello* first performed; first Paris performances of Wagner's *Lohengrin*, Fauré's *Messe de Requiem* and Chabrier's *Le Roi malgré lui*
- Vischer and Borodin die

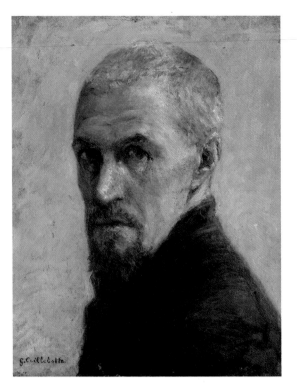

CAILLEBOTTE
Self-Portrait
1892

Caillebotte's self-portrait is one of the most revealing and perceptive of those produced by the Impressionists. Painted two years before his untimely death in 1894, it shows him at the age of 43.

IMPRESSIONIST DINNERS AT THE CAFÉ RICHE

Around this time the Impressionists started to hold dinners at the Café Riche in the boulevard des Italiens, and were to continue to do so well into the 1890s. One of those who attended was Gustave Geffroy, a journalist, novelist and critic, whose *La Vie artistique*, issued in eight volumes between 1892 and 1903, included a comprehensive history of Impressionism. In his book *Claude Monet, sa vie, son temps, son œuvre* published in 1922, Geffroy described what the dinners were like:

They were evenings dedicated to gossip and conversation, in which the happenings of the day were discussed with that freedom of spirit peculiar to artists free from any contact with official organizations. It must be admitted that the Impressionists' table was very lively and noisy, and that, relaxing from the burden of work, they behaved rather like children just let out of school. The discussions sometimes got quite heated, especially between Renoir and Caillebotte. The former – nervous and sarcastic, with his mocking voice and a kind of Mephistopheleanism that showed with an irony and a strange mirth in his face, already ravaged by illness – took a mischievous delight in taunting Caillebotte, a choleric and irascible man, whose face would change colour, from red to puce and even to black, whenever his opinions were contradicted by the sprightly flow of words which Renoir loved to employ against them. He would then display a fierceness that turned to anger, though that was harmless enough. The discussions covered not only art but politics, philosophy and every possible literary topic – subjects that appealed to Caillebotte's enthusiasm, as he was a great reader of books, reviews and newspapers. Renoir kept abreast by buying an encyclopaedia, from which he culled arguments to floor Caillebotte. Mirbeau would throw himself headlong into these intellectual combats, and was always listened to when he pronounced his considered judgments. Pissarro and Monet were also devotees of literature, both of them possessed of an assured and refined taste. I well remember a veritable duel, for and against Victor Hugo, that unleashed a spate of passion, ardour and wisdom – from which everybody emerged reconciled, to go and sit on the café terrace and contemplate the fairy-like appearance of Paris by night. On other occasions the arguments continued outside on the boulevard, and I'm sure some of them were never resolved.

RENOIR'S NEW STYLE

Renoir's three-month tour of Italy in 1881 had been a revelation to him. In Italian art he found a clarity of form, a precision of outline and a compositional skill that seemed just the qualities his own work lacked. He had, in fact, been unhappy with his work for some time and destroyed many of his paintings during this period, later confessing to Vollard that in the late 1880s he felt he had 'reached the end of Impressionism'; he had become averse to the depiction of the ephemeral, of the fleeting moment, and started to seek 'an art of the museums'.

This involved a far greater concentration on the relationship between drawing and painting, and resulted in a 'hardness' of outline that was expressed in its most spectacular form in *The Bathers* of 1887. His new approach was emphasized by the fact that he undertook a large

This large work was painted at the height of Renoir's 'classical period', during which he consciously developed his abilities as a draughtsman to achieve a more controlled linear effect in his canvases. The composition *The Bathers* (below) was arrived at through a long sequence of preparatory studies in pencil, chalk, ink and watercolour, such as the chalk *Study of Three Nudes* (right), which he drew in 1886–7.

number of preliminary drawings for the work, which was as carefully constructed as a Poussin or an academic painting. Indeed his main inspiration seems to have been a bas-relief at Versailles by the seventeenth-century sculptor François Girardon, and the monumental quality of the work was emphasized by its size – approximately 120 x 180cm (4 x 6ft). Moreover, as is apparent from some of Renoir's preliminary drawings, at one stage he thought of surrounding the painting with a decorative frame; and he first exhibited it, at the International Exhibition in May 1887, under the title *Bathers: Trial for a Decorative Painting*.

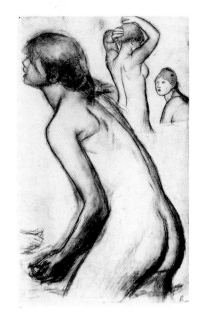

But it was not only in form and composition that Renoir's work altered. He had been impressed by the smooth texture and clear colours of Italian painting and sought to recapture these qualities. With this in mind, he adopted a new technique, first laying down a thin coat of white lead then applying his colours very thinly and with great care, to create a smooth

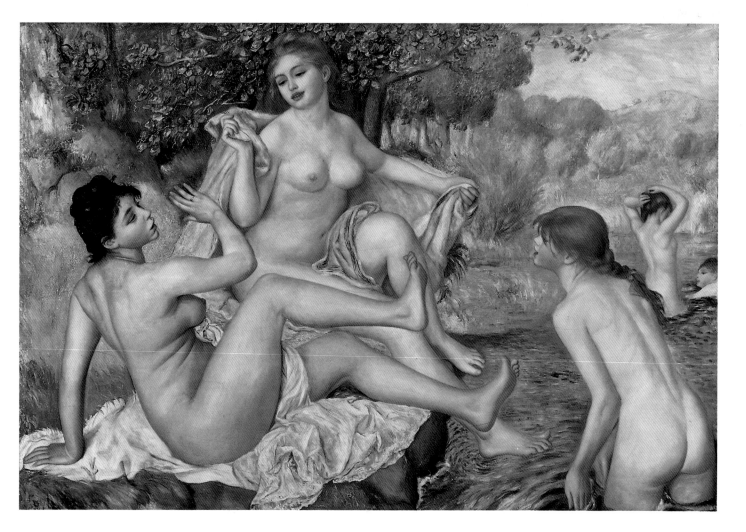

enamel-like finish; in addition, he used restrained colours – red and yellow ochre, dark green, and black. It could be said that all art alternates between the classical and the Romantic, between restraint and the prevalence of emotion. Renoir was going through his classical phase.

He was to persist in this phase for some three years, then abandoned it partly of his own volition and partly from necessity – as nobody, with the possible exception of Monet, liked the new paintings. Indeed Durand-Ruel not only disliked them but thought they would be difficult to sell, since collectors tended to be conservative and, having been coaxed into an appreciation of Renoir's earlier work, might well be reluctant to accept a different style.

MONET
Women in the Garden
1866–7

Two photographs taken at Bazille's home near Montpellier were the starting point for *Women in the Garden*. The painting was refused by the Salon of 1867 and later purchased by Bazille for 2500 francs.

◆ IMPRESSIONISM AND THE CAMERA

It was especially appropriate that the first Impressionist exhibition should have been held in a photographer's studio, for the camera was to have an important influence on the style and techniques of the movement. In the first place, it had provided images that could be copied. Manet based an etched portrait of Baudelaire on a photograph by Nadar, and one of Edgar Allan Poe on a daguerreotype. Monet's *Women in the Garden* (opposite), painted for Bazille in 1866–7, was based on two photographs taken at Bazille's home near Montpellier and, although Monet (who had four cameras) always stressed the advantages of painting *en plein air*, he certainly made use of photography for his series paintings, especially those of Rouen cathedral. Cézanne's self-portrait of 1866 was copied from a photograph, and in 1868 one of his friends wrote to another: 'Cézanne is planning a painting for which he will use some snaps. I have your photograph, and you will be in it.'

More significant than the use of photography as a means of providing subjects to paint was the fact that it reinforced the Impressionists' concern with realism and what Degas called 'magical instantaneity'. It caught people in the act and, especially after the invention of the snapshot type of photograph in the 1880s, provided abruptly cut-off images, unusual perspectives, and views taken from a great height or from a window – all of which gave an enhanced impression of immediacy. The critic Ernest Chesneau recognized this when, in 1874, he wrote of Monet's *Boulevard des Capucines* (p.86): 'Never has the amazing animation of the public thoroughfare, the ant-like swarming of the crowd on the pavement and the vehicles on the roadway, nor the elusive, fleeting nature and instantaneity of movement, been caught in its incredible flux and fixed as in this extraordinary picture.'

But the most notable instance of the influence of photography on the Impressionists occurred in 1887 when Degas bought a copy of *Animal Locomotion* by Eadweard Muybridge, whose work he had known about for some time. Muybridge had set out to establish whether a galloping horse had all four legs off the ground at any moment. After much experimentation, he evolved a system of cameras, each triggered by a trip wire activated by the movement of the animal, which enabled him to produce a series of photographs using techniques analogous to those of cinematography. Later he continued his exploration of movement with human beings and birds. His photographs greatly influenced many artists – but especially Degas ▲ (p.204), who made use of Muybridge's discoveries in his drawings, paintings and sculptures of horses.

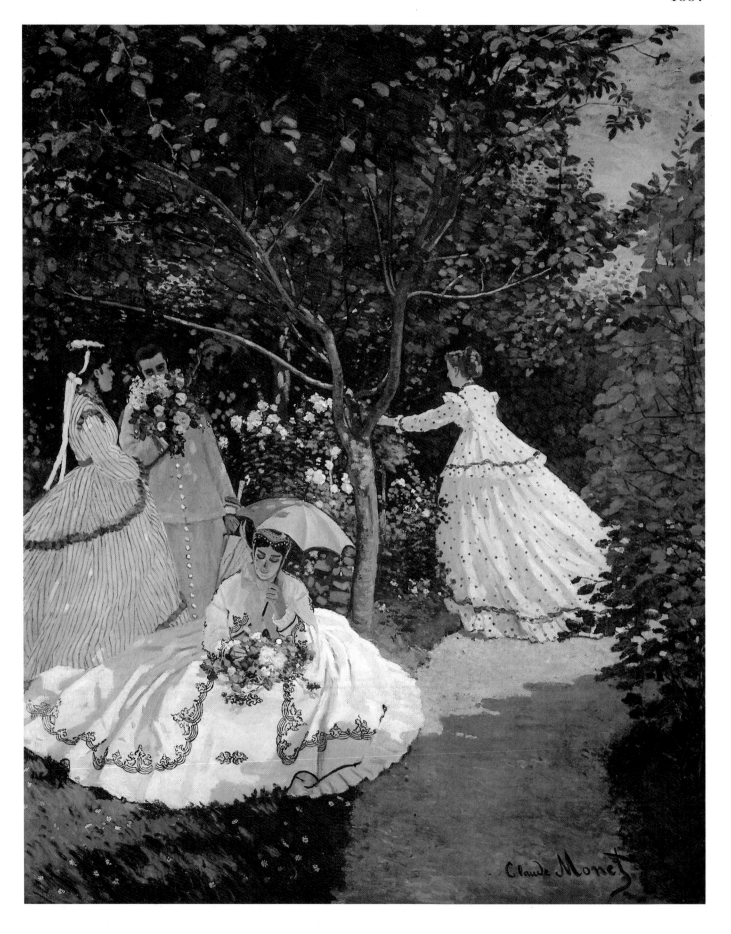

1888

Durand-Ruel Opens in New York

The growing vogue for Impressionist painting in America, a country without the prejudices of the French academic tradition, gives Durand-Ruel the courage to open a gallery in New York. Cassatt helps foster the popularity of Impressionism in the USA by nurturing the enthusiasm of American friends such as Henry and Louisine Havemeyer.

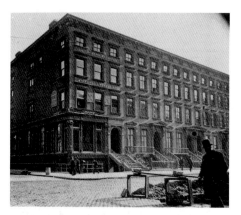

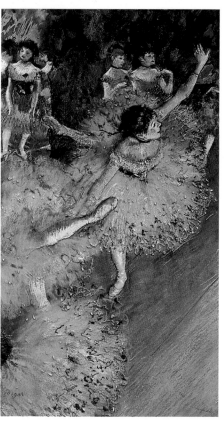

JANUARY

Durand-Ruel opens a gallery in an apartment on Fifth Avenue, New York (left and right).
Monet paints in Antibes (opposite), where he remains till April.
8th Pissarro exhibits some etchings at the offices of *La Revue indépendante*.
15th Mallarmé ◆ (pp.220–1) plans to have his prose poem *Le Tiroir de laque* illustrated by Degas, Renoir and Morisot. (When it is published in 1891, there is only one illustration – by Renoir.)
27th The Ministry of Fine Arts buys Sisley's *September Morning* (1887) for 1000 francs.

FEBRUARY

2nd Renoir, who has been staying at Cézanne's home, the Jas de Bouffan at Aix-en-Provence, moves to a hotel 'because the household is so wretchedly mean.'

MARCH

4th Renoir goes to Louveciennes, where his mother is seriously ill.

APRIL

3rd Degas' *Dance Class at the Opéra* (1872) is shown at the Glasgow International Exhibition, and his *Green Dancer* (left) at the New English Art Club in London ◆ (p.253).

MAY

1st Guillaumin has a one-man exhibition at the offices of *La Revue indépendante*.
25th A mixed exhibition opens at Durand-Ruel's gallery in Paris. It includes twenty-six Pissarros, twenty-four Renoirs and twenty-four Sisleys.

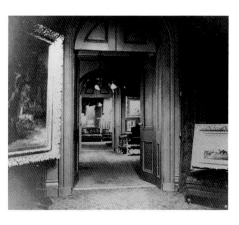

The exterior (left) and interior (above) of Durand-Ruel's gallery on Fifth Avenue, New York.

DEGAS
Green Dancer
c.1880

There is an interesting dichotomy in this work between the vibrant figures on stage and the static line of dancers waiting in the wings – a contrast that is highlighted by the two groups wearing dresses of a different colour. The pose of the central ballerina can be traced to *The Star* (p.101) and subsequent drawings of dancers by Degas.

Much admired in the 1880s, the pastel belonged to Sickert, who gave it to his second wife, Ellen.

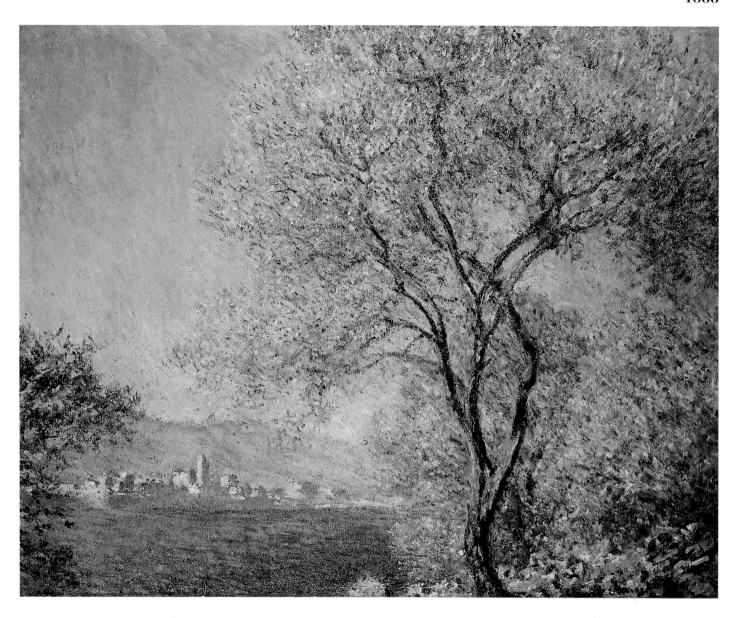

JUNE

Renoir spends the summer working in Argenteuil, with occasional trips to Essoyes.

Sisley – who has an English passport – toys with the idea of becoming a French citizen, but does not do so.

4th The dealer Theo van Gogh takes ten views of Antibes from Monet. (He sells them during the course of the year for 27,720 francs, out of which Monet receives 11,400 francs.)

5th An influential exhibition of historic Japanese prints opens at Siegfried Bing's gallery in Paris.

6th Degas buys *The Ham* and *A Pear* by Manet at the sale of part of the collection belonging to Eugène Pertuiset, the big-game hunter whose portrait Manet had painted in 1880–1. (Pertuiset had acquired nine pictures by Manet, not all of which are included in the sale.)

8th An exhibition of works by Pissarro, Renoir and Sisley opens at Durand-Ruel's gallery in Paris.

MONET
Antibes Seen from the Jardin de la Salis
1888

After painting the granite scenery off the coast of Brittany (*see* p.150), Monet chose, as a contrast, to go back to the Mediterranean. 'After terrible Belle-Ile', he wrote, 'this is going to be tender, here there's nothing but blue, rose and gold.' The Antibes canvases are similar in mood to those he produced in Bordighera (p.138), but there is a new harmony of colour flowing throughout these paintings.

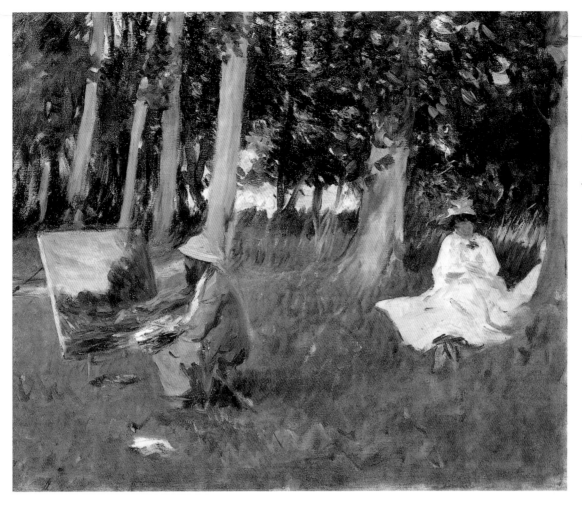

SARGENT
Claude Monet Painting at the Edge of a Wood
1888

Monet first met the gregarious and gifted American painter John Singer Sargent around 1876, and the two artists developed a close and mutually profitable friendship.

This portrait, produced while they were working together at Giverny in the summer of 1888, emphasizes Monet's taste for *plein-air* painting, and is a companion piece to Sargent's *Claude Monet in his Studio Boat* (1887).

JULY

Monet refuses the Legion of Honour, and pays a visit to London. Vincent van Gogh writes to Theo suggesting that Boussod & Valadon send them both to London 'to sell Impressionist paintings'. Degas works feverishly on sculptures of racehorses ◆ (p.235).

AUGUST

Degas visits Pau, where his friend Paul Lafond is director of the museum – Lafond had been responsible for buying Degas' *Portraits in an Office* (p.97) for the Société des Amis du Musée de Pau in 1878.

Sargent works with Monet at Giverny.

SEPTEMBER

Renoir stays in Petit-Gennevilliers with Caillebotte. He begins to suffer from rheumatoid arthritis.

Pissarro contracts an eye infection (which persists for the rest of his life).

OCTOBER

Renoir spends three months in Essoyes 'in order to get away from

GAUGUIN
L'Arlésienne Mme Ginoux
1888

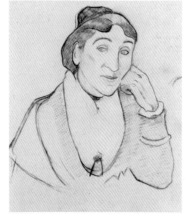

This charcoal sketch of the owner of the Café de la Gare at Arles was a preparatory study for Gauguin's painting *The Café at Arles* of the same year. Van Gogh had already used Mme Ginoux as the model for his *Arlésienne* canvases.

RENOIR
Washerwomen
1888

During his three-month visit to Essoyes, Renoir used less sophisticated models to produce some of his most important canvases of rustic life. Constantly searching for a new style of painting ▲ (pp.177–8), and at that time interested in eighteenth-century pastoral scenes, Renoir wrote to Durand-Ruel of this work: 'I have begun some washerwomen…I think it will work out all right this time. It is very soft and coloured, but luminous.'

expensive Parisian models, and paint washerwomen and laundresses on the river banks.'
23rd Gauguin joins van Gogh in Arles.

NOVEMBER
The painters Sérusier, Denis, Bonnard and Ranson – subsequently founder members of the Nabis group – begin to work together. (The influence of Gauguin and Cézanne is apparent in their emotive use of line and colour.)
Degas turns down an invitation from the avant-garde society Les Vingt ◆ (pp.214–5) to participate in an exhibition in Brussels.

DECEMBER
Renoir has an attack of facial paralysis.
Degas starts writing sonnets on themes from his paintings, dedicating each to an individual – including Mary Cassatt. (The poems are passed round in manuscript, but remained unpublished until 1946.)
24th After a violent quarrel with Gauguin, van Gogh cuts off part of his ear and makes a present of it to a prostitute. Gauguin contacts Theo to come and tend his brother, and immediately leaves Arles.
26th Gauguin arrives in Paris, where he stays with his friend and former colleague, Émile Schuffenecker.

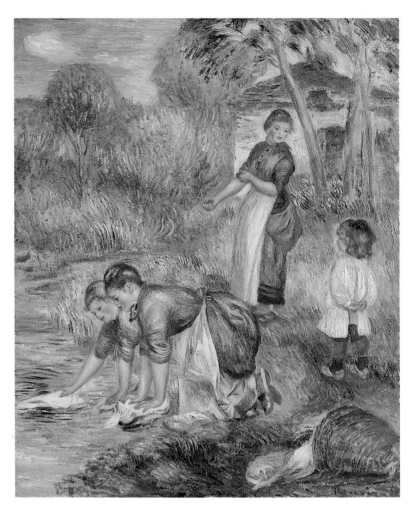

OTHER EVENTS

- Wilhelm II (the 'Kaiser') becomes Emperor of Germany
- Britain guarantees neutral status of Suez Canal
- General Boulanger elected to French Chamber of Deputies
- Benjamin Harrison elected President of the USA
- Jack the Ripper murders at least six prostitutes in London
- Hertz and Lodge independently identify radio waves as belonging to the same family as light waves
- John Boyd Dunlop invents the pneumatic tyre
- Charles Henry publishes *Cercle chromatique*, exploring the emotional significance of colours
- Publication of Loti's *Madame Chrysanthème*, Maupassant's *Pierre et Jean*, Kipling's *Plain Tales from the Hills* and George Moore's *Confessions of a Young Man*
- First performance of Rimsky-Korsakov's *Scheherazade*

THE IMPRESSIONISTS 'TAINT' BRITISH ART

By 1888 the Impressionist 'craze' had spread beyond the confines of France. In England, in the June issue of the well-established and highly regarded periodical *The Magazine of Art*, William Powell Frith, one of the country's most popular artists, addressed himself to the task of demolishing Impressionist pretensions in terms that no doubt delighted most of his readers:

We have now done, long ago, with the Pre-Raphaelitic, and another, far more dangerous craze has come upon us. Born and bred in France, what is called 'Impressionism' has tainted the art of this country. It is singular that this phase of art, if it can be called art, is in exact opposition to the principles of the Pre-Raphaelites. In the one we had overwrought details, in the other no details at all. So far as my feeble powers allow me to understand the Impressionist, I take him to propose to himself an 'impression' – probably a momentary one – that Nature has made upon him. If the specimens of the impressions that I have seen are what have been made on any human being, his mind must be strangely formed. There is an exhibition every year at Mr Wallis' gallery in Pall Mall where admirable examples of foreign art may be studied, and a comparison of our own school with the examples of others ought to be a lesson to students and professors alike. And when there is so much to instruct and stimulate in the best of these, it has always seemed to me strange in the extreme that painters can be found who seem only to strive to reproduce their faults. It is to be hoped that the 'Impressionists' will not be allowed to play their pranks in the Royal Academy exhibition; we have enough evidence there of the seeming forgetfulness of the good that may be obtained by foreign training in the occasional display of sooty flesh, and dingy, unmeaning, not to say unpleasant subjects. I have sometimes been surprised to find that a picture of which – to use a vulgarism – I could make neither head nor tail, had found a purchaser. It might have had a strange roughness entirely uncomprehensible [sic] to me, a kind of affectation of cleverness which the purchaser may have mistaken for genius. I fear my experience of public knowledge of art leads me to the conclusion that a picture simply true to Nature has no chance against one in which

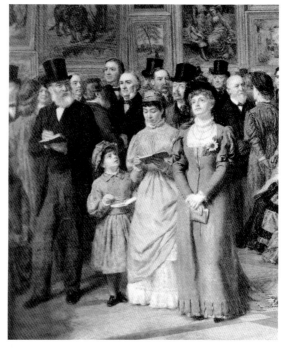

A detail of William Powell Frith's painting of a *Private View at the Royal Academy* (1881), which typifies the British establishment's attitude towards art and its position in society.

the painter has indulged in eccentricity, which the buyer thinks wonderful because he cannot understand it.

In the way of a final word to the gentlemen who record their momentary impressions of Nature, I venture to advise them to dwell longer on their impressions; let them keep Nature before their eyes for hours, days and weeks, and then perhaps their impressions will be more what they ought to be. This advice is not likely to be taken and these artists (?) may do much mischief to our modern school, the effects of which may be disastrously permanent; but the craze itself will as assuredly pass away as everything foolish and false does sooner or later.

Frith was not alone in his reactions. A few weeks after his article was published, Vincent van Gogh wrote to his sister from Arles recalling his own reactions when he first encountered the Impressionists' work:

One has heard about the Impressionists, one expects much and…when one has seen them for the first time, one is very much disappointed, and thinks they are ugly, sloppily and badly painted, badly drawn, of a poor colour; everything that is miserable. That was my first impression when I came to Paris.

THE IMPRESSIONIST CRAZE IN THE USA

In 1888 the critic Théodore Duret visited the USA. In his book *Manet and the French Impressionists*, published in 1910, he included the following account of the Impressionist paintings he found in America, adding details of subsequent acquisitions by some of the collectors:

This was still the heroic age of the new painting. It was still only appreciated by a very small minority. But the ardent enthusiasm, the birth and growth of which I had witnessed in France, manifested itself here also. Moreover, America is free from the prejudices of the Old World; the atmosphere is favourable to novelties. Hence, Manet and the Impressionists did not encounter there that desperate resistance which they had to overcome in France and Germany.

The Metropolitan Museum in New York now possesses two works by Manet, presented by Mr Irwin Davis in 1889: 'Boy with a Sword' and 'Young Woman with a Parrot'. 'Boy with a Sword' found more favour when it first appeared than any of Manet's other pictures. Pleasing in its subject, executed in softly blended tones, it received nothing but praise from the very first. 'Young Woman with a Parrot', on the other hand, was strongly condemned at the Salon of 1866, and has been more or less debated ever since. The collection has since been enriched by 'Portrait of Mme Charpentier and her Children' by Renoir, purchased at the Charpentier sale in 1907 for the sum of 84,000 francs.

The private collections of the United States contain a very large number of the works of Manet and the Impressionists. The following is a list of the works of Manet, with the names of their owners:

'The Guitar Player'	*Mr Osborn, New York*
'The Tragic Actor'	*Mr George Vanderbilt, New York*
'The Repose'	*Mr George Vanderbilt, New York*
'The Guitarist'	*Mr Pope, New York*
'The Water Drinker'	*Mr McCormick, New York*
'The Dead Torero'	*Mr Widener, Philadelphia*
'The Bullfight'	*Mr Inglis, New York*
'The Street Singer'	*Mrs Sears, Boston*
'The Racecourse'	*Mr Wittemore, Boston*
'The Philosopher'	*Mrs Eddy, Chicago*
'Races in the Bois de Boulogne'	*Mrs Potter-Palmer, Chicago*
'View of Venice'	*Mr Crocker, San Francisco*
'Battle of the Kearsage and the Alabama'	*Mr John Johnson, Philadelphia*

The works of Claude Monet in private collections are so numerous, that it is impracticable to compile a list of them here.

By far the most important collection of works of Manet and the Impressionists which exists in the United States is that brought together by Mr and Mrs H. O. Havemeyer ● (p.233), in New York. It was formed partly with the advice of their friend Miss Mary Cassatt. After having gathered together one of the finest collections of the old Italian and Dutch masters, and of the French masters of the nineteenth century, Ingres, Corot and Courbet, they turned their attention to the most recent of the French painters. Mrs Havemeyer, to whom the collection passed after the death of her husband, possesses the following works by Manet: 'Mlle V. in the Costume of an Espada', 'A Young Man in the Costume of a Maja', 'A Torero Saluting', 'Christ with Angels', 'The Garden', 'Ball at the Opera', 'The Port of Calais', 'The Railway', 'View of Venice', 'En Bateau', and other less important works and pastels. She has also a large number of works by Degas, representing every aspect of his art, also by Claude Monet and Cézanne, including the latter painter's 'The Rape'.

MANET
Masked Ball at the Opéra
1873–4

This painting was one of the first to be bought from the artist by Faure ● (p.81). The singer sold it to Durand-Ruel in 1894, and it was purchased by Mr and Mrs H. O. Havemeyer ● (p.233) the following year.

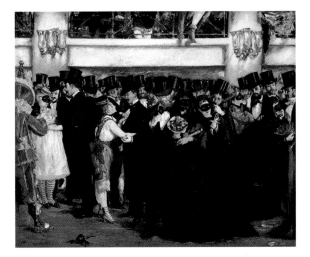

1889

Smaller Groupings

Clusters of Impressionist artists exhibit along with non-Impressionists: Pissarro and Bracquemond with Redon; Monet with Rodin. Works by Cézanne, Manet, Monet and Pissarro are shown at the Centennial Exhibition of French Art, but Degas and Renoir stand aloof.

JANUARY

23rd Durand-Ruel holds an exhibition of the newly formed Société des Peintres-Graveurs (a group organized by Durand-Ruel to take advantage of the growing fashion for collecting prints and engravings). It includes works by Bracquemond, Pissarro and Odilon Redon.

FEBRUARY

6th Cézanne, Gauguin, Monet, Pissarro and Signac exhibit at the avant-garde society Les Vingt in Brussels ◆ (pp.214–5).
20th Monet has an exhibition at Boussod & Valadon's Gallery in Montmartre.

MARCH

Monet paints at Fresselines, on the River Creuse, where he stays until May ▲ (pp.171–2).

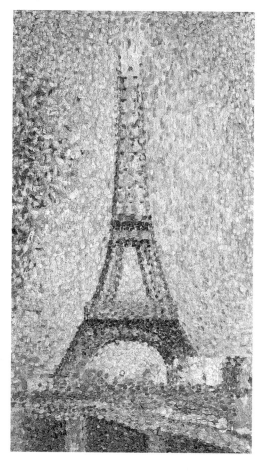

SEURAT
The Eiffel Tower
1888–9

A symbol of progress and French self-confidence, the Eiffel Tower was the most significant product of the Universal Exhibition.

A photograph of the Greek Pavilion at the Universal Exhibition of 1889.

APRIL

2nd Goupil's gallery in London shows 'Twenty Impressions by Claude Monet'. They are, unexpectedly, well received by the British press.
5th Durand-Ruel buys *Blue Dancer* from Degas for 500 francs and *Red Dancer* for 250 francs.
24th Renoir tells Dr Gachet that his health is improving and he is hoping to see him in Auvers after a visit to his brother in Villeneuve. Renoir and Degas refuse to participate in the Centennial Exhibition of French Art, which is being organized to coincide with the Universal Exhibition. Renoir writes to Roger Marx: 'Everything that I have done is bad and it would cause me a great deal of pain to see it exhibited.'

MAY

3rd Van Gogh is admitted to the Asylum of Saint Paul at St-Rémy-de-Provence, near Arles.

12th Pissarro's mother dies. He inherits nothing.

25th The collection of paintings belonging to Henry Hill of Brighton ◆ (pp.76–7) is sold at Christie's in London. Six works by Degas go for around 60 guineas each, although the Scottish collector Alexander Reid pays £180 for *The Absinthe Drinker* ◆ (pp.190–1). Sickert purchases *The Rehearsal of the Ballet on the Stage* at the auction, and later buys three more works by Degas from Durand-Ruel.

JUNE

5th The Centennial Exhibition of French Art, at the Universal Exhibition, includes works by Cézanne, Manet, Monet and Pissarro.

8th An exhibition organized by Gauguin, described as 'Paintings of the Impressionist and Synthetist Group', opens at the Café Volpini, near the Universal Exhibition. It includes works by Augustin, Bernard, Gauguin, Laval and Schuffenecker.

21st An exhibition of works by Monet and Rodin opens at Georges Petit's gallery. Of the 145 works by Monet, only six are for sale. Many visitors to the Universal Exhibition, however, are exposed to Monet's work for the first time and his popularity is enhanced. In *L'Art moderne*, Octave Maus ◆ (pp.214–5) states that 'Nature has never been rendered with more intensity and truth.' Other reviews are no less enthusiastic.

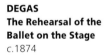

DEGAS
The Rehearsal of the Ballet on the Stage
*c.*1874

This is one of three very similar works by Degas, all painted around 1874, that show a ballet rehearsal on stage. In this version an ink underdrawing was covered with watercolour, built up with opaque layers of essence and, finally, oil paint. The resulting tones are particularly effective in suggesting the artificial stage lighting.

The Rehearsal of the Ballet on the Stage was included in the sale of Henry Hill's collection in 1889 ◆ (pp.76–7), and was purchased by Sickert for his wife, Ellen. It changed hands a number of times during the next few years and was eventually bought by Mrs Havemeyer ◆ (p.233) in 1902.

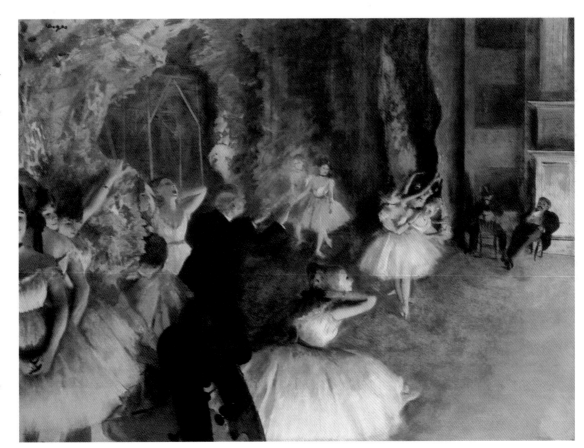

JULY

Monet starts a collection in order to raise 20,000 francs to buy Manet's *Olympia* for the nation ▲ (p.179).

10th Degas' sister Marguerite Fevre and her family sail from Le Havre for Buenos Aires.

AUGUST

8th Renoir writes to Monet refusing to contribute to the *Olympia* fund. (He later relents and sends 50 francs.)

SEPTEMBER

5th Degas, accompanied by the Italian portrait painter Giovanni Boldini, arrives in Madrid, then goes on to Andalusia.

18th Degas visits Tangier, before returning to Paris via Cadiz and Granada.

OCTOBER

30th The Society of the Friends of Art in Copenhagen holds an exhibition entitled 'Scandinavian and French Impressionists', which includes works by Cassatt, Cézanne, Degas, Guillaumin, Pissarro and Sisley.

DECEMBER

Pissarro completes an album of political drawings, entitled *Turpitudes sociales* (left), paying tribute to the anarchist movement and deploring the condition of the working classes.

An exhibition of work by British 'Impressionists', including Steer and Sickert, opens at Goupil's gallery in London.

The cover of the album *Turpitudes sociales*. Compiled by Pissarro for his British niece Esther Isaacson, the album gave examples of social injustice. It was never published.

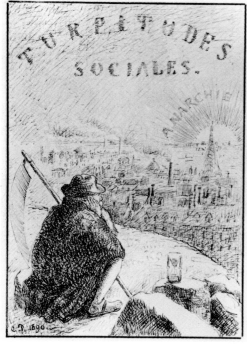

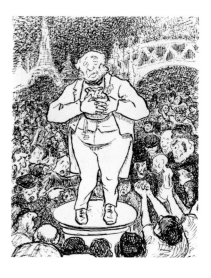

A caricature of the 'Synthetists' by Émile Bernard, showing (from the left) Schuffenecker, the artist and Gauguin. The words 'Un cauchemar' (a nightmare) appear at the bottom.

An anarchist sketch by Pissarro entitled *Capital* (1889).

OTHER EVENTS

- Crown Prince Rudolf of Austria commits suicide at his hunting lodge in Mayerling
- General Boulanger flees to Brussels, after being accused of attempting a coup d'état
- Panama Canal Company declared bankrupt; the construction of the canal is abandoned
- The Eiffel Tower is completed in time for the Universal Exhibition (held to celebrate the centenary of the French Revolution)
- First May Day celebration in Paris
- George Eastman introduces the Kodak camera
- André Gide begins his journal
- Maurice Maeterlinck's *Princesse Maleine*, Jerome K. Jerome's *Three Men in a Boat* and Mark Twain's *A Connecticut Yankee at the Court of King Arthur* first published
- First performance of Richard Strauss's *Don Juan*
- Robert Browning dies

▲ **THE PROBLEMS OF PAINTING 'EN PLEIN AIR'**

MONET
Ravine of the Petite Creuse
1889

Deeply impressed by the landscape of the Massif Central, Monet spent several weeks in the small town of Fresselines, painting the rocky gorges of the two rivers the Grande Creuse and the Petite Creuse. Of the twenty-four paintings he produced there, five were included in his exhibition in June, held at Georges Petit's gallery (*see* p.169).

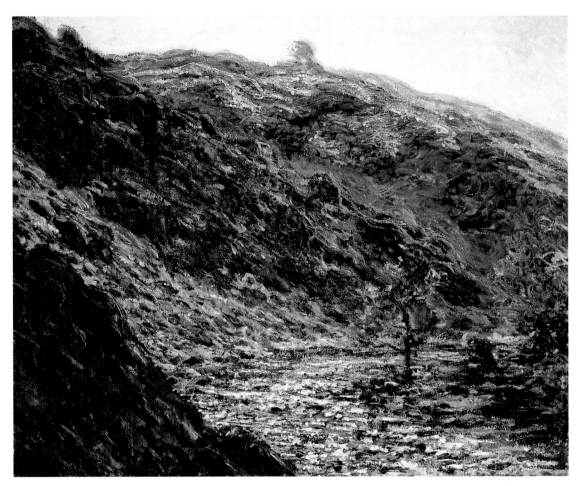

Monet's letters to his future wife, Alice Hoschedé ◆ (pp.146–7), are touching in their display of affection, and revealing in their account of the constant problems that beset the production of his seemingly spontaneous and joyous paintings. The following extracts are taken from letters written to her during the spring of 1889 when he was working on his *Valley of the Creuse* series at Fresselines in the Massif Central:

March 9th

I'm back from work; a bad session, and I wiped out everything I did this morning. It wasn't well expressed, and I hadn't got the feeling of it. It's always like this to start with. I worked better yesterday. On top of all this, the weather has been very changeable today; grey skies and sunshine.

Forgive me for not writing to you at greater length today. It will soon be midday, and I must see about

sending your letter off. Till tomorrow. Kisses to the children. Best wishes to Marthe. All my love and tenderness to you.

March 22nd

I'm utterly desolate. Snow came this morning, accompanied by wind, and a glacial coldness. What a curse!

I was a bit more content with myself last night, despite the rain, or perhaps because of it, since both paintings had a gloomy look about them which I couldn't quite get right.

Anyway, they were coming along well, and I was buoyed up with the highest hopes for today; but what am I going to do about this snow, which is settling enough to be a nuisance, but not enough to paint it? Still, if it persists after lunch I'll have a go at something.

But troubles never cease; the struggle is endless.

March 31st

As I said last night, work has been going much better these last few days, and I'm beginning to think that I might have some interesting work to bring back with me. By looking hard I've really entered into the spirit of the countryside. I understand it now, and have a clearer idea of what to do with it.

The most recent work I had to start on when the weather changed is much better than the early paintings and less hesitant; in the end it's the result of a great deal of effort.

Your old Claude, who loves you tenderly.

April 4th

So, with this damnable weather, which is too awful for words, progress is slow, and the sight of my paintings terrifies me; they're so dark, moreover several are skyless. It will be a gloomy series. A few have some sunlight in them, but they were started so long ago that I'm very much afraid that when the sun finally re-emerges I shall find my efforts considerably altered. Apart from this, the Creuse is bound to rise with all the rain we're having now, and it will change colour, so I live in a state of continual suspense, and I'll have to consider myself fortunate if I can manage to bring off a quarter of the canvases I've begun.

April 17th

Briefly, yesterday was a very bad day and this morning was worse still; a painting which might have been very good is utterly spoilt, and I fear for the others. What's more, the weather is wearing me down, a terrible cold wind, which wouldn't have bothered me in the slightest if I'd captured my effect, but the endless succession of clouds

and sunny intervals couldn't be worse, especially when I'm getting to the end. But the thing that is upsetting me most is that with the drought the Creuse is sinking visibly, and its colour is altering so radically that everything around it is transformed. In places where once the water fell in green torrents, all you see now is a brown bed. I'm desperate and don't know what to do, as this arid weather is here to stay. None of my paintings are right as they are, and I was counting on these last few days to rescue a good number of them; to give up now would mean that all my efforts have been wasted, but the struggle terrifies me. I am worn out, and longing to come home.

Advise me, comfort me.

Yours,

Claude

May 8th

I'm going to offer 50 francs to my landlord to see if I can have the oak tree's leaves removed. If I can't, I'm done for, since it appears in five paintings and plays a leading part in three; but I fear it won't do any good as he's an unfriendly old money bags, who has already tried to prevent access to one of his fields, and it was only because the priest intervened that I was able to continue going there.

May 9th

I'm overjoyed, having unexpectedly been granted permission to remove the leaves from my fine oak tree! It was quite a business bringing long enough ladders into the ravine. Anyway, it's done now, two men having worked on it since yesterday. Isn't it the final straw to be finishing a winter landscape at this time of year?

HUYSMANS ON CÉZANNE

When Joris-Karl Huysmans' novel *A Rebours* was published in 1884 its advocacy of uninhibited hedonism created a sensation. As a result, it became one of the seminal works of the Decadent movement in art and literature, which numbered among its enthusiasts Aubrey Beardsley and Oscar Wilde. In addition to being a novelist, Huysmans was a prolific art critic (and also a full-time civil servant), his first collection of criticism, *L'Art moderne* ▲ (pp.136–7),

appearing in 1883. This was followed in 1889 by a second collection, *Certains*, which included the following praise for Cézanne, who was then still largely disregarded:

Seen in a bright light, in porcelain compotes or on a white tablecloth, coarse pears and apples, shaped with a trowel, emphasized with a twist of the thumb. Seen close to, they appear to be a rough mixture of vermilion and yellow, of green and blue, but viewed from a

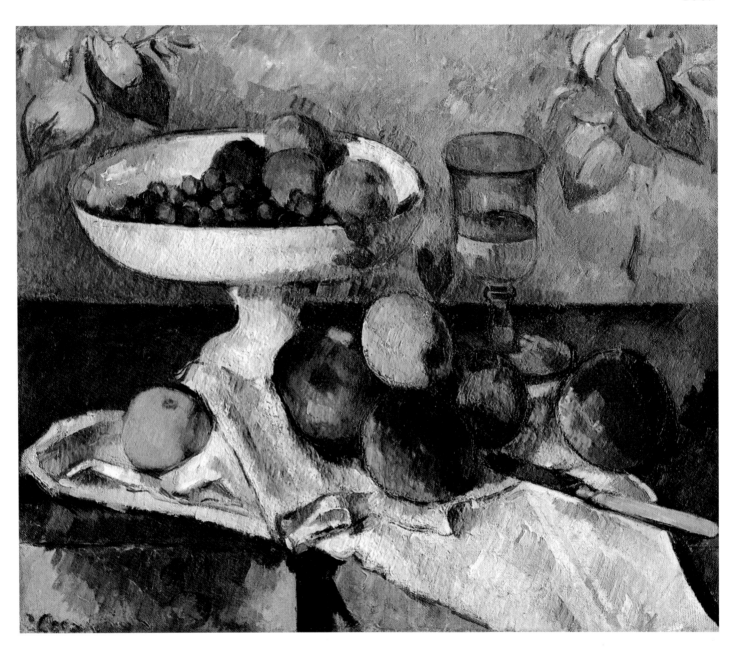

CÉZANNE
Still Life with Compotier
1879–80

Corresponding almost exactly to Huysman's description of a Cézanne still life in *Certains*, this is one of the most formal of the artist's works in this genre. The objects are paired and centred, from the fruit to the foliate pattern on the wall, but the colours establish a different pairing, which creates a competing axis.

distance … they become fruits of the kind that can be found in the window of a high-class fruit merchant, full-flavoured, savoury, enticing.

Truths until then unnoticed become apparent: strange and true tones, convincing splashes of colour, the shading on the tablecloth, vassals of the shadows spreading from the curves of the fruits, scattered in vague and charming traceries of blue – which make these canvases works that initiate us into mysteries, in contrast to the usual still lifes one sees, caked with bitumen, against unintelligible backgrounds.

Then there are sketches of landscape, done in the open air: some remain unfinished, in limbo; some are fresh sketches spoiled by retouching; childish and

savage sketches. And finally there are stupefying distortions in drunken pottery, nude bathers, delineated by insane but entrancing lines, for the gratification of the eye, done with the energy of a Delacroix but without the refinement of vision and the skillful fingers, whipped on by a fever of confused colours, clashing in relief, on the overburdened canvas that bends in defeat.

In conclusion, a colourist of revealing powers, who contributed more than Manet to the Impressionist movement, an artist with diseased retinas who, in the exasperated distortions of his sight, discovered the beginnings of a new art – that is how the too often disregarded painter, Cézanne, can be summed up.

1890

'Olympia' Accepted by the State

Monet's campaign to buy 'Olympia' culminates in the painting being offered to the State. His motives are threefold: to aid Manet's widow, to win official recognition for Impressionism, and to establish his own position as the leader of the movement.

FEBRUARY

Pissarro shows twenty-five works at Boussod & Valadon, including *The Gleaners* (p.176). The owners of the gallery say they are unhappy with his Pointillist style because 'it frightens the buyers.'

Foundation of the Société Nationale des Beaux-Arts, a splinter group of the Société des Artistes Français (which took over the running of the Salon following the reforms of 1880). Sisley becomes a member of the new society.

7th Monet writes to the Minister of Fine Arts, Armand Fallières, formally offering Manet's *Olympia* to the nation ▲ (p.179) – the fund, which was launched in July 1889, having now almost reached its target of 20,000 francs.

MARCH

The Ministry of Fine Arts buys two etchings by Pissarro.

Cézanne, Pissarro, Seurat and van Gogh feature in the biographical publication *Les Hommes d'aujourd'hui*.

5th An exhibition of the Société des Peintres-Graveurs, including paintings by Pissarro, opens at Durand-Ruel's gallery.

12th In a letter to Monet, Degas agrees to make a belated contribution of 100 francs to the *Olympia* fund.

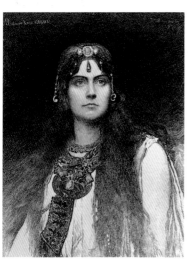

An engraving of Rose Caron ◆ (pp.146–7), Degas' favourite opera singer (1898).

APRIL

14th Renoir marries Aline Charigot ◆ (pp.146–7) at the Town Hall of the 9th arrondissement in Paris.

25th An exhibition of Japanese woodblock prints opens at the École des Beaux-Arts.

MAY

Degas visits Brussels to see his favourite opera singer, Rose Caron ◆ (pp.146–7), in Delibes' *Salammbô*.

Renoir refuses the offer of a decoration from the Government.

Pissarro visits London, where he paints views of Charing Cross Bridge (opposite), Hampton Court Green, Hyde Park and Kensington Gardens.

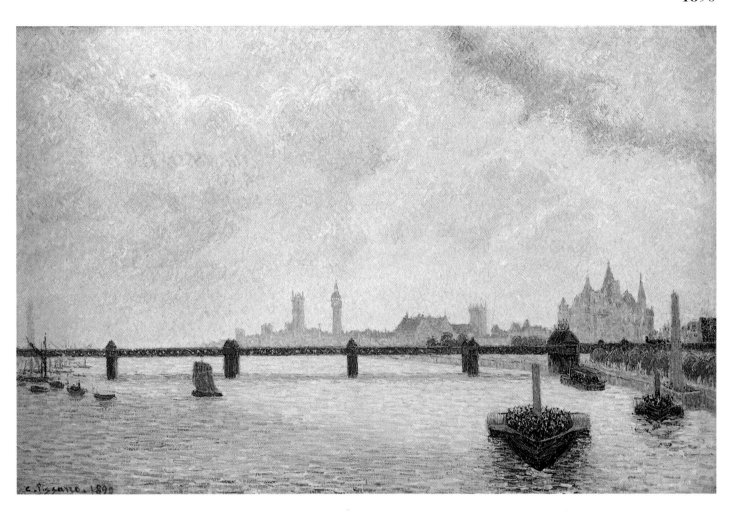

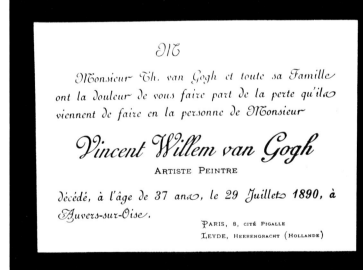

A card from Theo van Gogh announcing Vincent's death on July 29th, 1890.

JUNE

8th Renoir spends at least two weeks at La Rochelle.

28th Publication of the first issue of *The Whirlwind*, a magazine launched by 'The London Impressionists'.

JULY

29th Van Gogh dies in Auvers from a self-inflicted bullet wound (left).

AUGUST

Degas takes the waters at Cauterets in the Pyrenees. At nearby Pau he sees Paul Lafond. He goes on to visit his brother Achille in Geneva.

Monet starts work on his *Haystacks* series ▲ (pp.182–3).

SEPTEMBER

Renoir stays with Berthe Morisot and her family at Mézy.

1st An article by George Moore ◆ (pp.46–7) entitled 'Degas:

**PISSARRO
Charing Cross Bridge,
London**
1890

Painted during Pissarro's visit to London in May with the Neo-Impressionist Maximilien Luce, this view is from Waterloo Bridge. In the centre are the Houses of Parliament, and to the right can be seen Westminster Hall, Westminster Abbey, Whitehall and Cleopatra's Needle. That Pissarro was beginning to abandon Neo-Impressionism when he painted this work is evident from his use of a much fuller brushstroke.

1890

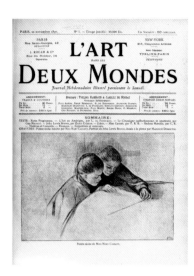

The front cover of the first edition of *L'Art dans les deux mondes*, with an etching by Cassatt, published on November 22nd, 1890.

The Painter of Modern Life', is published in the influential British periodical *The Magazine of Art*. It praises Degas' realism and also mentions his family's financial problems.

26th Degas goes to Burgundy in a tilbury (an open two-wheeled carriage) drawn by a white horse.

OCTOBER

12th Theo van Gogh goes into hospital.

14th Degas breaks with George Moore over the revelations about his family published in *The Magazine of Art* in September. Monet buys the freehold of his house in Giverny and starts replanning the gardens.

NOVEMBER

Lucien Pissarro settles in London.

22nd Durand-Ruel launches a magazine called *L'Art dans les deux mondes* (left), which publishes articles about the Impressionists in order to generate publicity for their work in Europe and the USA. (It only survives until May 1891.)

DECEMBER

6th Téodor de Wyzewa publishes an important essay on Renoir in *L'Art dans les deux mondes* ▲ (pp.177–8).

27th Publication of the last issue of *The Whirlwind* (the magazine of 'The London Impressionists').

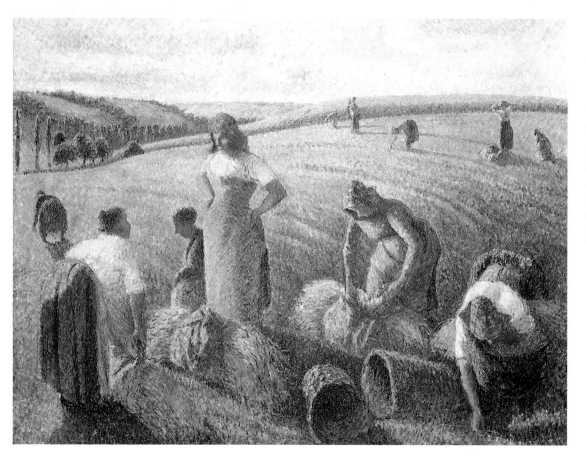

PISSARRO
The Gleaners
1889

This composition was first used by Pissarro for a fan in 1887, the year in which Millet's *The Gleaners* was shown at his retrospective at the École des Beaux-Arts. Painted in a field at Éragny-sur-Epte, Pissarro's version shows a greater realism than Millet's idealized portrayal of life in the fields.

OTHER EVENTS

- Bismarck dismissed by Kaiser
- Cecil Rhodes becomes Premier of Cape Colony
- Queen Wilhelmina accedes to throne of Netherlands
- First Japanese general election

- Right-wing Catholic political party, the Ralliment, formed in France
- Massacre of Sioux by US troops at Wounded Knee
- Daughters of the American Revolution founded in USA
- Emil von Behring discovers anti-toxins for tetanus and diphtheria

- Stage début of Ibsen's *Hedda Gabler*
- Publication of Tolstoy's *The Kreutzer Sonata*, Anatole France's *Thaïs* and Oscar Wilde's *The Picture of Dorian Gray*
- Borodin's *Prince Igor* and Mascagni's *Cavalleria Rusticana* first performed
- César Franck dies

  RENOIR'S 'TWENTY STYLES'

RENOIR
Place Clichy
c.1880

In this painting there is a striking contrast between the highly detailed figure in the foreground and the shimmering secondary figures, which are reminiscent of those in *Dancing at the Moulin de la Galette* (p.105).

Durand-Ruel had never approved of Renoir's 'hard' style ◆ (pp.158–60), and when the dealer commissioned Téodor de Wyzewa – a young Polish-born critic who had been a friend of Renoir's since 1886 – to write an article about the artist (published in *L'Art dans les deux mondes* on December 6th, 1890) it was clearly with the intention of explaining to prospective buyers the artist's various changes of style.

M. Renoir had become famous; of all the Impressionists he was the most delicate, the most feminine, the one in whom we recognized the less praise-worthy of our sensual feelings. And at this point in his career he started to react against this weaker, feminine characteristic of his work. For several years he felt disquiet, and sometimes despair, as he looked at the Old Masters whose dedicated and respectful admirer he had always been. He was searching for a more solid, a more classical way of painting, one which was sufficient unto itself, independently of the sensual charm he was able to add to it. 'The Bathers', which he exhibited at the rue de Sèze in 1887 [at Georges Petit's gallery], will

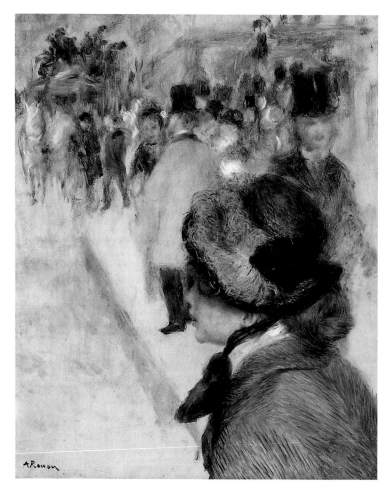

continue to bear witness to those years of quest and hesitation. I cannot forget the quite unearthly emotion aroused in me by this strong but gentle painting, this delicious mixture of looking and dreaming.

The effort of so many years ended in triumph: M. Renoir finally took possession of this pure and perceptive beauty of form, and never lost it. So far, he is the only one amongst us who knows its secret. Some of the portraits, nude studies and heads of children that he painted after his 'Bathers' are works which have all the lifelike qualities of relief, the sobriety and trenchancy of execution of the Old Masters. All he had to do now was to add the apparent grace of his early paintings – ennobled and raised to the level of an art that had by now become completely classical. And it is upon this mingling of life-giving power and grace of expression that M. Renoir has been working ever since. Today each of the pictures he paints represents a particular style, for he has not spent ten years on these patient and varied studies in vain – studies to which none of our young painters has the time or the inclination to devote themselves. He has not stopped being a master for ten

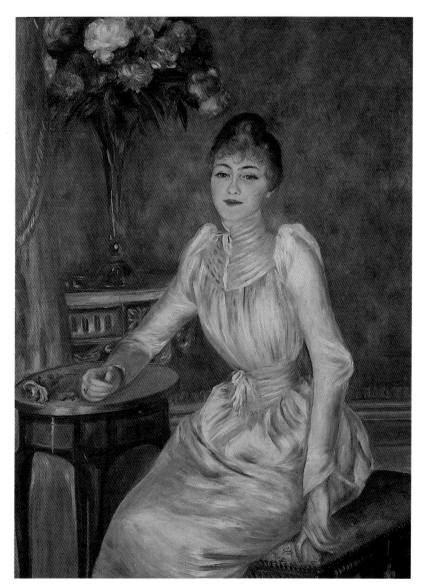

**RENOIR
Portrait of Mme
de Bonnières**
1889

Not content with writing articles in praise of Renoir's work, Téodor de Wyzewa persuaded Robert de Bonnières, a writer for *Le Figaro*, to commission Renoir to paint this portrait of his wife. At the time it was fashionable for women to be pale, and the canvas does give the impression of a woman wearing heavy make-up. Renoir was frustrated by this and later confided in Vollard: 'Just imagine – I come across one of the most charming women it is possible to meet, and she doesn't want to have any colour in her cheeks!'

years to become a pupil once more, without gaining a richness and variety of vision capable of bringing to different subjects the forms appropriate to each of them...

What constitutes the artistic merit of the work of M. Renoir is that beneath his twenty successive styles he has always remained the same, absolutely the same, so that it is enough to have seen one of his early pictures in order to recognize him in his present works. No painter has brought more personal, innate and individual qualities to the service of art.

These innate and individual qualities are, unfortunately, easier to appreciate than to define in words. I believe they may be summed up as an extraordinary feeling for those aspects of nature that are elusive, capricious, feminine. Unknown to himself, M. Renoir brings life to everything he sees, with a characteristic touch of his own that is at once naïve and sophisticated,

agitated and serene. His type of young girl has tried to alter herself, but in all her poses and beneath all her guises we find the same delicious little being, like a cat in a fairy tale, peering sleepily out at the world through strange little eyes, both tender and mischievous. And this expression is not just the result of the form of the body and the facial features. It is to be found in the half-imaginary settings that serve the figures as a background; it may be found even in those simple and powerful landscapes that M. Renoir loves to paint from time to time, knowing, as the Old Masters did, that nothing does more to imbue the eye with a feeling of life. One may recognize M. Renoir's very soul in his painting of flowers – the loveliest flower paintings ever created, marvellously alive, bursting with colour, and ever seductive by virtue of a very feminine intermingling of gentle languor and disturbing capriciousness.

▲ MONET OFFERS 'OLYMPIA' TO THE NATION

Having accumulated 19,415 francs for the purchase of Manet's *Olympia* (p.36) for the nation, on February 7th Monet wrote a letter to Armand Fallières, the Minister of Fine Arts, that reveals the extent to which he was using a basically philanthropic gesture, intended to aid Manet's widow, in order to boost Impressionism and, indirectly, his own standing in the movement.

Monet was clearly apprehensive that the State would accept *Olympia* and then relegate it to some obscure provincial museum. He therefore not only had the letter published in *Le Figaro* but also returned the agreement to the Minister when he discovered that a clause placing the picture in the Luxembourg had been omitted. Eventually *Olympia* was hung in the Luxembourg where it remained for seventeen years, before being moved to the Louvre in 1907.

Cartoon from the magazine *La Vie parisienne* entitled *La Belle Olympia au Louvre*, February 22nd, 1890.

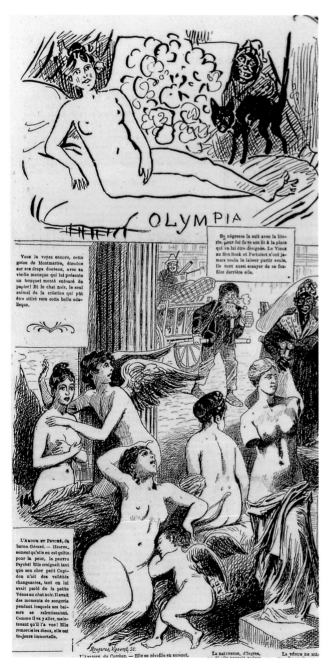

Monsieur le Ministre,

In the name of the group of subscribers below, I have the honour of offering the State 'Olympia' by Édouard Manet.

We come to you as representatives and spokespersons of a large number of artists, writers and art lovers who have recognized for a long time now how considerable a place this painter, prematurely taken from his art and his country, should occupy in the history of this century. The discussions that swirled around Manet's paintings and the hostilities that they provoked have now subsided. The struggle will go on against those people who are less convinced than we of the importance of Manet's œuvre and his definitive triumph. However, we need only recall figures once decried and rejected such as Delacroix, Corot, Courbet and Millet, to cite only a few names who suffered anonymity at the beginning of their careers only to enjoy incontestable posthumous fame, figures who are today celebrities.

But the vast majority of those people who concern themselves with French painting believe that Édouard Manet's role was effective and decisive. Not only did he play a large part individually; he was the representative of a great and rich evolution as well.

It seems to us inconceivable that such a work as the 'Olympia' should not have its place in our national collections; that the master is not represented where his disciples already reside. In addition, we have been concerned about the incessant movement of the market, the extraordinary purchase of works from us by the Americans, the easily predicted departure for another continent of so many works of art that are the joy and glory of France. We have wanted to retain one of Édouard Manet's most characteristic canvases, one in which he appeared victorious in the fight, master of his vision and of his craft.

It is the 'Olympia' that we put back in your hands, Monsieur le Ministre. Our desire to see it take its place in the Louvre, in its time, among the productions of the French school. If regulations bar its immediate entry, if it is objected, despite the precedent of Courbet, that a period of ten years has not elapsed since Manet's death, then we believe the Musée du Luxembourg is perfectly appropriate to receive the 'Olympia' and keep it until the appointed time. We trust that you will want to give your approval to the work with which we are associated, with the satisfaction of having accomplished what is simply an act of justice.

1891

Success of Monet's 'Haystacks'

Monet exhibits fifteen paintings from his 'Haystacks' series at Durand-Ruel's gallery in Paris and the exhibition meets with astonishing success. Within three days of opening all have been sold, but even this triumph does not stop the artist from selling his work privately.

JANUARY

25th Theo van Gogh dies in Utrecht.

FEBRUARY

1st The British art magazine *The Portfolio* publishes an enthusiastic survey of Impressionism by its editor, Philip Hamerton, as part of its series 'The Present State of the Fine Arts in France'.

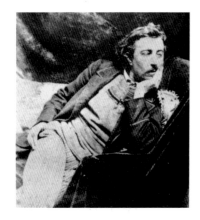

A photograph of Gauguin taken February 13th, 1891.

5th The Renoirs go to stay, until April, with Téodor de Wyzewa ▲ (pp.177–8) and his wife at their house, the Villa des Roses, in Tamaris-sur-Mer.

7th Les Vingt in Brussels ◆ (pp.214–5) shows works by Cézanne, Gauguin, Camille and Lucien Pissarro, Seurat and van Gogh at their annual exhibition.

13th The critic Paul Alexis writes to Zola saying Cézanne has become a fervent Catholic because he is frightened of death and doesn't want to 'run the risk of roasting for all eternity.'

30th Gauguin auctions thirty of his pictures at the Hôtel Drouot ◆ (p.102). All but one are sold, and his target of 10,000 francs for the sale is nearly reached. At the auction Degas buys *La Belle Angèle* for 450 francs and a landscape of Martinique for 260 francs – he later acquires several other works by Gauguin, including the copy Gauguin made of Manet's *Olympia* (p.36).

MARCH

5th The Salon of the Société Nationale des Beaux-Arts (*see* p.174) opens. It includes several works by Sisley (who was to exhibit there regularly).

7th Gauguin visits his wife and family in Copenhagen (it is the last time that he will see them). He returns to Paris a fortnight later.

17th An exhibition described as 'Paintings by the Impressionists of Paris from the galleries of Durand-Ruel, Paris and New York' opens at the Chase Gallery in Boston.

29th Seurat dies of an infection at the age of 32.

31st Gauguin departs for Marseilles by train, en route to Tahiti.

APRIL

Renoir spends the month at Le Lavandou in the south of France.

4th An exhibition of watercolours, pastels and prints by Pissarro and

Cassatt opens at Durand-Ruel's gallery (right).

7th The art patron Victor Chocquet ▲ (p.224) dies at Yvetot in Normandy.

14th Van Gogh's friend Alexander Reid ◆ (p.190) opens a gallery in Glasgow called the Société des Beaux-Arts, dealing in contemporary French paintings. His first exhibition includes works by Degas and van Gogh.

MAY

Publication of the last issue of Durand-Ruel's short-lived magazine *L'Art dans les deux mondes* (*see* p.176).

4th Monet shows fifteen of his *Haystacks* series at Durand-Ruel's gallery ▲ (pp.182–3). The catalogue includes a laudatory preface by the radical journalist and critic Gustave Geffroy. The exhibition is an enormous success, all the paintings being sold within three days of the opening.

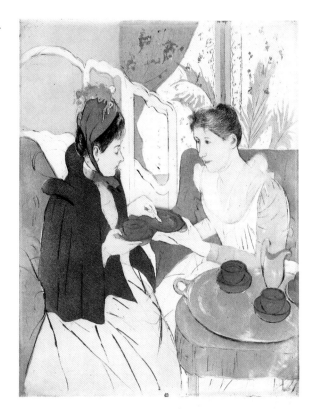

CASSATT
Afternoon Tea Party
1890–1

JULY

1st Durand-Ruel holds an exhibition of recent works by Renoir.

12th Manet and Monet are represented in the Internationale Kunstausstellung in Berlin.

20th Pissarro has an eye operation, after which he does not paint outdoors for some time.

AUGUST

5th Renoir visits Berthe Morisot and her husband, Eugène Manet, at Mézy and introduces them to his wife, Aline ◆ (pp.146–7).

SEPTEMBER

In a letter to his mother, Toulouse-Lautrec mentions that 'Degas has encouraged me by saying my work this summer wasn't too bad.' Renoir spends a week with Caillebotte at the latter's home in Petit-Gennevilliers, near Argenteuil.

DECEMBER

During December and January Degas sees *Sigurd*, a mediocre opera by Reyer, twenty-nine times – as it features Rose Caron (p.174), the singer with whom he is infatuated ◆ (pp.146–7).

1st Alexander Reid's Société des Beaux-Arts holds an exhibition at Mr Collier's Rooms, 39B Old Bond St, London. It includes works by Degas, Monet, Pissarro and Sisley.

3rd Sisley exhibits at Georges Petit's gallery.

5th Monet visits London. He and Degas have works shown at the annual exhibition of the New English Art Club ◆ (p.253).

12th Guillaumin wins 100,000 francs in the Paris city lottery.

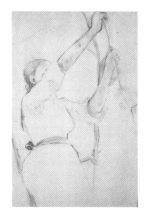

MORISOT
Girl Picking Cherries
1891

Shortly after his visit to Mézy in August, Renoir wrote to Morisot urging her to finish her 'painting with the cherry trees'. He was referring to *The Cherry Tree*, a large painting of Morisot's daughter Julie and her niece Jeanne picking fruit. It was developed from the largest group of preliminary studies Morisot had ever made for a painting, which included this red chalk drawing.

This colour print with drypoint and aquatint ably demonstrates Cassatt's extraordinary skill as a printmaker. In a letter to his son Lucien the day before the joint exhibition of works by Cassatt and Pissarro opened, Pissarro wrote, 'You remember the effects that you strove for in Éragny? Well, Miss Cassatt has realized just such effects and admirably: the matt tone, subtle but delicate, without stains or smudges; adorable blues, fresh rose…The result is admirable, as beautiful as Japanese work.'

OTHER EVENTS

- Triple Alliance between Austria, Germany and Italy renewed for twelve years
- France and Russia form an alliance
- Troops shoot nine French workers during strike for eight-hour day
- General Boulanger commits suicide
- Alexandre and Thadée Natanson launch *La Revue blanche*
- Trans-Siberian railway begun
- Publication of Hardy's *Tess of the D'Urbervilles* and Maurice Barrès' *Le Jardin de Bérénice*
- Mahler composes his First Symphony
- Rimbaud and Delibes die

MONET'S DEALINGS WITH DURAND-RUEL

The first showing of the *Haystacks* series in May 1891 was Monet's most successful exhibition to date, and it confirmed his reputation as the most financially successful of the Impressionists. His correspondence with Durand-Ruel gives an indication of the interplay between artist and dealer that characterized their professional relationship. Monet was anxious to avoid having Durand-Ruel as his sole agent, and wished to continue selling privately and through others.

The following letters were all written from Monet's home in Giverny. In the absence of Paul Durand-Ruel, the letter of June 30th was addressed to the dealer's son Joseph.

February 23rd

Dear M. Durand,

In response to your request that I myself should make a selection of my most recent works and reserve them for you, I must confess frankly that to do so would be most embarrassing for me, as well as involving a matter of some delicacy. I would prefer therefore to wait till it is possible for you to come to Giverny, so that you can make your own choice according to your taste.

I have enough here at the moment to offer you an ample choice, and in case others come here before you I shall arrange not to show them everything.

With my best wishes,
Yours truly,
Claude Monet

April 10th

Dear M. Durand,

Here is my catalogue. I have been tardy in sending it, so will you please make sure that it gets to the printer immediately so that I can correct the proofs straight away?

In haste. See you soon.
Yours sincerely,
Claude Monet

April 13th

Dear M. Durand,

I am a little late in sending you the measurements of the frames...for the pictures I have to deliver to you – the haystacks and others. I shall exhibit twelve, including the one of the haystacks that I delivered to you the other day. There are therefore twelve frames that you must have for May 2nd or 3rd:

6 frames measuring 92 x 65cm, one of them being white
5 frames measuring 1m x 60cm, one of them being white
1 frame measuring 1m x 65cm.

I shall look after the ones that I have – but if I am short, perhaps I can rely on you to supply the difference?

In haste.
With my best wishes,
Claude Monet

April 28th

Dear M. Durand,

I think that by now you will have received my telegram correcting the mistake in my catalogue. As I have told you, I shall have twenty-two pictures to exhibit, including a series of fifteen paintings of haystacks. I hope that by now my friend Geffroy has sent you the text of his preface. In any case, as he is coming here shortly, I shall chivvy him up about it.

I am hoping to come up to Paris myself either on Thursday evening or Friday morning. Could you kindly let me know immediately when the Peintres-Graveurs will have left the gallery reserved for me? And then I would like you to collect the paintings from M. Paul Gallimard and M. G. Clemenceau, 12 rue Clémont-Marot. Get this done on Thursday morning. Have all the frames ready for the same day.

Till we meet.

Yours very sincerely,
Claude Monet

May 8th

Dear M. Durand,

Would you be good enough to let me know how my exhibition is coming on? I have hardly seen any notices about it in the papers – but despite this, I am sure those who are interested in my painting will come to see it anyway.

In the hope of hearing some news from you,
Yours sincerely,
Claude Monet

June 30th

Dear M. Durand,

I shall send to your address tomorrow morning the six paintings that your father bought from me on his last visit. Two of these canvases need a little retouching (they are the haystack ones). Keep the other four, and send me back these two in the same case. I would have liked to have sent them to you today, but it was impossible to get them down to Vernon [the station nearest to Giverny]. *As to what you said to me in your previous letter, I would retort that it is impossible for me to tell people who come to my house that I don't have anything to sell them, no matter whether they are Americans or anyone else. The important thing is that I should not put you at a disadvantage. In fact, you can absolutely rely on the contrary: although collectors hope to buy pictures from me directly on the cheap, I often demand prices higher than those which you charge. Sometimes I sell sketches at a reduced price, but that is to other artists or friends.*

As to commercial prices, you can rest assured that I have always favoured your father, and I am sure that to charge on an agreed scale is the right thing, especially for you, but also for me.

With best wishes,
Claude Monet

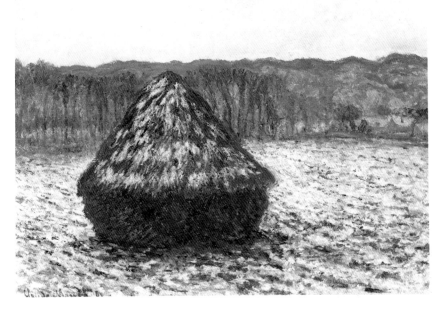

October 19th

Dear M. Durand,

I have constantly been hoping to receive a visit from you, and indeed even yesterday was still expecting you. So I am now writing to you with the request that you should take steps to send me the sum of 20,000 francs, which I need by the 25th of this month in order to complete the purchase of this house. If I can, I shall come and collect the money myself this week, but I cannot be more precise because of the weather – indeed, since your last visit here I have had nothing but problems and difficulties with my poor trees, about which I am not at all happy. However, if I cannot come myself, I shall send my son – or perhaps you yourself could bring me the money next Sunday, which will be the 25th. But in that case, it is essential that I should be absolutely certain [that you will bring it]. *In any event, I expect a word from you to let me know, one way or another, whether I can rely on you.*

I am all the more regretful that you were not able to come before, since M. Valadon [of Boussod & Valadon] *came here three days ago and chose several paintings. But don't be alarmed – there are still plenty left for you, and I put on one side those that you marked as being likely to sell. Finally, I hope that if you have to go away soon you will find time to come here first.*

With all my best wishes,
Claude Monet

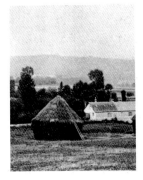

MONET
Haystack in Winter, Giverny
1891

In later years Monet said that the origin of the *Haystacks* series were the rapid changes in atmospheric conditions while he was trying to paint the haystacks behind his house at Giverny, which can be seen in the contemporary photograph (above). Each time the light changed he asked Blanche Hoschedé to fetch him another canvas.

Monet worked on the series from the summer of 1890 to the end of the winter of 1891. Fifteen of the twenty-five canvases were included in Monet's exhibition at Durand-Ruel's gallery in May.

1892

Monet's Series Paintings

While the 'Poplars' paintings are being exhibited at Durand-Ruel's Paris gallery, Monet is hard at work on his 'Rouen Cathedral' series, which – canvas by canvas – shows the building's façade under different effects of light and atmosphere. Meanwhile, the dealer Ambroise Vollard rapidly develops his relationship with the Impressionist artists.

JANUARY

12th Boussod & Valadon purchase their first Renoir, for 600 francs. They also buy three landscapes from Pissarro for 2400 francs, and four from Monet for 3750 francs each.

15th Monet starts work on his *Rouen Cathedral* series ▲ (p.209).

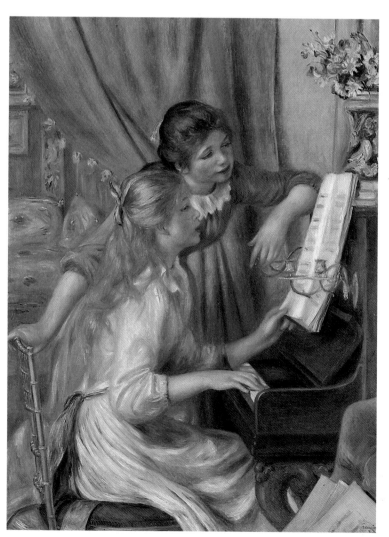

FEBRUARY

5th Pissarro has a one-man exhibition at Durand-Ruel's gallery. The catalogue has an introduction by Georges Lecomte. Seventy-five works are on show, of which Durand-Ruel buys ten.

8th An exhibition of Les Vingt opens in Brussels ◆ (pp.214–5), with works by Cassatt, Pissarro, Signac and Toulouse-Lautrec.

MARCH

3rd Monet exhibits fifteen out of the twenty-three paintings in his *Poplars* series at Durand-Ruel's gallery. They are very well received, by even the more reactionary critics, and he sells some of the paintings to other dealers ▲ (pp.182–3).

APRIL

The State buys Renoir's *Young Girls at the Piano* for the Musée du Luxembourg.

RENOIR
Young Girls at the Piano
1892

Late in 1891 or early in 1892 Renoir was asked informally by the State to paint a work for the Musée du Luxembourg. He took great pains over the commission, producing six large versions – five oils and one pastel. The State chose this version and purchased it for 4000 francs.

The subject of the work was closely related to many of Renoir's recent paintings. He had already depicted two girls at the piano in *The Piano Lesson* (1889), and was generally preoccupied throughout the 1890s with the theme of the innocence and beauty of young people.

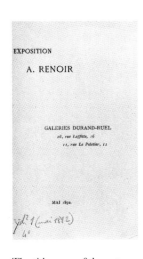

The title page of the catalogue for the Renoir exhibition held at Durand-Ruel's gallery in May 1892.

13th Eugène Manet, brother of the artist and husband of Berthe Morisot, dies.

16th Octave Mirbeau criticizes unfavourably the paintings by Sisley exhibited at the Salon of the Société de Beaux-Arts.

MAY

2nd A Renoir retrospective opens at Durand-Ruel's gallery. The catalogue (left), which lists forty works, includes an introduction by Arsène Alexandre.

4th Berthe Morisot has an exhibition at Boussod & Valadon's gallery (probably arranged by Theo van Gogh before his death). Monet buys one of her works, and the show is a success.

12th Monet marries Alice Hoschedé ◆ (pp.146–7).

23rd Pissarro visits London, where he stays first with his son Lucien, at 7 Colville Square, Bayswater, and then above a bakery in Gloucester Terrace, Kew. He paints several views of the Kew area.

26th Renoir makes a trip to Spain with his friend Paul Gallimard (owner of the Théâtre des Variétés) and is especially impressed by the works of Velázquez in the Prado.

JULY

Renoir and his family visit Brittany, staying till October.

AUGUST

11th Pissarro's son Lucien, who has been living in London since 1890, marries Esther Bensusan in Richmond.

12th Durand-Ruel stages a small Impressionist exhibition in a rented gallery at 13 King Street, St James's, London.

14th Pissarro returns to Éragny and, with 15,000 francs lent to him by Monet, buys the house he had previously rented there.

27th Degas goes to stay with his friends the Valpinçons (below) at Ménil-Hubert, where he paints a number of interiors including two canvases of the billiard room (above).

DEGAS
The Billiard Room at Ménil-Hubert
1892

Throughout his life Degas visited his friends the Valpinçons regularly at their home at Ménil-Hubert. During his stay in August 1892 the artist was interested in different perspectives, and produced a number of interiors of the house, including this one of the billiard room.

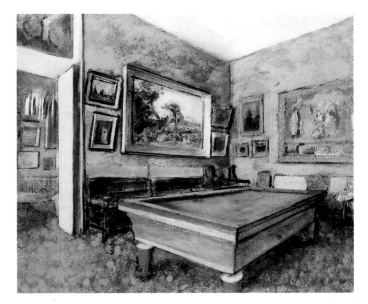

M. and Mme Fourchy (*née* Hortense Valpinçon) and Degas playing charades in front of the Valpinçons' house at Ménil-Hubert.

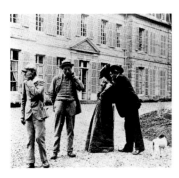
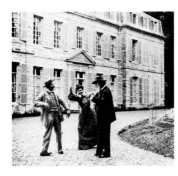
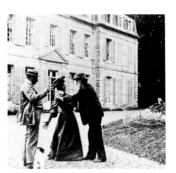
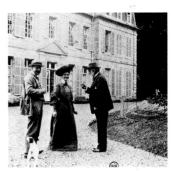

The collection of the actor Coquelin, which includes Impressionist works by Monet and Pissarro, is exhibited at the Barbizon Galleries in Piccadilly, London.

SEPTEMBER

Degas has an exhibition of landscapes at Durand-Ruel's gallery – the first of the only two exhibitions known to have been devoted to Degas' work during his lifetime.

DECEMBER

Renoir paints a portrait of Mallarmé ◆ (pp.220–1).

OTHER EVENTS

- Grover Cleveland elected President of the USA for second time
- Gladstone becomes Prime Minister of Britain for fourth time
- Anarchist bombs explode in the rue de Clichy
- Cholera epidemic in France

- Viscose patented by C. S. Cross; reinforced concrete by François Hennebique; and the Diesel engine by Rudolf Diesel
- Comte de Chardonnet sets up world's first artificial-silk factory in Besançon
- Publication of George and Weedon Grossmith's *The Diary of a Nobody*

- Stage débuts of Ibsen's *The Master Builder*, Maeterlinck's *Pelléas et Mélisande* and Oscar Wilde's *Lady Windermere's Fan*
- Leoncavallo's *I Pagliacci* and Tchaikovsky's *The Nutcracker* first performed
- Ernest Renan, Walt Whitman and Alfred, Lord Tennyson die

 VOLLARD MEETS DEGAS

In 1888 Ambroise Vollard arrived in Paris from the island of Réunion, in the Indian Ocean, and began laying the foundations of his career as one of the most astute art dealers of his generation. The following is an extract from his *Recollections of a Picture Dealer* (1934) – a greatly embellished account of his life.

I got into touch with Degas in this way. I had given the frame-maker Jacquet some planks of foreign wood from the [Universal] Exhibition of 1889. I intended having frames made from them. One day Jacquet said to me, 'You know M. Degas is always scheming out frames. He has seen your wood and told me to ask if you would let him have it.' I replied that I would not take any money for it, but that I would be delighted to accept the smallest sketch. Degas agreed. That was how I made my way into his studio.

When he moved from the rue Ballu to settle into the rue Victor-Massé [in 1890], everything for which there was no room in the new apartment was taken up to the studio. Consequently, the most heterogeneous objects were to be seen there side by side. A bath, little wooden horses, used by the artist in composing his pictures of racecourses that have such marvellous colour and movement. Easels too, with half-finished canvases on them – for after he had started working on an oil painting, he would soon give way to discouragement, not being able to fall back, as he did with his drawings, on tracing after tracing by way of correction.

RENOIR
Portrait of M. Ambroise Vollard
1908

The dealer Ambroise Vollard began to buy work from Renoir soon after they met around 1894, and after 1900 he became one of the artist's three principal dealers (the other two being Durand-Ruel and Bernheim-Jeune). Vollard commissioned many portraits of himself from the artists with whom he dealt, and of these Renoir's version is among the most flattering. He is shown here holding the statuette *Crouching Woman* (1900) by Maillol, who was working on a bust of Renoir at the time.

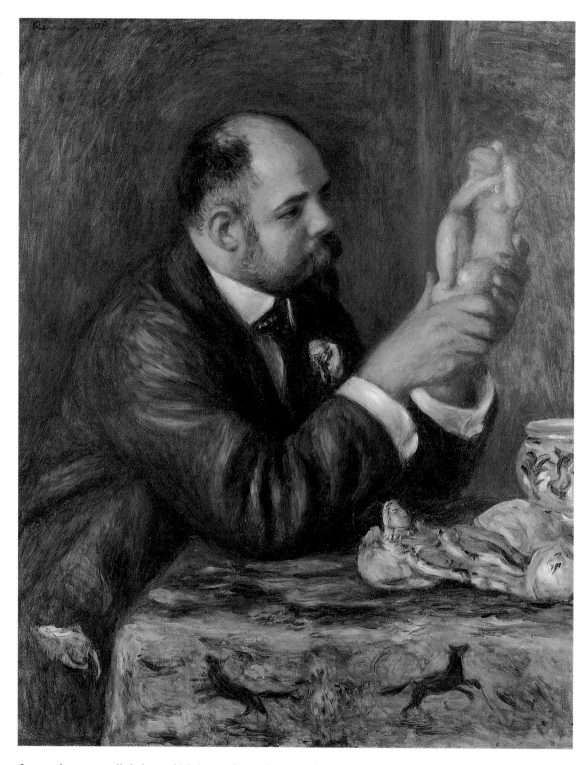

I remember too a tall desk at which he stood to write. Once an object had found its way into his studio, it never left it or changed its position, and gradually it would become covered with a layer of dust that no flick of a feather duster came to disturb. The painter would have been astonished if he had been told that his studio was not perfectly tidy. One day I brought him a picture that he had asked to see. As I undid the parcel, a scrap of paper, no bigger than a piece of confetti, flew out and landed on the floor. Degas pounced on it, exclaiming 'Do be careful, Vollard! You will make my studio untidy.'

1893

Degas' Painting Shocks London

'The Absinthe Drinker' causes a furore when exhibited at the Grafton Galleries in London and is derided for the 'ugly', 'depraved' and 'boozy' appearance of the figures depicted. In France, the Impressionists were drifting apart – physically as well as temperamentally. Sisley had forsworn Paris altogether; Renoir was spending more time in the south; Cézanne had settled permanently in Aix-en-Provence; and Monet's heart was in Giverny, although he visited Paris from time to time.

A cartoon by Draner ridiculing the proliferation of exhibitions. The caption reads: 'Oh, these painters …they have become more stupid than we musicians.'

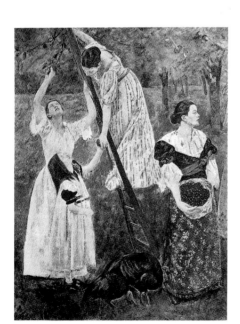

JANUARY

Durand-Ruel has an exhibition of Japanese prints. Mary Cassatt arranges shipment of *The Modern Woman* (below left), a mural specially commissioned for the World's Columbian Exhibition building in Chicago.

FEBRUARY

Ambroise Vollard ▲ (pp.186–7) opens a small gallery in the rue Lafitte, and for his first exhibition presents a selection of Manet pastels.

MARCH

3rd Pissarro has a one-man exhibition at Durand-Ruel's gallery. Forty-one works are on show.
5th Degas' *The Absinthe Drinker* ◆ (pp.190–1) is exhibited at the Grafton Galleries in London. It is attacked for its 'immorality' and defended by George Moore.
7th Sisley has a one-man exhibition at Boussod & Valadon's gallery.

APRIL

Renoir meets Jeanne Baudot (who subsequently becomes a pupil and lifelong friend).
5th Death of Père Tanguy ● (p.192).
An exhibition of the Société des Peintres-Graveurs opens at Durand-Ruel's gallery. Cassatt and Pissarro have a separate exhibition of coloured prints in two small adjoining rooms.
9th Degas, Monet and Morisot exhibit at the New English Art Club in London.

CASSATT
The Modern Woman
1893

In April 1892 Cassatt was engaged to paint a large mural, showing modern women, for the World's Columbian Exhibition. The mural was destroyed after the exhibition, and the detail of the centre section (below left) is a typogravure published in 1893.

PISSARRO
Women Weeding
1893

Since 1886 Pissarro and his son Lucien had been working on a series of prints of aspects of country life – *Travaux des champs*. The six woodcuts were drawn by Camille and engraved and printed by Lucien. *Women Weeding* is one of two multi-coloured prints in the series.

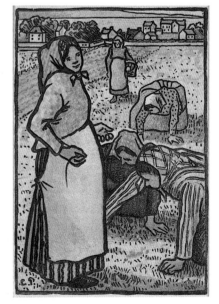

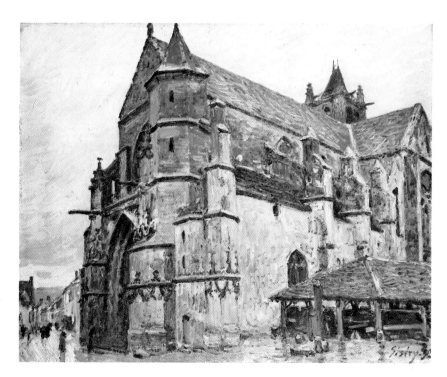

SISLEY
The Church at Moret
Rainy Morning
1893

Sisley painted the church at his home town of Moret-sur-Loing a dozen times between 1893 and 1894 (pp.154–5), producing a series of paintings comparable with Monet's thirty views of *Rouen Cathedral* ▲ (p.209). Like Monet, Sisley attempted to show the changing appearance of the church throughout the day, in different seasons and through a succession of atmospheric changes. (Detail on pp.154–5.)

MAY

1st Pissarro contributes a drawing to a special issue of the magazine *La Plume* devoted to the anarchist movement, which he actively supports.
3rd Durand-Ruel puts on an exhibition of works by Zandomeneghi – largely because he is a friend of Degas.
23rd Degas and Puvis de Chavannes are witnesses at the marriage of Paul Durand-Ruel's daughter Marie-Thérèse.

JULY

15th Pissarro has another operation on his infected eye. (This time it is more successful.)
Sisley begins to paint views of the church at Moret-sur-Loing, where he is living, seen at different times of day and in different light.

AUGUST

Renoir visits Pont-Aven in Brittany for the second time, accompanied by his family. He stays two weeks.
Monet begins to create his water garden at Giverny ▲ (p.193).

NOVEMBER

4th Durand-Ruel holds an exhibition of Gauguin's Tahitian pictures at the instigation of Degas, who buys *The Moon and the Earth*. Renoir expresses his dislike of the exhibition, which has a mixed reception.
Pissarro exhibits fans, engravings and prints at the Arts and Crafts exhibition held at the New Gallery in London.

DECEMBER

Durand-Ruel relieves Pissarro from money troubles by buying a number of his paintings for a total of 23,600 francs.
Mary Cassatt has an exhibition at Durand-Ruel's gallery.

OTHER EVENTS

- Panama Canal corruption trial in Paris; Ferdinand de Lesseps and associates are jailed
- France gains protectorate over Laos

- Hawaii proclaimed a republic
- Edison builds first film studio
- First production of Oscar Wilde's *A Woman of No Importance*
- Publication of Anatole France's *La Rôtisserie de la Reine Pédauque*

- Dvořák's Symphony No.9 ('From the New World'), Tchaikovsky's Symphony No.6 ('Pathétique') and Sibelius' *Karelia Suite* completed
- Verdi's *Falstaff* first performed
- Maupassant and Tchaikovsky die

DEGAS' 'THE ABSINTHE DRINKER'

Between 1875 and 1876 Degas painted a picture which he called *Dans un café*, now known as *The Absinthe Drinker*, showing his friend the actress Ellen Andrée seated at a café table with a glass of absinthe in front of her. Beside her is the engraver Marcellin Desboutin smoking a pipe, with what looks like a glass of tea – or possibly beer – at his elbow, although he was in fact a teetotaller. Degas had intended the painting for the second Impressionist exhibition ■ (pp.96–7), held in April 1876, and included it in the catalogue. He was, however, unable to complete it in time for the exhibition and decided to send it to London, where it was bought by Henry Hill ◆ (pp.76–7), a tailor who lived in Brighton and sometimes described himself as Captain Hill. In September, Hill lent the painting to Brighton Museum, where it was shown in the winter art exhibition under the title *A Sketch in a French Café*. The following year, Degas borrowed it for the third Impressionist exhibition ■ (pp.104–5) and, although it did not feature in the catalogue, it was hung as part of a group of paintings depicting café interiors. After the exhibition, Degas returned it to Hill and it remained in his collection until his death in 1889.

In 1892 the painting was auctioned, along with others from Hill's collection, at Christie's in London – where it was acquired by the Glasgow dealer Alexander Reid for £180, despite being hissed by the audience. A few weeks later he sold it for £200 to Arthur Kay ◆ (pp.76–7), who had been a fellow-student of Roger Fry in Paris, and Kay lent it to the Grafton Galleries for their exhibition in March 1893. There it created a furore among the public and was castigated by the press for its 'immorality' and 'vulgarity'. To the *Westminster Gazette* it was 'a picture of two rather sodden people', and among the disparaging adjectives lavished on it by other periodicals were 'boozy', 'sottish', 'loathsome', 'revolting', 'ugly', 'depraved' and 'repulsive'. The following month Kay sold the picture to the Parisian dealers Martin & Camentron, from whom it was bought by the well-known collector Count Isaac de Camondo for 21,000 francs under the title *L'Apéritif*. On Camondo's death it was left as a bequest to the Louvre, where it was hung in 1911, subsequently being transferred to the Musée d'Orsay, where it now forms part of the museum's formidable collection of Impressionist paintings.

**DEGAS
The Absinthe Drinker**
1875–6

In terms of composition, this is one of Degas' most interesting works, using the 'cut-off' technique derived in equal parts from Japanese prints and the influence of photography. The oblique viewpoint parallels the disorientation of the subjects.

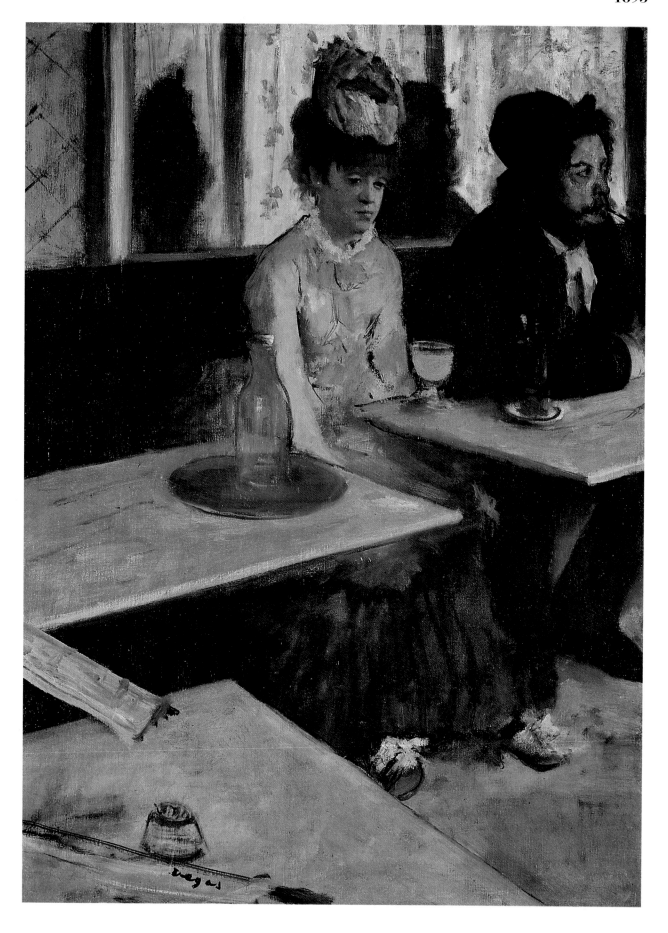

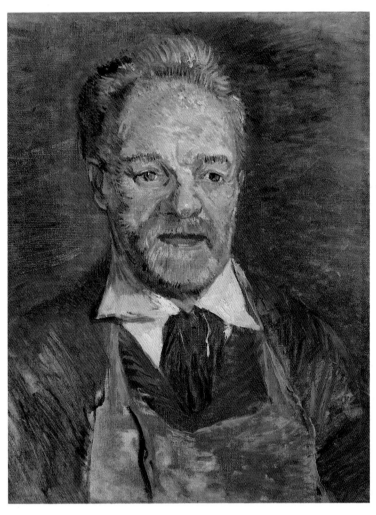

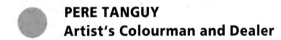

VAN GOGH Le Père Tanguy 1887

PERE TANGUY
Artist's Colourman and Dealer

In 1873, after being imprisoned in Brest as a Communard and released through the intervention of Henri Rouart, Julien Tanguy (1825–93), the artist's colourman who was also a painter and a friend of several of the Impressionists, opened a small shop in the rue Clauzel in Montmartre. This rapidly became one of the most important centres of the Impressionist world, as Tanguy not only took paintings and drawings in exchange for materials but acted as a dealer and patron as well. In this respect he was especially helpful to Cézanne (who in 1885 owed him 4015 francs for materials at a time when Tanguy was facing eviction for non-payment of rent) and to van Gogh, who painted two subsequently famous portraits of him. The prices he paid were necessarily low – at one time Cézanne received only 50 francs per picture from him – but as the painter and critic Émile Bernard recalled, 'People would go there [to Tanguy's shop] as they might to a museum. It had become a Parisian legend, the talk of every studio.'

In an article published in *Atlantic Monthly* in April 1892, the American critic Charles Warren described the wonders of the shop, where he found 'violent or thrilling van Goghs, dusky or heavy Cézannes, daring early Sisleys, all lovingly preserved.' Nor was the owner less remarkable. 'Père Tanguy', he wrote, 'is a short, thickset, elderly man, with a grizzled beard and large beaming dark-blue eyes. He had a curious way of first looking down at his pictures with all the fond love of a mother, and then looking up at you over his glasses, as if begging you to admire his beloved children. I could not help feeling, apart from any opinions of my own, that a movement in art which inspired such devotion must have a deeper final import than the ravings of a mere coterie.'

▲ A VISIT TO GIVERNY

On October 30th 14-year-old Julie Manet and her mother, Berthe Morisot, visited Monet at his house in Giverny and were shown the *Rouen Cathedral* series, on which he was currently working. The following is an account of their visit taken from Julie's diary:

We left early this morning for Giverny. It rained all day. M. Monet showed us his 'cathedrals'. There are twenty-six of them; they're magnificent, some all violet, others white, yellow with a blue sky, pink with a greenish sky; then one in the fog, two or three with shadow at the bottom and lit with rays of sunshine on the towers. These cathedrals are admirably painted in broad areas, and yet one can see every detail. They're so confusing. It seems so hard to me not to draw all the details. These pictures by M. Monet are an admirable lesson in painting. The house has changed since we *last went to Giverny. M. Monet has made himself a bedroom above the studio, with big windows, doors and a floor in pitch pine, decorated in white. In this room lots of paintings are hung, among them Isabelle combing her hair, Gabrielle at the basin, Cocotte with her hat on, a pastel of Maman's, a pastel by Uncle Édouard [Manet], a very attractive nude by M. Renoir, some Pissarros, etc.*

Mme Monet's bedroom has blue panelling, those of Mlles Blanche and Germaine are mauve. We didn't see Mlle Marthe's bedroom. Mlle Blanche showed us some of her own paintings, which have lovely colours; two of them, of trees reflected in the Epte, are very like M. Monet's paintings.

The drawing room is panelled in violet – lots of Japanese prints are hung there, as well as in the dining room, which is all yellow. We walked beneath the poplars to see the greenhouse, where there are magnificent chrysanthemums. Then on to the ornamental lake, across which there is a green bridge that looks rather Japanese. M. and Mme Butler came – their little boy is sweet; he kept on trying to pull my hair (he's six months old).

We came home before dinner, still in the pouring rain, on the new line from Mantes to Argenteuil.

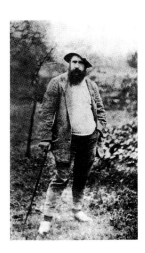

MORISOT
Julie Manet and Jeannie Gobillard Practising
1893

A sketch of Morisot's daughter on violin with her cousin on piano.

Above: A photograph of Monet (*c*.1893) taken by the American painter Theodore Robinson.

Right: This photograph was taken in 1893 during a visit to Giverny by Paul Durand-Ruel (in the bowler hat).

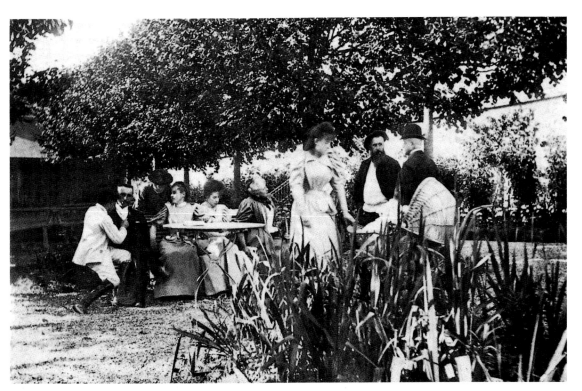

1894

The Caillebotte Bequest

The year is dominated by negotiations over the Caillebotte bequest – which, in retrospect, can be seen as the final acceptance of the status of Impressionism in France. That most of the main figures of the movement are now financially secure is a sign of the increased prestige the Impressionists are beginning to enjoy.

JANUARY

5th Degas buys Gauguin's *Day of the Gods* from Durand-Ruel. Guillaumin has a one-man exhibition at Durand-Ruel's gallery. Several works by Renoir are included in a mixed exhibition at the Grafton Galleries of Bond Street in London.

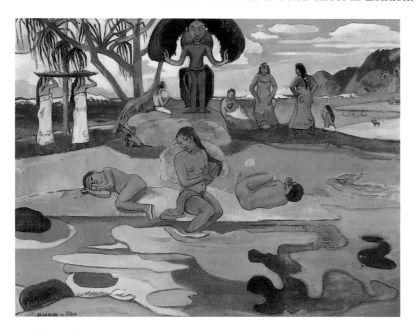

FEBRUARY

15th Morisot, Camille, Georges and Lucien Pissarro, Renoir and Sisley exhibit at the first show of La Libre Esthétique – a new organization headed by Octave Maus which had replaced Les Vingt in 1893 ◆ (pp.214–5).
21st Caillebotte dies at the age of 46.

MARCH

7th Pissarro has a one-man show consisting of ninety-eight works at Durand-Ruel's gallery.

GAUGUIN
Day of the Gods
1894

In this canvas Gauguin drew from native and classical mythology as well as Egyptian tomb paintings to create an extraordinary vision of an imaginary primitive paradise. The painting was purchased by Degas, who was one of the first to recognize Gauguin's genius, calling him 'the collarless wolf'.

11th Renoir writes to Henri Roujon, the Director of Fine Arts, informing him that Caillebotte has bequeathed his collection to the nation ◆ (pp.197–8).
13th Morisot visits Brussels to see her paintings at La Libre Esthétique.
18th Sale at the Hôtel Drouot of the collection belonging to the critic Théodore Duret ▲ (p.199). Monet's *The White Turkeys* (opposite) attracts the highest bid, going for 12,000 francs.
19th Representatives of the Ministry of Fine Arts examine the Caillebotte bequest. The works are temporarily housed in Renoir's studio at 11 boulevard de Clichy, as Caillebotte has named Renoir as his executor ◆ (pp.197–8).

APRIL

25th Degas buys El Greco's *Saint Ildephonsus* from Millet's collection.

MAY

4th The Director of Fine Arts, Henri Roujon, accepts Caillebotte's *The Floor Strippers* (p.96) for the nation.
6th An exhibition of lithographs by Toulouse-Lautrec opens at Durand-Ruel's Paris gallery.

JUNE

2nd Sale of the collection belonging to Père Tanguy ● (p.192) – including six paintings by Cézanne, which fetch between 45 francs and 215 francs each.
3rd Pissarro visits Brussels.
6th A Caillebotte retrospective opens at Durand-Ruel's gallery.
Mary Cassatt buys and renovates the Château de Beaufresne at Mesnil-Théribus, about 80 kilometres (50 miles) northwest of Paris.

AUGUST

Gabrielle Renard – a distant cousin of Renoir's wife, Aline ◆ (pp.146–7) – comes to stay at their house. (She remains with them for twenty years, becoming one of Renoir's favourite models.)
Berthe Morisot paints in Brittany; she invites Renoir to join her, but he is unable to do so.

SEPTEMBER

15th Birth of Renoir's second son, Jean (who would achieve fame as a film director during the 1930s). Durand-Ruel's son Georges agrees to be the godfather.
Cassatt, Cézanne, Rodin and the critic Gustave Geffroy visit Monet in Giverny and stay at the same inn ▲ (p.196).

NOVEMBER

Degas buys two fragments of one of Manet's paintings of the execution of the Emperor Maximilian ◆ (pp.56–9), which had been cut up by Léon Leenhoff ◆ (pp.146–7). (Degas hoped to reconstitute the work and mounted the fragments on a single piece of canvas the size of the painting, having already acquired the third piece.)

DECEMBER

Renoir meets the dealer Ambroise Vollard (p.187) for the first time.

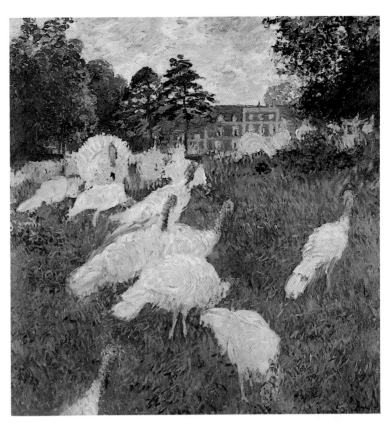

MONET
The White Turkeys
1877

This work was painted for Ernest and Alice Hoschedé ◆ (pp.146–7), and is set in the park of their country estate near Montgeron. Hoschedé lent the painting for the third Impressionist exhibition ▦ (pp.104–5) shortly before he was declared bankrupt in 1878 (*see* p.109). When Hoschedé's collection was consigned for auction, Monet's paintings were fetching an average of 184 francs. *The White Turkeys* was purchased by Duret and was the top lot (selling for 12,000 francs) at the subsequent sale of his collection in March 1894 ▲ (p.199).

d'Orsay

OTHER EVENTS

- Japan declares war on China
- Tsar Alexander III dies and is succeeded by Nicholas II
- French President Sadi Carnot assassinated by Italian anarchist; Jean-Casimir Perier succeeds him
- Anarchist bombings in Paris and elsewhere – thirty anarchists arrested, including Félix Fénéon
- Captain Dreyfus is court-martialled and deported to Devil's Island
- First motor show held at Palais de l'Industrie in Paris
- First bottles of Coca Cola produced
- First production of G. B. Shaw's *Arms and the Man*
- Publication of George Du Maurier's *Trilby*, George Moore's *Esther Waters*, Anthony Hope's *The Prisoner of Zenda* and Rudyard Kipling's *The Jungle Book*
- Debussy composes *L'Après-midi d'un faune*
- Robert Louis Stevenson and Oliver Wendell Holmes die

CASSATT ON CÉZANNE'S TABLE MANNERS

In the autumn of 1894 Mary Cassatt, Cézanne, Rodin and the journalist Gustave Geffroy visited Monet in Giverny. Cassatt, who was staying at the same inn as Cézanne, was fascinated by his personality and behaviour, which she described in a letter:

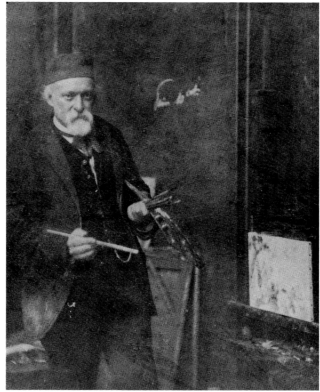

A photograph taken around 1894 of Cézanne working in his studio.

When I first saw him, he looked like a cut-throat, with large red eyebrows standing out from his head in a most ferocious manner, a rather fierce-looking, pointed beard, quite grey, and an excited way of talking that positively makes the dishes rattle. I found later on that I had misjudged his appearance, for far from being fierce or a cutthroat, he has the gentlest nature possible – 'comme un enfant', as he would say. His manners at first rather startled me – he scrapes his soup plate, he then lifts it and pours the remaining drops into his spoon; he even takes his chop in his fingers and pulls the remaining meat from the bone. He eats with his knife, and accompanies every gesture, every movement of his hand with that implement, which he grasps firmly when he commences his meal and never puts down till he leaves the table. Yet in spite of the total disregard of the dictionary of manners, he shows a politeness towards us that no other man here would have shown. He will not allow Louis to serve him before us in the usual order of succession at the table; he is even deferential to that stupid maid, and when he enters the room pulls off the old tam-o'-shanter that he wears to protect his bald head. I am gradually learning that appearances are not to be relied on here.

The conversation at lunch and dinner is mainly on art and cooking. Cézanne is one of the most liberal artists I have ever met. He prefaces every remark with 'pour moi' it is so and so, but he grants that everyone may be just as faithful to nature from their own convictions. He doesn't believe that everybody should see alike.

196

◆ THE CAILLEBOTTE CONTROVERSY

Caillebotte's generosity towards his fellow artists, as well as his innate artistic discrimination, were responsible for his accumulating a formidable collection of Impressionist works, which eventually consisted of nineteen Pissarros, fourteen Monets, ten Renoirs, nine Sisleys, seven Degas, five Cézannes and four Manets. By his will, originally drawn up in 1876, when he was twenty-eight, and subsequently modified and made more explicit, he left his collection to the French nation on condition that 'it should go neither to an attic, nor a provincial museum, but straight to the Luxembourg [the museum devoted to the work of living artists] and later to the Louvre.' The terms of Caillebotte's bequest showed shrewdness and foresight. 'It is necessary,' he stated, 'that a certain time goes by before this clause can be put into effect and until the public may, I don't say understand, but accept this painting. This time could be twenty years or more; in the meantime my brother Martial, or failing him, another of my heirs, will keep them. I ask Renoir to be my executor and would like him to accept a picture that he may choose. My heirs will insist that he takes an important one.'

On March 11th, 1894, Renoir wrote to Henri Roujon, the Director of Fine Arts, informing him of the bequest – but problems arose immediately. There was vehement opposition from artists who were officials of the Salon – the sculptor and painter Jean-Léon Gérôme, for instance, objecting that if works by Manet and Pissarro were accepted by the State it would be a sign of 'moral turpitude' and would signify the end of the nation. There was also opposition from the bureaucrats, including Roujon and the Director of the Luxembourg, partly on practical grounds. The museum, they argued, did not have space to hang the

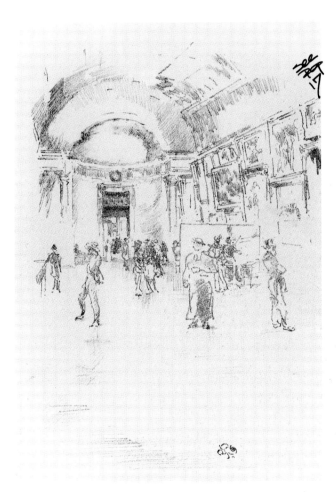

A lithograph of *The Long Gallery in the Louvre* (1894) by Whistler, reproduced in the magazine *The Studio*.

collection, and some artists (such as Monet and Pissarro) would be heavily over-represented.

On March 24th the bequest was considered by the Comité Consultatif des Musées Nationaux, which decided that it should be accepted in its entirety 'for the national museums with placement in the Luxembourg.' But what the representatives of the State clearly wanted was first of all to get hold of the collection – and then decide what *they* would do with it. Reinforced by legal advice, Renoir and Martial Caillebotte (the late artist's brother) insisted, however, that all the provisions of the will had to be carried out. By way of compromise, the

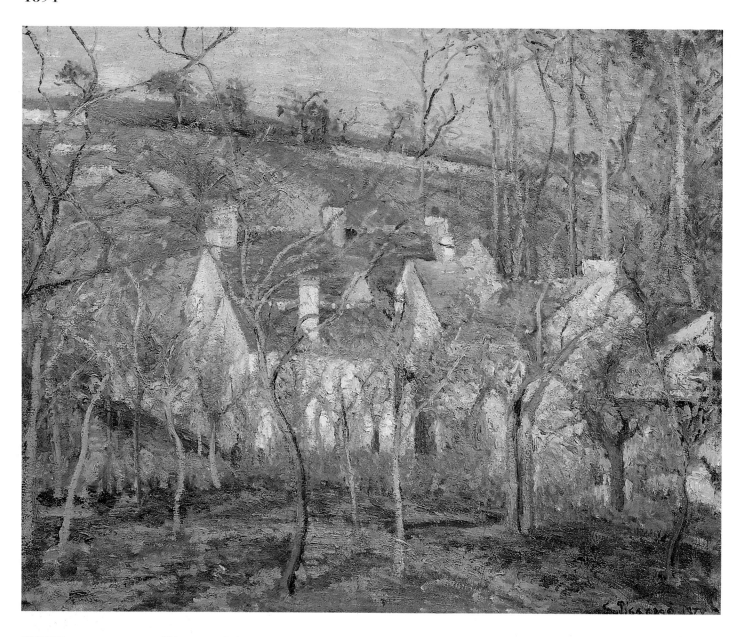

PISSARRO
The Red Roofs: Corner of the Village, Winter Effect
1877

Of the eighteen works that Caillebotte bought from Pissarro, seven – including this one of farm buildings near Pontoise – were accepted by the State.

Director of the Louvre, Léonce Bénédite, suggested that he should hang as many works as he could and assign the rest to museums at Fontainebleau and Compiègne. This was rejected by Renoir and Martial Caillebotte. Eventually, in January 1895 it was agreed that the Musée du Luxembourg should accept only those pictures which it could hang, the number finally agreed on being thirty-eight. In the autumn of 1895 the Conseil d'État gave its stamp of approval, and the final decree accepting the bequest was signed in February 1896. The remaining twenty-nine pictures were left in the hands of Martial Caillebotte, who reoffered them to the government, again unsuccessfully, in 1904 and 1908. Ironically, when in 1928 the government at last expressed a desire to have them, Martial Caillebotte's widow repudiated the terms of the bequest. Meanwhile, the whole saga had become a *cause célèbre* illustrative of the tribulations and vicissitudes of modern art.

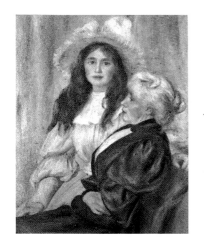

THE DURET SALE

On March 18th a large number of Impressionist paintings owned by the critic Théodore Duret were auctioned at the Hôtel Drouot ◆ (p.102), fetching a record price of 160,000 francs. Author of *Les Peintres impressionnistes* and *Critique de l'avant-garde* ▲ (p.145), published in 1878 and 1885 respectively, Duret was a loyal supporter and patron of the Impressionists – but faced with severe losses due to the failure of the 1893 grape harvest, he was forced to sell the greater part of his collection. On March 17th Julie Manet – the 15-year-old daughter of Berthe Morisot and Manet's brother Eugène – went to see the pictures and wrote the following account in her diary:

The collection includes one of Maman's paintings – of a woman in a low-cut white dress, on which is a garland of glorious white flowers (right); several of Uncle Édouard's large canvases; 'Repose' (p.78), a portrait of Maman, dressed in white on a red sofa, with one foot stretched out; 'Le Père Lathuille' (p.117); and a small portrait of Maman in three-quarter profile, dressed in black with a bouquet of violets and wearing a small hat. I adore this portrait – the brushwork is so good, and the blacks are quite magnificent, as are the whites in the other portrait. What wonderful brushwork Uncle Édouard had!

There is also a very attractive picture by M. Monet in the collection, of some white turkeys on a great lawn and beyond them a castle made of brick, surrounded by pine trees (p.195). As for M. Renoir's paintings, they're really lovely – one landscape, and one picture of a nude combing her hair; the head, which is slightly foreshortened, is delightful, and the whole picture is painted in very attractive, pleasant colours.

The one painter whom I like very much, from what I have seen of his here, is Cézanne; above all it's his well-modelled apples that I like (I only know these three paintings by him). I almost forgot to mention that there's an unfinished painting of Albert Wolff by Uncle Édouard, a wonderful portrait such as only Manet could have painted, which must be an extremely good likeness. Looking at this portrait, one has to say 'what a marvellous thing' – especially considering how stupid and ugly the sitter is! Also in the collection are some of M. Degas' racehorses, and some of the beautifully drawn dancers of this great master.

RENOIR
Berthe Morisot and her Daughter, Julie Manet
1894

A few weeks after the Duret sale Morisot and her daughter Julie posed for this double portrait. Renoir was an intimate friend of the family, and helped to look after Julie following her mother's death in 1895.

MORISOT
Young Woman in a Ball Gown
c.1876

The significance of the large body of works donated to the State by Caillebotte ◆ (pp.197–8) was obvious to Mallarmé ◆ (pp.220–1), who also realized that as Morisot was not represented in the collection, her key role in the movement might be overlooked. He therefore persuaded the Ministry of Fine Arts to buy this painting at the Duret sale.

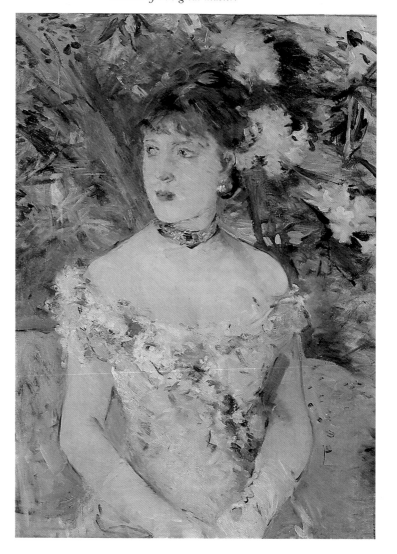

1895

Monet Triumphant

Monet enjoys an extremely successful and prolific trip to Norway, producing some twenty-six paintings, including several of Mount Kolsaas. On his return, he has fifty paintings from various series exhibited at Durand-Ruel's Paris gallery. As with the 'Haystacks' exhibition of 1891, the critical response is rapturous.

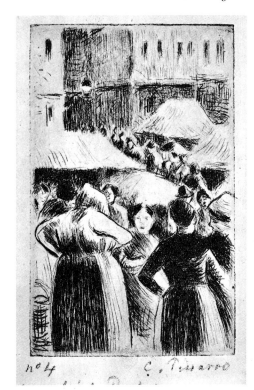

PISSARRO
Market at Pontoise
1895

Pissarro frequented the marketplaces of Gisors and Pontoise, even after he had moved to Éragny-sur-Epte in 1884, and produced market scenes in a variety of media.

JANUARY

Monet goes to Christiania (now Oslo) in Norway to visit his stepson Jacques Hoschedé, taking with him one of the paintings of Rouen cathedral on which he is still working. He stays at Sandviken, about 20 kilometres (twelve miles) from Christiania, and paints some twenty-six views of the village and surrounding countryside – including nearby Mount Kolsaas in different atmospheric conditions ▲ (p.203).

12th Renoir visits the home of his pupil Jeanne Baudot and her parents in Carry-le-Rouet, near Martigues.

FEBRUARY

7th Pissarro exhibits with La Libre Esthétique ◆ (pp.214–5) in Brussels.

24th In a letter to his son Lucien, Pissarro bemoans his lack of success: 'They say there is no money around, which is only comparatively true. Monet sells, doesn't he? And gets high prices. Renoir and Degas sell, don't they? No, I remain in the same boat as Sisley, bringing up the rear of Impressionism.'

MARCH

3rd Berthe Morisot (right) dies of pneumonia at the age of 54. In her last letter to her daughter, Julie Manet, she bequeaths paintings to Degas, Monet and Renoir.

7th An exhibition of works by Manet opens at Durand-Ruel's New York gallery.

12th Gauguin sails for Tahiti.

A photograph of Berthe Morisot (1894), taken the year before her death.

APRIL

3rd Monet returns to Giverny from Norway ▲ (p.203) and, together with Durand-Ruel, starts organizing a major exhibition of his work.

16th Cassatt has an exhibition at Durand-Ruel's gallery in New York (right), consisting partly of items from the exhibition held at his Paris gallery in 1893 and partly of new work.

25th–26th The American Art Association in New York holds a sale of works by Degas, Guillaumin, Monet, Pissarro, Renoir and Sisley on behalf of the American dealer and collector James F. Sutton.

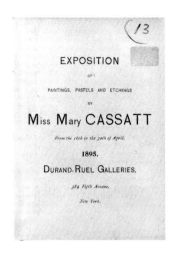

EXPOSITION
OF
PAINTINGS, PASTELS AND ETCHINGS
BY
Miss Mary CASSATT
From the 16th to the 30th of April,
1895.
DURAND-RUEL GALLERIES,
389 Fifth Avenue,
New York.

The title page of the catalogue of Mary Cassatt's exhibition at Durand-Ruel's gallery in New York.

MAY

Pissarro helps the anarchist paper *Les Temps nouveaux* by contributing money and drawings.

9th Monet's exhibition opens at Durand-Ruel's gallery. Fifty paintings are on show, including the *Rouen Cathedral* series ▲ (p.209), priced 12,000 francs each; several views of Vernon (near Giverny); thirteen of Mount Kolsaas (p.203); one work from the *Haystack* series ▲ (pp.182–3); one from the *Poplars* series; two *Ice Floe* paintings (p.118); and several of the Dutch tulip fields (from 1886). The exhibition is a huge success. The critic Camille Mauclair asserts that Monet is 'the most prodigious virtuoso that France has seen since Manet'; and Clemenceau ▲ (p.209) declares that Monet has 'made the stones themselves live.'

12th Murer puts on an exhibition of works by Monet, Pissarro, Renoir and Sisley at his hotel in Rouen.

JUNE

15th Degas purchases Delacroix's portrait of Baron Schwitter (now in the National Gallery, London) from the dealer Michel Montaignore in exchange for three of his own pastels valued at 12,000 francs.

JULY

3rd Renoir spends a week in La Roche-Guyon. He visits Monet at Giverny, which is nearby, and receives a visit from Cézanne.

AUGUST

8th The Renoir family visit Brittany and stop in Pont-Aven, where they entertain Morisot's daughter Julie and her cousins Jeanne and Paule Gobillard (the children of her sister Yves, who had died in 1883).

11th Degas, who has become an obsessive photographer ▲ (p.204), starts employing the colour merchant and framer Tasset to develop and enlarge his prints.

SEPTEMBER

Monet, Pissarro and Sisley exhibit at the Ghent Triennale in Belgium.

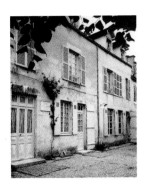

A photograph of the house Renoir somewhat reluctantly bought in Essoyes, the home village of his wife, Aline ◆ (pp.146–7), to which he later added a studio.

RENOIR
Gabrielle and Jean
1895

The birth of Renoir's second son, Jean, in 1894 resulted in Mme Renoir's distant cousin, Gabrielle Renard, being invited to stay with the family as nursemaid. She remained for the next twenty years and became Renoir's favourite model.

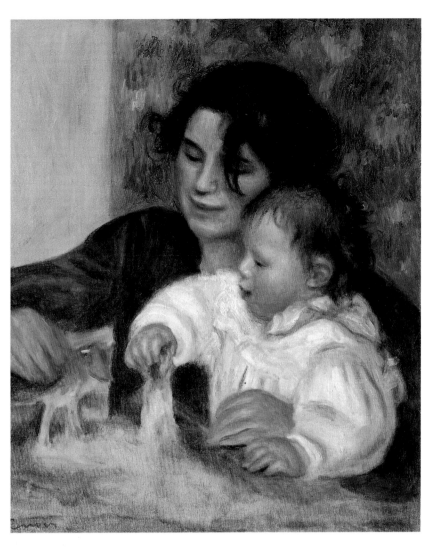

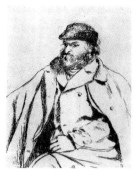

This etched *Portrait of Paul Cézanne* (1874) by Pissarro was reproduced in the catalogue of Cézanne's exhibition, held at Vollard's gallery in November.

NOVEMBER
Degas works on a bust of his friend the artist Federico Zandomeneghi.
7th Vollard exhibits Cézanne's paintings ▲ (p.205) at his gallery in the rue Lafitte, establishing his reputation as a dealer in avant-garde art.
24th Works by Monet and Sisley are shown at the annual exhibition of the Carnegie Institute in Pittsburgh.
29th Julie Manet buys an early Cézanne, *The Assassination*, from his exhibition at Vollard's gallery.

DECEMBER
Renoir buys a house in Essoyes (above left).

OTHER EVENTS

- China loses war with Japan
- First road race for petrol-driven cars, between Paris and Bordeaux
- Oscar Wilde loses libel suit against Marquess of Queensbury
- Röntgen discovers X-rays
- Lumière brothers develop a motion-picture camera
- Publication of Freud's *Studies in Hysteria*, H. G. Wells' *The Time Machine* and the last volume of Marx's *Das Kapital*
- Engels, Dumas *fils* and Pasteur, die

▲ **MONET IN NORWAY**

MONET
Mount Kolsaas
1895

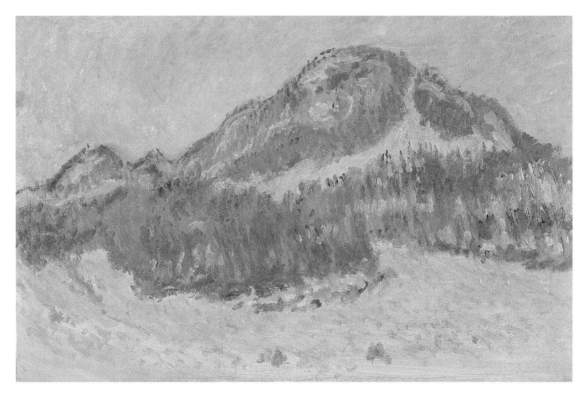

Monet's trip to Norway was primarily to see his stepson Jacques. While there, however, he produced twenty-six landscapes, thirteen of which were views of Mount Kolsaas. The artist found the countryside 'very difficult to understand', feeling that 'one needed to live here for a year to do anything good.' He also complained about the weather's variability. Almost all of the Mount Kolsaas canvases are painted from the same viewpoint, and are the same size.

Monet's fame had preceded him before his arrival in Norway, and on April 6th, shortly before his departure, a national newspaper, the *Bergens Tiede*, published an article about him by a young poet, Henri Bang:

After tea, when Claude Monet was sitting in the corner of the sofa, looking rather like a peasant after a long day's work, the conversation turned to interviews, writers and reporters, and this led Monet to say: 'Anyway what do you want? What can be said about me? What indeed can be said about a man who is interested in nothing but his painting? It's a pity if a man can only interest himself in one thing. But I can't do anything else. I only have one interest. Work is nearly always a torture. If I could find something else I would be much happier, because I could use this other interest as a form of relaxation. Now I cannot relax. Colours pursue me like a constant worry. They even trouble me in my sleep.'

One evening when he came back after ten hours of work in the bitterly cold Norwegian air, watching the sun and the colours of the landscape, this 60-year-old man said: 'No, it was no real hardship. And anyway, what else could I have expected? I am chasing a dream. I want the unobtainable. Other artists paint a bridge, a house, a boat, and that's the end. They've finished. I want to paint the air which surrounds the bridge, the house, the boat, the beauty of the air in which these objects are located, and that is nothing short of impossible. If only I could satisfy myself with what is possible!'

Monet has twelve or thirteen canvases which he is working on at different times, and each moment of the day has its own canvas. At each time of day he goes to work on the canvas connected with it, so as to find, as closely as possible, the same light which has the same beauty, and perhaps only to work on that part of each which his eye sees and his spirit understands at that particular moment. But nature mocks his art, and his dream fades as his hands cannot express what he wants them to. There are days when, in a blind rage, furious with himself and with the ineffectiveness of his colours, he tears his canvas in pieces and treads it into the snow. 'Ah,' he says, 'how often when I was working in Le Havre have I thrown my colour box into the sea, and been forced the next morning to telegraph to Paris for a new one – because you always have to start again.'

DEGAS' PHOTOGRAPHY

In October 1895 Julie Manet noted in her diary: 'Monsieur Degas can think of nothing but photography. He's invited us all to have dinner with him next week, and he's going to take us all by artificial light'. Although all the Impressionists were influenced by the camera, Degas was especially sensitive to its impact and particularly intrigued by Eadweard Muybridge's photographs of horses in motion ◆ (p.160).

But it was not until 1895 – curiously enough at a moment in his career when he had virtually given up painting the portraits which had constituted a major part of his earlier output – that he began using the camera as a creative tool. Although glass plates were now giving way to celluloid roll film and he himself bought one of the new Eastman-Kodak cameras in 1896,

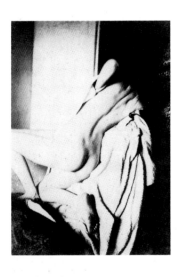

nevertheless, whenever possible, Degas persisted in using the older technique, for which a tripod was essential. Moreover, he always took his photographs at night – explaining to his friend Daniel Halévy that 'Daylight is too harsh, what I need is the light of lamps, or of the moon.' In fact, the effect he constantly strove to achieve was that of the calotypes (the process invented by Fox Talbot) of the 1840s and 1850s. The most impressive of Degas' photographs were the ones he took of the Halévy family ▲ (p.208), and Daniel gave this account of a photographic session at the house of his uncle Jules Tascherau on December 29th, 1895:

The social part of the evening having concluded, Degas, his voice having assumed an authoritarian tone, ordered that a lamp should be brought into the small drawing room and that anybody who was not going to pose should leave…One had to obey Degas' fierce will; his artist's ferocity. At moments like this all his friends always spoke of him with absolute terror. If you invite him for the evening, you know what to expect – two hours of military obedience.

Despite the command that anyone who was not going to pose should leave, I sneaked into the room and, silent in the shadow, I watched Degas. He had seated Uncle Jules, Mathilde and Henriette on the little sofa in front of the piano. He walked up and down in front of them, running from one side of the room to the other with a look of infinite happiness. He moved the lamps, changed the reflectors, and tried to light their legs by putting a lamp on the floor – so as to catch Uncle Jules' legs, the most slender and agile in the whole of Paris, about which Degas always spoke ecstatically.

'Tascherau,' he said, 'get hold of that leg for me with your right arm, and pull it in towards you – like that – then look at the young person beside you. More affectionately! Come on, come on. You can smile so nicely when you want to. And you, Mlle Henriette, bend your head – more, go on, still more. Really bend it, rest it on your neighbour's shoulder.' And when she didn't do it properly, he got hold of her by the nape of her neck and posed her as he wanted. He then got hold of Mathilde and turned her face towards her uncle. Then he stepped back, and happily exclaimed 'That's it!'

The pose was held for two minutes, and then repeated. We shall see the photographs tonight or tomorrow night. He is coming to show them to us – he seems so happy about the whole thing.'

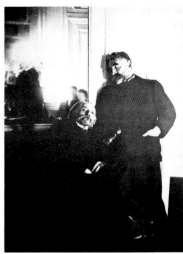

A photograph by Degas showing Renoir (left) and Mallarmé (right).

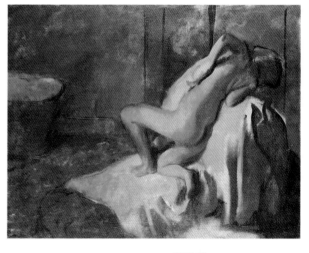

DEGAS
After the Bath
1896

Recently a bromide photograph (left) was discovered which is clearly related to three paintings Degas produced in 1896, all entitled *After the Bath*. This one is painted so thinly that bare canvas can be seen in places, and it contains only four colours, leading to a debate as to whether it is a sketch or finished work.

▲ **PISSARRO ON CÉZANNE**

CÉZANNE
Bathers
1875–6

Cézanne often recalled days of his childhood spent with Zola and other friends, swimming, playing, talking and reciting verses on the river bank, and throughout his life he returned to the theme of *Bathers*. This painting was once in the collection of Victor Chocquet ▲ (p.224).

After viewing Cézanne's one-man exhibition, Pissarro pondered about the qualities of Cézanne's paintings, and on November 20th aired his thoughts in a letter to his son Lucien:

I have been thinking about Cézanne's show, in which there were exquisite things, still lifes of irreproachable perfection, others much worked on, and yet unfinished, of even greater beauty, landscapes, nudes and heads that are unfinished, but yet grandiose and so painted, so supple. Why? Sensation is there ...

Curiously enough, while I was admiring this strange, disconcerting aspect of Cézanne's work, familiar to me for many years, Renoir arrived. And my enthusiasm was nothing compared to his. Degas himself is seduced by the charms of this refined savage. Monet, all of us, are we mistaken? I don't think so. The only ones who are not subject to Cézanne's charm are those artists and collectors who have shown by their errors of judgment that their sensibilities are defective. They properly point out the faults that we all see, but are oblivious to the charm. As Renoir put it so well, these paintings have an indefinable quality – like the murals at Pompeii, so crude and so admirable. Nothing of the Académie Julian! I exchanged a small sketch of Louveciennes for an admirable small canvas of bathers and one of his self-portraits.

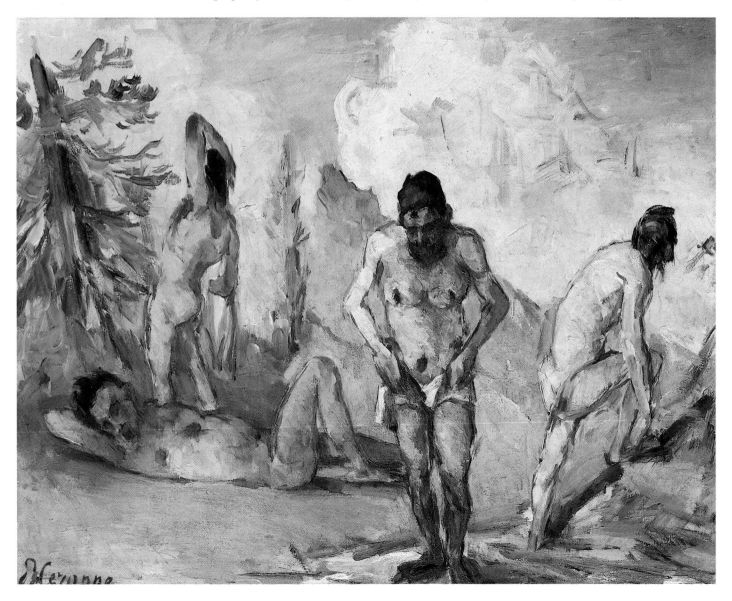

1896

Morisot's Retrospective

In memory of Berthe Morisot, who had died the previous year, the Impressionists organize a retrospective exhibition at Durand-Ruel's Paris gallery. Degas, Monet and Renoir hang her canvases, which, with their vibrant colour, loose brushwork and attractive subjects, are widely admired. The show is a considerable success.

JANUARY

1st Degas ▲ (p.204) has an exhibition of photographs at the premises of Tasset, the frame-maker who develops and enlarges his prints.

5th Pissarro goes to paint in Rouen, where he remains till March.

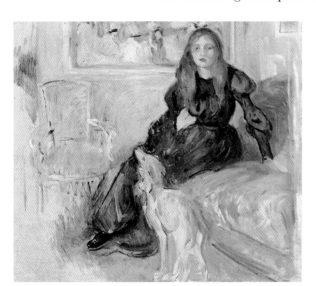

MORISOT
Girl with a Greyhound
(Julie Manet)
1893

Included in Morisot's retrospective exhibtion in March, this portrait of her daughter and greyhound Laërtes (a present from Mallarmé) was described by Julie Manet in her diary: 'It shows me in the rue Weber drawing room, in front of a Japanese print, leaning slightly towards Laërtes, in front of me.'

23rd Durand-Ruel buys Ingres' portraits of Jacques-Louis Leblanc and his wife for Degas at a public auction, paying 11,000 francs. At about the same time, Degas – who is intent on building up his personal collection – purchases two paintings by Cézanne, *Three Pears* and *Green, Yellow and Red Apples,* from Vollard.

FEBRUARY

4th Monet goes to Pourville-sur-Mer, near Dieppe, where he paints a number of seascapes.

20th Monet has several works included in an exhibition at Glasgow Institute.

MARCH

2nd–4th Degas, Monet and Renoir hang a retrospective exhibition of Morisot's works at Durand-Ruel's gallery.

5th Opening of the Morisot retrospective. It is favourable received both by the public and the press.

14th Hugo von Tschudi ◆ (pp.214–5), the newly appointed Director of the Nationalgalerie in Berlin, acquires Manet's *In the Conservatory* (p.114) for the gallery.

APRIL

15th Pissarro has a one-man exhibition at Durand-Ruel's gallery. 'All my artist friends', he writes to his son Lucien, 'say the exhibition is very

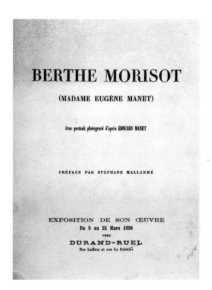

BERTHE MORISOT

(MADAME EUGÈNE MANET)

Avec portrait photogravé d'après ÉDOUARD MANET

PRÉFACE PAR STÉPHANE MALLARMÉ

EXPOSITION DE SON ŒUVRE
Du 5 au 21 Mars 1896
CHEZ
DURAND-RUEL
Rue Laffitte et rue Le Peletier

The title page from the retrospective exhibition of Morisot's works at Durand-Ruel's gallery, which ran from March 5th to 21st.

beautiful.' Durand-Ruel buys eleven of the pictures for 14,000 francs. (As a consequence, Pissarro is able to repay the balance of the money lent to him by Monet for the purchase of his house in Éragny.)

MAY

2nd Murer holds an exhibition of works by Guillaumin, Monet, Pissarro, Renoir and Sisley at his Hôtel du Dauphin et d'Espagne in Rouen. It includes thirty works by Renoir.
6th Renoir has a one-man exhibition of forty-two works at Durand-Ruel's gallery.

JUNE

15th *La Revue blanche* – the mouthpiece of the Symbolist movement, founded by the Natanson brothers in 1891 – publishes a laudatory article on Renoir by Thadée Natanson.

JULY

15th Renoir makes a trip to Germany with Caillebotte's brother Martial. They see a Wagner opera at Bayreuth, which Renoir finds immensely boring. Later in the month they go to Dresden, where they visit the museums.

SEPTEMBER

4th Pissarro goes to paint in Rouen again.

OCTOBER

Renoir rents a studio in the rue de la Rochefoucauld.

NOVEMBER

4th Degas buys El Greco's *Saint Dominic* for 3000 francs from the writer Zacharie Astruc ● (p.37).
5th Five works by Degas are included in the annual exhibition at the Carnegie Institute in Pittsburgh (probably through the influence of Cassatt.)
11th Pissarro has another eye operation.
21st Renoir's mother dies in Louveciennes at the age of 89.

RENOIR
The Apple Seller
c.1890

Exhibited at Durand-Ruel's gallery in May, *The Apple Seller* is an idyllic representation of rural life, reminiscent of an eighteenth-century French landscape. The seated woman is possibly the artist's wife, Aline.

PISSARRO
The Rooftops of Old Rouen, Grey Weather (the Cathedral)
1896

Painted during Pissarro's visit to Rouen at the beginning of the year, the viewpoint of this work is from the Hôtel de Paris, looking over the old section of the city. The artist treated the subject in a totally modern way, using a remarkable blend of greys, reds, oranges and browns on the roofs and chimneys.

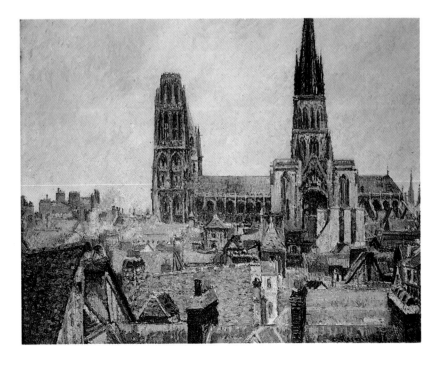

▲ DEGAS AND OSCAR WILDE

A photograph of Oscar Wilde, taken before his unsuccessful libel suit against the Marquess of Queensbury in 1895.

The family of Daniel Halévy was very much involved with the theatre. His father, Degas' friend Ludovic Halévy, was a dramatist and wrote the libretto for several of Offenbach's works as well as Bizet's *Carmen*, and his Aunt Geneviève (Ludovic's sister) married first Bizet and then the operetta composer Oscar Straus. The following extract is from the entry in Daniel's diary for January 2nd, 1896:

Degas said: 'Let's hope we shall soon have finished with art, with aesthetics; they make me sick. Yesterday I dined at the Rouarts'. There were his sons and some young people – all talking art. I blew up. What interests me is work, business, the army.'

I think that this outburst was triggered by a visit to Liberty's shop in Paris. He went there with his friend Bartholomé (p.239), *the sculptor, and said to him:* 'All this good taste will lead to prison.' This remark he repeated last year to Oscar Wilde. He met Wilde at Aunt Geneviève's, where they had a long, brilliant conver-sation, [full of exchanges] *like this:*

WILDE: *'You know how well known you are in England.'*

DEGAS: *'Fortunately less so than you.'*

All the experiments in furnishing in the artistic style during the last few years exasperate

A gelatin silver print of the dramatist Ludovic Halévy (c.1895), who was at school with Degas at the Lycée Louis le Grand.

him. At the Champ de Mars exhibition he was hailed by Montesquiou [Comte Robert de Montesquiou, dandy and homosexual, one of the prototypes for Baron de Charlus in Proust's *A la recherche du temps perdu*], *who was standing in front of an apple-green bed he had designed. Degas delivered himself of a great harangue in front of a crowd of about a hundred people (unfortunately, I cannot remember it all):*

'Do you think', he said, 'that you will conceive better children on an apple-green bed? Watch out M. de Montesquiou, taste is a vice.' And he turned his back on Montesquiou, whose reputation is not too good – this was after the Oscar Wilde affair.

Pederasty and taste, Degas makes no distinction between them. It seems that a 'Maison de l'Art Nouveau' has recently opened in which young women sell objects of good taste. Degas said: 'It's a good thing they use women shop assistants. If they'd had men, the police would already have closed the place.'

This morning he stamped his foot as he was walking along the rue Mansard. 'Taste, it doesn't exist!' he exclaimed. 'An artist makes beautiful things without being aware of it. Aesthetes beat their brows and ask themselves how they can make a pretty chamber pot. Poor creatures, their chamber pots may be works of art, but they'll make them stop urinating! Instead, they'll gaze at their pots and say to their friends "Look at my chamber pot. Isn't it pretty?"'

◤ CLEMENCEAU ON MONET'S 'ROUEN CATHEDRAL' SERIES

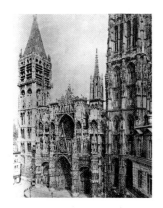

Radical politician, journalist, outstanding orator and one-time mayor of Montmartre, who later led France to victory in World War I, Georges Clemenceau (right) was a staunch friend and supporter of the Impressionists, being especially close to Monet, whom he helped in a variety of ways. Clemenceau had always been deeply interested in art, and in 1896 he published a volume of essays entitled *Le Grand Pan* – which included a piece on the mutability of vision, with special reference to Monet's *Rouen Cathedral* series:

The one thing that should give us pleasure in a constantly changing world is an awareness of that vital sense of life which powers the earth, the sea and the whole of nature. It is this constant sense of movement, to be found in every part of our planet, this ever changing miracle, which itself engenders others and which is to be found not only in men and animals but also in grass, trees and rocks, that provides for us a spectacle of which we never tire. Wherever I go, I analyse what I see: I try to grasp the fleeting, to understand the inexpressible mystery of things, and to savour the endlessly changing spectacle of life with a heightened awareness.

Rouen cathedral is an unchanging and unchangeable object, yet it is one which provokes a constant movement of light in the most complex way. At every moment of every day the changing light creates a new view of the cathedral, which seems as though it were constantly altering. In front of Monet's twenty views of the building, one begins to realize that art, in setting out to express nature with ever growing accuracy, teaches us to look, to perceive, to feel. The stone itself becomes an organic substance, and one can feel it being transformed as one moment in its life succeeds another. The twenty chapters of evolving light patterns of the building have been skilfully selected to create an ordered pattern of evolution. The great church itself, a testament to the vivifying light of the sun, hurls its mass against the brightness of the sky.

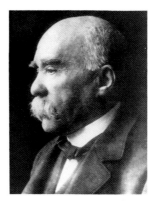

Far left: A contemporary photograph of the façade of Rouen Cathedral.

Left: A photograph of Clemenceau (*c*.1920).

MONET
Rouen Cathedral (Sunset)
1892

The Cathedral façade, is 'broken' into distinct upper and lower portions by the creeping shadows of evening (below left).

MONET
Rouen Cathedral: Façade and Tour d'Albane (Full Sunlight)
1894

The overhead sun casts the façade into high, sculptural relief (below right).

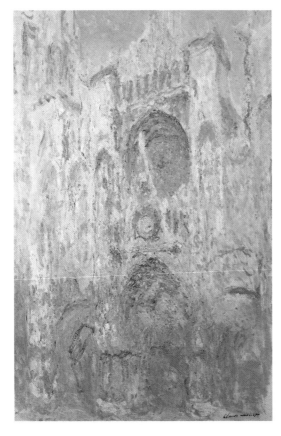

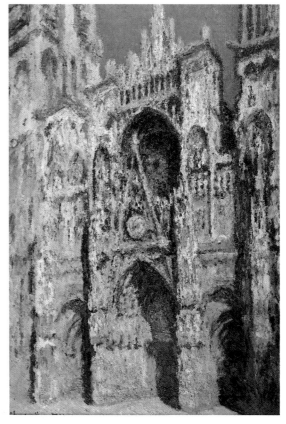

1897

Sisley's One-Man Show

This year Sisley finally begins to receive some recognition for his work. Georges Petit holds a one-man show for the artist at his gallery, and he travels to Britain on an all-expenses-paid trip, where he paints some twenty-five canvases. His prices improve too – a painting bought in 1887 for 150 francs sells this year for 2350 francs.

JANUARY
Pissarro begins a series of paintings of the Paris boulevards.

12th Monet goes to Pourville-sur-Mer on the Normandy coast (left), where he works till April, producing thirty paintings of the sea and cliffs – several of them featuring the custom house at Varengeville (right).

FEBRUARY
1st The collection of the jeweller André Vever is auctioned at Georges Petit's gallery; a Monet fetches 21,000 francs, a Degas 10,000 francs, a Sisley 2500 francs and a Pissarro 900 francs.

3rd Durand-Ruel sends eleven Impressionist paintings to an exhibition in Dresden.

5th Sisley has a one-man exhibition at Georges Petit's gallery. There are 146 paintings and five pastels on show, modestly priced at between 800 and 1500 francs, but the exhibition is not a great success.

7th The Caillebotte bequest ◆ (pp.197–8) is hung in an extension to the Musée du Luxembourg, where it is generally well received.

20th An Impressionist exhibition opens in Stockholm, mounted by Durand-Ruel at the instigation of the painter Prince Eugen of Sweden.

MARCH
23rd Degas is reconciled with his brother René (with whom he had not been on speaking terms since 1876).

APRIL
Monet begins a series of paintings of the Seine near Giverny. (He finishes thirty by the end of the year, sometimes getting up at 3.30 a.m.

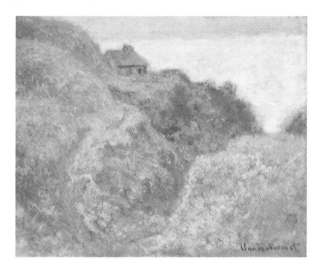

MONET
Gorge of the Petit Ailly (Varengeville)
1896–7

Between 1896 and 1897 Monet produced more than fifty paintings of the scenery in and around Pourville-sur-Mer. The artist was especially attracted to the custom house at Varengeville, which perches precariously on the cliff, high above the sea.

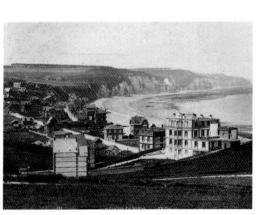

A contemporary photograph of Pourville-sur-Mer in Normandy.

to catch the dawn.) He exhibits at the second Venice Biennale.

7th Renoir exhibits at the New English Art Club in London.

MAY

10th Pissarro visits London – where he stays until July and paints a series of views of Bedford Park.

12th Sale of the collection belonging to Pierre Aubry, including a number of Impressionist works, mostly purchased from Theo van Gogh. Two paintings by Monet – *Umbrella Pines, Cap d'Antibes* (which Aubry had bought for 2800 francs) and *Antibes, View of Salis* (bought for the same price) – fetch 6300 francs and 7500 francs respectively. A Sisley, acquired for 150 francs in August 1887, goes for 2350 francs.

JULY

3rd Sisley and his family visit Britain, his expenses being met by the Rouen businessman and collector François Depeaux as advance payment for three paintings.

9th After spending several days painting in Falmouth, Sisley moves to the seaside resort of Penarth, near Cardiff, which he finds stimulating for his work.

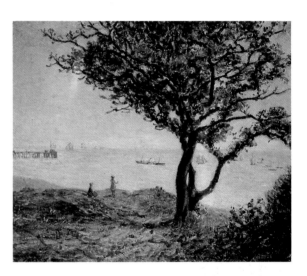

AUGUST

5th Sisley marries Marie-Adélaide-Eugénie Lescouezec, with whom he has been living since 1866 ◆ (pp.146–7), at the Registry Office in Cardiff.

10th Renoir falls off his bicycle in Essoyes and breaks his arm.

15th Degas spends several days in Montauban studying the works of Ingres in the museum there.

SEPTEMBER

14th Julie Manet stays with Renoir in Essoyes, and he gives her advice on her paintings.

OCTOBER

Sisley and his family return to Moret-sur-Loing, with some twenty-five canvases painted by him in England and Wales.

NOVEMBER

7th The Nationalgalerie in Berlin buys one of Pissarro's paintings.

26th Pissarro's third son, Félix, dies of tuberculosis ▲ (p.212).

DECEMBER

Murer has to sell his hotel in Rouen.

8th Degas introduces Julie Manet to Ernest Rouart, the son of his friend and patron Henri Rouart (p.131), who she is later to marry.

23rd Degas, who is vehemently anti-Dreyfus, breaks with the Halévy family ▲ (p.208) over the Dreyfus affair and refuses to see them.

SISLEY
Cardiff Roads
1897

In May Sisley made his last trip to Britain. After touring London and the South of England he travelled to Penarth, near Cardiff. On July 16th he wrote to the critic Gustave Geffroy: 'The countryside is pretty, and the Roads [an area where ships can lie at anchor], with the big ships sailing into and out of Cardiff, is superb…'

There are echoes in this painting of Monet's views of Cap d'Antibes (p.163). Sisley included the figures of his wife and daughter to add a human element.

OTHER EVENTS

- Turkey declares war on Greece over Crete and is defeated
- Russia occupies Port Arthur in North-East China
- Matthieu Dreyfus discovers that forged evidence has been used to incriminate his brother
- First Zionist Congress held in Basel
- Queen Victoria's Diamond Jubilee
- World Exhibition in Brussels
- Marconi sets up the Wireless & Telegraph Signal Company
- J. J. Thomson discovers electrons
- First performance of Edmond Rostand's *Cyrano de Bergerac*
- Publication of Beatrice and Sidney Webb's *Industrial Democracy* and H. G. Wells' *The Invisible Man*
- Brahms and Alphonse Daudet die

▲ PISSARRO AND HIS SONS

PISSARRO
Portrait of Félix Pissarro
1881

This portrait of Pissarro's third son, Félix (known as Titi), was painted when he was aged 7. The rather uncomfortable pose, with the head in three-quarter profile, gives the impression of a reluctant sitter.

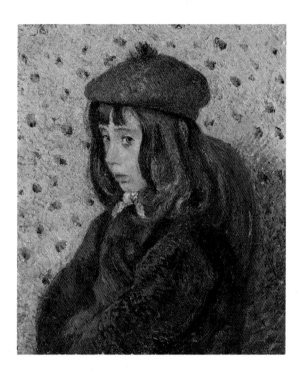

In December 1897 an article about the Pissarro family by the novelist and critic Octave Mirbeau appeared in *Le Journal*. Although Pissarro's third son, Félix, who died on November 26th, is not mentioned in the following extract, like other members of the family he was a talented artist. A painter, engraver and caricaturist, in order to avoid confusion with his father and brothers he generally used the pseudonym Jean Roch.

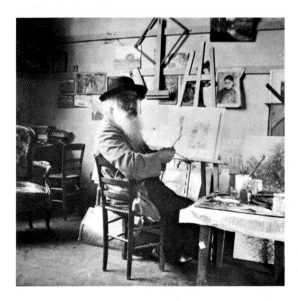

A photograph of Camille Pissarro at work in his studio at Éragny-sur-Epte (c.1897).

What an admirable family, that reminds us of the heroic periods of art! In his old age, a man still young in heart and revered, surrounded by five sons, all of them artists; all different! Each one follows his own nature. The father doesn't impose on any of them his own theories and doctrines, his own way of seeing and feeling. He concentrates instead the flower of their individuality. Lucien, a subtle and luminous landscape painter of exquisite sensibility, is not content to express himself on canvas alone. He has been living in England for the past few years and has tried his hand in every medium. In everything he does – wood engraving, etching, book decoration – he shows delightful and discreet taste, charming composition. Georges leans towards the broader aspects of decoration, and is attracted by the mystery of form, which he tries to capture on canvas, wood, copper. Rodolphe is sarcastic and always quiet. As a 10-year-old he was always out of doors. One day, to everyone's astonishment, large numbers of sketchbooks were discovered in his room. A strangely precocious feeling for caricature, a taste for composition, mass, and even landscape stands out. Even the youngest son, who is still in short pants, is involved. One evening his father confiscated a little watercolour from him of an old white horse in the snow. It showed surprisingly original qualities.

Such is this family, where art is in the home, where each one of them, young and old, cultivates the rarest flowers of beauty – quietly, without publicity, proudly and joyously independent.

▲ RENOIR'S PARIS HOME

Although Renoir was the most inveterate traveller of all the Impressionists and at various times rented studios in different parts of Paris, his home during most of the 1880s and 1890s was the grandiosely named Château des Brouillards at the seedier end of Montmartre – then still surrounded by market gardens and fields with grazing cows. The house, which had a fine garden, was part of a ramshackle group of buildings occupying the site of an eighteenth-century folly.

Renoir's second son, Jean (p.251), who was to achieve fame as a film director in the 1930s, was born there in 1894 and described it in his book *Renoir: My Father.*

A contemporary photograph of the Château des Brouillards, Renoir's home at 13 rue Girardon.

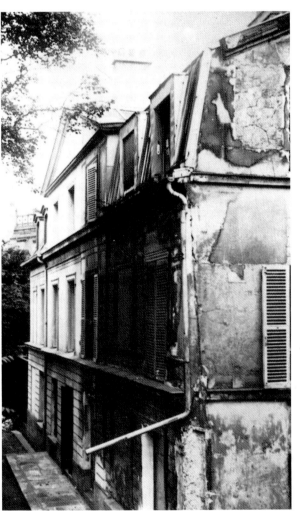

Our house at the Château des Brouillards was No.6 in the row of dwellings at 13 rue Girardon. It had two upper floors, plus the attic, which had been transformed into a studio. The garden, about fifty feet by seventy-five feet, had rose-bushes in it and one fruit tree. The central path led to the entrance of the house, which consisted of four or five stone steps. The iron ramp was painted black. The front hall, which ended in a staircase, opened on the left into a drawing-room and on the right into the dining-room. At the back was the kitchen, and also a butler's pantry. The staircase was circular, as in a tower, giving the kitchen, which was behind it, a peculiar shape. The steps were comfortably wide, but became narrower as you went down into the cellar. My father had the walls of the room painted white, and the doors a Trianon grey, just as he did wherever he lived. He had an obsession about the preparation of the Trianon grey, insisting that it should contain the best quality of linseed oil and that the white should be mixed with 'animal' black, and not 'peach' black. He wanted a pure grey obtained from a pure white and the best ivory black. The chief fault he had to find with 'peach black' was that it made the grey look 'sentimental' by giving it a bluish tone.

The largest rooms were about twelve feet by fifteen. In the dining-room Renoir had painted mythological subjects on the window-panes in translucent colours. I have no idea what became of these panes. The two upper floors were divided on the same plan as the ground floor. My mother slept upstairs over the dining-room; my brother Pierre, when he came home from school on Saturdays, over the drawing-room; Gabrielle above the kitchen. There was a primitive sort of bathroom over the pantry. It was an ordinary room, provided with drains for emptying the dirty water. We washed our faces in basins placed on marble-topped tables. Regular baths were taken in round zinc tubs about a foot deep. We washed our bodies with enormous sponges. We had to fetch our water from the pump at the entrance to the main pathway. Renoir slept on the second floor next to a guest-room, and at the back, over Gabrielle's room, was still another for a servant whenever extra help was needed.

THE CONQUEST OF EUROPE

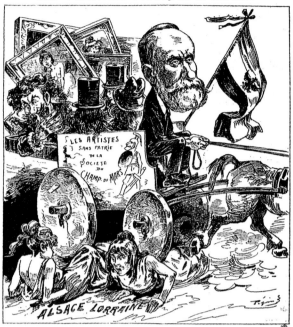

Voir en tête de la deuxième page les conditions auxquelles on peut recevoir gratuitement le **GRELOT**

LES PEINTRES FRANÇAIS A BERLIN

L'art n'a pas de patrie! Possible, mais M. Puvis de Chavannes en a une.

In April 1895 French artists were invited to participate in an exhibition in Berlin sponsored by Kaiser Wilhelm II of Germany. Right-wing nationalists boycotted the event, but many artists decided to take part, including Puvis de Chavannes. The caption of this caricature by Pépin, from *Le Grelot* (March 10th, 1895), reads: 'Art has no fatherland! Perhaps, but M. Puvis de Chavannes has one.'

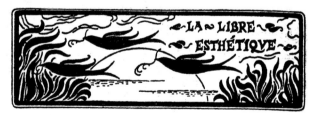

A decorative title promoting La Libre Esthétique, c.1894.

One advantage the Impressionists had over their predecessors was the existence of greater opportunities to make themselves known outside France. In 1897, for instance, their works were shown in Stockholm and Venice; and in other years they exhibited in Berlin, Brussels, Florence, Munich and Vienna. This was partly because of a new phenomenon, the international exhibitions of contemporary art, which had been made possible by more extensive railway and postal services, improved education and an increasingly sophisticated media, as well as the development of photography and the superior reproduction processes available to art magazines.

It was inevitable perhaps that the first of these international exhibitions should have taken place in Belgium – which was bound to France not only by a common language but by the fact that Brussels was a convenient haven for French artists seeking refuge from the political turmoils of the times. Durand-Ruel had opened a branch there in the 1870s, and in October 1883 a group of twenty 'undisciplined artists', as they called themselves, got together to form a society known as Les Vingt (often written as Les XX) that would hold annual exhibitions devoted to progressive artists from Belgium and other countries. Their success in doing so was largely due to the vigour and pertinacity of their secretary, the lawyer, journalist and art critic Octave Maus, who stated in *L'Art moderne* in 1886 that their aim was 'to make these exhibitions a realization of modern art in all its forms, enhanced by the fact that they include foreign artists and all who, rejecting the formulae of official art, would boldly proclaim a new art, proud and free, which would pay no heed to the timid protests of the general public or the juvenile or senile remonstrances of the critics.' In 1893, because of internal dissensions, Les Vingt was dissolved and its place taken by La Libre Esthétique, which was run not by artists but by Maus himself. During their existence, the two organizations showed work by all the Impressionists save Caillebotte.

The Venice Biennale, which was first held in 1895 and at which Monet exhibited in 1897, was a much more elaborate and more truly international affair, with national pavilions where each nation could show the artists of its choice. Its full impact on the reputation of the Impressionists did not begin to take effect until after World War I. During the next two decades there were exhibitions devoted to the work of Cézanne (1920), Degas

(1924 and 1936), Manet (1934), Monet (1932) and Renoir (1938). It was not until this period that the Italians really accepted French Impressionism, which they had previously thought of as being too imprecise, preferring the works of their own Macchiaioli (from *macchie*, meaning 'spots'), who by the 1870s had become a significant force in Italian art.

In Germany the various Secession exhibitions of Munich and Berlin had aims not dissimilar to those of Les Vingt and La Libre Esthétique; but, although Impressionist works were shown, they tended to prefer the Post-Impressionists – including Gauguin, who was to have a particularly strong influence on German painting. The real promoters of Impressionism in Germany were commercial galleries such as Gurlitt's (which held its first Impressionist exhibition in 1883) and that of Paul Cassirer, who acted as Durand-Ruel's agent in Berlin and was involved with the art magazine *Pan*. In addition, certain individuals played a vital role in promoting the movement. Chief of these was Hugo von Tschudi, a wealthy collector who became Director of the Nationalgalerie in Berlin in 1896. Shortly after accepting the post, he purchased works by Manet, Monet and Pissarro; and when, owing to the Kaiser's disapproval of his policy, he had to move to the Neue Pinakothek in Munich, he was responsible for acquiring works by Cézanne, Guillaumin, Manet, Monet, Pissarro and Renoir. Inspired by his example, other institutions eventually followed suit.

German critics too were in the forefront so far as the recognition of Impressionism was concerned. Richard Muther's *History of Modern Painting*, which appeared in German in 1893 and in English in 1895, contained a long, sympathetic chapter on Impressionism. Then in 1902 Julius Meier-Graefe published a book on Manet that included sections on Cézanne, Monet, Pissarro and Renoir, followed in 1908 by a magisterial work on modern art in which he gave due weight to the Impressionists' seminal role. By the first decade of this century there were several important collections of Impressionist paintings in Germany, including those of Franz Thurneyssen, Paul von Mendelssohn-Bartholdy and the artist Max Liebermann, who had started his collection in the 1890s.

Russia got to know Impressionism through the activities of three collectors. In 1897 a wealthy Moscow merchant, Sergei Shchukin, discovered the Impressionists thanks to one of his mother's relatives – who had lived in Paris – and bought Monet's *Lilac in the Sun* (1873), which was the first Impressionist painting to reach Russia. He proceeded to purchase further works by Monet covering every stage of the artist's development. Later Shchukin bought works by other Impressionists – including Cézanne, Pissarro and Renoir – and hung them in the gallery of his huge house, which was open to the public on Sundays. His friendly rivals were the brothers Mikhail and Ivan Morozov, who for several years spent, between the two of them, as much as 500,000 francs yearly on acquiring Impressionist and Post-Impressionist paintings.

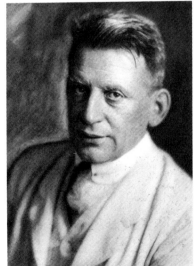

A photograph of the German critic Julius Meier-Graefe, used as the frontispiece to his book *Widmungen* (1927).

1898

Embracing Europe

Having participated in a number of international exhibitions, the artists are now enjoying significant prestige in Europe. This year works by Degas, Manet, Monet, Renoir and Sisley are included in an exhibition of the International Society of Artists in London, and Durand-Ruel stages Impressionist exhibitions in Munich and Berlin.

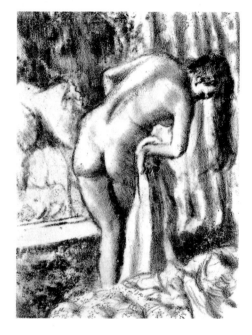

DEGAS
After the Bath (No.1)
1891–2

In 1891 Degas embarked upon a series of nude women at their toilet, all of whom are seen from behind, with their long hair loose. It is thought that a possible source for these lithographs was Delacroix's *The Entry of the Crusaders into Constantinople.* This painting (which Degas had copied thirty years earlier) shows a grieving woman from a similar angle, with her hair also tumbling forward.

JANUARY

1st The dealers Boussod & Valadon publish a portfolio of twenty reproductions of drawings by Degas, dating from 1861 to 1896, and executed by his friend the engraver and printer Michel Manzi.

8th Works by Manet and Monet are included in an exhibition at the South London Art Gallery, Camberwell.

9th Degas buys a still life of a glass and napkin by Cézanne from Vollard for 400 francs.

31st Sisley (who is still British) applies to the Ministry of Justice to become a naturalized French citizen.

FEBRUARY

4th Renoir visits Cagnes-sur-Mer in the south of France for the first time. He is most enthusiastic about this exceptionally beautiful resort (which would later become his home).

APRIL

14th In connection with Sisley's application for French nationality, the gendarmerie at Moret-sur-Loing report: 'His behaviour, morality and integrity are very sound; he is quiet and peace-loving, he does not visit anybody, and leads a very secluded life. His views do not seem to pose a threat to national security.'

MAY

1st Sisley exhibits five pictures – all painted during his visit to Britain in 1897 – at the Société Nationale des Beaux-Arts.

14th Durand-Ruel holds an exhibition of work by Monet, Pissarro, Renoir and Sisley.

JUNE

1st An exhibition of recent work by Pissarro opens at Durand-Ruel's gallery (opposite), plus a selection of pictures by Monet, Renoir, Sisley and Puvis de Chavannes.

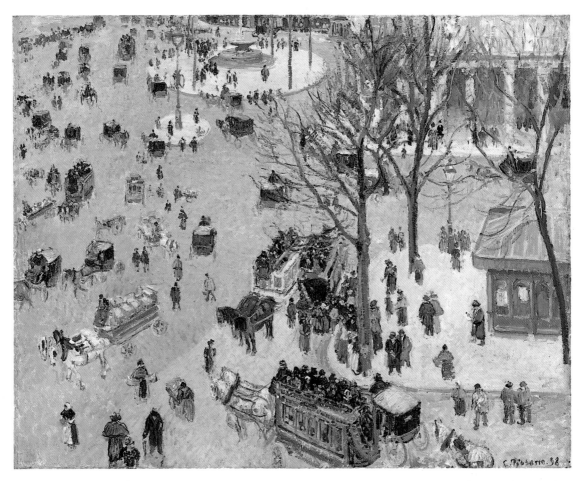

3rd Monet has a successful exhibition at Georges Petit's gallery (below).
12th Works by Degas, Monet, Pissarro and Renoir are exhibited at the Guildhall Art Gallery in London.

PISSARRO
The Place du Théâtre
Français
1898

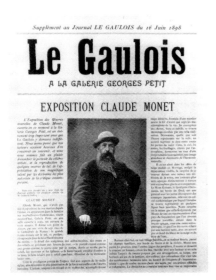

Supplement to *Le Gaulois* (June 16th, 1898) reviewing Monet's exhibition at Georges Petit's gallery.

JULY

1st Renoir and his family, accompanied by Julie Manet, go to Berneval, near Dieppe, where they rent a chalet.
4th An exhibition of the International Society of Artists organized by Whistler opens at the Prince's Skating Rink, in Kensington, London. It includes six works by Degas and one each by Monet, Renoir and Sisley, as well as Manet's *Vagabond Musicians* (1862) and the version of his *Execution of the Emperor Maximilian* ◆ (pp.56–9) that had been pieced together by Degas (*see* p.195).
15th Pissarro visits Rouen, where he stays till October.
22nd Degas paints his last landscapes in St-Valéry-sur-Somme (p.218), where his parents had taken him as a child.

SEPTEMBER

10th Mallarmé dies ◆ (pp.220–1).

OCTOBER

8th Sisley's wife, Marie-Adélaïde-Eugénie ◆ (pp.146–7), dies of cancer. He is suffering from the same disease.

Towards the end of 1897 Pissarro rented a room in the Hôtel du Louvre, which gave him a view of the Rue St-Honoré, the Avenue de l'Opéra and the Place du Théâtre Français. During the next few months he worked on a series of paintings of these streets.

In this work the viewer looks down on the Place du Théâtre Français (now the Place André Malraux). The theatre itself is in the top right-hand corner, while the Avenue de l'Opéra leads off to the left of the roundabout. The painting was one of a number of Pisssarro's recent works exhibited at Durand-Ruel's gallery in June.

DEGAS
The Return of the Herd
*c.*1898

Degas produced this painting during his visit to the village of St-Valéry-sur-Somme in July. Its harmonious colour and strong outlines are reminiscent of Gauguin's work, which Degas greatly admired.

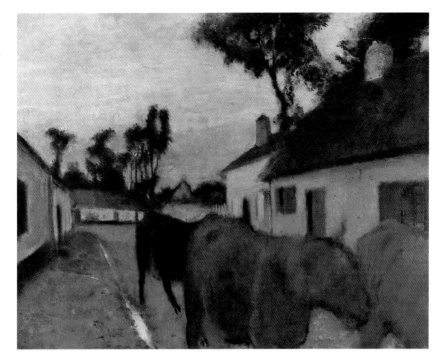

10th Renoir and Durand-Ruel's son Paul go to see a Rembrandt exhibition in Amsterdam. While in Holland, they also visit The Hague.

NOVEMBER

Renoir produces designs for decorative panels in the house of the impresario Paul Gallimard, but does not paint the panels themselves. Durand-Ruel stages Impressionist exhibitions in Munich and Berlin. Pissarro congratulates Zola on his pro-Dreyfus polemic *J'Accuse* (left).

A caricature from the anti-Dreyfus magazine *Psst…!* (1898) showing Zola as an incendiary with his controversial article *J'Accuse*.

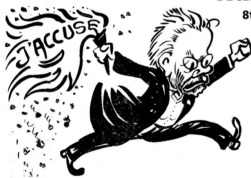

DECEMBER

8th–24th Monet visits London to see his son Michel, who is learning English there. He produces no work during his visit.

12th Renoir sells Degas' *The Dance Lesson* (*c.*1879), which he had chosen as a gift from Caillebotte's collection after the latter's death ◆ (pp.197–8). With the money it fetches, he buys a view of La Rochelle by Corot. Consequently, a coldness ensues between Degas and Renoir.

OTHER EVENTS

- Colonel Henry of the French army admits forging evidence against Dreyfus and commits suicide
- United States and Spain go to war over Cuba; Spain cedes Cuba, the Philippines, Puerto Rico and Guam
- China leases Port Arthur to Russia
- Kitchener scores decisive victories in Sudan
- Marie and Pierre Curie discover radium
- Paris Métro opens
- Corn flakes first marketed in USA
- Publication of Huysmans' *La Cathédrale*, H. G. Wells' *The War of the Worlds*, Henry James's *The Turn of the Screw* and Oscar Wilde's *The Ballad of Reading Gaol*
- Bismarck and Gladstone die

▲ MONET THE EPICURE

In his fascinating book about his stepfather *Claude Monet: ce mal connu*, published in 1960, Jean-Pierre Hoschedé – the son of Alice and Ernest Hoschedé ◆ (pp.146–7) – provided an intriguing account of Monet's favourite dishes and the painter's eating and drinking habits at the Giverny dinner table:

Monet… had a very good appetite… He loved good wine, and would never put water in it. That would have been sacrilege. Nevertheless, we never saw him less than in control of himself, and the reason for this was that, although loving a fine wine, he never abused it, being a gourmet and not a glutton. For the same reason, although he appreciated good cooking, he preferred simple dishes. He did, however, have his preferences. For instance, he liked asparagus very lightly cooked, and would have a separate dish of more thoroughly cooked asparagus for his guests. Salads he liked to season himself – and in what a manner! He would fill the spoon with ground black peppercorns, coarse salt, a lot of olive oil and a little wine vinegar, all well mixed up, and then douse the salad with the contents, making it almost black. Once it had been treated like this, the only people who could eat it were Monet and my sister Blanche, who always ate whatever he did. He had similar preferences for everything he ate. With duck for instance, he always took the wings off… and before they were cooked drenched them in a mixture of ground pepper, coarse salt and grated nutmeg. For lobster, Monet had a special sauce made of ground pepper beaten with the 'cream' taken out of the shell – something which is not usually eaten. When there was an especially copious meal, Monet always had 'le trou normand', a glass of Calvados taken between courses. Similarly, every day, after coffee had been served in the studio, Monet would always have a glass of plum brandy, made from the plums in the garden. He was particularly fond of game, especially grouse, which I always had to provide for him during the season – especially for Christmas and New Year's Day. It did not have to be fresh, as Monet liked his grouse well hung. He never followed any particular diet.

A photograph of Monet in his dining-room at Giverny (*c.*1898), which was painted in two different shades of yellow. Monet's treasured Japanese prints can be seen covering the walls.

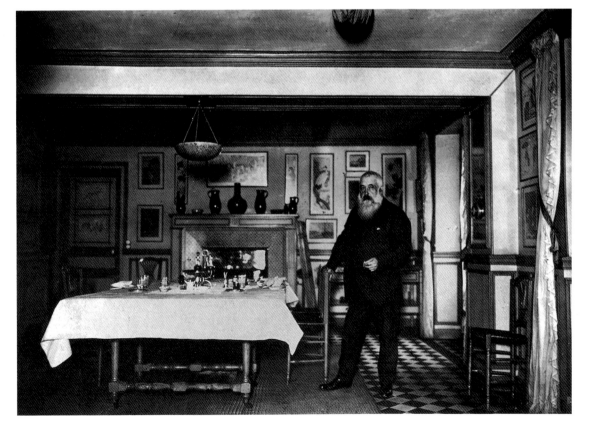

◆ LITERARY LINKS

GAUGUIN
Portrait of Stéphane Mallarmé
1891

Throughout his career Gauguin produced a great many wood engravings lithographs and monotypes, but this is his only known etching (right). It dates from a period in early 1891 when Gauguin was seeking publicity for a fund-raising sale of his work from Martinique, Brittany and Arles. Mallarmé had helped the artist by persuading the novelist and critic Octave Mirbeau to write a eulogistic article about Gauguin, which appeared in *L'Écho de Paris* a week before the sale.

A watercolour sketch by Edmond de Goncourt of his brother Jules, painted shortly before the latter's death in 1870.

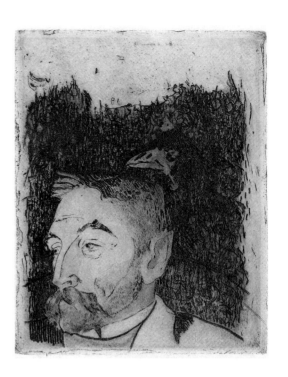

The death of Stéphane Mallarmé was a great blow to the surviving Impressionists. Never before had the links between art and literature been as close as they were in nineteenth-century France. Baudelaire had written extensively about art, and in the 1870s Zola had been not only a friend of the Impressionists but for a considerable time their stoutest defender. There was, not surprisingly, a natural camaraderie between the writers and artists that the establishment classed as 'rebels', and a two-way traffic of ideas and images flowed between them. Flaubert, for instance, who lived near Giverny and counted Monet among his friends, was very receptive to Impressionist ideas; and in *L'Éducation sentimentale* (1869) the artist Pellerin's painting *The Republic: Progress or Civilization* – showing Christ driving a railway engine through a virgin forest – was intended as a metaphorical reference to the Impressionists' concern with contemporary life, which became an important element in their approach to art.

The novelist and critic Edmond de Goncourt was particularly interested in the work of Degas – whom he saw almost as a rival, commenting in 1891: 'He is enamoured of modernity, and within this context has concentrated on washerwomen and dancers. I find this quite an admirable choice, especially since in *Manette Salomon* (1867) I myself cited these two professions

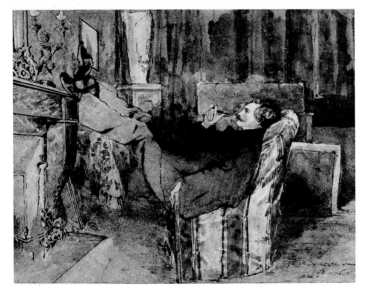

as providing the most pictorial examples in our age that a painter could think of.' Conversely, in *Parisian Sketches*, published in 1880, Huysmans included an account of an acrobatic turn at the Folies-Bergère that was obviously based on Degas' *Miss La La at the Cirque Fernando* (p.115).

The publisher Georges Charpentier – who subsidized the avant-garde art journal *La Vie moderne* (*see* p.112), which held exhibitions of work by the Impressionists – was a committed patron of the movement. Similarly, Marcel Proust and other writers who had no personal links with the Impressionists lent them their support and expressed their admiration for them in their writings.

With Mallarmé, however, the links were personal as well ideological. He had met Manet in 1873, soon after arriving in Paris – and in 1885, two years after the painter's death, he wrote to Verlaine 'I saw my dear Manet every day for ten years, and I find his absence today incredible.' It was at Manet's studio – where Mallarmé used to drop in on his way home from teaching at the Lycée Fontane (now the Lycée Condorcet) – that he become acquainted with Zola, Monet and Morisot, as well as Degas and Renoir, who became his close friends. In 1875 Manet illustrated Mallarmé's prose translation of Edgar Allan Poe's *The Raven* (p.91); and the following year – during which he painted a portrait of the poet – he illustrated one of his most famous poems, *L'Après-midi d'un faune*. Mallarmé, for his part, wrote enthusiastic articles about Manet ▲ (p.99),

Morisot and Whistler; and on the death of Morisot he became one of the guardians of her daughter Julie, a duty which he fulfilled with enthusiasm during the three remaining years of his life. Nevertheless, despite his links with the Impressionists, Mallarmé was one of the founders of the Symbolist movement – which reacted

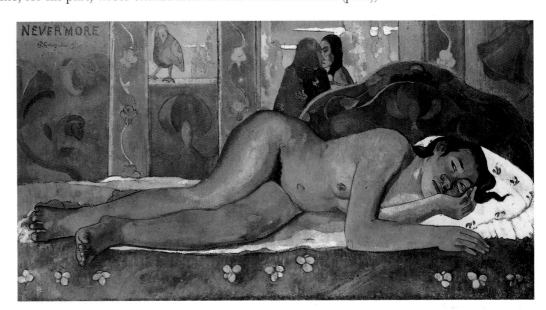

GAUGUIN
Nevermore, O Tahiti
1897

against both Romanticism and Realism, emphasizing the mystical and the religious. He was therefore closer in feeling to the Post-Impressionists, and was one of Gauguin's earliest supporters.

The poet Paul Valéry – Mallarmé's disciple and successor as the leading literary Symbolist, who was a talented draughtsman and sculptor as well as a writer – enjoyed equally close links with the Impressionists and married Jeannie Gobillard, Morisot's niece. Valéry was particularly close to Degas – one of his first major works, *La Soirée avec M. Teste* (1896), was partly based on his views of Degas – and in 1937 he published a book on the artist entitled *Degas, danse, dessin* (p.243).

Several of the Impressionists displayed a strong interest in literature. Degas wrote a number of sonnets, which were passed around among his circle in manuscript form, and his letters are models of wit and acuity. Renoir's literary ability is apparent from the introduction he wrote in 1911 to a new translation of Cennino Cennini's *Il Libro dell'Arte*; Monet read widely and had an extensive library at Giverny; and Cézanne, who wrote a considerable number of poems in his youth, retained his interest in poetry throughout his life, his favourite books being Virgil's *Eclogues* and Baudelaire's *Les Fleurs du mal*.

This reclining nude recalls Manet's *Olympia* (p.36), which Gauguin had copied in 1891, but has a much more overt symbolic content. Despite the title and the unexplained presence of the bird, however, Gauguin denied more than a passing reference to Edgar Allan Poe's narrative poem *The Raven* (see p.91).

1899

Sisley Dies in Poverty

The death of Sisley at the beginning of the year leaves his family in a state of crippling penury, and Monet – always quick to take up a cause – organizes a sale of his paintings at Georges Petit's gallery, which realizes the respectable sum of 115,640 francs. Sisley's clothes and furniture are also sold, and fetch 50 francs and 950 francs respectively.

**RENOIR
Self-portrait**
c.1899

Painted shortly after an attack of rheumatoid arthritis, this self-portrait shows Renoir looking sad and haggard, although he was in fact only 58. Julie Manet wrote: 'He is finishing a self-portrait that is very nice, but he has made himself look old and wrinkled.'

JANUARY

Mary Cassatt visits the USA for the first time in twenty years.
Pissarro rents an apartment at 204 rue de Rivoli in Paris in order to paint the Tuileries Gardens.
15th Degas refuses to provide an illustration for an edition of poems by Mallarmé ◆ (pp.220–1) because the publisher is a supporter of Dreyfus.
21st Monet writes to the critic Gustave Geffroy: 'Sisley is said to be extremely ill. He is a truly great artist, and I believe he is as great a master as any who has lived. I looked at some of his works again, which have a rare breadth of vision and beauty, especially one of a flood, which is a masterpiece.'

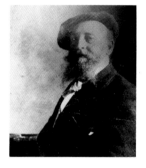

A photograph of Sisley taken a year before his death.

29th Sisley (right) dies of cancer of the throat at his home in Moret-sur-Loing.
30th The Ernst Arnold gallery in Dresden organizes an exhibition of twenty works by Degas, Monet, Pissarro, Renoir and Sisley.

FEBRUARY

Renoir (left) goes to Cagnes-sur-Mer with his former pupil Jeanne Baudot to receive treatment for his rheumatism.
Toulouse-Lautrec is admitted to a sanatorium for alcoholics.
9th The Bernheim-Jeune gallery exhibits fourteen paintings by Sisley.
27th An exhibition of twenty-eight paintings by Sisley opens at Durand-Ruel's gallery in New York.

MARCH

4th Pissarro has a one-man show at the Bernheim-Jeune gallery, consisting of some twenty-three works. Sales are reasonably good.

APRIL

30th Georges Petit puts on an 'exhibition of paintings, studies and pastels from Sisley's studio and those given to his children by other artists.' Together with his furniture and clothes (sold for 950 francs and 50 francs respectively), these form Sisley's total estate. Organized by Monet on behalf of Sisley's two orphans, the exhibition succeeds in raising a total of 115,640 francs.

3rd An exhibition of the International Society of Artists at the New Gallery in London includes works by Monet, Pissarro, Renoir and Rodin.

Siegfried Bing holds an exhibition at the Grafton Galleries in London, featuring works by the same artists with the addition of Morisot.

JUNE

4th Renoir stays in Saint-Cloud, where he receives a visit from Vuillard.

JULY

1st–4th The dealer Victor Chocquet's collection is auctioned at Georges Petit's gallery ◆ (p.224), his widow having died earlier in the year.

SEPTEMBER

15th Monet goes to England to begin work on a series of paintings of London. He stays at the Savoy Hotel and paints several views of Charing Cross Bridge ◆ (p.231).

16th Julie Manet mentions in her diary that Renoir and Degas are reconciled (*see* p.218).

19th Pissarro visits Varengeville, near Dieppe, in search of 'fresh motifs'.

NOVEMBER

Monet is taken ill with influenza in London.

DECEMBER

Renoir gives his *Portrait of Jean Renoir as a Child* to the municipal museum in Limoges.

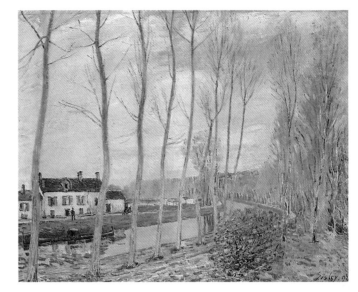

SISLEY
The Loing Canal
1892

One of many views that Sisley painted of the Loing Canal near Moret-sur-Loing, this work was donated to the Musée du Luxembourg in 1899 by a group of the artist's friends, led by Monet.

OTHER EVENTS

• Beginning of the Second Boer War
• Riots in Paris over Dreyfus affair; French President is assaulted by an anti-Dreyfusard; Dreyfus is retried and again found guilty, but subsequently accepts a pardon
• First Hague Peace Conference
• Tape recorder invented by Valdemar Poulsen
• Aspirin goes on sale to public
• Publication of André Gide's *Le Prométhée mal enchaîné*
• Elgar composes *Enigma Variations*
• First performance of Schoenberg's *Verklärte Nacht*
• Johann Strauss dies

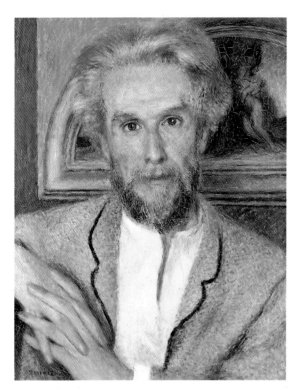

RENOIR
Portrait of Victor Chocquet
1875–6

This is the second of two portraits that Renoir painted of Victor Chocquet soon after he first met him in 1875. Although only recently introduced to the work of the Impressionists, Chocquet was already a discerning collector and owned several paintings by Delacroix, one of which can be seen behind the sitter in this painting. It is likely that Chocquet habitually interlaced his fingers, as he is similarly depicted in two portraits by Cézanne, c.1877.

An invoice made out to Durand-Ruel, dated July 5th, 1899, which lists three paintings from the Chocquet collection sold *hors catalogue*. According to Durand-Ruel's records, No. 493 was the *Portrait of Victor Chocquet* by Renoir (above), which sold for 1400 francs.

THE CHOCQUET SALE

The collection belonging to Victor Chocquet was auctioned at Georges Petit's gallery between July 1st and 4th, major works being offered for sale on July 1st, and watercolours, drawings and other items on July 3rd. Chocquet's furniture came under the hammer on July 4th. The catalogue was a sumptuous one, with numerous illustrations – including one of Renoir's portraits of Chocquet, which was reproduced as the frontispiece, but was not listed in the catalogue. A precise breakdown of what was auctioned is difficult, as at least twenty works were not catalogued and there was a supplementary sale, *hors catalogue*, the extent of which is unknown. Among the known works for sale were thirty-five Cézannes, fourteen Renoirs, twelve Monets, five Manets, one Pissarro and one Sisley. In general, prices were quite high (even the Cézannes surpassed their estimates). The top price paid for a Cézanne was 6200 francs for *The House of the Hanged Man* (p.88), but the main interest focused on his still lifes. Durand-Ruel bought three – two of them entitled *Le Dessert*, for 2000 francs and 3500 francs respectively, and one of flowers and fruit for 1300 francs.

Julie Manet attended the auction and noted the event in her diary:

The Chocquet sale. I was very excited at the prospect of perhaps buying a Delacroix. We followed the sale with Fauché and saw M.

Degas from afar looking very comical the way he examined each item through his magnifying glass. He was sitting next to the Rouarts. I was quite emotional when Maman's painting came up for sale, but was quickly reassured when the price went straight up to 8000 francs and finally stopped at 10,100.

The Renoirs did well, as did the Monets and the Cézannes, thanks to Vollard, but not the Manets, which was suprising. The Delacroix paintings went for practically nothing. 'Ovid amongst the Scythians', which I thought was so wonderful, only made 1800 francs. I'm almost sorry I didn't risk bidding for it, it would have been worth having a fling. Still I was pleased, as in the end I got the little sketch for 460 francs.

After the sale M. Degas asked us to go to his house with him in his carriage, with the Delacroix, so we took our leave of the Rouarts. M. Degas was very sorry not to have got the Chocquet portrait [by Renoir] – 'the portrait of one madman by another,' as he said. He liked it enormously. Durand-Ruel bought it for only 3500, but M. Degas had been afraid that Camondo would get it.

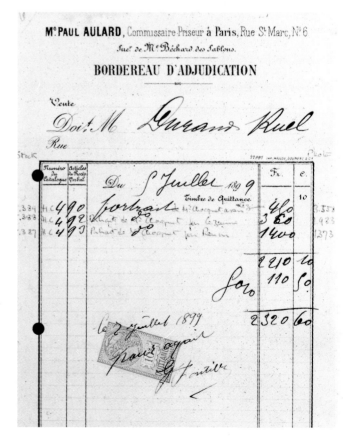

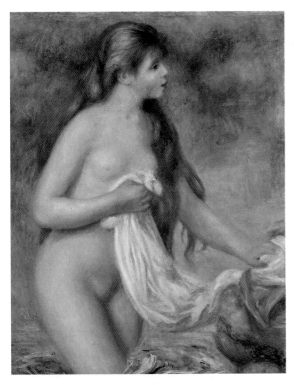

RENOIR
The Bather
c.1895

This portrait of a young bather, with its nymph-like pose and woodland setting, recalls a French eighteenth-century painting.

DEGAS
Waiting (2nd version)
1876–7

One of more than fifty monotypes of brothel scenes by Degas, this work was later bought by Picasso.

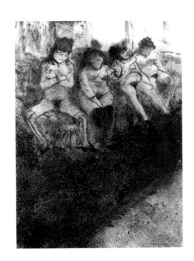

◆ THE IMPRESSIONIST NUDE

Renoir once said: 'The simplest subjects are eternal. A nude woman getting out of the briny deep or out of bed, whether she is called Venus or Nini, one can invent nothing better.' During the last two decades of his life a constant stream of nudes poured from his brush – making him one of the essential links in a tradition encompassing Praxitiles, Giorgione, Rubens and Ingres. Apart from early exercises in the genre, such as his *Bather with a Griffon* (1870), Renoir paid little attention to the nude until the 1880s, partly because the philosophy of Impressionism did not lend itself easily to such 'academic' subjects (being more concerned with contemporary life, which afforded few occasions for undressing in public) and partly because the Impressionist technique tended to lack the precision of outline that such subjects demanded.

But Renoir was also deeply ambivalent towards women ◆ (pp.146–7), and once claimed that he painted women as he would carrots. Moreover, since the Renaissance the nude had been an essential part of an artist's education, and it is significant that those Impressionists who painted nudes – Bazille, Degas, Manet, Renoir and to a lesser extent Cézanne – were basically traditionalists. Nor was it a coincidence that both of the paintings which effectively heralded the advent of Impressionism, Manet's *Déjeuner sur l'herbe* (p.27) and *Olympia* (p.36), featured nudes who could be prostitutes, and both were painted in a traditional manner – a formula that allowed the artist to present the 'reality of modern life' under the guise of classical expression.

Degas was particularly aware of the possibilities offered by this formula. Some of his early nude drawings are superb examples of straightforward academic studies. By the 1880s, however, he was exploring what was to become his most characteristic approach to the nude – images of women bathing or washing themselves, far removed from idealized poses or mythological settings. They were, as the critics put it, 'keyhole pictures' that stripped women of their mystery, showing them as unidealized creatures engaged in mundane activities.

Degas was a lifelong bachelor and it has been suggested that he was impotent – which would partly explain the character of his most extensive excursion into the nude, the fifty monotypes of brothel scenes produced between 1876 and 1877 (left). The images that pervade these works are characterized by an unflattering portrayal of women's bodies and faces and, in some pictures, the frank depiction of pubic areas. Nevertheless, they are a remarkable expression of a conception of the nude that was later to attract Toulouse-Lautrec, and they aroused the admiration of Picasso, who bought four of them in 1958.

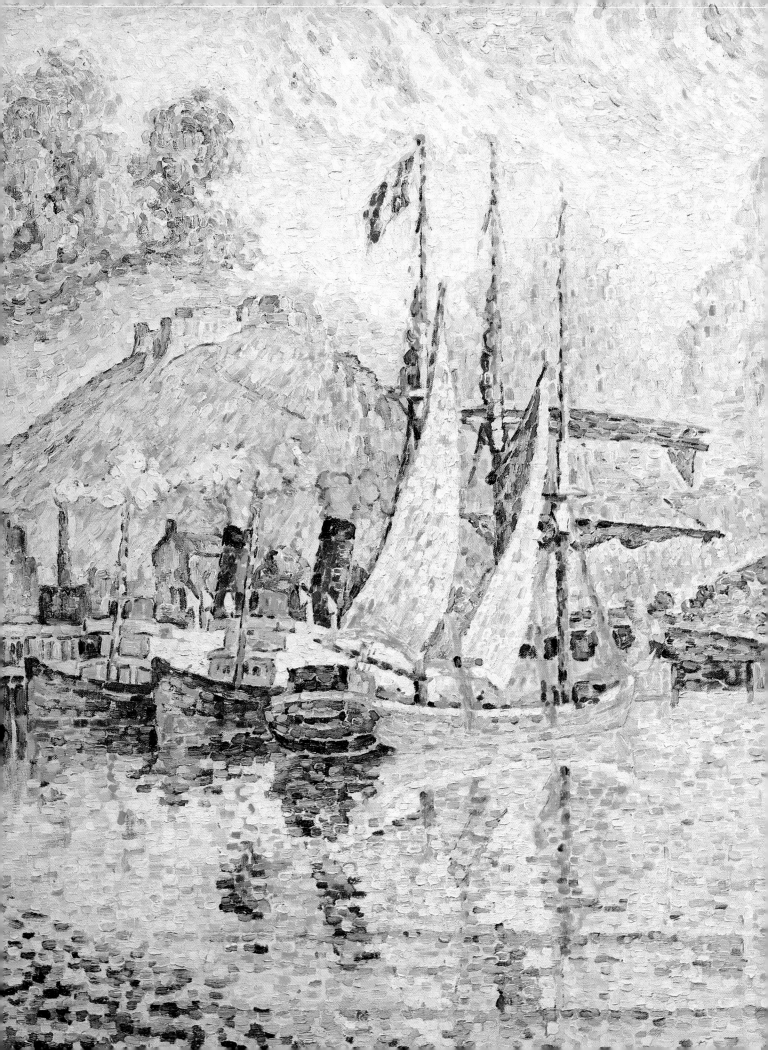

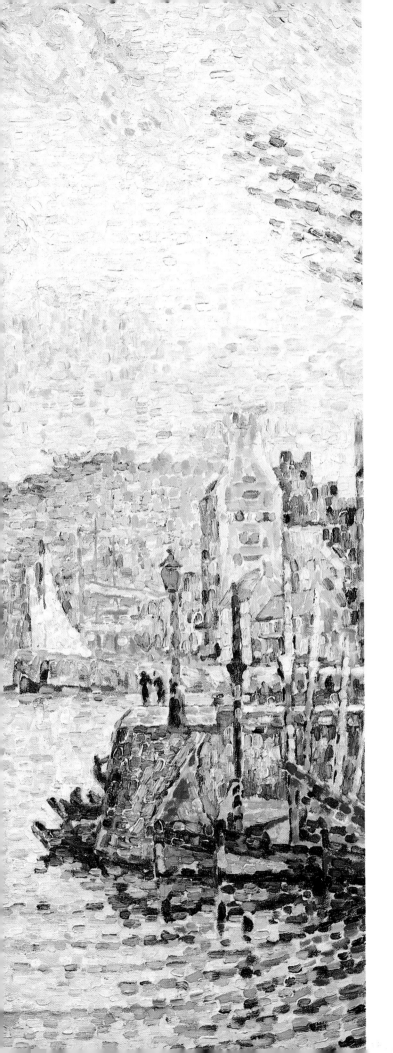

THE IMPRESSIONIST
LEGACY
1900–Today

SIGNAC **Cherbourg, Forte de Roule** (detail) 1932

1900–1903

Recognition Arrives

At the start of the new century the status of the Impressionists has greatly improved. They are given recognition in histories of art, and monographs are written about them; their prices have stabilized; they are selling well in America (especially Monet); and they are represented in official exhibitions and increasingly in museums.

1900

JANUARY: **3rd** Renoir has an exhibition at the Bernheim-Jeune gallery in Paris. He sells most of the sixty-eight paintings on show.

FEBRUARY: Monet takes a suite at the Savoy Hotel in order to paint views of London ◆ (opposite).

APRIL: **3rd** Opening of the Universal Exhibition in Paris (left) to mark the beginning of the new century. It includes a Centenary Exhibition of French Art, with works by the Impressionists. **20th** Berlin Secession exhibition ◆ (pp.214–5) shows works by Pissarro and Renoir.

MAY: **9th** Sale of the collection of Eugène Blot. Works by Cézanne, Monet, Morisot, Renoir and Sisley all achieve good prices.

JUNE: **1st** Munich Secession exhibition ◆ (pp.214–5) includes works by Degas, Monet, Pissarro and Renoir.

JULY: **4th** The dealer Georges Petit dies.

AUGUST: **16th** Renoir accepts the Legion of Honour.

OCTOBER: Cézanne has a one-man show in Berlin.

NOVEMBER: **22nd** Twelve paintings by Monet of his water garden at Giverny are greatly admired when exhibited by Durand-Ruel.

1901

JANUARY: **1st** Durand-Ruel organizes an exhibition at the Hanover Gallery in London of works by Monet, Pissarro, Renoir and Sisley. **4th** Pissarro has an exhibition of forty-two works at Durand-Ruel's gallery. **21st** Musée de Lyon buys Renoir's *Woman Playing the Guitar* (left).

APRIL: **15th** Monet, Pissarro and Renoir accept an invitation to participate in a Berlin Secession exhibition.

MAY: Durand-Ruel buys Abbé Gaugain's collection of Impressionist paintings for 101,000 francs (*see* p.15).

OCTOBER: **27th** Major exhibition of Impressionist paintings held at Paul Cassirer's gallery in Berlin. **30th** The International Society of Artists in London shows works by Monet, Pissarro, Renoir and Sisley.

DECEMBER: Monet returns to London ◆ (opposite).

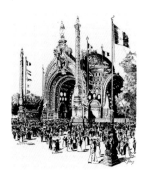

An engraving by L. Fillol showing the Monumental Gate at the entrance to the Universal Exhibition.

RENOIR
Woman Playing the Guitar
1896–7

The first of a group paintings, executed by Renoir in the late 1890s, of men and women playing the guitar, this work was apparently inspired by a dancer at the Folies-Bergère called 'La Belle Otéro'. It was bought by the Musée de Lyon in 1901.

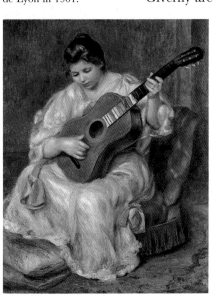

OTHER EVENTS

1900
- Boxer risings in China
- Commonwealth of Australia created
- King Umberto of Italy shot dead by anarchist
- Conrad's *Lord Jim* and Freud's *The Interpretation of Dreams* published
- Puccini's *Tosca* first performed
- Nietzsche, Ruskin and Oscar Wilde die

1901
- Queen Victoria dies and is succeeded by Edward VII
- President McKinley is assassinated; Theodore Roosevelt succeeds him
- Publication of Thomas Mann's *Buddenbrooks*
- Verdi dies

1902
- Boers surrender to Lord Kitchener
- USA buys Panama Canal concession for $40,000,000
- First performance of Chekhov's *Three Sisters*
- Publication of André Gide's *L'Immoraliste*
- Firs performance of Debussy's *Pelléas et Mélisande*

1903
- Russian socialists split into Bolsheviks and Mensheviks
- Mrs Pankhurst founds women's union
- Henry Ford founds Ford Motor Company
- Wright brothers make first sustained flight in a powered aircraft
- Shaw's *Man and Superman* first performed
- Butler's *The Way of All Flesh* published

1902

MAY: Julius Meier-Graefe's book on Manet is published ◆ (pp.214–5).

JUNE: Signac has an exhibition at the Galerie d'Art Nouveau.

JULY: Pissarro stays at a studio under the arcades of the fish market in Dieppe, where he finds 'first-rate subjects'.

AUGUST: Renoir suffers partial atrophy of the nerves in his left eye.

SEPTEMBER: 29th Zola dies of asphyxiation at his home in Médan due to a blocked flue.

OCTOBER: Publication of Théodore Duret's *Histoire d'Édouard Manet et son œuvre.*

DECEMBER: Renoir informs Durand-Ruel that two of the dealer's 'Renoirs' are forgeries.

1903

APRIL: Works by Monet, Pissarro, Renoir and Sisley are shown at the Venice Biennale.

MAY: 7th Durand-Ruel sells Cézanne's *The Rape* (1867), formerly owned by Zola, to the Havemeyers ● (p.233). **8th** Gauguin dies at Atuona in the Marquesas Islands, aged 54, possibly of a morphine-induced heart attack.

SEPTEMBER: Monet buys a motor car. **9th** Toulouse-Lautrec dies, aged 36.

OCTOBER: Opening of the progressive Salon d'Automne (left). It includes a vibrant display of Gauguin's works as a memorial to him.

NOVEMBER: 13th Pissarro dies, aged 73.

DECEMBER: Georges Viau – a dentist, collector and amateur painter – is accused of possessing forged Renoirs.

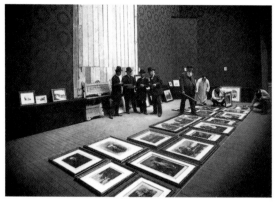

A photograph of the hanging committee at work on the Salon d'Automne of 1903.

 MONET IN LONDON

While he was in London in 1899, 1900 and 1901, Monet produced more than a hundred paintings – including forty-two views of Waterloo Bridge, thirty-five of Charing Cross Bridge and twenty of the Houses of Parliament.

During each visit he stayed in a small suite on the fifth floor of the Savoy Hotel. In addition to his vantage point at the Savoy, he obtained use of a room in St Thomas's Hospital on the south bank of the Thames.

In an interview given in 1920, Monet described his working method: 'At the Savoy Hotel or at St Thomas's Hospital, from which I took my viewpoints, I had up to a hundred canvases on the go – for a single subject. By feverishly searching among my sketches, I would choose one that did not differ too much from what I saw before me – but would then often modify it completely.'

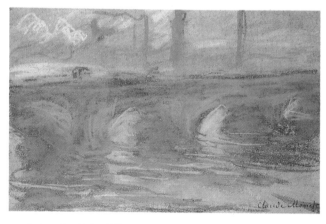

**MONET
Waterloo Bridge
1900**

Drawn from his room in the Savoy Hotel, this is one of the few pastels that Monet produced.

1904–1906

The Apogee

Durand-Ruel's exhibition at the Grafton Galleries in London in January 1905 marks the apogee of Impressionism as a contemporary movement. The three hundred or so paintings on show include most of the great works of its exponents, gathered in one place on a scale both unprecedented and impossible to repeat.

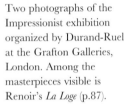

Two photographs of the Impressionist exhibition organized by Durand-Ruel at the Grafton Galleries, London. Among the masterpieces visible is Renoir's *La Loge* (p.87).

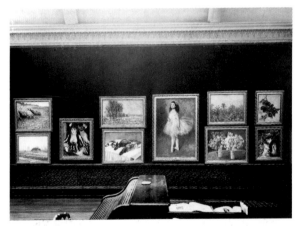

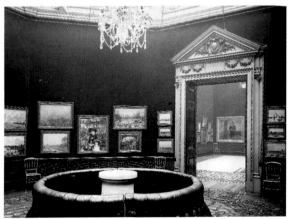

1904

JANUARY: Renoir registers a complaint with the authorities regarding forgery of his work by Georges Viau (*see* p.229).
FEBRUARY: 12th Works by Cassatt, Cézanne, Degas, Manet, Monet and Pissarro are shown at La Libre Esthétique ◆ (pp.214–5) in Brussels.
MAY: 4th Monet exhibits thirty-seven paintings of London at Durand-Ruel's gallery in Paris. **10th** Works by Monet, Pissarro and Renoir are on show at the World Exhibition in St Louis, Missouri.
JULY: Cassatt is made a Chevalier of the Legion of Honour.

OCTOBER: 2nd Opening of the Salon d'Automne (*see* p.229). Cézanne and Renoir are given individual rooms. **5th** Works by Degas, Manet and Monet are exhibited at Paul Cassirer's gallery in Berlin ◆ (pp.214–5).
NOVEMBER: 1st Monet and Renoir are included in an exhibition in Dublin.

1905

JANUARY: Durand-Ruel organizes a vast Impressionist exhibition at the Grafton Galleries, London. Among the 315 works shown are fifty-nine Renoirs, fifty-five Monets, forty-nine Pissarros, thirty-seven Sisleys, thirty-five Degas, nineteen Manets, thirteen Morisots and ten Cézannes.
APRIL: 9th The sixth Venice Biennale shows works by Monet, Pissarro and Sisley.
15th Degas stays with Henri Rouart at La Queue-en-Brie, near Créteil, and paints two portraits of the family (opposite).
20th Death of Antonin Proust (p.124).
MAY: The collection of Renoir's friend Paul Berard ● (opposite) is auctioned at Georges Petit's gallery. Prices are high.

OTHER EVENTS

1904
- France and Britain sign 'Entente Cordiale'
- Russia and Japan go to war
- Bakelite invented by L. H. Baekland
- Rolls-Royce Company formed
- Stage débuts of Wedekind's *Pandora's Box* and Chekhov's *The Cherry Orchard*
- Puccini's *Madame Butterfly* and Janáček's *Jenufa* first performed
- Chekhov dies

1905
- General strike in Russia; mutiny on the *Potemkin*; Tsar concedes reforms
- Separation of Church and State in France
- Norway declares independence from Sweden
- Einstein formulates his special theory of relativity
- Amundsen discovers location of North Pole
- Publication of E. M. Forster's *Where Angels Fear to Tread* and H. G. Wells' *Kipps*
- Richard Strauss' *Salome* first performed
- Jules Verne dies

1906
- Dreyfus rehabilitated and awarded Legion of Honour
- Opening of Simplon Tunnel between Switzerland and Italy
- Bergson's *L'Évolution créatrice*, Galsworthy's *The Man of Property* and Upton Sinclair's *The Jungle* published
- Ibsen dies

**DEGAS
Mme Alexis Rouart
and Her Children**
c.1905

Mme Alexis Rouart was the daughter-in-law of Degas' great friend Henri Rouart (p.131), and a favourite of the artist. In this large pastel, Degas' use of harmonious colours is at odds with the emotional tensions between the sitters – while one tearful child seeks comfort from his mother, the other turns her back on her.

JULY: 13th Cézanne visits Paris for the last time and stays at Fontainebleau.
SEPTEMBER: 5th Cassatt refuses to serve on the jury at the Carnegie Institute's annual exhibition, on the grounds that it is against 'the rules of les Indépendants'.
OCTOBER: Georges Charpentier, publisher of *La Vie moderne* (*see* p.112), dies. **18th** The Salon d'Automne opens. Seeing the bold colours used by Matisse and others, the critic Louis Vauxcelles dubs them 'Les Fauves' (the wild beasts). **24th** Death of Renoir's patron Paul Berard ● (below).

1906
Publication of George Moore's *Reminiscences of the Impressionist Painters* and Théodore Duret's *Histoire des peintres impressionnistes* (an expanded version of his 1878 publication).
MARCH: Durand-Ruel exhibits works by Manet and Monet from Jean-Baptiste Faure's collection ● (p.81).
MAY: Bernheim-Jeune open a new gallery at 15 rue Richepanse and become increasingly interested in Impressionist paintings. **23rd** Death of the restaurateur and hotelier Eugène Murer.
JUNE: 11th The American critic James G. Huneker writes an article about Cézanne in the *New York Sun*.
OCTOBER: 22nd Cézanne dies at his home in Aix-en-Provence, aged 67. Degas visits Naples.
DECEMBER: 5th Degas is robbed of 1000 francs in Marseilles.

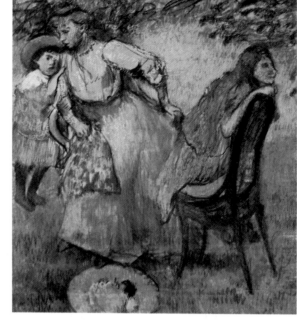

● PAUL BERARD
Banker, diplomat and patron

With the death of Paul Berard on October 24th, 1905, Renoir lost one of his closest friends and most devoted patrons, with whom he had been in regular contact since 1879. Descended from a family of Huguenot bankers, Berard was a diplomat as well as a businessman. He had a town house in the rue Pigalle and a mansion, built in Second-Empire style, called the Château de Wargemont, just outside Dieppe – an area much favoured by members of the bourgeois intelligentsia, such as Degas' friends the Halévys ▲ (p.208) and the portrait painter Jacques-Émile Blanche.

Between 1879 and 1884 Renoir produced numerous paintings for the Berards, many of them portraits of their children – including the delightful *Children's Afternoon at Wargemont* (p.140) painted in 1884, which at the auction of Berard's collection in 1905 fetched 14,000 francs. The flow of commissions then stopped, though the family remained on friendly terms with the painter. Berard also introduced Renoir to business friends such as the Gimpels and the Clapissons; and when, in 1900, Renoir was awarded the Legion of Honour, he requested that 'M. Paul Berard, Chevalier of the Legion of Honour of 20 rue Pigalle, Paris, represent me, and deliver to me at Grasse [in Provence] the insignia of the Legion of Honour.'

Life at Wargemont seems to have been enchanting. Blanche described the three girls as 'unruly savages, with wind-tossed hair, who refused to learn to write or spell', preferring to 'slip away into the fields to milk the cows'. Renoir himself participated fully in the life of the estate, where he spent a good deal of time with the servants, and greatly enjoyed the family's weekly shopping trips in Dieppe.

1907–1910

Entering the Museums

The arrival of Manet's 'Olympia' in the Louvre and Renoir's 'Madame Charpentier and her Children' in the Metropolitan Museum of Art, New York, marks the final acceptance of the Impressionist movement into the official 'pantheon' of art history.

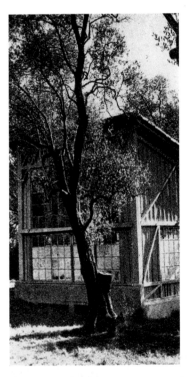

A contemporary photograph of the studio that Renoir built in the grounds of the Villa de la Poste at Les Collettes in Cagnes.

1907
JANUARY: 6th Manet's *Olympia* ▲ (p.179) is hung in the Louvre.
APRIL: 11th The collection belonging to Georges Charpentier (*see* p.231) is sold in Paris. The Metropolitan Museum of Art buys Renoir's *Madame Charpentier and her Children* (p.110) for 84,000 francs, the Kunsthalle in Bremen purchases his portrait of Madame Chocquet, and the Nationalgalerie in Berlin his *Chestnuts in Bloom*. **27th** Monet tells Durand-Ruel that he has destroyed thirty water-lily paintings with which he was unhappy.
MAY: Major Impressionist works from the Moreau-Nélaton collection (*see* p.242) are hung in the Musée des Arts Décoratifs – including Manet's *Déjeuner sur l'herbe* (p.27) and *Berthe Morisot with a Fan*, nine Monets (among them *The Field of Poppies*), Morisot's *Chasing Butterflies*, seven Sisleys and two Pissarros.
JUNE: Monet's eyesight deteriorates. **28th** Renoir buys Les Collettes, an estate at Cagnes, and starts to build a house there.
OCTOBER: 4th Opening of the Salon d'Automne (*see* p.229), which includes a Cézanne retrospective of fifty oils and watercolours. **20th** The critic Zacharie Astruc ● (p.37) dies.
NOVEMBER: 1st The Bernheim-Jeune gallery shows works by Cassatt, Cézanne, Degas, Manet, Monet, Morisot and Sisley.

1908
JANUARY: 1st Mary Cassatt makes her last visit to the USA.
MARCH: Durand-Ruel buys Manet's *Reading* (c.1865) from Faure ● (p.81) for 1500 francs, and sells it to the Museum of Cincinnati for 15,000 francs.
MAY: Monet departs for a visit to Venice. Ivan Morozov ◆ (pp.214–5) buys Renoir's *Bathing on the Seine* (1869) from Vollard for 20,000 francs.
JULY: The sculptor Aristide Maillol stays with Renoir in order to model a bust of him ◆ (p.235). **17th** Paul Cassirer sells Manet's portrait of Zacharie Astruc (p.37) to the Kunsthalle in Bremen for 21,000 marks.
AUGUST: 21st Degas mentions in a letter to Henri Rouart's son Alexis that he fears he is going blind and is concentrating on sculpture ◆ (p.235).
NOVEMBER: 12th A Renoir exhibition opens at Durand-Ruel's gallery in New York.

OTHER EVENTS

1907
- Russia hit by famine
- French gunboats bombard Casablanca
- British suffragettes clash with police
- Pope denounces modernism in France
- Huysmans and Grieg die

1908
- King Carlos and Crown Prince Luiz of Portugal assassinated
- Franco-British Exhibition held in London
- First newsreels
- First Model 'T' Ford goes on sale
- Anatole France's *L'Ile des pingouins* and E. M. Forster's *A Room with a View* published
- Bartók composes String Quartet No.1
- Rimsky-Korsakov dies

1909
- Aristide Briand succeeds Clemenceau as Premier of France
- Robert E. Peary reaches North Pole
- Louis Blériot flies the English Channel
- *L'Enchanteur pourrissant* by Apollinaire published
- Swinburne and George Meredith die

1910
- George V succeeds Edward VII
- Portugal declared a republic after coup
- Arthur Evans finishes excavating Knossos
- Tango craze sweeps Europe and USA
- Stravinsky's *Firebird* first performed
- Tolstoy and Mark Twain die

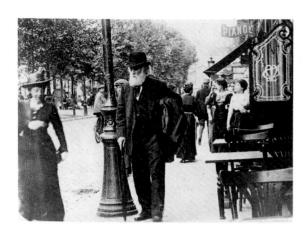

A photograph of Degas walking in the Boulevard de Clichy (*c*.1910).

1909

APRIL: 19th Death of Dr Gachet – patron, friend and physician to the Impressionists.
MAY: Durand-Ruel exhibits some of Monet's water-lily paintings. **19th** Degas attends the Paris début of Diaghilev's Ballets Russes.
DECEMBER: Monet proposes a monument to Cézanne, but it comes to nothing. **3rd** Paul Cassirer holds a Cézanne exhibition in Berlin.

1910

JANUARY: 4th Opening of a Cézanne exhibition at the Bernheim-Jeune gallery.
MARCH: Works by Cézanne, Monet and Renoir are shown in Berlin. The Frankfurt Museum purchases Renoir's *Young Girl Reading*.
APRIL: Renoir retrospective held at the Venice Biennale. **20th** Monet, Pissarro and Renoir participate in an exhibition entitled 'The Evolution of Landscape' at the Libre Esthétique ◆ (pp.214–5) in Brussels.
JUNE: 20th Durand-Ruel, Bernheim-Jeune and Paul Cassirer pay 1,000,000 francs for some major Impressionist works owned by the margarine manufacturer Auguste Pellerin (*see* p.241).
JULY: Renoir visits Franz Thurneyssen ◆ (pp.214–5) in Germany and paints a portrait of his wife.
OCTOBER: Renoir writes a preface to Victor Mottez's translation of Cennino Cennini's *Il Libro dell'Arte*, a fifteenth-century artists' handbook ◆ (pp.220–1).
NOVEMBER: 8th Works by Cézanne and Manet appear in a Post-Impressionist exhibition, organized by Roger Fry, at the Grafton Galleries in London.

● THE HAVEMEYERS

Head of the American Sugar-Refining Company, Henry Osborne Havemeyer had begun collecting Japanese artefacts after seeing the 1876 World Exhibition in Philadelphia, with its wealth of oriental art. But following his marriage in 1883 to Louisine Waldron-Elder – who had been a childhood friend of Mary Cassatt and lived with her while studying art in Paris – he started collecting paintings on a large scale, including the works of the Impressionists. Cassatt was the Havemeyers' guide during their frequent excursions to Europe in search of art – and inevitably she promoted the work of her friends, especially that of Degas.

After her husband's death in 1907, Louisine continued collecting energetically (she was among the first Americans to recognize the importance of Cézanne). She became a suffragette and scandalized her family by being arrested at a demonstration.

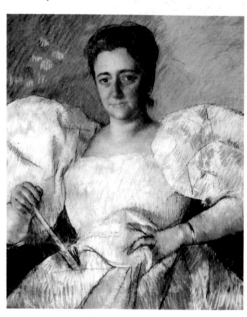

CASSATT *Portrait of Mrs H. O. Havemeyer* 1896

Her long friendship with Cassatt foundered in 1923, after a dispute over some of the latter's prints (*see* p.239).

On her death in 1929, Louisine left most of her collection to the Metropolitan Museum of Art and the balance to her son and two daughters, who donated the greater part of their legacy to the museum. As well as a wealth of Old Masters, the collection (which was largest the museum had ever been given) included thirty-six Degas, twenty Courbets, nine Manets, eight Monets, five Cézannes, four Corots, three Cassatts and two Renoirs.

1911–1913

Changing Attitudes

Impressionist works are being exhibited extensively in most European countries as well as in the USA and a surprising development is the enhancement of Cézanne's reputation, which stems from a reaction against the 'incoherence' of artists such as Monet.

1911

JANUARY: Cézanne's widow and son stay with the Renoirs in Cagnes.
MARCH: 4th Alfred Stieglitz's photographic gallery in New York mounts the first Cézanne exhibition to be held in the USA.
APRIL: Twelve paintings by Degas are shown at Harvard University's Fogg Art Museum (the second of the two solo exhibitions of Degas' work held during his lifetime).
MAY: 1st Monet and Renoir are included in the International Exhibition in Rome. **14th** Monet's second wife, Alice ◆ (pp.146–7), dies.
JUNE: Renoir attends a performance of Diaghilev's Ballets Russes.
JULY: The banker Count Isaac de Camondo dies, leaving his collection of Impressionist and Post-Impressionist paintings to the French nation.
OCTOBER: 3rd A Pissarro exhibition opens at the Stafford Gallery, London. **20th** Renoir is elevated to Chevalier of the Legion of Honour.
NOVEMBER: An exhibition of works by Cézanne and Gauguin opens at the Stafford Gallery, London.
DECEMBER: Cassatt visits Egypt with her brother Alexander and family.

1912

JANUARY: Degas reluctantly moves to an apartment at 6 boulevard de Clichy, as his house in the rue Victor-Massé is to be demolished. Renoir temporarily rents an apartment in Nice to be more mobile.
FEBRUARY: 1st An exhibition of forty-one works by Renoir opens at the Thannhauser gallery in Munich. It subsequently transfers to Paul Cassirer's gallery in Berlin ◆ (pp.214–5).
APRIL: Works by Manet, Monet and Renoir appear at the 'Centennial Exhibition of French Art' in St Petersburg. **9th** Rouart dies, aged 79.
10th The annual exhibition of the International Society of Artists in London includes works by Degas, Manet, Monet, Pissarro and Renoir.
MAY: Monet's Venice paintings are shown at the Bernheim-Jeune gallery.
JUNE: 7th Durand-Ruel mounts an exhibition of thirty-eight portraits by Renoir. **15th** Renoir has an attack of paralysis, but soon regains the use of his arms and hands ▲ (p.237).
JULY: 1st An Impressionist exhibition in Mannheim shows works by Cézanne, Degas, Manet, Monet and Renoir.

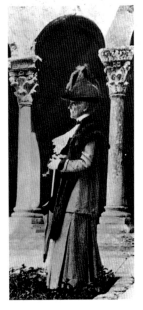

A photograph of Cassatt in the cloisters of St-Trophime in Arles (1912).

OTHER EVENTS

1911

- Revolution in China; Sun Yat-sen becomes President of new Chinese Republic
- Assassination attempt on French Premier Aristide Briand in Chamber of Deputies
- Women riot in France over price of food
- Amundsen beats Scott to South Pole
- Publication of Rupert Brooke's *Poems* and Katherine Mansfield's *In a German Pension*
- First performance of Stravinsky's *Petrushka* and Richard Strauss' *Der Rosenkavalier*
- Mahler dies

1912

- Morocco becomes a French protectorate
- Shipping embargo on Dardanelles by Turkey
- Outbreak of war in Balkans
- Woodrow Wilson elected US President
- Stainless steel and cellophane first made
- *Titanic* sunk by iceberg
- Jung's *The Theory of Psychoanalysis* published
- Ravel's *Daphnis et Chloé* first performed
- Strindberg dies

1913

- Poincaré becomes French President
- Opening of Grand Central Terminal in New York
- Publication of Proust's *Du côté de chez Swann* and D. H. Lawrence's *Sons and Lovers*
- Stravinsky's *Rite of Spring* causes uproar at first performance

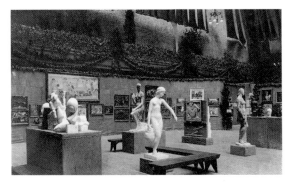

A photograph of the densely-hung Armory Show.

DECEMBER: 9th–11th Sale of Rouart's collection at the Manzi-Joyant gallery. Degas' *Dancers Practising at the Barre* (1876–7) goes for 478,000 francs to the American collector Mrs H. O. Havemeyer ● (p.233), who subsequently presents it to the Metropolitan Museum of Art. **10th** Dr Albert C. Barnes of Philadelphia acquires one of Cézanne's *Bathers* (1888) from Vollard for 14,980 francs.

1913

Publication of G. L. Borgemeyer's *The Master Impressionists* (the first major book on Impressionism to appear in the USA).

FEBRUARY: 17th Opening of the Armory Show in New York (above), the most comprehensive exhibition of modern art so far held in America. The Impressionists, including Cézanne, Degas, Manet and Renoir, are well represented. Approximately 87,000 people see the show.

JUNE: 9th The collection belonging to Count Mariczell of Budapest is auctioned at the Hôtel Drouot ◆ (p.102).

AUGUST: Renoir takes up sculpture. He employs 23-year-old Richard Guino as his teacher and assistant ◆ (below).

SEPTEMBER: 12th Cassatt writes to Horace Havemeyer – the son of Henry and Louisine Havemeyer ● (p.233) – that Degas is only a shadow of his former self.

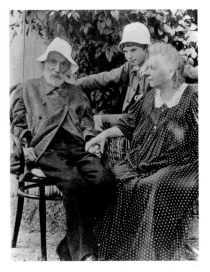

A photograph taken in 1912 of Renoir with his son Coco (Claude) and wife Aline.

◆ **THE IMPRESSIONISTS AND SCULPTURE**

With failing sight, both Renoir and Degas turned to sculpture to express themselves and also to experiment with form. Degas had taken his first steps in the medium before 1870, and was greatly helped by his friend the sculptor Paul-Albert Bartholomé. All his sculptures were modelled in wax, but during his lifetime only one of them, the *Little Dancer of 14 Years* (p.126), was cast in bronze. Visitors to his studio were surprised by the number of small wax figures that cluttered the place and by how, especially in old age, he would constantly play with them. After his death, the most presentable ones were cast in bronze ◆ (p.239). Renoir's interest in sculpture was aroused when Aristide Maillol made a bust of him at Essoyes in 1906. This had been commissioned by Vollard ▲ (pp.186–7), and in the summer of 1913 he suggested that Renoir should collaborate with Richard Guino, who had been working as Maillol's assistant. Fourteen figures and bas-reliefs resulted from this partnership, including a clock case entitled *Hymn to Life* (left), a bas-relief version of Renoir's *Judgment of Paris*, a study of his wife with their son Jean on her knee, and several medallions of famous artists, including Cézanne, Delacroix, Ingres and Rodin.

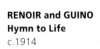

RENOIR and GUINO
Hymn to Life
c.1914

The theme of this clock case is the continuity of life: a man and woman look up to a torch-bearing child.

1914–1918

Successful Survival

Despite the war and the death of Degas, Impressionism survives and the prices of Impressionist works continue to rise significantly.

1914

FEBRUARY: 10th Monet's son Jean dies at the age of 47. Monet is deeply affected by his death.

MARCH: Construction begins of a large studio for Monet's *Nymphéas* cyclorama ◆ (p.241) at his home in Giverny. Renoir works on a tapestry of Neptune and Venus for the State-owned Gobelins factory.

APRIL: The Prince de Wagram sells sixteen Renoirs to Durand-Ruel (several of which would subsequently be bought by Dr Albert C. Barnes.)

JUNE: 3rd Count Isaac de Camondo's collection is hung in the Louvre (*see* p.234). It includes works by Cézanne, Degas, Monet, Morisot, Pissarro, Renoir, Sisley, Toulouse-Lautrec and van Gogh.

SEPTEMBER: Mary Cassatt is awarded the Gold Medal of the Pittsburgh Academy of Fine Arts. Because of the approach of German forces, she leaves her house at Mesnil-Théribus to live in Nice. **15th** Bracquemond dies, aged 81.

OCTOBER: Renoir's sons Jean and Pierre are wounded in action.

1915

MAY: 3rd The Knoedler Galleries in New York stage an exhibition of 'Old Masters and Works by Edgar Degas and Mary Cassatt' in aid of the suffragette movement.

JUNE: 27th Renoir's wife, Aline ◆ (pp.146–7), dies in Nice on her way home from visiting their wounded son Jean in hospital.

NOVEMBER: Degas becomes very deaf and rarely leaves his flat, except for daily outings to the Place Pigalle.

DECEMBER: 15th In a letter to Durand-Ruel, Renoir says he has had a stomach infection and a six-week bout of bronchitis but is still painting.

1916

FEBRUARY: 4th At the suggestion of Mary Cassatt, Degas' niece Jeanne Fevre comes to look after him.

AUGUST: 5th Degas goes to stay with his friend the sculptor Paul-Albert Bartholomé ◆ (p.235) in Auteuil.

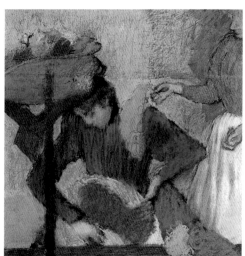

DEGAS
At the Milliner's
c.1905–10

One of a number of scenes of milliners that Degas produced late in his life, this pastel was still in the artist's possession on his death, and was sold to the Comte de Beaumont for 13,000 francs in 1918.

OTHER EVENTS

1914
• Austrian Archduke Ferdinand murdered in Sarajevo
• Start of World War I
• Germany invades France and Belgium

1915
• Poison gas first used on Western Front
• Disastrous Allied assault on Gallipoli
• Sinking of the *Lusitania*
• Einstein proposes his general theory of relativity

1916
• Italy declares war on Germany
• First Zeppelin raid on Paris
• Tanks first used on Western Front
• Irish Easter Rising
• Henry James dies

1917
• Russian monarchy collapses; Bolsheviks seize power
• USA enters the war
• Mata Hari executed for spying
• Début of Cocteau's *Parade* (with music by Satie and set designs by Picasso)

1918
• Woodrow Wilson proposes 'Fourteen Points' peace plan
• Civil war in Russia
• Russian royal family murdered
• Armistice between Germany and Allies
• Killer flu sweeps world
• Spengler's *Decline of the West* published
• Apollinaire, Debussy and Wedekind die

1917
MAY: Renoir starts to sculpt medallions of famous artists ◆ (p.235).
JUNE: 1st Death of the novelist and critic Octave Mirbeau.
AUGUST: Renoir spends the month in Essoyes.
SEPTEMBER: Renoir teaches his son Claude to make pottery in Cagnes.
27th Degas dies of a stroke at the age of 83. **28th** Degas' funeral is attended by over a hundred mourners, including Bartholomé, Cassatt, Joseph and Georges Durand-Ruel, Monet, Vollard and Zandomeneghi.
DECEMBER: 2nd Richard Guino, who has been helping Renoir with his sculpture, leaves Cagnes after a disagreement with him ◆ (p.235).
31st Matisse visits Renoir in Cagnes.

1918
The collections of Sergei Shchukin and Ivan Morozov ◆ (pp.214–5) are nationalized but left in their owners' houses in Moscow, becoming the First and Second Museums of Modern Western Painting.
MARCH: 26th–27th Degas' collection of Old Masters is auctioned at the Galeries Georges Petit. It fetches 1,966,200 francs.
MAY: 4th Cézanne's widow, Hortense ◆ (pp.146–7), dies.
NOVEMBER: 3rd Monet proposes to Clemenceau that he give his *Nymphéas* cyclorama to the nation in honour of the victory ◆ (p.241).
DECEMBER: 11th–13th The contents of Degas' studio are auctioned at the Galeries Georges Petit.

 RENOIR IN 1918

In March the art dealer René Gimpel and his wife visited Renoir at his home in Cagnes. The following extract from Gimpel's *Journal d'un collectionneur, marchand de tableaux*, published in 1963, reveals the desperate condition of the artist during the last years of his life:

Through the partly open door I caught sight of him; they were bringing him down, two women carrying him in a kind of litter … Before me was a shell of a man …

Seated he is a frightful spectacle, elbows clamped to his sides, forearms raised; he was shaking two sinister stumps dangling with threads and very narrow ribbons. His fingers are cut almost to the quick; the bones jut out, with barely any skin on them. Ah, no, he has his fingers pressed in and spread against the palms of his hands, his pitiful, helpless hands, like the claws of a chicken plucked and trussed ready for the spit.

But I still had not seen his head; it was sunk on a carved, humped back. He was wearing a tall, large English travelling cap. His face is pale and thin;

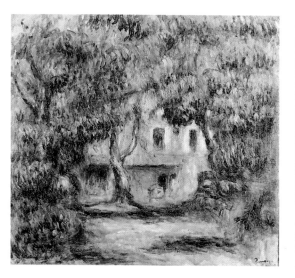

his white beard, stiff as gorse, hangs sideways as if wind-blown …

'How can he paint?' we asked the woman. 'I place the brushes between his fingers and fasten them with the strings and ribbons. Sometimes they fall, and I put them back – but what's so astonishing about M. Renoir are those lynx eyes of his. Sometimes he calls me and tells me to remove a hair that's come off the brush and got stuck on the canvas. I look and see nothing till Monsieur shows it to me; a minuscule, hidden in a daub of paint.'

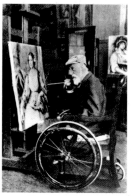

A photograph of Renoir in a wheelchair, working on his portrait of the German Actress Tilla Durieux (1914).

RENOIR
The Farm at Les Collettes
c.1915

Renoir never painted the house he built at Les Collettes, but preferred to depict this farmhouse on the estate, which he saw as a symbol of a continuing rural tradition.

237

1919–1924

Impressionism in a New World

Once seen as a new and revolutionary art form, Impressionism has now become virtually the art of the establishment – its leading position in the avant-garde having been taken over by Cubism, Surrealism and other movements. But due to improvements in education, printing and reproduction processes, and exhibition facilities, it is beginning to attract a larger public than any of its predecessors.

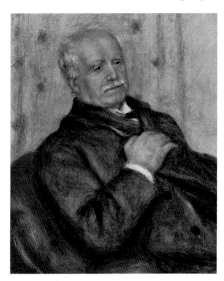

RENOIR
Portrait of Paul
Durand-Ruel
1910

This was Renoir's only portrait of Durand-Ruel, the man to whom he owed much of his success. Painted when the dealer was in his late 70s, it seems an affectionate rendering, with the red armchair reflecting the warm hues of the sitter's face.

1919

FEBRUARY: 12th Renoir's *Madame Charpentier and her Children* (p.110) is acquired by the Louvre.
MARCH: 25th Renoir is promoted to Commander of the Legion of Honour (the highest grade).
MAY: 14th Death of Octave Maus ◆ (pp.214–5).
AUGUST: At the invitation of the Director of the Louvre, Renoir goes to see his *Madame Charpentier and her Children*.
DECEMBER: 3rd Renoir dies of pneumonia, aged 78.

1920

FEBRUARY: 14th Death of Zoé Closier, Degas' housekeeper for thirty-five years ◆ (pp.146–7).
SEPTEMBER: It is proposed that the government build a pavilion in the grounds of the Hôtel Biron (now the Musée Rodin) to house Monet's *Nymphéas* cyclorama ◆ (p.241).

1921

MAY: 1st An exhibition of Degas bronzes ◆ (opposite) opens at Adrien Hébrard's gallery in the rue Royale.
JUNE: The Ministry of Fine Arts says that Monet's *Nymphéas* cyclorama will be hung in specially adapted rooms in the Orangerie ◆ (p.241).
JULY: 14th Durand-Ruel is awarded the Legion of Honour.

1922

FEBRUARY: The British textile magnate Samuel Courtauld starts to buy Impressionist paintings (*see* p.242). **5th** Durand-Ruel dies, aged 91.
MARCH: 20th Renoir's heirs sell 130 of his works for 1,500,000 francs to Barbazanges, a new firm of art dealers financed by the banker Orosdi.
APRIL: 22nd Monet signs an agreement donating his as yet unfinished *Nymphéas* cyclorama to the nation ◆ (p.241).
JUNE: Death of Pissarro's widow, Julie ◆ (pp.146–7).
AUGUST: 3rd An exhibition entitled 'Les maîtres de l'Impressionnisme et leurs temps' opens at the Musées Royaux in Brussels.

OTHER EVENTS

1919
• Versailles Peace Conference begins
• Weimar Constitution adopted in Germany
• Publication of Somerset Maugham's *The Moon and Sixpence* (based on Gauguin)

1920
• First meeting of League of Nations
• Prohibition comes into force in USA
• Holst's *The Planets* first performed

1921
• Paris conference fixes German reparations
• Début of Pirandello's *Six Characters in Search of an Author*
• Saint-Saëns dies

1922
• Hyperinflation in Germany
• Mussolini seizes power after march on Rome
• T. S. Eliot's *The Waste Land* and James Joyce's *Ulysses* published
• Marcel Proust dies

1923
• Hitler arrested after Munich putsch
• Primo de Rivera seizes power in Spain
• Gershwin's *Rhapsody in Blue* first performed
• Pierre Loti and Sarah Bernhardt die

1924
• Death of Lenin; power struggle in USSR
• Greece becomes a republic
• Conrad, Anatole France, Kafka and Puccini die

1923

JANUARY: Prince Kojiro Matsukata of Japan starts buying Impressionist works (*see* p.247). **10th** Monet has an operation for a cataract.
MARCH: The American collector Duncan Phillips buys Renoir's *Luncheon of the Boating Party* (p.132) from Durand-Ruel's sons for $125,000 and begins to collect Impressionist paintings on a large scale.
APRIL: The First and Second Museums of Modern Western Painting in Moscow – which contain the collections of Impressionist paintings amassed by Sergei Shchukin and Ivan Morozov ◆ (pp.214–5) – are merged to create the State Museum of Modern Western Art.
JUNE: Cassatt has a dispute with the Metropolitan Museum of Art about a set of 20-year-old drypoint plates. She falls out with Louisine Havemeyer ● (p.233), who has been acting as an intermediary.

1924

FEBRUARY: 12th The dealer Édouard Gerbineau is sentenced to three months' imprisonment for selling a forged Renoir.
APRIL: 7th A Degas retrospective opens at the Galeries Georges Petit. The introduction to the catalogue is by Daniel Halévy ▲ (p.208).
10th Barbazanges, in partnership with Bernheim-Jeune, purchase further paintings by Renoir from his heirs. **15th** Mrs Arthur Sachs of New York buys Manet's *The Plum* (1877) for 1,000,000 francs.
JUNE: The Tate Gallery buys Degas' *Young Spartans Exercising* (painted in 1860–2, but largely reworked in 1882) from Goupil.

◆ THE DEGAS BRONZES

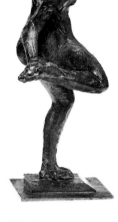

DEGAS
Dancer Looking at the Sole of Her Right Foot
1895–10

Several of the wax figures found in Degas' studio were of dancers in this naturalistic stance. Alice Michel, who posed for the artist in 1910, related that he worked excruciatingly slowly, and often had to start again when the waxes fell apart. The bronze above was first modelled in green wax, and the original wax for that on the right was destroyed.

According to a letter written by Joseph Durand-Ruel in June 1919 to the art critic of the *New York Herald*, approximately 150 wax figures were found in Degas' studio after his death, many of them in fragments. The viable figures were entrusted to Paul-Albert Bartholomé ◆ (p.235), who, in conjunction with Degas' heirs, sold the reproduction rights to the founder and art dealer Adrien Hébrard.

In May 1921, the bronzes were exhibited at Hébrard's gallery and were widely acclaimed. The Italian founder Albino Palazzolo, who had done the casting, was awarded the Legion of Honour in recognition of his work on Degas' and Rodin's sculptures. The process used was quite complex. First of all moulds were made from the figures in order to produce working models in bronze, from which the final casts were taken using the *cire perdue* process. Working from the durable bronze models, it proved possible to make at least twenty-two casts of each figure.

The price for a set of thirty bronzes was between 600,000 and 700,000 francs. One set was bought by Cassatt, who lent it to the Metropolitan Museum of Art, and the Louvre acquired a set through Degas' heirs. The original wax figures were bought by Paul Mellon in 1955, and the bronze working models by another American collector, Norton Simon, in 1976.

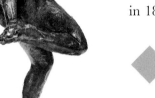

1925–1929

Deaths and Bequests

With the deaths of the last Impressionists – Cassatt, Monet and Guillaumin – the final active phase of the movement draws to a close. A number of important bequests enrich the major museum collections.

1925

APRIL: 13th Death of Léon Leenhoff ◆ (pp.146–7).

MAY: Zola's widow dies, leaving Manet's portrait of her husband (p.53) to the Louvre.

JUNE: The Durand-Ruel gallery sells Renoir's *La Loge* (p.87) to Percy Moore Turner who, in turn, sells it to his client Samuel Courtauld.

JULY: The Wildenstein Galleries sell a Cézanne still life for $1,500,000.

DECEMBER: The Durand-Ruel gallery moves to 39 Avenue Friedland.

1926

JANUARY: Renoir's *Cabaret of Mère Antony* (p.38) is donated to the Nationalmuseum in Stockholm.

MARCH: The Tate Gallery buys Monet's *Lady in a Park* (*c*.1878) for £525.

APRIL: 12th Death of the critic Gustave Geffroy ▲ (p.158).

15th Auction of pictures belonging to the American collector James Quinn in Paris. Pissarro's *The Jetty at Le Havre* is sold for 40,000 francs, and one of Cézanne's paintings of Mont Ste-Victoire for 280,000 francs.

JUNE: 14th Cassatt dies at the age of 82.

DECEMBER: 6th Monet dies at Giverny, aged 86.

1927

JANUARY: Roger Fry's influential *Cézanne: A Study of his Development* is published in London.

MAY: 17th Monet's *Nymphéas* cyclorama ◆ (opposite) opens to the public. **19th** The critic Théodore Duret ▲ (pp.145 and 199) dies. Shortly after his death it is discovered that his collection of Impressionist works has been stolen and forgeries substituted.

OCTOBER: Death of Guillaumin, the sole survivor of the exhibitors at the Impressionist exhibitions, aged 86.

NOVEMBER: 10th The collection of Degas' brother René is sold in Paris.

1928

FEBRUARY: 8th An important Manet exhibition opens at the Matthiesen Gallery in Berlin.

APRIL: The Louvre acquires Manet's portrait of Mallarmé (p.99).

The cover of Roger Fry's influential book on Cézanne, from a design by the author. The work was published by the Hogarth Press (run by Leonard and Virginia Woolf) and received much acclaim in England.

OTHER EVENTS

1925
- European powers sign Locarno peace pact
- Hitler's *Mein Kampf* published
- John Logie Baird makes his first TV transmission
- Kafka's *The Trial* and Scott Fitzgerald's *The Great Gatsby* published
- Alban Berg's *Wozzeck* first performed

1926
- Hirohito becomes Emperor of Japan
- Britain paralysed by general strike
- Publication of Gide's *Les Faux-Monnayeurs*
- Rilke and Rudolph Valentino die

1927
- Stalin emerges as leader of USSR
- Release of *The Jazz Singer* (the first 'talkie')
- Hermann Hesse's *Steppenwolf* published
- Isadora Duncan dies

1928
- Chiang Kai-shek becomes President of Chinese Republic
- Alexander Fleming discovers penicillin
- Publication of D. H. Lawrence's *Lady Chatterley's Lover*
- Janáček and Thomas Hardy die

1929
- Wall Street crash
- Publication of Cocteau's *Les Enfants terribles*, Faulkner's *The Sound and the Fury* and Hemingway's *A Farewell to Arms*
- Diaghilev dies

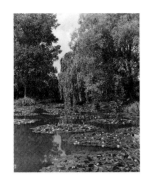

1929
Following the recent death of Louisine Havemeyer, the Metropolitan Museum of Art receives the Havemeyer bequest ● (p.233).
MARCH: 20th Clemenceau dies at the age of 88.
OCTOBER: 14th The margarine manufacturer Auguste Pellerin dies, leaving an Impressionist collection worth 80,000,000 francs (*see* p.233).
NOVEMBER: 7th New York's Museum of Modern Art opens in temporary premises with a loan exhibition of thirty-five Cézannes, twenty-one Gauguins, seventeen Seurats and twenty-eight van Goghs.

A recent photograph of Monet's water garden at Giverny. The house and gardens were restored in the late 1970s and now look very much as they did during the artist's life.

 ## MONET'S 'NYMPHÉAS' CYCLORAMA

Monet decided to create a work on a monumental scale that would act as a distraction from the horrors of the war, establish his reputation as a national figure, and symbolically pay tribute to the greatness of France. The subject was to be his water garden, and he saw the project as a 'cyclorama' of twelve panels, each about 4m (13ft) long and 2m (6ft) high. He decided to offer the work to the nation through Clemenceau, provided that it was displayed suitably and that the government bought his *Women in the Garden* (1866).

Unfortunately Clemenceau lost the elections of 1920, and the project became increasingly tortuous. In September 1920 it was suggested that the panels should be exhibited in a pavilion in the grounds of the Hôtel Biron. Finally, Monet having been paid 200,000 francs for *Women in the Garden*, it was decided in June 1921 that the panels would be hung in specially adapted rooms in the Orangerie. Nine months later a formal agreement was signed by the artist and the Director of Fine Arts. In 1925 Monet visited the Orangerie to inspect the gallery, but he continued altering the panels until his death in 1926, and the gallery was not opened to the public until May 1927.

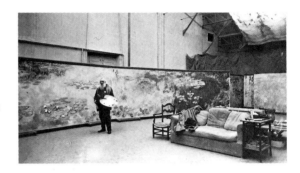

A photograph of Monet in his third studio at Giverny (*c*.1924–5), in front of the *Nymphéas* panel *Morning*.

MONET
Nymphéas: The Setting Sun
1916–26

This panel shows the evening light reflecting in the dark shadows of the pool. It hangs in the first of the specially adapted rooms in the Orangerie between *Morning* and *Clouds*.

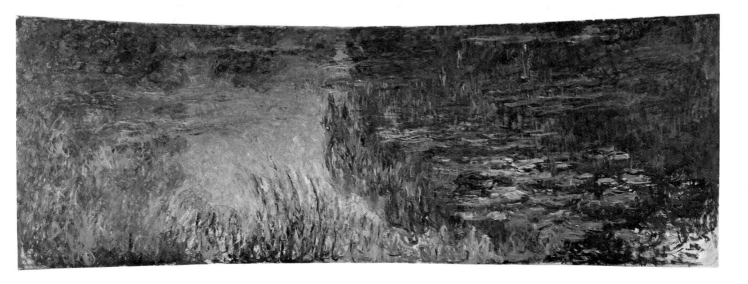

1930–1939

Major Retrospectives

The development of more modern museum practices, together with the increasing number of exhibitions being held throughout the world, helps to promote public awareness of the significance of the Impressionists and brings about a wider recognition of their astonishing achievements.

1930
FEBRUARY: A Pissarro retrospective is held at the Orangerie in Paris to mark the hundredth anniversary of his birth.
MARCH: 10th The Havemeyer bequest ● (p.233) is exhibited at the Metropolitan Museum of Art in New York.

1931
JULY: 19th An exhibition entitled 'Degas, Portraitist and Sculptor' opens at the Orangerie.
SEPTEMBER: 8th The Courtauld Institute, housing Samuel Courtauld's collection of Impressionist paintings (*see* p.242), opens in London as a centre for the study of art history.

1932
JANUARY: 4th Opening of a major exhibition of French art at the Royal Academy in London, including a selection of important Impressionist paintings.
JUNE: A Manet retrospective is held at the Orangerie.

1933
FEBRUARY: The Knoedler Galleries in New York buy Degas' *Green Singer* (*c*.1884) from the State Museum of Modern Western Art in Moscow (*see* p.239).
MARCH: 4th Death of the novelist George Moore (p.46).
APRIL: A Renoir retrospective is held at the Orangerie.
JUNE: The American lawyer John G. Johnson bequeaths his collection of Impressionist paintings to the Philadelphia Museum of Art.

1934
APRIL: Manet's *Déjeuner sur l'herbe* (p.27) and other works from the Moreau-Nélaton collection (*see* p.232) are transferred from the Musée des Arts Décoratifs to the Louvre.
JUNE: 12th Sale of collection of works by Degas belonging to his niece, Jeanne Fevre.

1936
JUNE: The twentieth Venice Biennale features a Degas retrospective.

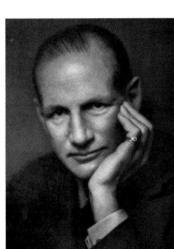

A photograph of the British textile magnate, Samuel Courtauld, who founded the Courtauld Institute in 1931.

OTHER EVENTS

1930
• France begins to build Maginot Line
• D. H. Lawrence dies

1931
• Spain becomes a republic

1932
• Franklin D. Roosevelt elected US President
• Cockcroft and Walton split the atom
• Aldous Huxley's *Brave New World* published

1933
• Hitler becomes German Chancellor
• Prohibition laws repealed in USA

1934
• Austrian Chancellor murdered by Nazis

1935
• Italy invades Abyssinia
• Show trials in USSR

1936
• German troops march into Rhineland
• Civil war starts in Spain
• Gorky and Lorca die

1937
• Japan invades China
• Ravel dies

1938
• Germany annexes Austria and the Sudetenland

1939
• Franco wins Spanish Civil War
• Hitler occupies Czechoslovakia and invades Poland
• Britain and France go to war with Germany

1937

MARCH: 1st A Degas retrospective opens at the Orangerie.
AUGUST: 3rd Works by Cézanne, Gauguin and van Gogh are included in the Nazis' exhibition of 'degenerate art' at the new Haus der Kunst in Munich (left).

1938

AUGUST: 20th In a letter to the *New Statesman*, Lucien Pissarro complains that a painting bearing the forged signature of his father has been sold as a genuine Pissarro and there is no legal mechanism for insisting that the signature be erased.

1939

Publication of *Degas, danse, dessin* (right) by the poet Paul Valéry ◆ (pp.220–1) and *Les Archives de l'impressionnisme*, a selection from the archives of the Durand-Ruel gallery, in two-volumes, edited by the art historian Lionello Venturi (one of the most important records of the history of Impressionism).

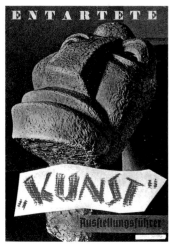

The cover of the exhibition guide to 'Degenerate Art' (*Entartete Kunst*), showing the sculpture *The New Man* by Otto Freundlich.

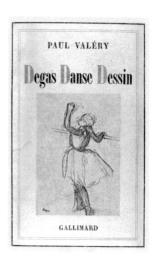

The cover of the poet Paul Valéry's book *Degas, danse, dessin* (1938).

◆ THE REACTION AGAINST IMPRESSIONISM

A reaction against Impressionism – among artists rather than dealers – had started in the 1880s, and was partly brought about by the Impressionists themselves. Renoir told Vollard in 1883 that 'he had reached the end of Impressionism', and for a period his work was characterized by carefully pre-meditated composition, culminating in *The Bathers* of 1887 ◆ (pp.158–60).

The next generation of painters – such as Seurat and Signac and their disciples – reacted against the visual self-indulgence of Impressionism, which they felt was isolating them from the mainstream of European art. They also complained that Impressionism did not display feeling nor endeavour to arouse it (as did Gauguin and van Gogh, who used emotive arrangements of lines and colours); and there was a yearning for an art that would engage the spectator through images possessing a political, spiritual or sensual appeal.

On these reactions to Impressionism were built the main artistic movements that emerged during the first few decades of the twentieth century. The desire for structural formality, for example, gave rise to Pointillism, Divisionism and Cubism, while the desire for feeling and involvement produced Fauvism, Expressionism and Surrealism.

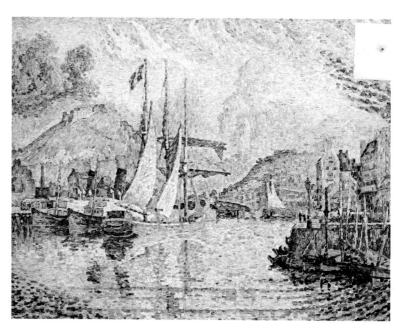

SIGNAC
Cherbourg, Fort de Roule
1932

Heavily influenced by Seurat, Signac was a fervent advocate of Pointillism, and this work, painted towards the end of his life, is an example of his loyalty to the style (p.227).

1940–1949

The Impact of War

During the war the survival of the Impressionist legacy is threatened by the perils of bombing and pillaging, and also by the Nazis' campaign against 'decadent' art. Nevertheless, partly thanks to the special units set up by the Allies to recover works of art, relatively few Impressionist paintings are lost or destroyed.

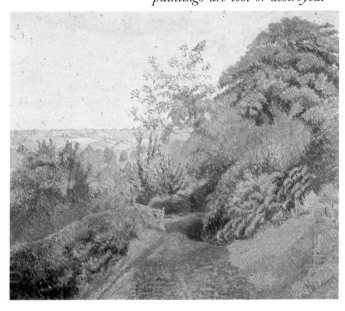

LUCIEN PISSARRO
A Muddy Lane, Hewood
1940

Lucien Pissarro settled permanently in England in the early 1890s. In his latter years he concentrated on intimate landscapes, such as this autumnul view of the village of Hewood, painted from the artist's garden.

1940
AUGUST: The Nazis confiscate more than two hundred paintings from Jewish collectors in France, including a number of Impressionist works.

1941
FEBRUARY: 6th An exhibition entitled 'French Painting from David to Toulouse-Lautrec' opens at the Metropolitan Museum of Art.
MARCH: 24th 'The Art of Camille Pissarro in Retrospect' opens at the Durand-Ruel Galleries in New York.
MAY: The Musée Fabre in Montpellier holds an exhibition to mark the centenary of Bazille's birth.

1942
MARCH: An exhibition of 'Nineteenth-Century French Paintings' opens at the National Gallery, London.

1943
The Princesse de Polignac (*née* Winaretta Singer) dies, leaving works by Manet and Monet to the Louvre, including Manet's *Reading* (1865).

1944
Pissarro's son Lucien ▲ (p.212) dies, aged 81.

1945
Many Impressionist paintings, including works by Renoir, Manet, van Gogh and Degas, are looted from Dresden by the Russians.

1946
John Rewald's *The History of Impressionism* ◆ (p.247) is published by the Museum of Modern Art, New York.
DECEMBER: 26th The Paul Rosenberg Gallery in New York stages a

OTHER EVENTS

1940
• Germany occupies Denmark, Norway, Holland, Belgium and France
• Churchill becomes British Prime Minister
• Pétain heads Vichy government in France

1941
• Germany invades USSR and Yugoslavia
• Pearl Harbor bombed
• USA enters the war

1942
• Battles of El Alamein and Midway

1943
• Battle of Stalingrad
• Italy surrenders

1944
• D-day landings
• Liberation of Paris

1945
• Germany surrenders; Hitler commits suicide
• Mussolini shot
• USA drops atomic bombs on Japan

1946
• Inaugural session of United Nations
• Paris Peace Conference
• War crimes trials

1947
• Partition of India and Pakistan

1948
• Gandhi assassinated
• State of Israel created

1949
• Chinese civil war won by Communists
• Division of Germany
• NATO founded

loan exhibition of 'Masterpieces by Manet for the Benefit of American Aid to France' (right).

1947

Publication of Adolphe Tabarant's *Manet et ses œuvres*.
The Jeu de Paume in the Tuileries Gardens becomes the Musée de l'Impressionnisme, and all the Impressionist paintings from the Louvre are moved there.
MARCH: The twenty-fourth Venice Biennale ◆ (pp.214–5) has an exhibition devoted to the work of the Impressionists.
30th An exhibition of drawings and pastels by Degas opens at the Phillips Memorial Gallery in Washington.

1948

The collection of Impressionist works in Moscow's State Museum of Modern Western Art (*see* p.239) is divided between the Hermitage and the Pushkin Museum of Fine Arts.
SEPTEMBER: 4th A Degas exhibition opens at the Ny Carlsberg Glyptotek in Copenhagen – then transfers to the Galerie Blanche in Stockholm on October 9th.

1949

SEPTEMBER: 3rd Impressionist show opens at the Kunstmuseum, Basel.

Loan Exhibition

MASTERPIECES

By

Manet

(1832 - 1883)

*for the benefit of
American Aid to France, Inc.*

December 26, 1946 to January 11, 1947

PAUL ROSENBERG & CO.
16 East 57th Street, New York 22, N. Y.

Title page of the exhibition catalogue of 'Masterpieces by Manet for the Benefit of American Aid to France'. The exhibition was held at Paul Rosenberg's gallery, New York, from December 1946 to January 1947.

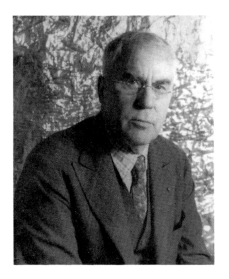

A photograph of Dr Albert C. Barnes, who established the Barnes Foundation at Merion near Philadelphia in 1924, taken by Carl van Vechten (*c*.1934).

 IMPRESSIONIST PRICES

The auction houses of London, New York and to a lesser extent Paris continued business almost as usual throughout the war – and in America the season that ended in July 1941 proved to be the best since 1929. Although this was largely due to the sale of Old Masters, in 1942 the Barnes Foundation in Philadelphia paid $57,600 for one of Cézanne's *Bathers* and $133,200 for Renoir's *Mussel Fishers of Berneval*. Works by Renoir, however, could still fetch as little as the £2200 paid for a portrait of Gabrielle Renard at Sotheby's in 1948. Cézanne maintained reasonably high prices in America – a portrait of his wife being sold at Parke-Bernet in 1940 for $22,800, although in England a watercolour landscape fetched only £450 at Sotheby's in 1946. As for Degas, in Paris in 1940 the Durand-Ruel gallery sold some of his pastels for the equivalent of £6–7000 each. In contrast, the value of Monet's works had declined since his death; a view of Hyde Park, for example, went for £640 at Sotheby's in 1940, and the maximum price paid for a Monet during the 1940s was the $11,052 obtained in 1946 by the Van Horne Gallery, New York, for a view of the Seine at Bougival. The same gallery achieved $6312 for Pissarro's *Old Chelsea Bridge*, and his *Village Street* was sold at Sotheby's in the following year for £1250, the undemanding nature of his work ensuring him steady popularity with the buying public.

1950–1959

Taking Impressionism Seriously

Largely thanks to the arrival of scholars and experts from Central Europe, the history of art begins to be regarded as a serious academic discipline in the English-speaking world. An increase in the number of publications on Impressionism leads to a greater appreciation of the paintings, resulting in a sharp rise in their market value.

1950

JUNE: A Bazille exhibition opens at the Wildenstein Galleries, New York.

1951

Death of Albert Barnes (p.248), an energetic collector of Impressionist paintings and creator of the Barnes Foundation in Philadelphia.

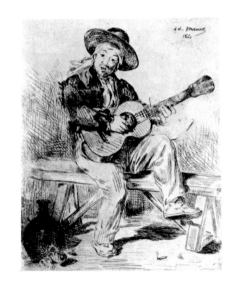

MANET
The Spanish Singer
1861–2

This etching was based on Manet's painting of the same name (1860), which, when shown at the Salon of 1861, brought him his first popular and critical success. The artist no doubt desired that the print, which was published several times during his lifetime, would introduce his work to a wider public.

1952

FEBRUARY: 8th A major Degas exhibition opens at the Stedelijk Museum in Amsterdam.

MAY: 14th At the sale of Gabriel Cognacq's collection at the Charpentier gallery in Paris, a Cézanne still life, *Apples and Biscuits* (*c.*1880), fetches 33,000,000 francs.

JUNE: 18th At a sale of prints owned by Henri Thomas, Manet's etching of *The Spanish Singer* fetches 130,000 francs.

AUGUST: An important Degas exhibition is shown at the National Gallery of Scotland in Edinburgh – then transfers to the Tate Gallery in London on September 20th.

1953

At the opening of the Ordrupgaardsamlingen Gallery in Copenhagen, a private collector donates Degas' *Children on a Doorstep (New Orleans)* to the gallery (p.75).

JULY: The Edinburgh Festival includes a Renoir exhibition.

1954

APRIL: 24th The Tate Gallery stages an exhibition entitled 'Manet and His Circle: Paintings from the Louvre'.

SEPTEMBER: 24th Opening of 'The Two Sides of the Medal: French Painting from Gérôme to Gauguin' at the Detroit Institute of Arts.

1955

APRIL: 14th The Californian art dealer Hans Goldenberg is sentenced to two months' imprisonment for forging a Degas and two Manets.

JUNE: The Sterling and Francine Clark Art Institute in Williamstown, Massachusetts opens; its collection includes thirty-seven Renoirs.

NOVEMBER: 9th The Knoedler Galleries in New York exhibit a selection of wax figures by Degas ◆ (p.239).

1956

Horace Havemeyer – son of Henry and Louisine ● (p.233) – gives Manet's *The Railroad* (p.153) to the National Gallery of Art, Washington.

1957

JANUARY: 14th Jeanne Baudot, Renoir's pupil and latterly his companion, dies at the age of 80.
JULY: An important Monet exhibition is shown at the Edinburgh Festival, before being transferred to the Tate Gallery.
OCTOBER: 15th Seven Impressionist paintings owned by Erwin Goldschmidt are sold at Sotheby's, London, including Manet's *The Rue Mosnier with Flags* (1878) for £113,000 and Cézanne's *The Boy in the Red Waistcoat* (1888–90) for £220,000.

1958

Picasso buys four of Degas' brothel monotypes ◆ (p.225) from the Lefevre Gallery in London and produces his own variation on the theme.

1959

The National Gallery in London values Renoir's *Umbrellas*, bought by Sir Hugh Lane ◆ (pp.76–7) for £1050 around 1910, at £250,000.
MAY: Four hundred pictures – including numerous Impressionist paintings – bought by Prince Kojiro Matsukata in the 1920s (*see* p.239), and impounded by the French authorities on the outbreak of war, are released and sent to the National Museum of Western Art in Tokyo.

◆ **THE STATUS OF IMPRESSIONISM**

In the second half of the twentieth century Impressionism attained a status, both in terms of popularity and market standing, superior to that of almost any other form of art. Much of this appeal was the result of advances made in the study of art history, attributable in part to the new vigour instilled into the discipline by the influx into the English-speaking countries of scholars from Germany and Austria (where it was regarded as a profession rather than a hobby), culminating in the publication of John Rewald's magisterial work *The History of Impressionism* (1946).

The study of art was also beginning to benefit from greater cross-fertilization with other disciplines. Curators of art galleries began to display and catalogue their treasures more skilfully and to take their educational responsibilities more seriously. Meanwhile, more and more books were being published about Impressionism, ranging from the popular to the erudite. Perhaps the most significant factor that enhanced the movement's status was the advent of huge travelling exhibitions in the 1950s and 1960s, which attracted millions of visitors.

THE

HISTORY

OF

IMPRESSIONISM

JOHN REWALD

THE MUSEUM OF MODERN ART, NEW YORK
DISTRIBUTED BY SIMON AND SCHUSTER, ROCKEFELLER CENTER, NEW YORK

The title page of Rewald's innovative book *The History of Impressionism*, published in New York (1946).

1960–1969

Impressionism in the Age of Pop

*A new interest in the Realist tendencies of the movement leads to a
Caillebotte retrospective and a reassessment of the artist's work.*

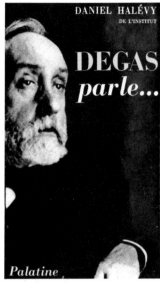

The cover of Daniel Halévy's
Degas parle… (1962).

A photograph of Julie
Rouart (*née* Manet), taken
in her Paris apartment
towards the end of her life.

1960

The Musée Marmottan in Paris is given a number of important
Impressionist paintings under the Donop de Monchy legacy,
including Monet's *Impression: Sunrise* ▲ (p.88).
JUNE: An exhibition entitled 'Claude Monet: Seasons and
Moments' opens at the Museum of Modern Art in New York.

1962

MAY: Daniel Halévy's *Degas parle…* (left), a selection of extracts
from a diary he started in 1888, is published in Geneva ▲ (pp.204
and 208). **4th** An exhibition of 'Paintings, Drawings and Graphic
works by Manet, Degas, Berthe Morisot and Mary Cassatt' opens
at the Baltimore Museum of Art.

1964

The Art Institute of Chicago purchases Caillebotte's *Street in Paris,
A Rainy Day* (p.103).
MAY: The National Gallery in London buys Cézanne's *Large Bathers*
(*c.*1895) from the daughter of Auguste Pellerin (*see* pp.233 and 241).

1965

MAY: 2nd Opening of 'Edgar Degas, His Family and Friends in New
Orleans' at the Isaac Delgado Museum in New Orleans. The catalogue
has articles by John Rewald, James B. Byrnes and Joan Sutherland Boggs.

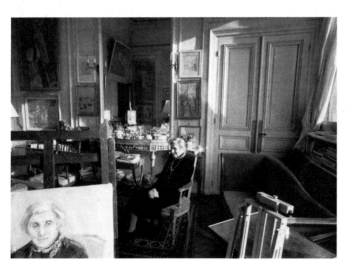

1966

JANUARY: 19th Michel Monet, the
painter's only surviving son, dies aged
87, leaving his father's collection of
paintings, as well as the house and
gardens at Giverny, to the Académie
des Beaux-Arts. The paintings are
subsequently transferred to the
Musée Marmottan.
FEBRUARY: The Marmottan
receives Renoir's portrait of Monet
(1872), which has been bequeathed
to the museum by Michel Monet.
JULY: 14th Death of Julie Rouart

(opposite), daughter of Berthe Morisot and Manet's brother Eugène, and wife of Ernest Rouart, grandson of the painter Henri Rouart, (pp.193, 199 and 224). **15th** The Wildenstein gallery in London mounts an exhibition of works by Caillebotte.

1968
MARCH: 21st An exhibition entitled 'Degas' Racing World' opens at Wildenstein's gallery in New York.

◆ VARIATIONS IN TASTE

Impressionism was more readily accepted in the USA than it was in France – and much more readily than in Britain, where Degas eventually occupied the favourite place assigned to Monet in the USA. It was also more enthusiastically received in northern Europe, especially Germany and Russia, than in the Mediterranean countries (consequently, there are few major Impressionist paintings in either Italy or Spain). Why this should have been so cannot be explained without resorting to dubious generalizations about national character. Specific reasons for variations in taste can, however, be discerned in the development of art: for instance, during the postwar period the emphasis on structure and form led to a reaction against Monet and in favour of Cézanne.

But less obvious fluctuations in taste had their influence too. One outstanding example is Caillebotte's reputation. During the first half of the century, when the generally accepted view of the Impressionists was as purveyors of the beauty of life and nature, he was almost completely disregarded; then, as historians and critics began to focus on the sociological dimensions of the movement and the significance of its 'realistic' aspects, interest in Caillebotte's work increased. This was initially stimulated by the exhibitions of his paintings held in London in 1966 and in New York in 1968. Then in 1976 the Houston Museum of Fine Arts mounted the first authoritative Caillebotte retrospective; and in 1978 Marie Berhaut produced a serious catalogue raisonné of his paintings, *Caillebotte, sa vie, son œuvre*. A decade later Caillebotte's works had been acquired by eight American museums and public art galleries, and could be seen in important general exhibitions such as 'The New Painting: Impressionism 1874–86' held in Washington and San Francisco in 1986.

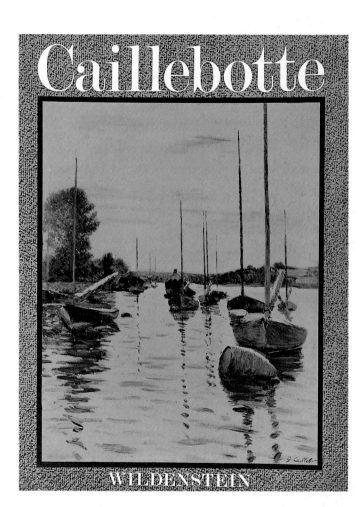

The cover of the catalogue for the Caillebotte exhibition held at the Wildenstein gallery, London (July 1966).

1970–1979

Escalating Prices

Inflation and other factors create new wealth for certain individuals on an astronomic scale. Consequently, the prices paid for Impressionist paintings outstrip those of most other works of art.

1970

MARCH: 3rd Renoir's *The Woman with the Rose* is sold at Christie's for 78,000 guineas. At the same sale, Pissarro's *The Hermitage at Pontoise* (1878) goes for 70,000 guineas.

APRIL: 3rd 'A Hundred Years of Impressionism: A Tribute to Paul Durand-Ruel' opens at the Wildenstein Galleries in New York.

SEPTEMBER: 'Monet et ses amis' opens at the Musée Marmottan. Works by Manet are shown in Tokyo, Osaka and Fukuoka.

1971

JUNE: 27th Manet's pastel *Head of a Woman in a Black Hat* (*c.*1880) is sold at Sotheby's for £47,250.

SEPTEMBER: 9th The American collector Norton Simon sells Monet's *The Wooden Bridge at Argenteuil* (1873) at Christie's for £168,000, having bought it seven years earlier at Sotheby's for £48,000.

1973

JANUARY: 'The Impressionists in London' opens at the Hayward Gallery.

MARCH: 27th Christie's sell Monet's *Antibes Seen from the Jardin de la Salis* (p.163) for £99,750 and Pissarro's *Avant-port de Dieppe* for £94,750.

JULY: 3rd Renoir's *Portrait of Jean Renoir Holding a Hoop* (1908) fetches £194,250 at Christie's.

1974

FEBRUARY: 9th 'Impressionism, its Masters, its Precursors and its Influence on Britain' opens at the Royal Academy in London.

JULY: 1st Christie's sell Degas' *Woman Putting on her Gloves* for £152,250.

SEPTEMBER: 21st The 'Centenaire de l'Impressionnisme' exhibition opens at the Grand Palais in Paris – then in December moves to the Metropolitan Museum of Art in New York.

1975

APRIL: 15th Christie's sell Degas' *After the Bath* for £141,750.

JULY: 1st Monet's *Rouen Cathedral: the Tour d'Albane in the Morning* (1892–4) is sold at Sotheby's for £210,000.

1976

MARCH: The Houston Museum of Fine Arts mounts a major exhibition of Caillebotte's works.

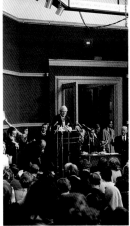

A photograph of an auction in Christie's saleroom (1971).

OTHER EVENTS

1970
• De Gaulle dies

1971
• Idi Amin seizes power in Uganda

1972
• First arms-limitations treaty signed
• Bangladesh becomes a sovereign state

1973
• Britain, Denmark and Eire join EEC
• Allende killed in coup in Chile
• Yom Kippur war in Middle East

1974
• Nixon resigns over Watergate

1975
• USA evacuates troops from Vietnam
• Civil wars in Lebanon, Angola and Eritrea

1976
• Jimmy Carter elected President of USA
• Soweto riots
• Mao Tse-tung dies

1977
• 'Boat people' flee from Vietnam

1978
• Camp David peace talks on Middle East

1979
• Shah of Iran ousted by Ayatollah Khomeini
• Soviet troops invade Afghanistan
• Sandinistas depose Somoza in Nicaragua
• Thatcher elected Prime Minister of UK

JULY: **7th** Sisley's *The Seine at Bougival in Spring* (1873) achieves £120,000 at Sotheby's. **28th** Christie's sell Morisot's *The Steamboat* for £24,000.
SEPTEMBER: A Degas exhibition opens at the Seibu Museum of Arts, in Japan, and then goes on to Kyoto and Fukuoka.

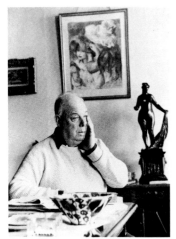

A photograph of Renoir's son Jean, taken in the 1960s.

1977

MAY: Gerald van der Kemp is appointed curator of Monet's house in Giverny (*see* p.248) and initiates a restoration programme.

1978

APRIL: 2nd Monet's *The Railway Bridge at Argenteuil* (1873) is sold at Sotheby's for £420,000 (in June 1963 it had fetched £77,000).
JULY: 4th Renoir's *Fisherman with His Line* (1874) – bought by Georges Charpentier at the ill-fated Impressionist sale (*see* p.90) at the Hôtel Drouot ◆ (p.102) in 1875 for 180 francs – is sold at Sotheby's for £610,000.

1979

FEBRUARY: 13th Renoir's son Jean (left), the film director ▲ (p.213), dies at the age of 84.

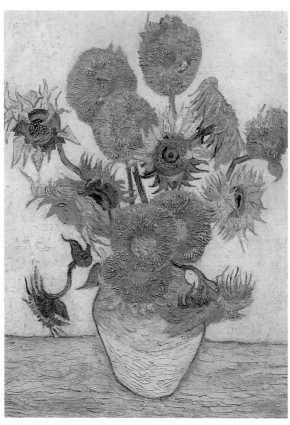

◆ THE 'MEGABUCK' PAINTINGS

During the 1970s and 1980s Impressionist paintings came to be sold for astronomic sums, far exceeding the prices of all but a few works of comparable aesthetic status. This frenetic escalation of prices was partly due to economic factors. In a world haunted by the spectre of inflation, works of art came to be regarded as a useful hedge against inflation. Moreover, in an era when entrepreneurs were accumulating wealth on an enormous scale, investment in paintings offered legitimate opportunities for avoiding or reducing taxation.

In the 1980s a new factor appeared, when Japanese collectors began to buy Impressionist paintings on a fantastic scale. This was stimulated by the International Plaza Agreement of 1985, which revalued the yen. The immediate effect was that the yen rose by 45 per cent against the dollar; and within two years it had risen by nearly 100 per cent. Within months of the agreement, the Matsuoka Art Museum in Tokyo spent $4,250,000 on works by Monet, Pissarro, Renoir, Chagall and Modigliani. At the same time, it became fashionable for Japanese businesses to collect paintings; and it was a Japanese financial institution, the Yasuda Fire and Marine Insurance Company, that bought van Gogh's *Sunflowers* at Christie's in March 1987 for £24,750,000 (right).

VAN GOGH
Sunflowers
1888

When it was auctioned in 1987, this was the only version of van Gogh's *Sunflowers* paintings to have remained in private hands. Its desirability was confirmed when it sold for £24,750,000 – more than three times the previous world record.

1980–Today

The Boom Years

The 1980s see Japanese private collectors and businesses paying unprecedented amounts for Impressionist works. The trend is tempered somewhat by the onset of global recession in the 1990s.

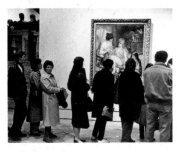

1980

OCTOBER: 31st 'Pissarro' (left) opens at the Hayward Gallery. (It moves to the Grand Palais and Boston Museum of Fine Arts.)

1983

APRIL: 22nd 'Manet, 1832–83' opens at the Grand Palais. (It moves to the Metropolitan Museum of Art.)

1984

NOVEMBER: 'A Day in the Country: Impressionism and the French Landscape' opens at Los Angeles County Museum of Art. (It moves to the Art Institute of Chicago and the Grand Palais.)

1985

JANUARY: 30th 'Renoir' (left) opens at the Hayward Gallery. (It moves to the Grand Palais and Boston Museum of Fine Arts.)

1986

JANUARY: 17th 'The New Painting – Impressionism 1874–86' opens at the National Gallery of Art, Washington. (It moves to the Fine Arts Museum of San Francisco).

DECEMBER: All the Impressionist and Post-Impressionist works from the Jeu de Paume (*see* p.245) and the Louvre are moved to the new Musée d'Orsay (opposite).

1987

NOVEMBER: 11th Van Gogh's *Irises* (1889) fetches $53,900,000 at Sotheby's, New York.

1989

'Monet in the '90s: The Series Paintings' opens at the Boston Museum of Fine Arts. (It transfers to the Art Institute of Chicago and the Royal Academy, London.)

1990

MAY: 17th Renoir's *Dancing at the Moulin de la Galette* (p.105) achieves $78,100,000 at Sotheby's, New York.

JUNE: The Courtauld Institute Galleries, London (*see* p.242), move to Somerset House, in the Strand.

Above (top): A poster for the Pissarro exhibition at the Hayward Gallery, London (October 31st, 1980 to January 11th, 1981).

Above: A photograph of visitors to the Renoir exhibition at the Hayward Gallery, London (January 30th to April 21st, 1985).

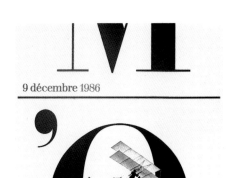

The poster, designed by Bruno Monguzzi, announcing the opening of the Musée d'Orsay in Paris (December 9th, 1986).

1994
- Opening of Channel Tunnel
- Genocide in Rwanda

1995
- Russia invades Chechnya

1997
- Economic crisis hits Asia
- Hong Kong handed back to China
- Princess Diana and Mother Teresa die

1999
- War in Kosovo
- Introduction of the euro

1992
JULY: 3rd 'Alfred Sisley' opens at the Royal Academy in London. (It transfers to the Musée d'Orsay and the Walters Art Gallery in Baltimore.)

1993
MAY: 11th Sotheby's, New York, sells Cézanne's *Still Life: Large Apples* (1890–94) for $26,000,000.

1994
APRIL: 19th 'The Origins of Impressionism' opens at the Grand Palais in Paris. (It transfers to the Metropolitan Museum of Art in New York.)

1995
SEPTEMBER: 25th 'Cézanne' opens at the Grand Palais in Paris. (It transfers to the Tate Gallery, London, and Philadelphia Museum of Art.)
JULY: 22nd 'Claude Monet: 1840–1926' opens at the Art Institute of Chicago.

1997
NOVEMBER: 13th Renoir's *Bather* (1888) fetches $19,000,000 at Sotheby's, New York.

1998
OCTOBER: 10th 'Mary Cassatt: Modern Woman' opens at the Art Institute of Chicago. (It transfers to the Museum of Fine Arts, Boston, and the National Gallery of Art, Washington, D.C.)
NOVEMBER: 19th Van Gogh's *Self-Portrait with a Clean-Shaven Face* (1889) fetches $65,000,000 at Christie's, New York.

1999
JANUARY: 23rd 'Monet in the Twentieth Century' opens at the Royal Academy in London. (It transfers to the Museum of Fine Arts in Boston.)

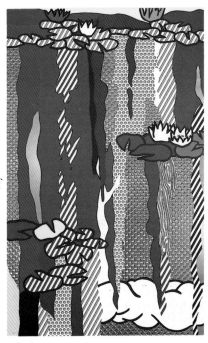

LICHTENSTEIN
Waterlilies and Clouds
1992

This screenprint is one of Lichtenstein's most recent tributes to Monet's series paintings; it is 'after' the Impressionist's *Nymphéas* cyclorama ◆ (p.241).

 THE INFLUENCE OF IMPRESSIONISM

In France Impressionism was soon supplanted by movements such as Pointillism, Fauvism and Cubism, though its techniques were absorbed in a diluted form into the mainstream of conventional painting. However, the influence of the emancipation that Impressionism brought to modern art should not be underestimated. Indeed, one of the most unexpected examples is Roy Lichtenstein (right), who in the 1960s made lithographs based on Monet's *Rouen Cathedral* ▲ (p.209) and *Haystacks* ▲ (pp.182–3) series, and whose most recent works have been variations on the *Nymphéas* cyclorama ◆ (p.241).

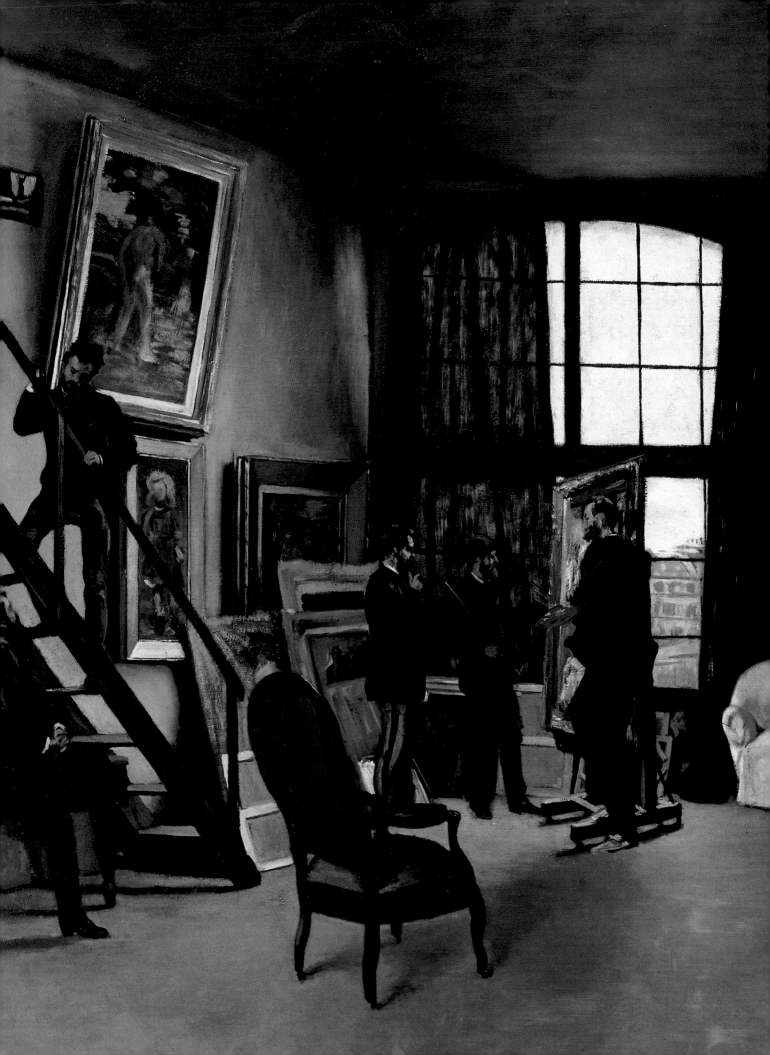

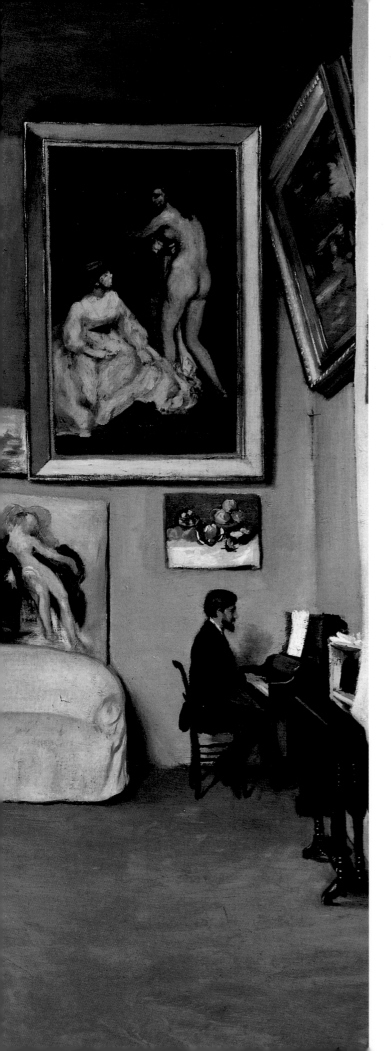

REFERENCE DATA

BAZILLE The Artist's Studio (detail) 1870

Biographical Index

ALEXIS, Paul (1847–1901)

A close friend of most of the Impressionists who, as a critic, was a staunch defender of their paintings (mainly in *L'Avenir*). A habitué of the Café Guerbois and the Nouvelle-Athènes ◆ (pp.46–7), he was a witness to the duel between Manet and Duranty. The author of Realist plays and stories, he supported Impressionism on the grounds that it was the visual equivalent of literary Realism.

ANDRÉE, Ellen (1857–c.1915)

After working as a model, she starred at the Folies-Bergère and then achieved success on the legitimate stage. She appears in Degas' *The Absinthe Drinker* (p.191), Manet's *La Parisienne* (1876) and *At the Café* (1878), and Renoir's *Luncheon of the Boating Party* (p.132). She married the painter Henri Dumont.

ASTRUC, Zacharie (1833–1907)

Sculptor, painter and critic ● (p.37) who participated in the first Impressionist exhibition. He brought out a daily paper supporting the participating artists during the Salon des Refusés in 1863, and helped write the preface to the catalogue of Manet's one-man show in 1867 ▲ (p.45).

BARNES, Albert (1872–1951)

An American collector who, having made his fortune from a purgative called Argyrol, began buying Impressionist paintings from Durand-Ruel. He built up an important collection of works by Renoir, including several previously owned by the Prince de Wagram. In 1924 he created the Barnes Foundation at Merion, near Philadelphia, to which he donated his paintings.

BARTHOLOMÉ, Paul Albert (1848–1928)

A sculptor in the tradition of Rodin, Bartholomé became a close friend of Degas and assisted him with his sculpting. After Degas' death, he supervised the casting in bronze of the wax figures found in the painter's studio ◆ (p.239).

BAUDELAIRE, Charles Pierre (1821–67)

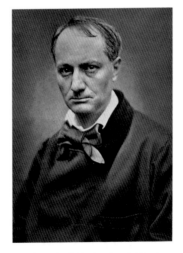

Photograph of Charles Baudelaire by Étienne Carjat (c.1863)

One of the most celebrated poets and of his day, his *Fleurs du Mal* ◆ (p.221) became a cult work among younger writers and painters. Deeply interested in the visual arts, about which he wrote with sympathy and understanding, he praised the work of Manet (who was a close friend) and the painters of the Barbizon school in his incisive reviews of the Salon.

BAZILLE, Frédéric (1841–70)

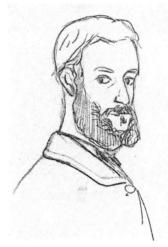

BAZILLE Self-Portrait c.1865

The son of a wealthy family of wine-producers near Montpellier, Bazille was introduced to painting by Alfred Bruyas, the patron of Courbet. Having come to Paris as a medical student, he enrolled as a pupil of Gleyre and, after failing his medical exams, decided to become an artist. A close friend of Monet, Pissarro, Renoir and Sisley, he was widely read, clear-minded and charitable. In 1867 he told his parents he was planning an independent exhibition together with Courbet, Corot and others, but was killed in action before the idea could be realized.

BÉLIARD, Édouard (1835–1902)

A painter who had studied with Gleyre, Béliard was a founder member of the Société Anonyme des Artistes and helped Renoir manage the finances. He participated in the first Impressionist exhibition and in 1875 joined Pissarro's short-lived *L'Union (see* p.91). A habitué of the Café Guerbois ◆ (pp.46–7), he was a close friend of Zola and often advised him about the artistic and musical details for his novels.

BELLIO, Georges de (1835–94)

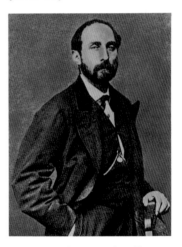

Photograph of Georges de Bellio

A successful homoeopath of Romanian origin who tended several of the Impressionists and their families and models, Bellio was a shrewd collector over a significant number of years, acquiring such important works as Monet's *Impression: Sunrise* (p.88) and Renoir's *Dancing at the Moulin de la Galette* (p.105).

BERARD, Paul (1823–1905)

Diplomat, businessman and banker who became a patron of Renoir ● (p.231).

BERNARD, Émile (1868–1941)

Painter and critic who played a key role in the development of Post-Impressionism. A tireless correspondent, he was friendly with Cézanne and van Gogh, whose reputation he helped to establish through his articles about them. He was also an admirer and close friend of Gauguin until they quarrelled bitterly in 1891.

BERNHEIM-JEUNE, Joseph (1870–1941) and Gaston (1870–1953)

Art dealers who succeeded their father, Alexandre, in 1904. Unlike him, they were keenly interested in contemporary art. In 1906 the brothers opened a new gallery in the boulevard de la Madeleine, where they staged major exhibitions, such as the two of Cézanne's works held in 1907 and 1910. For twenty-five years their main adviser was the critic Félix Fénéon, who eventually became one of the directors of the gallery.

BING, Siegfried (1838–1905)

Collector and dealer who in 1881 opened a gallery that specialized in Oriental prints and artefacts. Bing and his colleague Tadamasa Hayashi brought scholarship and discernment to the cultivation of the Japanese print.

BLANCHE, Jacques-Émile (1861–1942)

A socialite and portrait painter who had been a pupil of Henri Gervex, Blanche had a wide circle of friends, among them Degas and Sickert. He lived near Dieppe and was a passionate Anglophile, as well as being a dedicated admirer of Manet.

BOUDIN, Eugène (1824–98)

A self-taught painter from Le Havre who was one of the early practitioners of *plein-air* painting, Boudin had a great influence on the young Monet and made a significant contribution to the doctrines of Impressionism. He participated at the first Impressionist exhibition and, although he generally distanced himself from art politics, was often taken to be a member of the group.

BOUSSOD, Étienne (1826–96) and VALADON, Pierre (1848–1921)

Art dealers who succeeded Adolphe Goupil as owners of his gallery at 2 Place de l'Opéra in 1875 (Boussod being married to Goupil's grand-daughter). Although renamed Boussod & Valadon, parts of the business continued to be known as Goupil. As well as the luxurious main gallery, they had a branch at 19 boulevard Montmartre and a printing works at 9 rue Chaptal. In 1879 Theo van Gogh became manager of the Montmartre branch and began dealing in Impressionist paintings. After his breakdown in 1890, Theo was replaced by Maurice Joyant, who carried the interest of the firm into the new generation of painters such as Gauguin.

BRACQUEMOND, Félix (1833–1914)

After studying with Joseph-Benoît Guichard (who was a pupil of Ingres), Bracquemond made his reputation through lithographs and etchings. He participated in the Impressionist exhibitions of 1874, 1879 and 1880 largely because of his friendship with Manet and the other Impressionists. In 1871 he became art director of the Sèvres porcelain factory; he then moved to a similar position at the Haviland factory in Limoges. In 1886 he published *Du Dessin et de la couleur*, in which engraving featured prominently, and it was in this medium that he made his greatest achievements.

BRACQUEMOND, Marie (1841–1916)

The wife of Félix Bracquemond, Marie produced paintings that displayed a closer affinity to Impressionism and were more original than her husband's – a fact of which he was apparently aware (their son Pierre related that he was jealous of her work). Although she was an energetic supporter of the Impressionists, participating in the exhibitions

of 1879, 1880 and 1886, she was something of a recluse. Many of her paintings, such as *Young Woman in White* (p.119), were set in her own garden.

BURTY, Philippe (1830–90)

Critic and art historian who worked as an ornamental painter at the state-controlled Gobelins tapestry factory, then joined the *Gazette des Beaux-Arts* as editor of the sales and curiosities section. In 1881 he became an official Inspector of Fine Arts. He produced many scholarly catalogues, and in his critical writings was a strong supporter of the Impressionists.

CAILLEBOTTE, Gustave (1848–94)

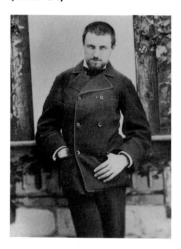

Photograph of Caillebotte (c.1874–5)

A painter of great originality, who was rediscovered in the 1960s and 1970s ◆ (p.249), Caillebotte had a penchant for startling perspectives and realistic details of urban life. Wealthy as well as gifted, he was a generous supporter of the Impressionists, buying their works at artificially high prices and making them gifts of money. He also designed racing yachts and succeeded in communicating his enthusiasm for gardening to Monet. He exhibited at the Impressionist exhibitions of 1876–80 and 1882, and when he died left his remarkable collection of Impressionist paintings to the nation ◆ (pp.197–8).

CASSATT, Mary (1844–1926)

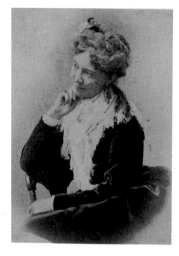

Carte-de-visite photograph of Mary Cassatt (1872)

Born in Pittsburgh of wealthy parents, Cassatt studied art at the Pennsylvania Academy of Fine Arts, then in 1868 came to Europe to complete her art education. After travelling extensively on the Continent, she settled in Paris in 1874. In that year she was accepted at the Salon, and in 1877 met Degas, who was to remain a close friend throughout his life. Cassatt was of great practical help to the Impressionists, providing them with direct financial support and persuading rich American friends such as the Havemeyers ● (p.233) to buy their works. A talented painter and exceptional print-maker who excelled at intimate scenes from everyday life, she participated in the Impressionist exhibitions of 1879–81 and 1886.

CASTAGNARY, Jules (1830–88)

A politician and critic who defended Realism in art and literature, Castagnary was a friend of Baudelaire and an ardent supporter of Courbet. Aware of the transition taking place in contemporary art from Realism to Naturalism, he was highly sympathetic to the aims of the Impressionists. In 1879 he became Minister of Religion, and eight years later Minister of Fine Arts.

CÉZANNE, Paul (1839–1906)

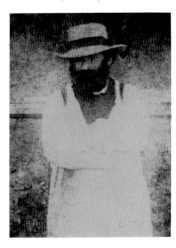

Photograph of Cézanne taken in the late 1870s

Son of a hat-maker turned banker from Aix-en-Provence, where one of his childhood friends was Zola, Cézanne came to Paris in 1861 to study at the Académie Suisse; there he met Pissarro, who had a considerable influence on him and introduced him to the circle at the Café Guerbois ◆ (p.46–7). He participated in the Impressionist exhibitions of 1874 and 1877, but soon began to diverge from the other members of the group, developing a closer concern with form and space. After inheriting his father's fortune in 1886, he spent the rest of his working life in Aix-en-Provence, taking the subject of many of his paintings from the surrounding landscape.

CHAMPFLEURY (1821–89)

Pseudonym of the novelist and critic Jules Husson. He met the Impressionists through the restaurateur Eugène Murer, defended them in print and collected their works. In 1868 Manet provided a lithograph for the poster advertising his book *Les Chats* (p.50).

CHARPENTIER, Georges (1846–1905) and Marguerite (1848–1904)

Publisher of authors such as Flaubert, the Goncourts, Maupassant and Zola, in 1872 Georges Charpentier married Marguerite Lemonnier (p.110),

who shared and encouraged his interest in art. Their salon became renowned as a meeting place for artists, writers and left-wing politicians. Enthusiastic patrons and supporters of the Impressionists, the Charpentiers founded the magazine *La Vie moderne* (see p.112), edited by Edmond Renoir, who also supervised the exhibitions held at its offices.

CHOCQUET, Victor (1821–91)

Collector, civil servant and friend of the Impressionists. In 1875, after seeing the works of the Impressionists at the Hôtel Drouot ◆ (p.102), he commissioned Renoir to paint portraits of himself (p.224) and his wife. His collection, which was sold in 1899 ▲ (p.224), included thirty-five works by Cézanne.

CLEMENCEAU, Georges (1841–1929)

Radical politician and journalist who made his mark as mayor of Montmartre. Twice Premier of France (1906–09 and 1917–20), he was one of the dominant figures of the Third Republic and led France to victory in World War I. After Manet had painted two portraits of him in 1879 (p.18), Clemenceau became friendly with Monet, who was a neighbour in Giverny. An active supporter of the Impressionists, he wrote perceptively about their works ▲ (p.209) and helped to ensure that Monet's *Nymphéas* cyclorama was hung in the Orangerie ◆ (p.241).

COROT, Camille (1796–1875)

One of the most important painters of the Barbizon school, Corot took a lively interest in the activities and experiments of the Impressionists, and gave advice to Pissarro and Morisot among others. He travelled widely throughout France and Italy, and his exact study of landscape had a strong impact on the Impressionists, especially Pissarro and Sisley, while Monet derived invaluable inspiration from his mastery of light.

COURBET, Gustave (1819–77)

As the accepted leader of the Realist school of painting, Courbet was largely responsible for the Impressionists' concern with 'contemporary reality', while the influence of his landscape painting can be seen in works such as Pissarro's *The Hermitage at Pontoise* (1867). After being imprisoned for his actions during the Commune (see pp.68–70), he died in exile in Switzerland.

COURTAULD, Samuel (1876–1947)

British silk and textile magnate, Courtauld started collecting Impressionist paintings in 1922 and gave the Tate Gallery £50,000 in 1923 with which to purchase modern French paintings. He donated his own impressive collection to the Courtauld Institute of Art, which he endowed at the University of London in 1931. In 1990 the Institute was moved to Somerset House, in the Strand.

COUTURE, Thomas (1815–79)

A history and portrait painter who achieved fame with his *Romains de la Décadence* (1847). He was a very successful teacher, counting Manet and Puvis de Chavannes among his pupils. Of the former, he said that he would be no more than the Daumier of his generation. He wrote two books on painting: one devoted to techniques and practice, the other to landscape.

DAUBIGNY, Charles-François (1817–78)

A pioneer of *plein-air* painting who had a strong influence on the Impressionists, Daubigny also offered practical help to the artists. He introduced Monet to Durand-Ruel and often ensured that works by Bazille, Manet, Morisot, Pissarro, Renoir and Sisley were accepted at the Salon through his membership of the jury. His own style was influenced by Dutch and English landscape painting.

DAUDET, Alphonse (1840–97)

A successful novelist and playwright, published by Georges Charpentier, Daudet was regarded as one of the leading literary Realists. His most popular works included *Lettres de mon moulin* (1866) and *Aventures prodigeuses de Tartarin de Tarascon* (1872). A regular visitor to the Nouvelle-Athènes ◆ (p.46–7), he was friendly with Degas and Renoir and bought a number of Impressionist paintings.

DEGAS, Hilaire Germain Edgar (1834–1917)

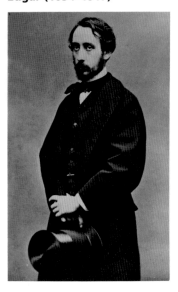

Photograph of Degas (c.1862)

Member of a Neapolitan banking family that had settled in Paris, Degas studied at the École des Beaux-Arts and then spent a few years in Italy. Although he participated in all the Impressionist exhibitions except the seventh, he sometimes caused disunity within the group ▲ (p.127) and was not deeply involved in their technical innovations – being more concerned with linear and compositional issues. His subject matter ranged from horse-racing and ballet to café and brothel scenes ◆ (p.225). He was also a keen photographer ▲ (p.204), and in his old age turned largely to sculpture ◆ (p.235). A lifelong bachelor ◆ (p.147), Degas was dandified, witty and opinionated.

DENIS, Maurice (1870–1943)
Painter and writer on art, Denis played an important part in the evolution of Post-Impressionism. He was a member of the Nabis group, and in his painting *Homage to Cézanne* (1901) depicted Bonnard, Roussel, Vollard Vuillard, and others admiring one of the master's still lifes.

DEPEAUX, Félix-François (1853–1920)
A wealthy businessman from Rouen with offices in Paris who was a client of Durand-Ruel. He bought many Impressionist paintings, including forty-six by Sisley, who virtually depended on him for his livelihood during the last decade of his life.

DESBOUTIN, Marcellin (1823–1902)

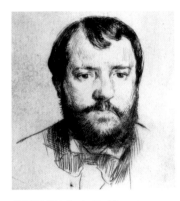

DESBOUTIN Portrait of Ernest Hoschedé 1875

Painter, engraver, writer and professional Bohemian who was a close friend of Manet. He sat for Manet's *The Artist* in 1875 and is the pipe-smoker in Degas' *The Absinthe Drinker* (p.191).

DEWHURST, Wynford (1868–1927)
British painter and critic who wrote extensively in *The Studio* about the Impressionists and in 1904 published a book entitled *Impressionist Painting: Its Genesis and Development*.

DIAZ DE LA PEÑA, Narcisse Virgile (1807–76)
Brought up in France but of Spanish descent, Diaz achieved early success as an academic

painter but, on coming into contact with Millet and Théodore Rousseau, rapidly became a leading member of the Barbizon school. His dramatic treatment of light and shade influenced Renoir. Lame from birth, he had a warm personality, and would often help younger artists by purchasing their paintings.

DU MAURIER, George (1834–96)
Caricaturist, illustrator and writer. Born in Paris, he studied chemistry at University College, London, then painting with Charles Gleyre in 1856–7. His autobiographical novel *Trilby* (1894) includes an account of his student days in Paris.

DURAND-RUEL, Paul (1831–1922)

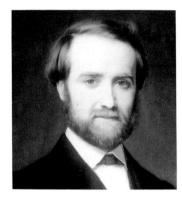

MERLE Paul Durand-Ruel 1866

Art dealer of great resourcefulness and energy who devoted the greater part of his working life to promoting the work of the Impressionists (*see* pp.14–15). The movement's success both in Europe ◆ (pp.214–5) and the USA ▲ (p.153) was largely due to Durand-Ruel's imaginative publicity ▲ (p.80) and attention to detail ▲ (pp.182–3).

DURANTY, Louis Émile Edmond (1833–80)
Novelist, art critic and founder of the short-lived periodical *Réalisme*, Duranty was a loyal and energetic defender of the Impressionists and helped to popularize their work. In 1876 he published the first study of

the Impressionists, entitled *La Nouvelle Peinture*. Impressionism also featured prominently in his posthumous novel *Le Pays des arts* (1881).

DURET, Théodore (1838–1927)
Aristocrat, politician, journalist and wine-grower, in 1868 Duret started *La Tribune française* with Zola and others. Author of *Les Peintres impressionnistes* (1878) and *Critique de l'avant-garde* ▲ (p.145), he was a loyal supporter and patron of the Impressionists. In 1894, because of business losses, he had to sell most of his collection ▲ (p.199).

FANTIN-LATOUR, Théodore (1836-1904)
Portraitist and flower painter whose works were very popular in England. He was friendly with the Impressionists and other progressive artists and writers, many of whom feature in his group portraits *Homage to Delacroix* (p.28) and *A Studio in the Batignolles Quarter* (p.62).

FAURE, Jean-Baptiste (1830–1914)
Famous baritone and patron, whose wide-ranging collection of Impressionist paintings was the product of a mutually advantageous friendship with Durand-Ruel ● (p.81). In 1880 Manet painted a portrait of Faure as Hamlet (p.81).

FÉNÉON, Félix (1861–1944)
Anarchist and critic who in 1884 founded *La Revue indépendante*. Although his enthusiasm for the founders of Impressionism never abated, in 1886 he published a pamphlet contending that the 'scientific' Impressionism of Seurat and Signac had replaced 'naturalistic' Impressionism as the most vital force in contemporary art. In 1900 he organized a Seurat retrospective at the offices of the Symbolist magazine *La Revue blanche*, to which he was a regular contributor; he also edited the first *catalogue raisonné* of Seurat's work.

FORAIN, Jean-Louis (1852–1931)
Painter, caricaturist and close friend of the Impressionists who participated in the exhibitions of 1879–81 and 1886. Nevertheless, apart from his subject matter (he shared Degas' concern with the realities of urban life), his painting had little in common with Impressionism. His drawings were remarkable for their incisive line, his caricatures for their trenchant wit.

FRY, Roger Eliot (1866–1934)
Influential British art critic, author and painter who between 1905 and 1910 was associated with the Metropolitan Museum of Art. In 1907 he persuaded the trustees to buy Renoir's *Madame Charpentier and her Children* (p.110). Fry did much to encourage the appreciation of Cézanne and organized the exhibitions of Post-Impressionism (a name that he invented) at the Grafton Galleries in 1910 and 1913.

GACHET, Dr Paul (1828–1909)
Socialist, Darwinian, homoeopathic doctor and psychiatrist, Gachet became a friend and medical adviser to many of the Impressionists. An enthusiastic engraver (exhibiting under the pseudonym Paul van Ryssel), he set up a press at his house in Auvers which he encouraged Cézanne and Pissarro to use. Gachet strongly opposed the fatal amputation of Manet's leg, and in 1890 looked after van Gogh (who shot himself in a field near the doctor's house). His large collection of Impressionist paintings is now housed in the Musée d'Orsay

GANGNAT, Maurice (1856–1924)
An engineer who was at one time a business associate of Alexandre Natanson (founder of *La Revue blanche*). He started collecting paintings in 1905 and subsequently became a close friend of Renoir, whom he often visited in Cagnes.

GAUGAIN, Abbé Paul-Octave (1850–1904)

Priest, teacher and collector who was a regular client of Durand-Ruel (*see* p.15). After serving as headmaster of the Cours Saint-Augustin in the boulevard Haussmann, he became mayor of Boulon, his native village near Caen.

GAUGUIN, Paul (1848–1903)

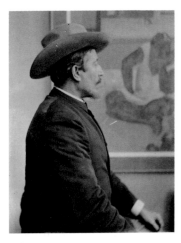

Photograph of Gauguin
1893–4

Born in Paris but brought up in Peru, Gauguin spent seven years as a sailor then became a successful stockbroker in Paris, where he met Pissarro and the other Impressionists. In 1883 he decided to abandon business for art. At first he employed an Impressionist style, participating in the exhibitions of 1880–6, but then began to develop a new approach which evolved into a highly distinctive style after he left Europe for Tahiti in 1891. Apart from a visit to France in 1893–5, he spent the rest of his life in the South Seas, dying in poverty in Atuana in the Marquesas Islands.

GAUTIER, Théophile (1811–72)

Critic, poet, painter and author of novels such as *Mademoiselle de Maupin* (1835), which promoted the idea of 'art for art's sake'. Usually supportive of new movements, he generally praised the Impressionists' work and was included in Manet's *Music*

in the Tuileries Gardens (p.25); however, he wrote a scathing review of *Olympia* in *Le moniteur universel* in 1865 ▲ (p.36).

GEFFROY, Gustave (1855–1926)

Probably the most perceptive contemporary writer about Impressionism, Geffroy was also a novelist, journalist and advocate of left-wing causes. His *La Vie artistique*, issued in eight volumes between 1892 and 1903, included the most comprehensive history of Impressionism to date. In 1924 he published the first authoritative book about Monet ▲ (p.158). He also wrote introductions to solo exhibitions by Monet, Morisot, Pissarro and Rodin. He ended his career as director of the Gobelins factory.

GLEYRE, Charles (1808–74)

Teacher of many of the Impressionists, including Bazille, Monet, Renoir, Sisley and also Whistler (*see* pp.18–19), Gleyre was born in Switzerland but moved to Paris in 1838 and became an instructor at the École des Beaux-Arts. His own paintings tended to use Romantic subjects and classical compositional ideas.

GOGH, Theo van (1857–91)

The younger brother of Vincent, Theo moved to Paris in 1878 and joined the well-known art dealers Boussod & Valadon. After supervising the firm's stand at the Universal Exhibition of 1878, Theo became manager of their Montmartre branch and, despite opposition from his superiors, began dealing in Impressionist works. Initially quite cautious, he sold one work each by Monet, Pissarro, Sisley and Renoir, but with the arrival of his brother in Paris in 1886 he became more confident, and also expanded his interests to include Post-Impressionist works. Prior to his breakdown in 1890, he sold 1 Cézanne, 23 Degas, 18 Gauguins, 5 Manets, 24 Monets, 23 Pissarros, 4 Renoirs and 7 Sisleys.

GOGH, Vincent van (1853–90)

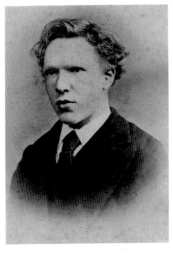

Photograph of van Gogh
(c. 1872)

The son of a Dutch pastor, Vincent joined his uncle's gallery in The Hague (which was part of the Goupil empire) when he was 16, and moved to Goupil's London branch when he was 20. In 1875 he worked as a lay preacher among the miners of the Borinage in Belgium, then in 1881 returned to Holland and decided to become a painter. After studying art in Antwerp, in 1886 he joined his brother Theo in Paris, where he first encountered the Impressionists' paintings ▲ (p.168). Following several bouts of madness, he shot himself in a field near Dr Gachet's house in Auvers.

GONCOURT, Edmond (1822–96) and Jules (1830–70)

Brothers famous for their *Journal* and critical writings, and joint authors of Realist novels such as *Manette Salomon* (1867), which was set in the Parisian art world. As art historians, they succeeded in rehabilitating the painters of the eighteenth century (then out of favour) and helped stimulate interest in Japanese art.

GONZALÈS, Eva (1849–83)

Daughter of a successful novelist, Gonzalès became, in 1869, the only pupil ever to be taken on by Manet and remained his devoted

disciple. From being his imitator, she evolved a style of her own, but did not exhibit at any of the Impressionist exhibitions. She married the engraver Henri Guérard in 1878, and died a few days after Manet of an embolism resulting from childbirth.

GUILLAUMIN, Armand (1841–1927)

The longest surviving Impressionist, at 15 Guillaumin went to work in an uncle's shop and studied drawing in the evenings, then pursued his interest in painting while employed on the Paris-Orléans railway. In 1861 he enrolled at the Académie Suisse, where he became friendly with Cézanne and Pissarro. As well as participating in most of the Impressionist exhibitions, he exhibited at the Salon des Refusés in 1863 and the Salon des Indépendants in December 1884. His later work was close to that of the Fauves.

GUILLEMET, Antoine (1843–1918)

A pupil of Corot, Guillemet was a mildly conservative painter whose work won approval at the Salon, where he was able to use his influence to help his Impressionist friends. These included Cézanne and Pissarro, who were fellow-students at the Académie Suisse, and Manet, to whom he introduced Cézanne. He appears with Berthe Morisot and the violinist Fanny Claus in Manet's *The Balcony* (p.60).

HALÉVY, Ludovic (1833-1908)

Novelist and dramatist, Halévy wrote the libretti for many of Offenbach's operas and for Bizet's *Carmen*. A close friend of Degas since school days, he had a house near Dieppe where the painter frequently stayed – but on the outbreak of the Dreyfus affair Degas broke off all contact with Halévy and his family. A selection from the diaries of his son Daniel, entitled *Degas parle…*, was published in 1962 ▲ (pp.204 and 208).

HAVEMEYER, Henry Osborne (1847–1907) and Louisine (1859–1929)
American collectors and friends of Mary Cassatt, who encouraged them to purchase Impressionist paintings ● (p.233).

HOSCHEDÉ, Ernest (1838–90)
Department-store owner who collected Impressionist works and often invited the artists to his home at Montgeron near Paris. He and his wife, Alice, were great friends of Monet, and came to live with him when Ernest became bankrupt in 1878. Soon after his death Alice married Monet ◆ (p.146)

HOUSSAYE, Arsène (1825–96)
Writer, art critic and official Inspector of Fine Arts, he was editor-in-chief of the influential periodical *L'Artiste*, which often gave favourable publicity to the Impressionists

HUYSMANS, Joris-Karl (1848–1907)

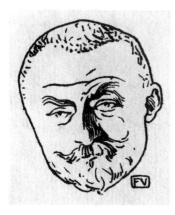

HUYSMANS Portrait of Félix Vallotton

French writer of Dutch extraction whose novels *A Rebours* ('Against the Grain') and *Là-bas* ('Down There') became virtual bibles of the so-called 'decadent' movement in art and literature. A prolific writer, he published two collections of writings on art, *L'Art moderne* ▲ (p.136–7) and *Certains* ▲ (p.172–3), and was one of the first critics to appreciate the work of the Impressionists (particularly that of Cassatt and Cézanne).

JONGKIND, Johann Barthold (1819–91)
Dutch painter, mainly of land- and seascapes, who moved to Paris in 1843. He was a frequent visitor to Honfleur and the Channel coast, where he met and formed a lasting friendship with Monet, on whose work he had a considerable influence ▲ (p.33). He suffered from a profound persecution neurosis and died in an asylum.

JOYANT, Maurice (1864–1930)
Childhood friend of Toulouse-Lautrec who replaced Theo van Gogh at Boussod & Valadon following Theo's breakdown in 1890. Because of opposition to his dealing in Impressionist and Post-Impressionist works, in 1893 he left Boussod & Valadon and went into partnership with Michel Manzi. Joyant's private income enabled him to build an important collection of works by the Impressionists. In 1926–7 he published a two-volume book on Toulouse-Lautrec.

LANE, Sir Hugh Percy (1875–1915)
One of the first British collectors of Impressionist paintings, he started buying from Durand-Ruel in 1905 with the intention of founding a gallery of modern art in Dublin ◆ (pp.76–7).

LE COEUR, Jules (1832–82)
Architect, painter and friend of Renoir ◆ (p.50). In 1865 he took a house and studio, where Renoir often painted, at Marlotte in the Forest of Fontainebleau. He appears in Renoir's *Cabaret of Mère Antony* (p.38).

LEGROS, Alphonse (1837–1911)
Despite successes at the Salon, Legros participated in the Salon des Refusés (partly influenced by his friend Whistler) and in the second Impressionist exhibition. Although his paintings were too academic to be Impressionist, he was attracted by the movement's doctrines. In 1863 he was made

head of the Slade School of Art in London, where his teaching influenced the founders of the New English Art Club (*see* p.148).

LEROY, Louis (1814–85)
Artist, engraver, playwright and critic (*see* p.14) whose satirical review in *Le Charivari* ▲ (p.88) led to the general adoption of the term Impressionism.

MALLARMÉ, Stéphane (1842–98)
A close friend of Degas, Manet, Morisot and Renoir, Mallarmé was one of the founders of the Symbolist movement in literature ◆ (pp.220–1). His apartment on the rue de Rome in Batignolles was a centre of Parisian cultural life. In 1876 he wrote an enthusiastic article about Impressionism for the British *Art Monthly Review* ▲ (p.99). Manet illustrated his poem *L'Après-midi d'un faune* (p.99) and his prose translation of Poe's poem *The Raven* (p.91).

MANET, Édouard (1832–83)

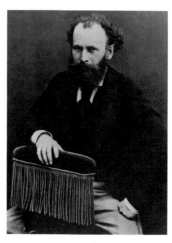

Photograph of Manet by Nadar

The son of a wealthy Paris magistrate, at 16 Manet sailed to Rio as a trainee seaman, then spent six years as a pupil of Couture. The reluctant leader of the Impressionists, in whose exhibitions he expressed no desire to exhibit, he claimed that he had 'no intention of overthrowing old methods of painting, or creating new ones' ▲ (p.45). His early notoriety

was based on the subject matter of paintings such as *Déjeuner sur l'herbe* (p.27) and *Olympia* (p.36) rather than their style, and it was not until the mid 1870s that he began to adopt Impressionist techniques. In 1870 he served in the National Guard during the siege of Paris ▲ (p.67). A staunch Republican, his lithograph of *The Execution of the Emperor Maximilian* was banned by the censor ◆ (p.56–9).

MANET, Julie (1879–1966)

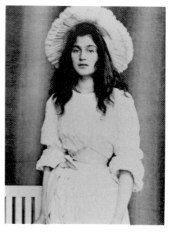

Photograph of Julie Manet (1894)

Daughter of Berthe Morisot and Manet's brother Eugène. After her parents died, the poet Stéphane Mallarmé became her guardian. The diary she kept as a teenager (of which an English translation, *Growing up with the Impressionists*, was published in 1987) provides a fascinating record of Impressionist life ▲ (pp.193, 199 and 224). She married Ernest Rouart, grandson of the painter Henri Rouart.

MANZI, Michel (1849–1915)
Engraver, printer and dealer who in 1893 opened a gallery in partnership with Maurice Joyant. From 1881 to 1893 he directed Boussod & Valadon's branch at 9 rue Chaptal, which specialized in reproductions. In 1896 he produced a remarkable volume of reproductions of Degas' drawings.

MARTELLI, Diego (1838–96)
Florentine painter and art critic who was an eloquent supporter of the Macchiaioli ◆ (pp.214–5). During a long stay in Paris in 1878–9 he became friendly with the Impressionists – especially Degas, who painted his portrait (p.121). After returning to Italy he publicized their achievements and gave a lecture on Impressionism, which was reprinted as a pamphlet ▲ (p.121).

MARTIN, 'Père' (c.1810–c.1880)
A small-time dealer who bought paintings from the Impressionists in their early days at very low prices (as little as 20 francs), often supplemented by unwelcome criticism. Pissarro and others nevertheless persisted in selling to him throughout the 1870s.

MARTINET, Louis (1810–94)
A painter and engraver who became a successful art dealer with a gallery in the boulevard des Italiens. He promoted eighteenth-century painting (then out of fashion) and in 1861 held one of the earliest exhibitions of works by Manet, who absorbed the influence of artists such as Chardin and Watteau displayed at the gallery.

MAUCLAIR, Camille (c.1872–1945)
Born Camille Faust, he was a poet, novelist and dramatist associated with the Symbolists and for many years art critic of their magazine, the *Mercure de France*. In 1903 he published a book on the Impressionists which helped to raise their status.

MAUS, Octave (1856–1919)
Lawyer, journalist and critic who founded the avant-garde organization Les Vingt (so called because it had twenty members) and its successor La Libre Esthétique ◆ (pp.214–5).

MELLON, Paul (1907–99)
Son of the American financier Andrew Mellon (1855–1937), who founded the National Gallery of Art in Washington. Paul and his wife built up a large Impressionist collection, which they donated to the museum.

MEURENT, Victorine (1844–c.1885)
A professional model who posed frequently for Manet, notably in *Déjeuner sur l'herbe* (p.27), *Olympia* (p.36) and *The Railroad* (p.153). A talented guitarist and competent artist, she had a self-portrait accepted by the Salon in 1876. After succumbing to alcoholism, she died in abject poverty.

MIRBEAU, Octave (1848–1917)
Novelist and critic who was an ardent defender of Impressionism and one of the first to recognize the genius of Gauguin. He wrote catalogue introductions for three of Monet's exhibitions, and an important study of Renoir published in 1917. One of his novels, *Le Calvaire* (1886), featured a misanthropic artist named Lirat based on Degas. A volume of his collected criticism, entitled *Des Artistes*, was published posthumously in 1921.

MONET, Claude (1840–1926)

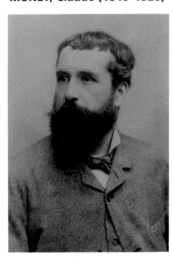

Photograph of Monet (c.1880)

Eldest son of a Parisian shopkeeper who moved to Le Havre in 1845, Monet enrolled at the Académie Suisse at the age of 19. After military service in Algeria, he studied with Gleyre, then went to paint in the Forest of Fontainebleau with Bazille, Renoir and Sisley. After a period of great financial hardship, he exhibited at the Impressionist exhibitions held in 1874–9 and 1882, by which time his paintings were earning him 35,000 francs a year from Durand-Ruel. In 1883 Monet moved to Giverny, where he created a remarkable garden and painted the *Nymphéas* cyclorama, which he donated to the French nation ◆ (p.241).

MOORE, George (1852–1933)
Irish-born novelist who lived in Paris for ten years and studied painting at Cabanel's *atelier*. A habitué of the Nouvelle-Athènes ◆ (pp.46–7), he included reminiscences of his friendship with the Impressionists in his books, such as *Confessions of a Young Man* (1888). As art critic of the *Speaker* (1891–5), he was a champion of Impressionism in Britain.

MORISOT, Berthe (1841–95)

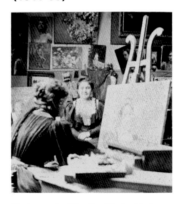

Photograph of Berthe Morisot in her studio

Daughter of a high-ranking civil servant, Morisot was given painting lessons by Joseph-Benoît Guichard, then was influenced by Daubigny and Guillemet. In 1868 she met Manet, whom she greatly admired, but soon developed a distinctive style that influenced his own painting and encouraged him to work *en plein air*. Morisot exhibited regularly at the Salon ▲ (p.61), and at all the Impressionist exhibitions except for 1879. She appears in many of Manet's paintings, such as *The Balcony* (p.60) and *Repose* (p.78). After her marriage to his brother Eugène in 1874, her house in the rue Villejust became a social and inspirational centre for the Impressionists.

MOROZOV, Mikhail (1870–1903) and Ivan (1871–1921)
Russian collectors whose family wealth was based on textiles ◆ (pp.214–5). They started buying Impressionist paintings in the 1890s from Durand-Ruel and others, employing an agent in Paris for that purpose. Their collection (including major works by Manet, Monet, Renoir and Sisley) is now divided between the Hermitage and the Pushkin Museum of Fine Arts.

MURER, Eugène (1845–1906)

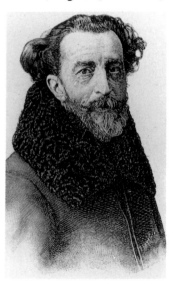

Engraving of Murer from the *Mariani Picture Book* (1900–3)

A schoolfriend of Guillaumin, he was a restaurateur and *pâtissier* who during the 1870s held free dinners for the Impressionists at his restaurant in the boulevard Voltaire. In 1883 he purchased a hotel in Rouen, where he exhibited their works, which he collected assiduously. The author of two novels, after his retirement he took up painting. On his tombstone in Auvers is the inscription 'Eugène Murer: Ouvrier–Littérateur–Peintre'.

NADAR
(1820–1910)
Professional name of Gaspard-Félix Tournachon. Originally an artist and caricaturist, he became one of the most celebrated pioneers of photography. In 1863 he took the first aerial photos of Paris, from a balloon. He got to know the Impressionists through frequenting the Café Guerbois ◆ (p.46–7), and arranged for them to rent his old studio for their first exhibition ■ (p.86).

NITTIS, Giuseppe de
(1846–84)

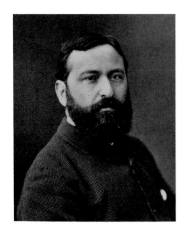

Photograph of de Nittis

An Italian painter, at one time associated with the Macchiaioli ◆ (pp.214–5), who settled in Paris in 1872. A lifelong friend of Degas and Manet, he attempted to imitate their style and took part in the first Impressionist exhibition, but later developed a more popular approach and became a successful painter of society portraits.

PETIT, Georges
(c.1835–1900)
A wealthy dealer who owned a fashionable gallery in the rue de Sèze. He became increasingly interested in the Impressionists and often exhibited their works at his series of annual Expositions Internationales de Peinture, launched in 1882 in partnership with Giuseppe de Nittis. During 1889 he successfully staged a three-month joint Monet-Rodin exhibition, which featured 145 works by Monet.

PHILLIPS, Duncan
(1899–1966)
Grandson of a steel magnate who started collecting in 1916 together with his brother Jim, who died a few years later. In 1921 he opened two rooms of his family home in Washington as the Phillips Memorial Gallery. With the help of his artist wife, Marjorie, he built up a superb collection of Impressionist and Post-Impressionist paintings.

PIETTE, Ludovic
(1826–77)
A landscape painter who met Pissarro at the Académie Suisse and was superficially influenced by Impressionism. The paintings by Piette shown at the Impressionist exhibition of 1877 and posthumously at the exhibition of 1879 were almost indistinguishable in style from those of Pissarro, who often stayed with him on his farm at Montfoucault in Normandy.

PISSARRO, Camille
(1830–1903)

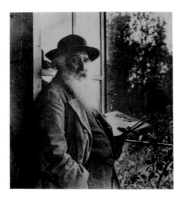

Photograph of Pissarro in his studio at Éragny-sur-Epte (c.1890)

Born in Saint Thomas in the West Indies of a fairly affluent mercantile family, Pissarro was sent to Paris to complete his education. In 1855 he enrolled at the Académie Suisse, where he got to know Monet, and by frequenting the Café Guerbois ◆ (p.46–7) he soon met the other artists. Influenced by Corot, he exhibited at the Salon between 1864 and 1869, and at the Salon des Refusés in 1863. During the Franco-Prussian War he joined

Monet in London ▲ (p.71), where they met Durand-Ruel. Actively involved in the creation of the Société Anonyme des Artistes, he took part in all the Impressionist exhibitions. Around 1865 Pissarro adopted a form of Pointillism, but eventually reverted to his earlier style. His versatility extended to fan and porcelain painting, engraving and illustration. Politically a radical, he had a strong leaning towards the anarchistic beliefs that were causing alarm throughout European society at the time.

PISSARRO, Félix
(1874–97)
Pissarro's second son. A painter, engraver and caricaturist, he used the pseudonym Jean Roch to avoid confusion with other members of his family.

PISSARRO, Lucien
(1866–1944)
Pissarro's eldest son, who, like his brothers, was a talented artist ▲ (p.212). He exhibited at the Impressionist exhibition of 1886 (when his painting was influenced by Seurat's Pointillist style) and also at the Salon des Indépendants. In 1893 he settled in England, maintaining a lively correspondence with his father. He founded the Éragny Press in Hammersmith in 1896, which specialized in small books illustrated with hand-engraved colour blocks made by himself.

PROUST, Antonin
(1832–1905)
A close friend of Manet since their schooldays at the Collège Rollin. He began his career as the founder of the periodical *La Semaine universelle*, then became secretary to the left-wing politician Léon Gambetta. As a result he was appointed Minister for Refugees during the Franco-Prussian war, and subsequently Minister of Fine Arts (1881-2) and Commissioner of Fine Arts for the Universal Exhibition of 1889. In all of these offices he was helpful to the Impressionists. He wrote a book about Manet –

who painted his portrait in 1880 (p.124) – which was published posthumously in 1913.

PUVIS DE CHAVANNES,
Pierre-Cécile (1824–98)
A trained engineer who studied painting in Italy and later with Delacroix and Couture, he became known for his mural-like paintings executed in a flat, decorative style. Although the naturalism and spontaneity of Impressionism was opposed to his own style of painting, he was a close friend of Degas and Morisot. His work frequently had symbolic undercurrents, which exerted a considerable influence on Seurat, Gauguin, Redon and the Nabis.

RAFFAELLI, Jean-François
(1850–1924)
Realist painter, lithographer and sculptor who participated in the Impressionist exhibitions of 1880 and 1881. A protégé of Degas and habitué of the Café Guerbois ◆ (pp.46–7), he was a gifted illustrator and produced landscapes and urban scenes that were praised by Huysmans. In 1886 he disassociated himself from the Impressionists, partly because of his growing success, and was subsequently dropped by the group.

RENOIR, Edmond
(1849–1923)
Younger brother of the painter, Edmond posed for *La Loge* (p.87) and many other of Renoir's works. His career as a journalist was interrupted by the war of 1870, but he was subsequently appointed editor of *La Presse*. When the Charpentiers founded *La Vie moderne* in 1879, he was appointed its editor and directed the art gallery on its premises. Edmond was disliked by some of the Impressionists – who felt that he favoured his brother's work over their own. From 1884 he became gradually less involved with the movement and when *La Vie moderne* ceased publication in 1893 he lost all contact with the artists.

RENOIR, Pierre-Auguste (1841–1919)

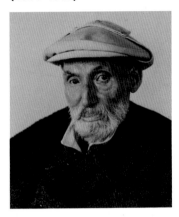

Photograph of Renoir (1914)

Son of a tailor and a dressmaker, after being apprenticed to a porcelain painter, Renoir became a student of Gleyre and enrolled at the École des Beaux-Arts (*see* p.19). Initially influenced by the Barbizon school, once he had come into contact with Monet and Sisley he evolved a broader approach to the treatment of light and shade. Although he played an active role in the creation of the Société Anonyme des Artistes and the Impressionist exhibitions of 1874–77 and 1882, Renoir continued exhibiting at the Salon, where he had some notable successes. Remarkably versatile, his work ranged from portraits and scenes of Parisian life to landscapes and eventually nudes ◆ (p.225) and sculpture ◆ (p.235). Despite an attack of paralysis in 1912, he continued painting almost to the end of his life ▲ (p.237).

RIVIÈRE, Georges (1855–1943)

Art critic who was a close friend of Renoir. The Impressionists had always wanted to have a publication of their own, and in 1877 Renoir persuaded Rivière to edit *L'Impressionniste*, which was published throughout the third Impressionist exhibition but received little attention. Many years later, he wrote valuable books of reminiscences about Renoir (1921), Cézanne (1923) and Degas (1935).

ROBINSON, Theodore (1852–96)

An American artist who worked in France from 1887 until 1892. He was a close friend of Monet and spent much time at Giverny, painting similar subjects and infecting Monet with his own enthusiasm for photography.

ROUART, Henri (1833–1912)

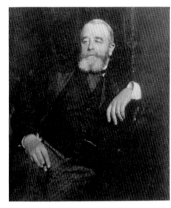

ANON Alexis Rouart c.1895

A successful industrial engineer who pioneered refrigeration machinery in France, Rouart was a keen amateur painter and participated in all the Impressionist exhibitions excepting that in 1882, when he paid the rent for the exhibition space. A close friend of Degas since school days, they served in the same unit during the Franco-Prussian War, and maintained an extensive and historically important correspondence. As a result of their friendship, Rouart started to buy Impressionist paintings and to help the artists both financially and with advice.

ROUSSEAU, Théodore (1812–67)

A landscape artist, strongly influenced by Constable and the Dutch landscape painters, who settled in Barbizon in 1848 and became the leader of the Barbizon school. His vision of nature and the spontaneity of his composition influenced the landscape painting of all the Impressionists, especially that of Pissarro.

RUTTER, Frank (1876–1937)

Art critic of the *Financial Times* and *Sunday Times* who was an enthusiastic supporter of the Impressionists. In 1905 he campaigned for the purchase of some of their works for the national collections of Britain.

SARGENT, John Singer (1856–1925)

Fashionable portrait painter who was born in America but spent most of his life in Europe. He was friendly with most of the Impressionists (especially Monet, with whom he stayed on several occasions) and helped to promote their work in England and the USA. In the 1880s he began to paint landscapes that had an Impressionist character, and in 1886 became a founder member of the New English Art Club (*see* p.148).

SCHUFFENECKER, Émile (1854–1912)

A colleague of Gauguin's at Bertins, the stockbrokers, who also decided to become a painter. A loyal and generous friend, he was ever willing to offer Gauguin help and accommodation. His work was shown at the Salons des Indépendants in 1884 and the eighth Impressionist exhibition in 1886. He also exhibited at and helped to organize the exhibition at the Café Volpini in 1889 (*see* p.169).

SEURAT, Georges (1859–91)

After studying at the École des Beaux-Arts, Seurat began evolving a scientific method of painting that would supplant what he saw as the amorphism of Impressionism. The system he evolved, which became known as Pointillism, entailed the juxtaposition of tiny dots of colour – which would blend in the eye of the spectator to produce the required hue – coupled with an almost geometric approach to form. He showed several such paintings at the Impressionist exhibition of 1886 ■ (pp.151–2), and temporarily converted

Pissarro and his son Lucien to Pointillism. After his death, aged 32, his doctrines were continued by Signac and others.

SHCHUKIN, Sergei (1851–1936)

A Moscow merchant who, after he succeeded his father as head of the family firm, became a keen collector ◆ (pp.214–5). He relied heavily on Durand-Ruel and built a special gallery for his collection, which included works by Gauguin, Matisse and Picasso as well as Cézanne, Degas, Monet and Renoir. His collection is now divided between the Hermitage and the Pushkin Museum of Fine Arts.

SICKERT, Walter Richard (1860–1942)

A British artist who studied at the Slade under Legros, then worked in Whistler's studio. He became friendly with Degas in 1883, and his paintings, which often depict scenes from urban life, show Degas' influence. From 1899 to 1905 he lived in Dieppe, where he got to know Gauguin. Sickert did much to popularize Impressionism, both through his writings and as a member of the New English Art Club (*see* p.148).

SIGNAC, Paul (1863–1935)

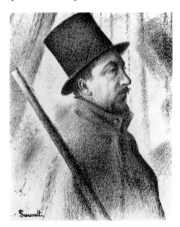

SEURAT Portrait of Signac c.1889

Helped by Monet while still in his teens, Signac started painting in the Impressionist style. Then in 1884 he met Seurat (both were members of the Société des Artistes Indépendants) and became a convert to Pointillism, which he eloquently defended in his book *D'Eugène Delacroix au néo-impressionnisme* (1899). In the Impressionist exhibition of 1886 Signac's and Seurat's paintings were hung in a separate room ■ (pp.151–2).

SILVESTRE, Armand (1837–1901)
Novelist, critic, poet and playwright who supplied the preface to the three-volume album of engravings by, among others, Degas, Manet, Monet, Pissarro and Sisley, that Durand-Ruel brought out in 1873 ▲ (p.80). He also wrote an autobiography, *Au Pays des souvenirs* (1892), which gives a fascinating account of the early days of Impressionism and the circle that met at the Café Guerbois ◆ (pp.46–7).

SISLEY, Alfred (1839–99)

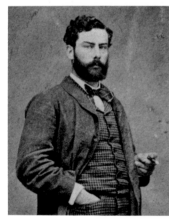

Photograph of Sisley
c.1872–4

The son of a wealthy English merchant who had settled in Paris, Sisley studied painting at Gleyre's *atelier*. There he met Bazille, Monet and Renoir, and in the 1860s painted with them in the Forest of Fontainebleau. Deeply influenced by Courbet and Daubigny, in 1866 he exhibited at the Salon as 'a pupil of Corot'. One of the circle that frequented the Café Guerbois ◆ (pp.46–7), he participated in the Salon des Refusés and the

Impressionist exhibitions held in 1874–7 and 1882. After the failure of his father's business in 1870, he suffered a long period of extreme financial hardship. His diffident nature inhibited him from promoting his own work, which mainly consisted of landscapes, and it was only towards the end of his life that his paintings began to receive the recognition they deserved.

TANGUY, 'Père' (1825–93)
Artist's colourman and dealer who befriended many of the Impressionists and displayed their works in his shop ● (p.192). He was especially helpful to Cézanne, and also to van Gogh.

TISSOT, Jacques-Joseph (James) (1836–1902)
As a painter of portraits and scenes from polite society, Tissot was influenced by Whistler and also by Japanese art. He was a close friend of Degas, who was jealous of his success, and broke with him in 1895 when Tissot sold a picture that Degas had given him. After the fall of the Commune, he spent eleven years in London. The later part of his life was devoted to painting religious subjects.

TRÉHOT, Lise (1848–1924)
Model who features in many of Renoir's most important paintings between 1867 and 1872 ◆ (p.50).

VALPINÇON, Paul (c.1830–1894)
Degas' lifelong friend whom he met at the Lycée Louis le Grand. His father Édouard Valpinçon introduced Degas to Ingres. Degas made regular visits to the family's château at Ménil-Hubert, in Normandy and painted various members of the family on many occasions.

VOLLARD, Ambroise (1868–1939)
Born in Réunion, he studied law at Montpellier, then moved to Paris and became an art dealer.

He opened his first gallery in the rue Lafitte with an exhibition of sketches by Manet. The following year he moved to larger premises and began vigorously to promote Cézanne. Vollard also dealt in works by Degas ▲ (pp.186–7), Pissarro, Renoir and Rodin, but his main achievement was in promoting the artists who succeeded the Impressionists.

WAGRAM, Louis-Marie Philippe Alexandre Berthier, Prince de (1883–1917)
A voracious collector, descended from one of Napoleon's generals. He acquired over a hundred Impressionist works, including 28 Cézannes, 11 Degas, 12 Manets, 40 Monets, 50 Renoirs and 47 van Goghs.

WHISTLER, James Abbott McNeill (1834–1903)

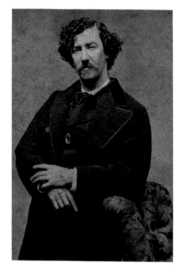

Photograph of Whistler by Étienne Carjat (c.1864)

Born in America, Whistler came to Paris in 1855 to study with Gleyre, then settled in London in 1859. He exhibited *The White Girl* (p.23) at the Salon des Refusés in 1863, and appears in Fantin-Latour's *Homage to Delacroix* (p.28). While in Paris Whistler became friendly with the Impressionists and he had a considerable influence on Degas and Manet. He was also encouraged the increasing enthusiasm for Japanese art.

WOLFF, Albert (1835–91)
Of German origin, he was a prolific author of novels, plays and essays, and became art critic of *Le Figaro*. Although he was a virulent opponent of Impressionism (*see* p.14), Manet insisted on painting his portrait.

ZANDOMENEGHI, Federico (1841–1917)
A member of the Macchiaioli group of painters in Florence ◆ (p.214–5), whose work was close to that of the Impressionists, he came to Paris in 1874, where he met Degas, Pissarro and Renoir. Regarded as a protégé of Degas, he participated in the Impressionist exhibitions of 1879–81 and 1886. Although he was taken up by Durand-Ruel and his pastels were praised by the critics, most of the Impressionists did not think very highly of his work.

ZOLA, Émile (1840–1902)

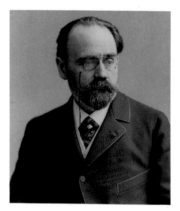

Photograph of Zola

One of the most celebrated novelists and critics of his time, Zola grew up with Cézanne and for many years energetically defended the Impressionists in articles and pamphlets such as *Mon Salon* ▲ (p.41). By 1879, however, his enthusiasm for them had begun to wane ▲ (p.114), and the final break came in 1886 with the publication of his novel *L'Oeuvre*, in which the unattractive central character was based on Cézanne and Manet ● (p.53).

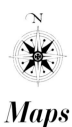

Maps

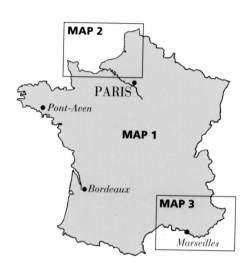

MAP 2

PARIS

Pont-Aven

MAP 1

Bordeaux

MAP 3

Marseilles

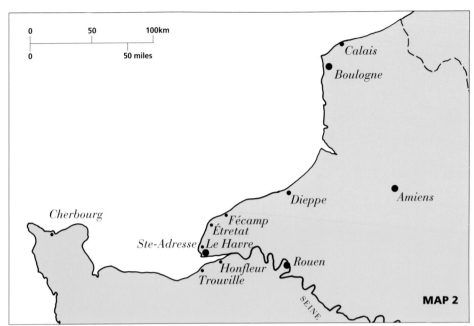

Calais

Boulogne

Dieppe

Amiens

Cherbourg

Fécamp
Étretat
Ste-Adresse *Le Havre*

Rouen

Honfleur
Trouville

SEINE

MAP 2

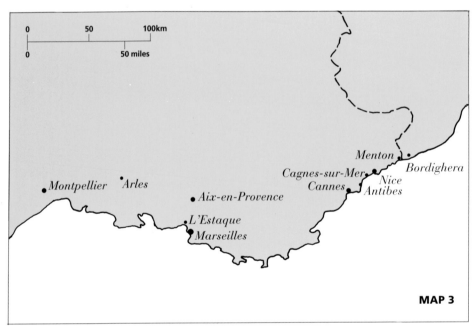

Menton

Cagnes-sur-Mer

Bordighera

Montpellier *Arles*

Nice

Cannes
Antibes

Aix-en-Provence

L'Estaque
Marseilles

MAP 3

THE CHANNEL COAST (Map 2)
Until the latter half of the eighteenth century, in genteel society the seaside was considered a place to be avoided. Then for a variety of reasons attitudes began to change, especially in England and France. Members of the medical profession started to recommend the therapeutic properties of sea water. Culturally, the quest for picturesque images engendered by the Romantic movement resulted in painters, poets and musicians visiting the coast in search of inspiration. And socially, as more and more people forsook the countryside for the city, the need to escape at least annually from the horrors of sprawling industrial conurbations became increasingly urgent. Together, these factors conspired to convert simple fishing villages into fashionable resorts for the elegant and the rich.

Easily accessible from Paris thanks to the development of the railways from the Gare St-Lazare and the Gare du Nord, a whole chain of resorts grew up – Deauville, Trouville, Le Havre, Ste-Adresse, Boulogne and the rest. The rich and the famous either built houses in or near the Channel resorts or visited the splendid hotels there on a regular basis, thus presenting painters such as the Impressionists with opportunities to maintain contact with existing patrons and the hope of meeting new ones.

THE MEDITERRANEAN COAST (Map 3)
As light railways began to spread out from Marseilles and Toulon through the old kingdom of Provence, the new accessibility of the area began to attract artists and holidaymakers from Paris and the north of France.

With its rich cultural heritage, its ancient capital, Aix-en-Provence, and its beautiful scenery, the region possessed a confidence that had recently found expression in the revival of its own language. Mediterranean fishing villages and towns such as Cagnes, Antibes and Nice began to achieve a status as resorts similar to that already enjoyed by their counterparts on the Channel coast.

Renoir, in common with many others, was drawn to the area by its mild climate, which was known to be beneficial for those who suffered from rheumatic complaints; Cézanne spent the greater part of his life in Provence, deriving constant inspiration from the landscape; and Monet found in its vivid colours and pellucid atmosphere a context in which he could carry forward his attempts to reproduce the intensity and varying effects of light. It was also the landscape and light of the south that provided Post-Impressionist painters such as Matisse, Raoul Dufy and van Dongen with the sense of vibrant colour that was to become a hallmark of their work.

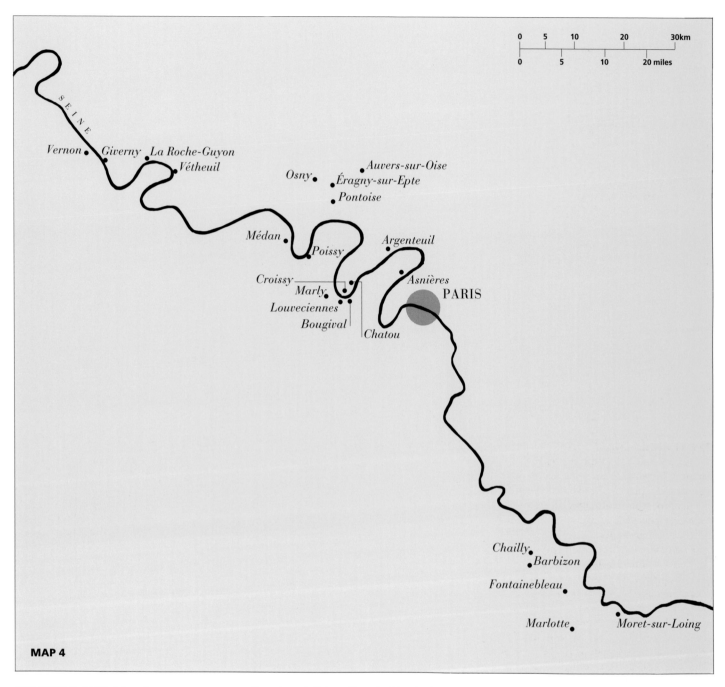

MAP 4

THE SEINE BASIN (Map 4)

In the mid nineteenth century, after a period when landscape painting was unfashionable, the countryside began to play an increasingly important role in art. For Parisian painters, the most accessible stretch of countryside was the neighbourhood of the old royal castle at Fontainebleau and the surrounding forest, especially after the extension of the railway south-eastwards from Paris in 1849. The area was still relatively wild, and its villages – Barbizon, Chailly and Marlotte – attracted artists such as Corot, Millet and Diaz de la Peña who were exploring new modes of naturalistic painting. Bazille, Monet, Pissarro,

Renoir and Sisley all worked in the Forest of Fontainebleau during the 1860s, staying at local inns and going on long walking expeditions. Consequently, most of the landscape paintings they produced at that time featured the scenery of the area.

The railway link between Paris and Rouen (opened in 1841) had been built by English engineers, and their influence permeated the Seine Basin, manifesting itself in the fashion for river sports and the style of domestic gardens. The banks of the Seine became a favourite destination for Parisians on weekend excursions, and to cater for them cafés and restaurants soon began to proliferate.

It was at Argenteuil that the characteristics of Impressionism began to emerge, and it was there that Manet first adopted a truly Impressionist style. It was there too that Renoir painted Camille and Jean Monet in their garden; that Manet painted Monet in his studio boat; and that Caillebotte sailed boats of his own design. At Croissy Island, near Bougival, both Monet and Renoir painted views of La Grenouillère ('The Froggery'), a restaurant and bathing place popular with Parisians (p.55).

Both the Forest of Fontainebleau and the riverside resorts of the Seine played a central role in Impressionist landscape painting.

Impressionist Locations

AIX-EN-PROVENCE (Map 3)
In medieval times capital of the
kingdom of Provence, in the
nineteenth century – as today –
Aix was a cultural centre, with a
university, an art school and a
well-stocked public art gallery.
Cézanne, who was born in Aix,
spent most of his life in and
around the city, taking the local
scenery for his subject matter –
especially the jagged profile of
Mont Ste-Victoire (right), which
features in so many of his
landscapes. Renoir, Pissarro and
other artists also painted in the
area when staying with Cézanne
at his home, the Jas de Bouffan.

ARGENTEUIL (Map 4)
Situated on the upper Seine at
the point where the river widens,
Argenteuil became a popular
leisure centre after the completion
of the railway line from Paris in
1841. It was greatly admired by

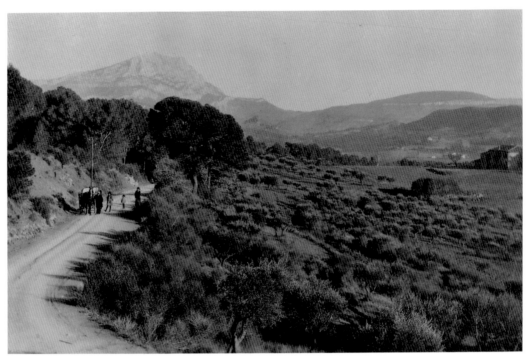
Photograph of Mont Ste-Victoire, near Aix-en-Provence

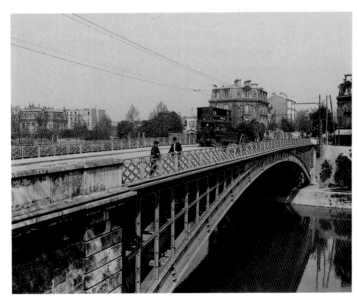
Photograph of the Pont de Clichy at Asnières

the Impressionists, whose new
ideas about painting developed
while they were working in the
area. Caillebotte, Manet, Monet,
Renoir and Sisley all painted
important pictures there in the
1870s, and it was at Argenteuil
that Monet built a floating
studio in 1873.

ASNIERES (Map 4)
The nearest to Paris of the Seine
pleasure haunts served by the
railway from the Gare St-Lazare,
the population of Asnières rose
from 1200 in 1856 to 15,200 in
1886. The writers Paul Alexis
and Armand Silvestre lived there;
Monet was especially attracted
by the place; and Seurat painted
his *Sunday Afternoon on the Island of
La Grande Jatte* (p.152) nearby.

AUVERS-SUR-OISE (Map 4)
A small, sparsely populated
village on the banks of the Oise.
The area became popular with
artists during the 1850s when
Daumier (who died in the
neighbourhood), Corot and
Daubigny worked there. Berthe
Morisot often came to the
village to visit her sister Yves. In
1872 Dr Gachet moved to a
house in Auvers, where he often
entertained his Impressionist
friends, including Cézanne,
Guillaumin, Pissarro, Renoir
and Sisley, who all produced
paintings of the area. When in
the 1890s Murer retired as a
hotelier, he moved to Auvers
from Rouen. In 1890 van Gogh
shot himself in a field near
Gachet's house.

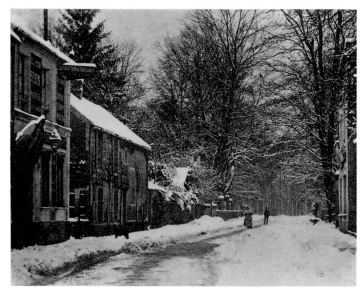

Photograph of an inn situated in the Forest of Fontainebleau (c.1875)

BARBIZON (Map 4)

A village in the Forest of Fontainebleau which in the 1840s and 1850s became a favourite location of Diaz de la Peña, Millet and Théodore Rousseau, who both went to live there, and other painters of the Barbizon school. In the late 1860s Bazille, Monet, Pissarro, Renoir and Sisley spent much time in and around Barbizon, staying in nearby villages such as Marlotte and Chailly. It was near Barbizon that Monet painted his *Study for Déjeuner sur l'herbe* (p.35) in 1865.

BOUGIVAL (Map 4)

When Asnières became over-popular, the Impressionists retreated to Bougival, further from Paris, which combined sawmills, docks, quarries and other industrial phenomena with stretches of pure country-side and places of entertainment. In the late 1860s Pissarro and Sisley began to paint the areas where industry and nature were in close juxtaposition – as did Monet, who in the late spring of 1869 came to live in the hamlet of St-Michel, just above the village. During that year Monet, Pissarro and Renoir all produced paintings of La Grenouillère (p.55), a popular bathing place on Croissy Island just a short walk from Bougival (right) that had converted barges for dining and dancing. Later, in 1881–4, Berthe Morisot rented a villa at Bougival, where she painted views of the river and portraits of her family.

BOULOGNE (Map 2)

By the 1870s the Channel ports, which were now accessible by train from Paris, had become increasingly popular as holiday resorts. During a visit to Boulogne in the summer of 1864 Manet made sketches of the battleship *Kearsage* (p.31); and in 1873 he painted several pictures of the port, some of which appear to have been directed at the popular market. While the Manet family were holidaying in Boulogne in 1869 they received a visit from Degas, who produced numerous pictures in pastel during his visit and worked on two oil paintings in the following months.

CAGNES-SUR-MER (Map 3)

A small village near Nice, which by the end of the nineteenth century was changing into a resort. In 1907 Renoir bought an estate named Les Collettes at Cagnes and built a house there, called the Villa de la Poste, where he spent most of the rest of his life.

CHAILLY (Map 4)

A village near Barbizon, on the edge of the Forest of Fontainebleau, first visited by Monet and Bazille in May 1863. The following June, after the closing of Gleyre's studio, Monet took Bazille, Renoir and Sisley there to paint in the forest. In the 1880s it became a favourite haunt of Seurat.

CHATOU (Map 4)

About 5km (3 miles) down-stream from Argenteuil and 15km (9 miles) from the Gare St-Lazare, Chatou was still delightfully rural when Renoir worked there, although it was a popular spot for rowing, and café-restaurants and dance places had begun to mushroom after the opening of the railway line from Paris. The Seine there was divided into two streams, the one used by commercial traffic, the other by pleasure craft. Facing the village was a small island where Renoir painted *Oarsmen at Chatou* in 1879 and *Luncheon of the Boating Party* (p.132), at Père Fournaise's restaurant, in 1880–1. In all, Chatou and the surrounding area provided Renoir with background material for nine figure paintings and six or seven riverscapes.

DIEPPE (Map 2)

By the 1870s, when it became a popular place of refuge during the Franco-Prussian War and the period of the Commune, Dieppe had already developed into a bustling resort. Ludovic Halévy and Jacques-Émile Blanche had houses in the neighbourhood, where Degas was a frequent guest. Gauguin, Eva Gonzalès and Monet also visited the port and painted in the surrounding area. Just outside the town was the Château de Wargemont, the country home of the Berards ● (p.231), where Renoir was a regular guest, producing numerous paintings between 1879 and 1884.

ÉRAGNY-SUR-EPTE (Map 4)

In 1884 Pissarro rented a house at Bazincourt-sur-Epte near Éragny, even though it was more than twice as far from Paris as his previous home in Pontoise. Gauguin visited him there, but when he offered accommodation to van Gogh his wife objected. In 1892 Pissarro bought the house with money borrowed from Monet and lived there for the rest of his life. Éragny and the landscape of the surround-ing countryside feature in many of his paintings.

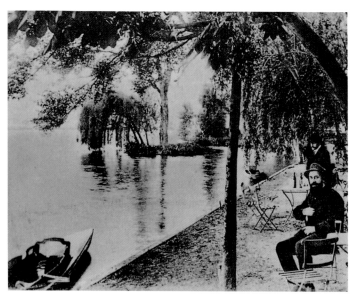

Photograph of La Grenouillère, near Bougival

ESSOYES

A small village about 20km (12 miles) south-east of Troyes, Essoyes was the birthplace of Renoir's wife, Aline ◆ (p.147). Renoir first visited Essoyes in 1885, and in 1895 he was persuaded by Aline to buy a house there, which they used as a holiday home and where he built a studio in 1905.

L'ESTAQUE (Map 3)

Spa and fishing village, about 50km (30 miles) from Marseilles, where Cézanne and his mistress Hortense Fiquet ◆ (p.146) went to live in 1870. Cézanne was enthralled by the village and the surrounding landscape, and continued to return there intermittently until he finally settled in Aix-en-Provence, following his father's death in 1886. Renoir stayed in L'Estaque in 1882, and he and Cézanne painted together in the neighbourhood until Renoir went down with pneumonia.

ÉTRETAT (Map 2)

Thriving, picturesque fishing port, with spectacular cliffs and rock arches, about 25km (15 miles) from Le Havre. Delacroix and Courbet had both painted there, and Monet was greatly attracted by the place. In 1885 Monet stayed with the singer Jean-Baptiste Faure ● (p.81) at his villa in Étretat. Offenbach and Michelet also had secondary residences there – as did Maupassant, who sometimes watched Monet painting *en plein air* and described his working practices in an article published in the periodical *Gil Blas* in 1885.

GIVERNY (Map 4)

A small village on the banks of the Seine, about 5km (3 miles) from the town of Vernon, where Monet rented a house in 1883. Seven years later he purchased the freehold, and immediately set about transforming the garden. Monet lived at Giverny for the rest of his life, receiving visits from Cassatt, Cézanne, Pissarro, Renoir, Rodin and

other famous figures, including Clemenceau, who was a neighbour. In 1914 he built a special studio in the grounds to accommodate his *Nymphéas* cyclorama ◆ (p.241). On the death of Monet's son Michel in 1966 the house and gardens were bequeathed to the nation and are now open to the public.

LE HAVRE (Map 2)

One of the major French ports, with a considerable English colony, Le Havre assumed a new importance in the 1860s with the introduction of a regular steamship service to the USA. Monet grew up in Le Havre, and at the outset of his career drew much of his inspiration from the surrounding area. It was here that he first met Boudin and Jongkind; and it was a local businessman, Louis-Joachim Gaudibert, from nearby Montivilliers, who became one of his first patrons and provided him with an allowance in 1868–9. Monet's *Impression: Sunrise* (p.88), the painting which gave its name to Impressionism, was originally entitled *Sunrise at Le Havre*.

HONFLEUR (Map 2)

An ancient fishing port on the other side of the Seine estuary from Le Havre, Honfleur was so popular with painters that it became known as the 'Barbizon of Normandy'. Boudin, Corot, Diaz de la Peña and Jongkind all worked there during the 1850s and 1860s, staying at the Ferme St-Siméon on a clifftop overlooking the estuary. In the summer of 1864 Monet painted in the area with Boudin and Jongkind, and was subsequently joined by Bazille, the two of them renting rooms from a baker ▲ (p.33).

LORIENT

Naval base, dockyard and fishing port at the confluence of the rivers Scorff and Blavet in Brittany. The Morisot family frequently stayed there, and in 1869 Berthe painted a delightful

picture, entitled *The Harbour at Lorient*, of her sister Edma (who was married to Adolphe Pontillon, a naval officer), sitting on a riverside wall with tall-masted boats in the background.

LOUVECIENNES (Map 4)

A village some 25km (15 miles) west of Paris where Pissarro lived in 1869–70, before the outbreak of the Franco-Prussian War, and again in 1871–2. In 1868 Renoir's parents retired to the Louveciennes neighbourhood; consequently, he spent a good deal of time there during the next few years. Pissarro, Renoir and Monet, who was then living at St-Michel, near Bougival, all painted in the area – as did Sisley, who moved to Louveciennes in 1871.

MARLOTTE (Map 4)

A small village in the Forest of Fontainebleau which achieved considerable fame in the 1850s through Henri Murger, author of *Scènes de la vie de Bohème*, who was a frequent visitor. When Renoir, Sisley and Le Coeur ▲ (p.50) painted in the neighbourhood in 1866, they stayed at the inn belonging to Mère Antony, which Murger had patronized. In Renoir's painting of the interior (p.38), a caricature of Murger is visible on the wall in the background. Bazille, Courbet, Monet and Pissarro also stayed at the inn; so did the Goncourts, who described its Bohemian ambience in their *Journal*.

MARLY (Map 4)

A village between St-Germain-en-Laye and Versailles, not far from Louveciennes. Sisley lived there from 1876 to 1879, when he moved to Sèvres. During that period he painted a great many views of the surrounding countryside and nearby river, including several of the floods at Port Marly (p.94) in 1876. He also painted his first series of flood paintings at Marly, when the Seine burst its banks in 1872.

MÉDAN (Map 4)

When published in 1877, Zola's novel *L'Assommoir* shocked polite society and was bought by everyone. With the money from it, the following year he purchased a country retreat at Médan, on a bend in the Seine beyond Chatou, about 15km (10 miles) from Pontoise. There he frequently entertained his Impressionist friends – especially Cézanne, who stayed with him for a few weeks every year until their friendship ended came to an end in 1886 ● (p.53).

MONTPELLIER (Map 3)

University city, built on the hills above the River Lez in Languedoc, with a medical school (which was founded in the thirteenth century) where Dr Gachet studied. Bazille grew up in the area; and his parent's home at Méric, where they owned vineyards, provided the setting for *The Artist's Family on a Terrace near Montpellier* (p.44). Several of Bazille's works that were painted in the neighbourhood are now housed in the city's Musée Fabre.

MORET-SUR-LOING (Map 4)

Picturesque village on the banks of the Loing near Fontainebleau, to which Sisley moved in 1880 and where he lived for the rest of his life, being buried there in 1899. He painted numerous views of the village, including a series of the impressive medieval church, modelled on Monet's paintings of Rouen cathedral. Pissarro also painted in Moret in 1901–2.

OSNY (Map 4)

A village near Pontoise where the Pissarro family lived for two years, from 1882 to 1883, before moving to Éragny-sur-Epte. His paintings of Osny show little of the enthusiasm for the landscape discernible in his paintings of Pontoise. Gauguin visited him there in the summer of 1883, a few months after making the decision to abandon stockbroking for painting.

PONT-AVEN (Map 1)

A Breton village in a valley at the mouth of the River Aven, near Lorient, which became an artists' colony in the 1860s, when Berthe Morisot often painted there. More than twenty years later, the village gave its name to the Pont-Aven school of painters – headed by Gauguin, who first worked there in 1886. It was during his second visit, in 1888, that he met Émile Bernard. Renoir was also a frequent visitor to Pont-Aven, and spent a fortnight there with his family in the summer of 1893.

PONTOISE (Map 4)

A village on the banks of the Oise, near Auvers, which had been 'discovered' by members of the Barbizon school. The landscape greatly appealed to Pissarro, who first lived there from 1866 to 1868. During this period he met Daubigny, who was already working in the area, and the two of them would often paint the same locations. Pissarro returned to Pontoise in August 1872, together with Cézanne – who, while they were working together, began to adopt Impressionist techniques. When the idea of forming a society to hold group exhibitions was broached in 1873, Pissarro advocated an elaborate constitu-

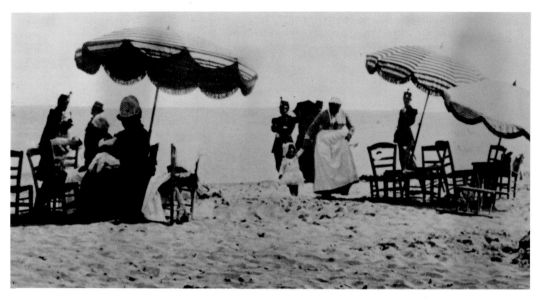

Photograph of the beach at Trouville (c.1890)

tion modelled on that of the bakers' co-operative in Pontoise. Eventually, in 1882, he moved from the village (below) because of encroaching urbanization.

ROUEN (Map 2)

Capital of Upper Normandy, about 60km (35 miles) by train from Giverny and little more than twice that distance from Paris. Monet was a frequent visitor to the city, and painted several views of it in the 1870s. The cathedral, which was the subject of his famous series of paintings ▲ (p.209) executed between 1892 and 1894, had

been sketched and painted by a variety of artists, including Turner, Bonington and Puvis de Chavannes. In 1883 Eugène Murer bought a hotel in Rouen, where he exhibited the works of the Impressionists and often invited them to stay. Gauguin and Renoir both painted in Rouen, as did Pissarro, who worked there for several weeks during the spring and autumn of 1896 and again in 1898.

STE-ADRESSE (Map 2)

A fishing village near Le Havre which became popular with British holiday-makers in the 1820s. Corot and Jongkind both painted there; so did Monet, whose parents lived in Le Havre. In 1867, while visiting an aunt who owned a villa overlooking the English Channel, he produced a variety of paintings, including *The Terrace at Ste-Adresse*, which shows his aunt's family and his father, Adolphe, relaxing on the terrace of the villa.

TROUVILLE (Map 2)

A fashionable resort on the Channel coast that was popular with artists, not least because of the chance of meeting potential patrons. Courbet had a studio there, where Monet first met him, and it was at Trouville, in

1863, that Whistler painted a picture of Courbet standing on the beach entitled *Harmony in Blue and Silver*. In 1870, while staying there with Camille and their infant son Jean, Monet painted *The Hôtel des Roches-Noires* and *On the beach, Trouville* (p.63), emphasizing the holiday mood of the resort (above).

VERNON (Map 4)

An old Norman town with a fourteenth-century church and half-timbered houses, about 5km (3 miles) from Monet's home at Giverny. Vernon provided Monet with subject matter for a number of his paintings, including a series of views of the church in different atmospheric conditions and in varying light.

VÉTHEUIL (Map 4)

A small town, about 50km (30 miles) from Argenteuil on a loop of the Seine between Médan and Giverny, where Monet rented a house in 1878 and where he lived until 1883. Monet was greatly attracted by the place and painted several pictures there, including some of the garden of the house he had rented. Later, when he was living in Giverny, he returned to Vétheuil to paint the church and its surroundings.

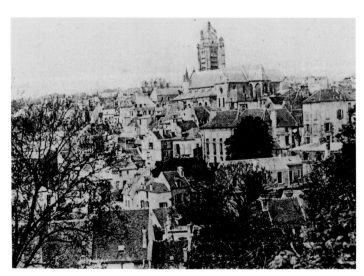

Photograph of Pontoise

Art in the Western World, 1863–Today

1863
- Salon des Refusés
- Gustave Doré illustrates Cervantes' *Don Quixote*
- Rossetti paints *Beata Beatrix*
- Delacroix dies

1864
- Gustave Moreau successfully exhibits *Oedipus and the Sphinx* at the Salon

1865
- Gustave Doré illustrates the Bible
- Yale University opens first Department of Fine Arts in USA

1866
- Winslow Homer paints *Prisoners from the Front*

1867
- Millais paints *The Boyhood of Raleigh*
- Japanese art exhibited for first time in West at Universal Exhibition in Paris
- Peter von Cornelius, Ingres and Théodore Rousseau die

1868
- Eugène Boudin Museum founded in Honfleur, France

1869
- Charles Cros invents colour photography

1870
- Bazille dies

1871
- Rossetti paints *The Dream of Dante*

1872
- Whistler paints *The Artist's Mother*

1873
- Corot paints *Souvenir d'Italie*

1874
- First Impressionist exhibition

1875
- Praxiteles' *Hermes* found at Olympia in Greece
- Corot and Millet die

1876
- Second Impressionist exhibition
- Puvis de Chavannes paints frescoes in the Panthéon in Paris
- Diaz de la Peña dies

1877
- Third Impressionist exhibition
- Winslow Homer paints *The Cotton Pickers*
- Rodin completes *The Age of Bronze*
- Courbet and Piette die

1878
- Publication of William Morris' *The Decorative Arts*
- Daubigny dies

1879
- Fourth Impressionist exhibition
- Couture and Daumier die

1880
- Fifth Impressionist exhibition

1881
- Sixth Impressionist exhibition

- *L'Art moderne* launched in Brussels

1882
- Seventh Impressionist exhibition
- *La Revue moderne* launched in Brussels
- Rossetti dies

1883
- Les Vingt founded in Brussels
- Manet, Gustave Doré and Eva Gonzalès die

1884
- First Salon des Indépendants
- Burne-Jones paints *King Cophetua and the Beggar Maid*
- De Nittis dies

1885
- Émile Guimet's collection of Japanese art moved from Lyon to Paris
- New Rijksmuseum opens in Amsterdam

1886
- Eighth Impressionist exhibition
- New English Art Club founded
- Jean Moréas publishes Symbolist Manifesto
- *Le Décadent* and *Le Symboliste* launched in Paris
- *L'Art libre* launched in Brussels
- Rodin completes *The Kiss*

1887
- James Ensor paints *The Entrance of Christ into Brussels*

1888
- Toulouse-Lautrec paints *Le Cirque Fernando*
- Sérusier, Denis, Bonnard and

Ranson (founders of the Nabis group) begin to work together
- Rodin completes *The Burghers of Calais*
- Adolfo Venturi launches *Archivio Storico dell'Arte*

1889
- Albert Aurier launches *Le Moderniste illustré*
- Sickert becomes art critic of *New York Herald*
- Vuillard and Ranson join the Nabis

1890
- Odilon Redon illustrates Baudelaire's *Les Fleurs du mal*
- Toulouse-Lautrec produces his first poster, *La Goulue*
- Musée des Arts Décoratifs opens in Paris
- First exhibition of Société Nationale des Beaux-Arts
- *La gravure japonaise* exhibition at École des Beaux-Arts
- 'The London Impressionists' launch *The Whirlwind*
- Vincent van Gogh dies

1891
- Gauguin arrives in Tahiti
- The Natansons launch *La Revue blanche*
- *Natura ed Arte* launched in Milan
- Jongkind, Meissonier, Seurat and Theo van Gogh die

1892
- Toulouse-Lautrec paints *Au Moulin Rouge*
- Lord Leighton paints *The Garden of the Hesperides*
- First Rose-Croix exhibition held in Paris

- Munich Secession founded
- Constantin Guys dies

1893
- Munch paints *The Scream*
- Les Vingt dissolved; replaced by La Libre Esthétique
- Art Nouveau style emerges in Europe

1894
- Rodin completes his sculpture of Balzac
- *The Yellow Book* launched in London
- Caillebotte dies

1895
- Siegfried Bing opens a new gallery in Paris named 'L'Art Nouveau'
- First Venice Biennale
- Censorship of art exhibitions lifted in Germany
- Stedelijk Museum opens in Amsterdam
- Berthe Morisot dies

1896
- William Morris publishes *The Kelmscott Chaucer*
- Art periodicals *Die Jugend* and *Simplicissimus* founded in Munich
- Millais and William Morris die

1897
- Max Klinger paints *Christ in Olympus*
- Douanier Rousseau paints *The Sleeping Gypsy*
- Corporation of Italian Artists founded
- Vienna Secession founded
- Sir Henry Tate donates Tate Gallery to British nation
- Félix Pissarro dies

1898
- Glasgow School of Art opens in buildings designed by Charles Rennie Mackintosh
- Aubrey Beardsley, Boudin, Burne-Jones, Gustave Moreau and Puvis de Chavannes die

1899
- Vollard publishes albums of colour lithographs by Denis, Bonnard and Vuillard
- Berlin Secession founded
- Sisley dies

1900
- Picasso paints *The Moulin de la Galette*
- The Wallace Collection, London, opens
- Ruskin dies

1901
- Munch paints *Girls on the Bridge*
- Max Liebermann paints *Self-Portrait*
- First Picasso exhibition in Paris
- Toulouse-Lautrec dies

1902
- *Arte Decorativa Moderna* launched in Turin
- Tissot dies

1903
- First Salon d'Automne
- Picasso paints *La Vie*
- Klimt paints *Philosophy, Medicine and Jurisprudence*
- Galleria d'Arte Moderna opens in Milan
- Gauguin, Pissarro and Whistler die

1904
- Max Beerbohm produces *Poet's Corner*
- Fantin-Latour dies

1905
- Matisse paints *Luxe, calme et volupté*
- Matisse, Derain and associates dubbed Les Fauves at Salon d'Automne
- Die Brücke group formed in Dresden
- Adolphe Bouguereau dies

1906
- Derain paints *The Port of London*
- Cézanne dies

1907
- First Cubist exhibition held in Paris
- Picasso paints *Les demoiselles d'Avignon*

- Derain paints *Blackfriar's Bridge, London*
- Klimt paints *The Kiss*
- Deutscher Werkbund formed by Hermann Muthesius
- Fitzroy Street Group founded in London by Sickert, Gore, Gilman and others

1908
- The term Cubism comes into common use
- Chagall paints *Nu rouge*
- Dufy paints *Landscape at Estaque*
- Utrillo's 'White Period' begins

1909
- Matisse paints *The Dance*
- Mondrian paints his *Tree* series
- William Orpen paints *Homage to Manet*
- Neue Künstlervereinigung formed by Kandinsky, Jawlensky and others
- Frederick Remington and William Powell Frith die

1910
- Roger Fry organizes Post-Impressionist exhibition in London
- Kandinsky paints *The Battle*
- *Der Sturm* magazine and gallery founded in Berlin
- Berlin Secession rejects the work of Die Brücke and other artists; New Secession founded in protest
- *Manifesto of the Futurist Painters* published in Italy
- Winslow Homer and Douanier Rousseau die

1911
- Cubist exhibition at Salon des Indépendants
- De Chirico paints *The Nostalgia of the Infinite*
- Der Blaue Reiter group formed in Munich
- Arts quarterly *Rhythm* launched by John Middleton Murry and Katherine Mansfield
- Sickert and associates form Camden Town Group
- Segantini Museum opens in St Moritz
- Legros dies

1912
- Duchamp paints *Nude Descending a Staircase*
- Schiele paints *Self-Portrait with Winter Cherry*
- Sonderbund exhibition in Cologne
- Publication of Kandinsky's *Concerning the Spiritual in Art*
- Boccioni's *The Technical Manifesto of Futurist Sculpture* published in Italy
- Rouart and Schuffenecker die

1913
- First German Autumn Salon
- Armory Show in New York
- Ernst Kirchner paints *Five Women in a Street*
- Larionov publishes Rayonist Manifesto
- Publication of Apollinaire's *The Cubist Painters*

1914
- Vorticist group formed in London
- Deutscher Werkbund exhibition in Cologne
- Futurists publish architectural manifesto
- Félix Bracquemond, August Macke and Spencer Gore die

1915
- Malevich exhibits Suprematist paintings in Moscow
- First Dada works produced
- Gaudier-Brzeska dies

1916
- First Dada manifestations at Cabaret Voltaire in Zurich
- Marie Bracquemond and Odilon Redon die

1917
- *De Stijl* founded in Amsterdam
- Degas, Rodin and Zandomeneghi die

1918
- November Group founded in Berlin
- Gerrit Rietveld designs *Red, Blue and Yellow Chair*
- Guillemet, Hodler, Klimt and Schiele die

273

1919
- Walter Gropius founds Bauhaus in Weimar
- Renoir dies

1920
- First Paris exhibition of works by Max Ernst
- First International Dada Fair
- Gabo and Pevsner publish Realist Manifesto
- Klinger and Modigliani die

1921
- Munch paints *The Kiss*

1922
- Constructivist Congress in Weimar
- Le Corbusier produces first reinforced-concrete building

1923
- André Breton publishes first Surrealist Manifesto

1924
- Miró paints *Harlequinade*
- Juan Gris gives 'Possibilités de la peinture' lecture in Paris
- Bakst and Raffaëlli die

1925
- First Surrealist group exhibition at the Galerie Pierre in Paris
- Exposition des Arts Décoratifs in Paris
- Bauhaus moves to Dessau from Weimar
- Stieglitz opens his Intimate Gallery in New York
- Sargent dies

1926
- Publication of Le Corbusier's *The Coming of Architecture*
- Monet and Mary Cassatt die

1927
- Edward Hopper paints *Manhattan Bridge*
- Guillaumin and Juan Gris die

1928
- Publication of André Breton's *Surrealism and Painting*
- Charles Rennie Mackintosh and Medardo Rosso die

1929
- Museum of Modern Art, New York, opens
- André Breton publishes second Surrealist Manifesto

1930
- Theo van Doesburg publishes pamphlet entitled *Art Concret*

1931
- Dali paints *The Persistence of Memory*
- Matisse starts *The Dance* mural for Barnes Foundation
- Whitney Museum of American Art opens in New York
- Forain and van Doesburg die

1932
- Major exhibition of Surrealist art held in New York
- Bauhaus moves to Berlin

1933
- Bauhaus occupied by Gestapo, its leaders go into exile
- Hans Hofmann opens art school in New York

1934
- Roger Fry dies

1935
- Max Liebermann, Malevich and Signac die

1936
- American Abstract Artists founded in New York
- International Surrealist exhibition in London

1937
- Picasso paints *Guernica* for Spanish Pavilion at Universal Exhibition in Paris

1938
- Ernst Kirchner dies

1939
- Solomon R. Guggenheim Foundation Museum of Non-Objective Painting opens in New York
- Gwen John and Alphonse Mucha die

1940
- International Surrealist Exhibition in Mexico City
- Paul Klee and Vuillard die

1941
- National Gallery of Art opens in Washington, D.C.
- Émile Bernard, Robert Delaunay and Jawlensky die

1942
- Peggy Guggenheim opens Art of This Century gallery
- Sickert and Steer die

1943
- Maurice Denis and Henri Laurens die

1944
- László Moholy-Nagy founds Institute of Design in Chicago
- 'Art Concrète' exhibition in Basel
- Kandinsky, Maillol, Mondrian, Munch and Lucien Pissarro die

1945
- Rothko has an exhibition at the Art of This Century gallery

1946
- Term 'Abstract Impressionism' coined by Robert Coates in the *New Yorker*
- Lucio Fontana publishes his 'White Manifesto'
- Frank Dobson, Moholy-Nagy and Paul Nash die

1947
- Institute of Contemporary Arts, London, founded
- Bonnard dies

1948
- Movimento Arte Concreta established in New York
- 'The Club' founded by Abstract Expressionist artists
- Jackson Pollock invents 'action painting'

1949
- First Cobra exhibition, in Amsterdam
- James Ensor dies

1950
- First Barnett Newman show, at the Betty Parsons Gallery in New York
- Peggy Guggenheim organizes Jackson Pollock exhibitions in Venice and Milan
- Max Beckmann dies

1951
- Exhibition of 'Abstract Painting and Sculpture in America' at Museum of Modern Art, New York

1952
- Gutai Concrete Group founded in Tokyo

1953
- First Rauschenberg exhibition, at the Stable Gallery, New York
- First São Paulo Bienal
- Raoul Dufy dies

1954
- The term Pop Art coined
- Derain and Matisse die

1955
- Fernard Léger, Yves Tanguy and Utrillo die

1956
- Emil Nolde, Jackson Pollock and Lyonel Feininger die

1957
- Richard Hamilton paints *Hommage à Chrysler Corp.*
- Brancusi, Wyndham Lewis, and Henri Van de Velde die

1958
- Works by Lucio Fontana, Rothko and Wols shown at Venice Biennale
- First Jasper Johns show, at the Leo Castelli Gallery, New York
- First 'happenings' take place
- Rouault and Vlaminck die

274

1959
- Guggenheim Museum, designed by Frank Lloyd Wright, opens in New York
- First Biennale of young artists held in Paris
- 'New Images of Man' show at Museum of Modern Art, New York, heralds New Figuration
- Epstein, Alfred Munnings and Stanley Spencer die

1960
- Pierre Restany publishes first 'New Realism' manifesto
- Fernand Léger Museum opens in Biot, France
- Museum of Western Art, designed by Le Corbusier, opens in Tokyo

1961
- 'Abstract Expressionists and Imagists' exhibition at Guggenheim Museum
- Augustus John dies

1962
- 'New Realists' show at the Sidney Janis Gallery, New York
- Pop Art symposium at Museum of Modern Art, New York

1963
- Pop Art show at Guggenheim Museum, including Johns, Rauschenberg and Warhol
- First exhibition of video art, by Nam June Paik, in Wuppertal
- Matisse Museum founded in Nice
- Picasso Museum founded in Barcelona
- Braque dies

1964
- Gallery of Modern Art opens in New York
- Maeght Foundation opens in St-Paul-de-Vence
- Giorgio Morandi dies

1965
- Op Art becomes popular
- National Foundation for the Arts and Humanities founded in Washington, D.C.
- Le Corbusier dies

1966
- Arp, Carlo Carrà, Giacometti, and Hans Hofmann die

1967
- Hockney paints *A Bigger Splash*
- Hopper and Magritte die

1968
- 'Dada, Surrealism and their Heritage' show at Museum of Modern Art, New York
- Light show at Whitney Museum, New York
- Van Dongen and Duchamp die

1969
- Dali Theatre Museum opens at Figueras in Spain
- First completely conceptual exhibition, at Seth Siegelaub gallery in New York
- Art Workers' Coalition established in New York
- Otto Dix, Walter Gropius and Ben Shahn die

1970
- Mark Rothko dies

1971
- Courbet Museum founded at Ornans in France

1972
- 'Sharp-Focus Realism' exhibition held at the Sidney Janis Gallery, New York
- Maurits Escher dies

1973
- Picasso and Lipchitz die

1974
- 'Open Circuits', conference on video art held at Museum of Modern Art, New York

1975
- Museum of the Barbizon School opens in France
- Joan Miró Foundation established in Barcelona
- Barbara Hepworth dies

1976
- 'Women Artists 1550–1950' exhibition at Los Angeles County Museum of Art
- Edward Burra, Alexander Calder, Max Ernst, L. S. Lowry and Man Ray die

1977
- Centre National d'Art et de Culture Georges Pompidou opens in Paris

1978
- De Chirico and Norman Rockwell die

1979
- 'Transformations in Modern Architecture' show at Museum of Modern Art, New York

1980
- Pissarro Museum founded in Pontoise
- Kokoschka, Clyfford Still, and Graham Sutherland die

1981
- Memphis design studio launched in Milan

1982
- Ben Nicholson dies

1983
- Miró dies

1984
- Sotheby's sell Turner's *Seascape: Folkestone* for £7,370,000

1985
- Chagall dies

1986
- Musée d'Orsay founded
- Henry Moore and Georgia O'Keeffe die

1987
- 'Avant-Garde in the Eighties' exhibition at the Los Angeles County Museum of Art
- William Coldstream, Renato Guttuso and Andy Warhol die

1989
- Completion of *grands projects* in Paris as part of French bicentenery celebrations
- Dali dies

1991
- Sainsbury Wing of National Gallery, London, opens
- Tinguely dies

1992
- Museum of Modern Art opens in Dublin
- Francis Bacon, John Bratby and John Piper die

1993
- Elizabeth Frink and Robert Jacobsen die

1994
- Andy Warhol Museum opens in New York
- Max Bill, Alighiero e Boetti and Paul Delvaux die

1995
- San Francisco Museum of Modern Art opens
- Manuel Rivera and Alberto Burri die

1996
- Duane Hanson dies

1997
- 'Sensation' exhibition opens at the Royal Academy, London
- The Guggenheim Museum Bilbao opens
- William de Kooning and Roy Lichtenstein die

1998
- Victor Pasmore dies
- American museums pledge to search their collections for Nazi war loot

1999
- Arthur Boyd dies

2000
- Tate Bankside opens in London

Select Bibliography

Adams, Steven, *The World of the Impressionists* (London/New York, 1989)

Adriani, G., *Degas: Pastels, Oil Sketches, Drawings* (London/New York, 1985)

Adhémar, Jean, and Françoise Cachin, *Degas: The Complete Etchings, Lithographs and Monotypes*, trans. Jane Brenton (London/New York, 1974)

Bataille, Marie-Louise, and Georges Wildenstein, *Berthe Morisot, catalogue des peintures, pastels et aquarelles* (1961)

Baudelaire, Charles, *The Painter of Modern Life and Other Essays*, trans. and ed. Jonathan Mayne (London, 1964)

Berhaut, Marie, *Caillebotte, sa vie, son œuvre: catalogue raisonné des peintures et pastels* (Paris, 1978)

Blunden, Maria and Godfrey, *Impressionists and Impressionism* (Geneva/London, 1981)

Boime, A., *The Academy and French Painting in the Nineteenth Century* (New Haven/London, 1971)

Braudel, F., and E. LaBrousse, *Histoire économique et sociale de la France*, Part III *L'Avènement de l'ère industrielle 1789–1880*, 2 vols (Paris, 1977–82)

Brettell, R., *Pissarro and Pontoise* (New Haven/London, 1990)

Bumpus, Judith, *Impressionist Gardens* (Oxford, 1990)

Cézanne, Paul, *Letters*, trans. and ed. John Rewald, revised edn (New York, 1984)

Champa, Kermit S., *Studies in Early Impressionism* (New Haven/London, 1973)

Clark, Timothy J., *The Painting of Modern Life: Paris in the Art of Manet and his Followers* (London/New York, 1985)

Cogniat, Raymond, *Pissarro* (Paris, 1974)

Constable, W. G., *Art Collecting in the United States of America* (London, 1964)

Cooper, Douglas, *The Courtauld Collection* (London, 1954)

Courthion, P., and P. Cailler (ed.), *Manet raconté par lui-même et par ses amis*, 2 vols (Vésenaz/Geneva, 1945–54)

Courtine, R., *La Vie parisienne, cafés et restaurants des boulevards 1814–1914* (Paris, 1984)

Coutagne, D., *Cézanne au Musée d'Aix* (Aix-en-Provence, 1984)

Crespelle, J-P., *La Vie quotidienne des impressionnistes* (Paris, 1981)

Daulte, François, *Alfred Sisley: catalogue raisonné de l'œuvre peint* (Lausanne, 1959)

— *Auguste Renoir: catalogue raisonné de l'œuvre peint*, Part I *Figures 1860–90* (Lausanne, 1971)

Degas, H. G. E., *Degas by Himself*, trans. and ed. Richard Kendall (London, 1987)

Denvir, Bernard, *Encyclopædia of Impressionism* (London/New York, 1990)

— *Impressionism: The Painters and the Paintings* (London/New York, 1990)

— *The Impressionists at First Hand* (London/New York, 1987)

Doran, P. M. (ed.), *Conversations avec Cézanne* (Paris, 1978)

Dufwa, J., *Winds from the East: A study in the Art of Manet, Degas, Monet and Whistler, 1856–86* (Stockholm, 1981)

Dunlop, J., *The Shock of the New* (London, 1972)

Finke, U. (ed.), *French Nineteenth-Century Painting and Literature* (Manchester, 1972)

Flint, Kate (ed.), *Impressionists in England: The Critical Reception* (London, 1984)

Garb, T., *Women Impressionists* (Oxford, 1986)

Gaunt, W., *The Impressionists* (London, 1970)

Geffroy, Gustave, *Claude Monet, sa vie, son temps, son œuvre* (Paris, 1922)

Gimpel, René, *Journal d'un collectionneur, marchand de tableaux* (Paris, 1963)

Gordon, Robert, and Andrew Forge, *Claude Monet* (New York, 1938)

Guest, Ivor, *The Ballet of the Second Empire, 1858–1870*, revised edn (London, 1974)

Halévy, Daniel, *Degas Parle…* (Paris/Geneva, 1960); trans. as *My Friend Degas* (London, 1964)

Hamilton, George H., *Manet and his Critics*, 2nd edn (New York, 1969)

Hanson, Anne Coffin, *Manet and the Modern Tradition* (New Haven/London, 1977)

Herbert, Robert L., *Impressionism: Art, Leisure and Parisian Society* (New Haven/London, 1988)

Hoschedé, J-P., *Claude Monet ce mal connu*, 2 vols (Geneva, 1960)

House, John, *Monet: Nature into Art* (New Haven/London, 1986)

Isaacson, Joel, *et al.*, *The Crisis of Impressionism: 1878–82* (Ann Arbor, 1979)

Jean-Aubry, G., *Eugène Boudin d'après des documents inédits* (Lausanne/Paris, 1968)

Lemoisne, P-A., *Degas et son œuvre*, 4 vols (Paris, 1946–9); rev. edn by P. Brame and T. Reff (New York, 1984)

Lloyd, C., and R. Thomson, *Impressionist Drawings* (Oxford, 1986)

Levine, Steven Z., *Monet and his Critics* (New York, 1976)

Manet, Julie, *Growing up with the Impressionists: The Diary of Julie Manet*, trans. and ed. R. de B. and J. Roberts (London, 1987)

Matthews, N. M. (ed.), *Cassatt and Her Circle: Selected Letters* (New York, 1984)

McMullen, R., *Degas: His Life, Times and Work* (Boston, 1984)

McQuillan, M., *Impressionist Portraits* (London, 1986)

Mainardi, P., *Art and Politics of the Second Empire: The Universal Expositions of 1855 and 1867* (New Haven/London, 1987)

Manet, Édouard, *Manet by Himself*, trans. and ed. Juliet Wilson-Bareau (London, 1991)

Milner, J., *The Studios of Paris: The Capital of Art in the Late Nineteenth Century* (New Haven/London, 1988)

Monet, Claude, *Monet by Himself*, trans. and ed. Richard Kendall (London, 1989)

Monneret, S., *L'Impressionnisme et son époque*, 4 vols (Paris, 1978–81)

Morisot, Berthe, *Correspondance de Berthe Morisot avec sa famille et ses amis*, ed. Denis Rouart (Paris, 1950); trans. Betty W. Hubbard as *The Correspondence of Berthe Morisot* (London, 1986)

Nochlin, Linda, *Realism* (London, 1971)

— (ed.), *Impressionism and Post-Impressionism 1874–1904: Sources and Documents* (Englewood Cliffs, New Jersey, 1966)

— *Pissarro, Camille, Correspondance de Camille Pissarro*, ed. Janine Bailley-Herzberg, 4 vols (Paris, 1980–9)

Pissarro, Camille, *Letters to his son Lucien*, trans. and ed. John Rewald, 4th edn (London, 1980)

Pollock, G., *Mary Cassatt* (New York, 1980)

Pool, Phoebe, *Impressionism* (London/New York, 1967)

Rearick, Charles, *Pleasures of the Belle Époque* (New Haven /London, 1985)

Reff, T., *Degas: The Artist's Mind* (New York, 1976)

— *The Notebooks of Edgar Degas* (Oxford, 1976)

— *Modern Art in Paris 1855–1900* (London/New York, 1981)

Renoir, Jean, *Pierre-Auguste Renoir, mon père,* (Paris, 1962); trans. as *Renoir, My Father* (London/Boston, 1962)

Rewald, John, *Cézanne: A Biography* (London/New York, 1986)

— *Cézanne and America* (London/New York, 1989)

— *The History of Impressionism,* 4th edn rev. (London/New York, 1985)

— *Post-Impressionism: From Van Gogh to Gauguin,* 3rd edn (London/New York, 1978)

— *Studies in Impressionism* (London/New York, 1985)

— *Studies in Post-Impressionism* (London/New York, 1986)

Rewald, J., and F. Weitzenhoffer (eds), *Aspects of Monet: A Symposium on the Artist's Life and Times* (New York, 1984)

Rivière, Georges, *Renoir et ses amis* (Paris, 1921)

Roos, Jane Mayo, *Early Impressionism and the French State, 1866–1874* (Cambridge, 1996)

Roskill, M., *Van Gogh, Gauguin and the Impressionist Circle* (London, 1970)

Samary, J., *Renoir* (Paris, 1962)

Sandblad, Nils G., *Manet: Three Studies in Artistic Conception* (Lund, 1954)

Seigel, Jerrold, *Bohemian Paris: Culture, Politics and the Boundaries of Bourgeois Life 1830–1930* (New York, 1986)

Shiff, Richard, *Cézanne and the End of Impressionism* (Chicago/London, 1984)

Skeggs, D., *River of Light: Monet's Impressions of the Seine* (London, 1987)

Sloane, J. C., *French Painting between the Past and the Present*

(Princeton, 1951)

Spate, Virginia, *The Colour of Time: Claude Monet* (London/ New York, 1992)

Tabarant, Adolphe, *Manet: Histoire catalographique* (Paris, 1931)

— *Manet et ses oeuvres* (Paris, 1947)

Thomson, Belinda, *Impressionism: Origins, Practice, Reception* (London/New York, 2000)

Tucker, Paul Hayes, *Monet at Argenteuil* (New Haven /London, 1982)

Varnedoe, Kirk, *Gustave Caillebotte* (New Haven /London, 1987)

Venturi, Lionello (ed.), *Les Archives de l'impressionnisme,* 2 vols (Paris/New York, 1939)

Vollard, Ambroise, *Degas: An Intimate Portrait* (London, 1928)

— *Recollections of a Picture-Dealer* (London, 1936)

Watson, P., *From Manet to Manhattan* (London, 1992)

White, Barbara Ehrlich (ed.), *Impressionism in Perspective* (Englewood Cliffs, New Jersey, 1978)

— *Renoir: His Life, Art, and Letters* (New York, 1984)

White, Harrison and Cynthia, *Canvases and Careers: Institutional Changes in the French Painting World* (New York, 1965)

Wildenstein, Daniel, *et al.,* *Claude Monet: Biographie et catalogue raisonné,* 4 vols (Lausanne/Paris, 1974–1985)

Wilson-Bareau, J., *Édouard Manet: Voyage en Espagne* (Caen, 1988)

Zeldin, Theodore, *France, 1848–1945,* 2 vols (Oxford, 1973 and 1977)

Zola, Émile, *Les Rougon-Macquart, Histoire naturelle et sociale d'une famille sous le Second Empire,* ed. Henri Mitterand, 5 vols (Paris, 1960–8)

— *Oeuvres complètes,* ed. Henri Mitterand, 15 vols (Paris, 1966–70)

EXHIBITION CATALOGUES

Adhémar, Hélène, *et al.,* *Centenaire de l'impressionnisme,* Grand Palais, Paris; Metropolitan Museum of Art, New York (1974–5)

— *Hommage à Claude Monet (1840–1926),* Grand Palais, Paris (1980)

Berson, Ruth, *The New Painting: Impressionism 1874–1886,* 2 vols, Fine Arts Museum of San Francisco (1996)

Boggs, Jean Sutherland, *et al.,* *Degas,* Grand Palais, Paris; National Gallery of Canada; Metropolitan Museum of Art, New York (1988)

Brettell, Richard, *et al., A Day in the Country: Impressionism and the French Landscape,* Los Angeles County Museum of Art (1984)

Cachin, François, Charles Moffett, *et al., Manet (1832–1883),* Grand Palais, Paris; Metropolitan Museum of Art, New York (1983)

Cachin, François, *et al., Pissarro,* Hayward Gallery, London; Grand Palais, Paris; Boston Museum of Fine Arts (1980)

Gowing, Lawrence, *et al., Cézanne: The Early Years 1859–1872,* Royal Academy of Arts, London; Musée d'Orsay, Paris; National Gallery of Art, Washington, D.C. (1988)

House, John, *Impressionism, its Masters, its Precursors, and its Influence in Britain,* Royal Academy of Arts, London (1974)

— *et al., Renoir,* Hayward Gallery, London; Grand Palais, Paris; Boston Museum of Fine Arts (1985)

— *et al., Landscapes of France,* Hayward Gallery, London; Boston Museum of Fine Arts (1995)

Ives, Colta F., *The Great Wave: The Influence of Japanese Woodcuts on French Prints,* Metropolitan Museum of Art, New York (1974)

Moffet, Charles S., *et al., The New Painting: Impressionism 1874–86,* Fine Arts Museum of San Francisco; National Gallery of Art, Washington,

D.C. (1986)

Moulin, Jean-Marie, Anne Pingeot, Joseph Rishel, *et al., The Second Empire 1852–70: Art in France under Napoleon III,* Philadelphia Museum of Art; Detroit Institute of Arts; Grand Palais, Paris (1978–9)

Reff, Theodore, *Manet and Modern Paris,* National Gallery of Art, Washington, D.C. (1982)

Thomson, Richard, *et al., Toulouse-Lautrec,* Hayward Gallery, London; Grand Palais, Paris (1991)

Tinterow, G., and H. Loyrette, *Origins of Impressionism,* Metropolitan Museum of Art, New York (1994)

Tucker, Paul Hayes, *Monet in the '90s: The Series Paintings,* Boston Museum of Fine Arts; Royal Academy of Arts, London, rev. edn (1990)

Wildenstein, Daniel, *Monet's Years at Giverny: Beyond Impressionism,* Metropolitan Museum of Art, New York (1978)

HISTORICAL EVENTS

The following books have been especially helpful in compiling the lists of contemporary events:

Chronicle of the 20th Century, Longman & Chronicle Communications Ltd (Harlow, 1988)

Collins Dictionary of the English Language, 2nd edn (London/Glasgow, 1986)

Eureka! An Illustrated History of Inventions from the Wheel to the Computer, ed. Edward de Bono (London, 1974)

Great Events of the 20th Century, Illustrated London News/Automobile Association, rev. edn (Basingstoke, 1992)

The Oxford Encyclopedic English Dictionary (Oxford, 1991)

The Shell Book of Firsts, Patrick Robertson, rev. edn (London, 1983)

The Timetables of History: A Chronicle of World Events Bernard Grun (London, 1975)

Gazetteer of Major Impressionist Collections

ALGERIA
ALGIERS Musée National des Beaux-Arts
The collection of European art includes one of Caillebotte's *Bathers* and a portrait of Renoir by Bazille.

BRAZIL
SÃO PAOLO Museu de Arte
The museum has some important paintings by Renoir (including *Jules Le Coeur in the Forest of Fontainebleau, Bather with a Griffon* and *Enfant portant des fleurs*); Cézanne's *Paul Alexis Reading to Émile Zola* and *Rocks at L'Estaque*; Manet's *The Artist*; Monet's *Japanese Bridge at Giverny*; and a number of works by Degas, Gauguin and van Gogh.

DENMARK
COPENHAGEN Ny Carlsberg Glyptotek
Because of his Danish connections, Gauguin is very well represented, with 25 paintings and 2 wood reliefs. The gallery also has 3 important Manets (*The Absinthe Drinker, The Execution of the Emperor Maximilian* and *Mlle Lemonnier*); 5 Monets, 3 Pissarros, 4 Renoirs and 3 Sisleys; works by Cézanne, Morisot and Guillaumin; and several Degas, including a complete set of bronzes.

FRANCE
PARIS Musée d'Orsay
The Impressionist paintings from the Jeu de Paume now form the core of this superb assembly of nineteenth-century French art and sculpture, in the converted Gare d'Orsay. Highlights include Bazille's *The Artist's Family on a Terrace near Montpellier*; Cézanne's *House of the Hanged Man* and *Still Life with Onions*; Caillebotte's *The Floor Strippers* and *Self-Portrait*; Degas' *The Bellelli Family, The Absinthe Drinker* and *The Orchestra at the Opéra*; Manet's *Olympia, Déjeuner sur l'herbe, Lola de Valence* and *The Balcony*, as well as his portraits of Clemenceau, Mallarmé and Zola; Monet's *Women in the Garden, The White Turkeys* and paintings from his *Rouen Cathedral, Gare St-Lazare, Haystacks* and *Water Lilies* series (also fragments of his *Déjeuner sur l'herbe*); Morisot's *The Cradle*; Pissarro's *Woman in a Field*; Renoir's *The Swing, Nude in the Sunlight, Gabrielle with a Rose* and *Dancing at the Moulin de la Galette*; Sisley's *Floods at Port Marly*; bronzes by Degas and Renoir; pastels by Cassatt, Degas, Manet and Morisot; Whistler's *Portrait of the Artist's Mother*; Fantin-Latour's *Homage to Delacroix* and *A Studio in the Batignolles Quarter*; and Maurice Denis' *Homage to Cézanne*.

Musée Marmottan
When Monet's son Michel died in 1966, he left his father's art collection to the museum – including 65 Monets (painted mainly in Giverny); oils by Morisot, Pissarro, Renoir and Sisley; watercolours by Boudin and Signac; and an ink sketch of Monet by Manet. The Donop de Monchy bequest of 1960 gave the museum its most famous painting, Monet's *Impression: Sunrise*.

Musée du Petit Palais
This museum has a number of Impressionist paintings, including Cézanne's *The Four Seasons*, Degas' *Mme Alexis Rouart and her Children*, Sisley's *The Tug* and Morisot's *Portrait of a Young Girl*.

Drawings and Prints
The Louvre's Cabinet des Dessins and the Cabinet des Estampes of the Bibliothèque Nationale both have major collections of Impressionist drawings, pastels and prints. The Bibliothèque d'Art et Archéologie at the University of Paris (Fondation Jacques Doucet) has an important collection of prints and drawings by Degas and Manet.

PROVINCIAL MUSEUMS
There are important Impressionist works in many French provincial museums and art galleries, including:

AIX-EN-PROVENCE Musée de l'Atelier de Paul Cézanne
This museum contains drawings and watercolours by Cézanne, as well as some of his personal possessions and painting equipment (including his easel and palettes).

Musée Granet
The museum has a section devoted to the works of Cézanne and his friends.

AIX-LES-BAINS Musée du Dr Faure
This collection includes works by Cézanne, Degas, Pissarro and Sisley.

CAGNES-SUR-MER Musée Renoir
Renoir's house the Villa de la Poste is now a museum (his studio and other rooms have been preserved as they were). On show are pictures painted by Renoir when he lived in Cagnes, plus works by friends such as Bonnard, Dufy and Maillol.

DIJON Musée des Beaux-Arts
Paintings include Monet's *Étretat* and

Manet's *Model at the Folies-Bergère*.

GIVERNY Musée Claude Monet
The house where Monet lived from 1883 until his death in 1926 is now a museum. As well as works by Monet and his contemporaries, it includes many of the artist's personal possessions and his collection of Japanese prints.

LE HAVRE Musée des Beaux-Arts
Destroyed by bombing during World War II, the museum reopened in a new building in 1961. The collection includes works by Monet, Pissarro and Sisley, among them Monet's *Water Landscape with Water Lilies*.

LIMOGES Musée Municipal
The museum has Guillaumin's *Portrait of Camille Pissarro Painting a Blind* and a number of works by Renoir (who was born in Limoges), including his *Portrait of Jean Renoir as a Child*.

LYON Musée des Beaux-Arts
Among the Impressionist paintings are Renoir's *Woman Playing the Guitar* and Monet's *Turbulent Sea, Étretat*.

MONTPELLIER Musée Fabre
Bazille's family home was just outside Montpellier, consequently the museum has a number of his works, including *La Toilette*. The museum also holds Caillebotte's *Portrait of Madame X*.

PAU Musée des Beaux-Arts
The collection includes Degas' *Portraits in an Office*, which the museum bought from him in 1878.

GERMANY
BERLIN Neue Nationalgalerie
Before World War II Berlin possessed one of the world's finest collections of nineteenth- and twentieth-century art. Although many French works were lost, those that remain include Renoir's *Children's Afternoon at Wargemont* and *Lise as a Gypsy Girl*; Manet's *In the Conservatory* and *The House at Rueil*; and several works by Monet and Cézanne.

BREMEN Kunsthalle
The collection includes Manet's *Portrait of Zacharie Astruc*, Monet's *Camille: Woman in the Green Dress*, Pissarro's *March Sunshine, Pontoise* and Gonzalès' *Morning Awakening*. There are also many works by German Impressionists.

COLOGNE Wallraf-Richartz Museum
The museum possesses Renoir's *The Engaged Couple*, Monet's *Rocks at Étretat*, Sisley's *Bridge at Hampton Court* and Pissarro's *The Hermitage at Pontoise*.

ESSEN Folkwang Museum
This collection includes 2 Cézannes, 4 Gauguins, 2 Manets (including his *Portrait of Faure as Hamlet*), a Monet *Water Lilies* canvas, Pissarro's *Snow at Louveciennes*, 4 Renoirs (including *Lise with a Parasol*), 1 Sisley and 4 van Goghs.

FRANKFURT Städelsches Kunstinstitut
Among the institute's Impressionist paintings are Degas' *Musicians in the Orchestra*, Manet's *The Game of Croquet*, Monet's *The Luncheon*, Renoir's *The End of the Luncheon* and Sisley's *The Banks of the Seine in Autumn*.

MANNHEIM Kunsthalle
The gallery has some important Impressionist works, including Manet's *The Execution of the Emperor Maximilian*, Monet's *A Village Street in Normandy*, Pissarro's *The Little Bridge* and Sisley's *Market Place*.

MUNICH Neue Pinakothek
The gallery has an excellent collection of works by Manet (including his *Luncheon in the Studio* and *Monet Working on his Boat at Argenteuil*), as well as works by Degas (*Women Ironing*), Cézanne, Gauguin and van Gogh.

HUNGARY
BUDAPEST Szépmüvészeti Museum
The museum has several Manets, including *Baudelaire's Mistress Reclining*.

IRELAND
DUBLIN Municipal Gallery of Modern Art
The gallery contains a number of important works by the Impressionists from the collection of Sir Hugh Lane.

JAPAN
Japan probably ranks third, after France and the USA, in its wealth of Impressionist works. Unfortunately many are either in private hands or owned by commercial organizations. Few galleries provide catalogues in European languages.

HIROSHIMA Museum of Art
Highlights of the collection include Renoir's *The Judgement of Paris* and Monet's *Morning on the Seine near Giverny*.

TOKYO National Museum of Western Art
The museum has major works by most of the Impressionists, many bought by Prince Kojiro Matsukata in the 1920s.

THE NETHERLANDS
AMSTERDAM Rijksmuseum
The museum's collection of Dutch art includes works by van Gogh. There are also 2 paintings by Monet and a superb group of prints and drawings by Degas, Manet and Renoir.
Stedelijk Museum
Devoted to modern Western art, the museum has works by Cézanne, Manet, Monet and van Gogh.
Van Gogh Museum
A superb collection of van Goghs. There are also works by Gauguin and Émile Bernard, and Vincent and Theo's collection of Japanese prints.
OTTERLO Kröller-Müller Museum
The museum has an important group of works by van Gogh and other Impressionists and Post-Impressionists (among them Renoir's *At the Café* and Seurat's *Le Chahut*).
ROTTERDAM Boymans-van Beuningen Museum
The museum contains both Old Masters and modern art, including a variety of Impressionist works.

NORWAY
OSLO Nasjonalgalleriet
The museum has a strong Impressionist and Post-Impressionist collection, comprising 4 Cézannes, 3 Degas, 6 Gauguins, 2 Guillaumins, 4 Manets (including *Mme Manet in the Conservatory* and *View of the Universal Exhibition, 1867*), 2 Monets (including *Rainy Weather, Étretat*), 1 Morisot and 2 Renoirs.

PORTUGAL
LISBON Calouste Gulbenkian Museum
The museum has an important collection of Impressionist works, including Manet's *Soap Bubbles*.

RUSSIA
MOSCOW Pushkin Museum of Fine Arts
There are 14 Cézannes (including *The Jas de Bouffan*, and *Pierrot and Harlequin*); 11 Monets (including *Study for Déjeuner sur l'herbe, Boulevard des Capucines*, and views of Rouen cathedral); 5 Renoirs; 4 Degas; Pissarro's *Avenue de l'Opéra* and *The Ploughed Field*; Sisley's *Frosty Morning at Louveciennes*; and 2 Manets.
ST PETERSBURG The Hermitage
An important collection with 15 Gauguins, 11 Cézannes, various Monets, Renoirs, and Degas pastels, and works by Pissarro and Sisley.

SWEDEN
STOCKHOLM Nationalmuseum
As well as Renoir's *Cabaret of Mère Antony* and *La Grenouillère*, there is an important group of prints by Manet.

SWITZERLAND
BASEL Kunstmuseum
The museum has a strong collection of Impressionist and Post-Impressionist works, including Pissarro's *The Gleaners*.

WINTERTHUR Oskar Reinhart Foundation
There are 12 Renoirs (including his *Portrait of Victor Chocquet*); 11 Cézannes; 4 Manets (including *At the Café*); 6 van Goghs; Monet's *Ice Floes on the Seine*; and works by Degas, Pissarro and Sisley.
ZURICH E. G. Bührle Foundation
This collection includes 7 Cézannes (among them *The Boy in the Red Waistcoat*), 5 Degas, 8 Manets, 4 Monets, 2 Pissarros, 2 Sisleys and 5 van Goghs.

UNITED KINGDOM
ENGLAND
CAMBRIDGE Fitzwilliam Museum
The university's collection includes Monet's *The Poplars (View from the Marsh)* and Pissarro's *Banks of the Marne*.
LONDON Courtauld Institute Galleries
Among the 45 Impressionist and Post-Impressionist works are 10 Cézannes (including *Mont Ste-Victoire* and *The Card-Players*), 3 Degas, 2 Manets (including *Bar at the Folies-Begère* and a study for *Déjeuner sur l'herbe*), 3 Monets (including *The Seine at Argenteuil, Autumn*), 3 Pissarros, 4 Renoirs (including *La Loge* and *Portrait of Vollard*) and 2 Sisleys.
National Gallery
The Impressionist collection contains 7 Cézannes (including *Large Bathers*); 9 Degas (including *Young Spartans Exercising* and *Miss La La at the Cirque Fernando*); 4 Manets (*Music in the Tuileries Gardens, Portrait of Eva Gonzalès, The Waitress* and fragments of *The Execution of the Emperor Maximilian*); 10 Monets (including *The Thames at Westminster*); 6 Pissarros (including *The Boulevard Montmartre at Night* and *Lower Norwood, London: Snow Effect*); 9 Renoirs (including *The Seine at Asnières* and *Umbrellas*); Seurat's *Bathing at Asnières*; and works by Morisot (*Summer's Day*) and Sisley.
Tate Gallery
The gallery's Impressionist collection has 13 works by Degas (including *Little Dancer of 14 Years*); 1 Manet; 3 Monets; 7 Pissarros; 1 painting and 3 bronzes by Renoir; and 3 Sisleys.
OXFORD Ashmolean Museum
As well as a number of Impressionist paintings, the museum contains the Pissarro Archive of manuscripts and drawings by Camille and his family.
SCOTLAND
EDINBURGH National Gallery of Scotland
The gallery's Impressionist paintings include 5 Renoirs, 4 Degas (among them *Portrait of Diego Martelli*) and 2 Monets (from the *Poplars* and *Haystacks* series), as well as works by Morisot, Pissarro, Sisley and van Gogh.
GLASGOW Burrell Collection
Among the paintings donated by the shipping magnate Sir William Burrell and his wife are Cézanne's *Château de Médan*; Degas' *The Rehearsal* and pastel portrait of Duranty; and works by Gauguin, Manet, Monet, Pissarro, Renoir and Sisley.

WALES
CARDIFF National Museum of Wales
Almost all the Impressionist works owned by the museum were donated by Gwendoline and Margaret Davies. There are 12 Monets, 4 Cézannes and 3 Manets, as well as paintings by Morisot, Pissarro, Renoir and Sisley; sculptures by Degas and Renoir; and works by Sickert, Whistler and Steer.

UNITED STATES
BOSTON Museum of Fine Arts
The museum has one of the largest Impressionist collections in the USA. There are 40 Monets (including *The Japanese Girl* and works from his *Water Lilies, Haystacks* and *Rouen Cathedral* series); 20 Renoirs (including *Rocky Crags at L'Estaque* and *Dance at Bougival*); 15 Degas (including *Carriage at the Races*); 7 Manets (including *The Execution of the Emperor Maximilian*); 5 van Goghs; 5 Cézannes; 5 Sisleys (including *Early Snow at Louveciennes*); one work each by Caillebotte, Guillaumin and Morisot; and several Cassatts (including *Woman in Black at the Opéra* and *Five O'Clock Tea*).
CHICAGO Art Institute of Chicago
The Institute's Impressionist works include a self-portrait by Bazille; Caillebotte's *Street in Paris, A Rainy Day*; Cassatt's *Afternoon Tea Party*; Cézanne's *Bay of Marseilles, Seen from L'Estaque*; Degas' *The Millinery Shop*; Manet's *Christ Mocked by Soldiers*; Monet's *Beach at Ste-Adresse*; Renoir's *Mme Clapisson (Lady with a Fan)*; and Seurat's *Sunday Afternoon on the Island of La Grande Jatte*.
CLEVELAND Cleveland Museum of Art
The museum possesses 3 landscapes by Cézanne, 5 Degas, 3 Gauguins, 5 Monets (including *Antibes* and *Water Lilies* canvases), 4 Renoirs (including *The Apple Seller* and *Three Bathers*), and important works by Cassatt, Morisot, Pissarro and Sisley.
KANSAS CITY Nelson-Atkins Museum of Art
The museum has a strong Impressionist collection, with paintings by Cézanne (including a *Mont Ste-Victoire*), Gauguin, Manet, Monet (including *Boulevard des Capucines* and a late *Water Lilies* canvas), Pissarro, Renoir, Seurat and van Gogh.
NEW YORK Brooklyn Museum
As well as works by Sargent and the American Impressionists (such as William Merritt Chase, Theodore Robinson and John Twachtman), the museum owns Cassatt's *Mother and Child*, Degas' *Mlle Fiocre in the Ballet 'La Source'*, Pissarro's *The Climbing Path, Pontoise*, 4 landscapes by Monet, a Cézanne, a Renoir and a van Gogh.
Metropolitan Museum of Art
One of the greatest Impressionist collections. There are many works by Cassatt, including *Lady at the Teatable, The Cup of Tea* and *Young Mother Sewing*; 18 Cézannes; 19 paintings by Degas

(including *The Ballet from 'Robert le Diable'* and *Woman with Chrysanthemums*); 4 Gauguins; 2 Guillaumins; 18 Manets (including *Boating, The Spanish Singer* and portraits of Faure and George Moore); 35 Monets (including *La Grenouillère*, and *Poplars* and *Haystacks* canvases); 1 Morisot; 16 Pissarros (including *Côte du Jallais, Pontoise*); 26 Renoirs (including *Mme Charpentier and her Children*); 5 Sisleys; and 9 van Goghs.
Museum of Modern Art
The museum's Impressionist works include 22 Cézannes (among them *The Bather* and *Still Life with Apples*), 1 Degas pastel (*At the Milliner's*), 3 Gauguins, 5 Monets (a whole room is devoted to his *Water Lilies*), 1 Renoir, 2 Sickerts and 3 van Goghs.
PHILADELPHIA Philadelphia Museum of Art
The museum holds paintings by all the major Impressionists. Highlights include Cassatt's *Woman and Child Driving* and *Family Group Reading*; Cézanne's *Large Bathers* and one of his *Mont Ste-Victoire* canvases; Degas' *The Ballet Class*; Manet's *Le Bon Bock*; Monet's *Poplars on the Banks of the Epte* and *The Japanese Footbridge and the Water Lily Pond, Giverny*; and Renoir's *The Bathers* as well as one of his portraits of Aline Charigot.
WASHINGTON, D.C. National Gallery of Art
Impressionist painting is one of the National Gallery's outstanding areas. The gallery has a very substantial collection of Manets, including *Dead Toreador, Masked Ball at the Opéra, The Plum, The Old Musician* and *The Railroad*. Other highlights include Cassatt's *The Boating Party, Girl Arranging her Hair* and *Mother Wearing a Sunflower*; Cézanne's *Portrait of the Artist's Father*; Degas' *Edmondo and Thérèse Morbilli*; a group of Monets, including views of Argenteuil, London and Rouen; Morisot's *In the Dining Room* and *The Mother and Sister of the Artist*; Pissarro's *Boulevard des Italiens* and *Orchard in Bloom, Louveciennes*; and Renoir's *Bather Arranging her Hair, The Pont Neuf* and *A Woman of Algeria*. There are also important works by Bazille, Guillaumin and Sisley.
Phillips Collection
This impressive collection includes a Cézanne self-portrait and one of his *Mont Ste-Victoire* canvases; Monet's *Road to Vétheuil* and *On the Cliffs, Dieppe*; Morisot's *Two Girls*; Renoir's *Luncheon of the Boating Party*; and a number of works by Degas, Manet, Sisley, Seurat and van Gogh.
OTHER MUSEUMS IN THE USA
Harvard University's Fogg Art Museum, Houston Museum of Fine Arts, Los Angeles County Museum of Art, Princeton University Art Museum, Fine Arts Museums of San Francisco, Sterling and Francine Clark Art Institute, Williamstown, Mass. and Yale University Art Gallery all have major holdings of Impressionist works.

Acknowledgments

The initial concept for this book is due not in the first instance to myself, but to the staff of Thames and Hudson, and its transformation into reality has been made possible by the tireless work of a dedicated team over the past year or so.

I should particularly like to thank Peter Leek, without whose tactful and meticulous editing my inaccuracies would be even more plentiful than in fact they probably are, and Slaney Begley, for her enthusiasm, accuracy and stamina.

I am also profoundly indebted to the many who, since the days when John Rewald's *History of Impressionism* first saw light, have followed in his footsteps to explore the movement with a vigour and clarity of quite exceptional a nature.

And I would like especially to recognize the editors of those magnificent exhibition catalogues, which, over the past three decades, have presented the works of the great figures of the movement with a remarkable acuity and breadth of vision.

SOURCE ACKNOWLEDGMENTS

Periodical sources are given in the text.

33 'Monet's letters from Honfleur': Kendall, Richard, *Monet by Himself*, Macdonald, London, 1989, pp.20–22
37 'Zacharie Astruc': Cachin, François, Charles Moffett, *et al.*, *Manet (1832-1883)*, exh. cat., Grand Palais, Paris; Metropolitan Museum of Art, New York, 1983, p.179
41 'Zola defends the Impressionists': Cézanne, Paul, *Letters*, trans. and ed. John Rewald, rev. edn, published by Hacker Art Books, Inc., New York, 1984, pp.110–2
45 'Manet's apologia for his exhibition': Cailler, Pierre (ed.), *Manet raconté par lui-même et par ses amis*, Geneva, 1953, vol. II, p.243
61 'The Salon of 1869': Morisot, Berthe, *The Correspondence of Berthe Morisot*, ed. Denis Rouart, trans. Betty W. Hubbard, Lund Humphries, London, 1959, pp.32–3
67 'Manet's letters from the siege of Paris': Wilson-Bareau, J., (ed.), *Manet by Himself*, Macdonald, London, 1991, pp.58–60
71 'Pissarro's reactions to life in London': (to Duret) Rewald, John, *The History of Impressionism*, 4th rev. edn, Martin Secker & Warburg Ltd, London, 1985, p.261; (to Dewhurst) Dewhurst, Wynford, *Impressionist Painting*, London, 1904, pp.31–2
75 'Degas writes from America': Kendall, Richard, *Degas by Himself*, Macdonald, London, 1987, p.92
80 'Durand-Ruel's catalogue': Venturi, Lionello, (ed.), *Les Archives de l'Impressionnisme*, Paris/New York, 1939, vol. II, pp.284-5

92 'Manet in Venice': Vollard, Ambroise, *Recollections of a Picture Dealer*, Constable, London, 1936, pp.149–51
111 'Cézanne's family problems': Cézanne, Paul, *Letters*, trans. and ed. John Rewald, rev. edn, published by Hacker Art Books, Inc., New York, 1984, pp.172-4
114 'Zola impugns the Impressionists': Rewald, John, *The History of Impressionism*, 4th rev. edn, Martin Secker & Warburg Ltd, London, 1985, p.426
121 'An Italian view of Impressionism': Martelli, Diego, 'Gli Impressionisti', *Scritti d'Arte di Martelli*, ed. A. Boschetto, Florence, 1952, pp.98–110
127 'Disunity in our midst': Rewald, John, *The History of Impressionism*, 4th rev. edn, Martin Secker & Warburg Ltd, London, 1985, p.447
133 'Behind the Scenes': Morisot, Berthe, *The Correspondence of Berthe Morisot*, ed. Denis Rouart, trans. Betty W. Hubbard, Lund Humphries, London, 1959, pp.109–10
136 'Huysmans on the Impressionists': Huysmans, Joris-Karl, *Certains*, Paris, 1889, pp.8–9
141 'The Society of Irregularists': Venturi, Lionello, (ed.), *Les Archives de l'Impressionnisme*, Paris/New York, 1939, vol. I, pp.127–9
145 'Duret on the Avant-garde': Duret, Théodore, *Critique d'avant-garde*, Paris, 1885, p.3
151 'The eighth Impressionist exhibition': Rewald, John, *The History of Impressionism*, 4th rev. edn, Martin Secker & Warburg Ltd, London, 1985, p.523
158 'Impressionist dinners at the Café Riche': Geffroy, Gustave, *Claude Monet, sa vie, son*

temps, son oeuvre, G. Cres & Cie, Paris, 1922, pp.55–6
167 'The Impressionist craze in the USA': Duret, Théodore, *Manet and the French Impressionists*, trans. J. E. Crawford Flitch, London, 1910, pp.75–6
171 'The problems of painting "en plein air" ': Kendall, Richard, *Monet by Himself*, Macdonald, London, 1989, pp.130–2
172 'Huysmans on Cézanne': Huysmans, Joris-Karl, *Certains*, Paris, 1889, p.41
177 'Renoir's "twenty styles" ': Wadley, Nicholas, *Renoir: a Retrospective*, Hugh Lauter Levin, New York, 1981, pp.181–2
179 'Monet offers *Olympia* to the nation': Wildenstein, Daniel *et al.*, *Claude Monet. Biographie et catalogue raisonné*, La Bibliothèque des Arts, Lausanne and Paris, 1974–85, vol. III, p.254
182 'Monet's dealings with Durand-Ruel': Venturi, Lionello (ed.), *Les Archives de l'Impressionnisme*, Paris/New York, 1939, vol. I, pp.336–41
186 'Vollard meets Degas': Vollard, Ambroise, *Recollections of a Picture Dealer*, Constable, London, 1936, pp.112–3
193 'A Visit to Giverny': Manet, Julie, *Growing Up with the Impressionists. The Diary of Julie Manet*, trans. and ed. Rosalind de Boland Roberts and Jane Roberts, Sotheby's Publications, London, 1987, pp.43–5
196 'Cassatt on Cézanne's table manners': Mathews, Nancy Mowll, (ed.), *Cassatt and her Circle. Selected Letters*, Abbeville Press, New York, 1984
199 'The Duret sale': Manet, Julie, *Growing Up with the*

Impressionists. The Diary of Julie Manet, trans. and ed. Rosalind de Boland Roberts and Jane Roberts, Sotheby's Publications, London, 1987, p.52
204 'Degas' photography': Halévy, Daniel, *Degas Parle...*, Paris, 1960, pp.91–3
205 'Pissarro on Cézanne': Rewald, John, *Camille Pissarro: Letters to his son Lucien*, Routledge & Kegan Paul, London, 1980, p.275
208 'Degas and Oscar Wilde': Halévy, Daniel, *Degas Parle...*, Paris, 1960, pp.95–6
209 'Clemenceau on Monet's "Rouen Cathedral" series': Clemenceau, Georges, *Le Grand Pan*, Paris, 1896, p.428
212 'Pissarro and his sons': Rewald, John, *Camille Pissarro: Letters to his son Lucien*, Routledge & Kegan Paul, London, 1980, pp.390–391
213 'Renoir's Paris home': Renoir, Jean, *Renoir, My Father*, Collins, London, 1962, p.245
219 'Monet the epicure': Hoschedé, Jean-Pierre, *Claude Monet: ce mal connu. Intimité familiale d'un demi-siècle à Giverny de 1883 à 1926*, Geneva, 1960, vol. II, 1960, pp.81–2
224 'The Chocquet sale': Manet, Julie, *Growing Up with the Impressionists. The Diary of Julie Manet*, trans. and ed. Rosalind de Boland Roberts and Jane Roberts, Sotheby's Publications, London, 1987, pp.176–7
237 'Renoir in 1918': Gimpel, René, *Diary of an Art Dealer*, trans. John Rosenberg, Hamish Hamilton, London, 1986, pp.12, 15

List of Illustrations

LIST OF ILLUSTRATIONS

Gardner Museum, Boston/Art Resource, New York
Frédéric Bazille, *View of the Village*, 1868, 132.3 x 90.4 (52⅛ x 35⅝). Musée Fabre, Montpellier
62 Frédéric Bazille, *The Artist's Studio*, 1870, 98 x 128.5 (38½ x 50⅝). Musée d'Orsay, Paris. © Photo R.M.N.
Henri Fantin-Latour, *A Studio in the Batignolles Quarter*, 1870, 204 x 273.5 (80¼ x 106¼). Musée d'Orsay, Paris. © Photo R.M.N.
63 Claude Monet, *On the Beach, Trouville*, 1870, 37.5 x 45.7 (14¾ x 18). Reproduced by courtesy of the Trustees, The National Gallery, London
Claude Monet, *The Hôtel des Roches-Noires, Trouville*, 1870, 80 x 55 (31¼ x 21½). Musée d'Orsay, Paris. © Photo R.M.N.
64-5 Pierre-Auguste Renoir, *A Woman of Algiera (Odalisque)*, 1870, 69.2 x 122.6 (27¼ x 48¼). Chester Dale Collection, © 1992 National Gallery of Art, Washington
66 Berthe Morisot, *The Mother and Sister of the Artist*, 1870, 101.0 x 81.8 (39½ x 32¼). Chester Dale Collection, © 1992 National Gallery of Art, Washington
67 Édouard Manet, *Queue at the Butcher's Shop*, 1870–71, etching, image17.1 x 14.8 (6¾ x 5⅞). George A. Lucas Collection on indefinite loan from the Maryland Institute. Courtesy of the Baltimore Museum of Art
A balloon leaving Paris during the siege of 1870, lithograph
View of the fort of Montrouge during the siege of Paris, 1870–71, photograph
68 Édouard Manet, *The Barricade*, 1871, lithograph, 46.5 x 33.4 (18¼ x 13⅛). Prints Division, the New York Public Library. Astor, Lenox and Tilden Foundations
Ticket to view the destruction of the column in the Place Vendôme, May 16th, 1871
Caricature of Gustave Courbet, *c.*1871, lithograph
69 Claude Monet, *The Thames at Westminster*, 1871, 47 x 72.5 (18½ x 28½). Reproduced by courtesy of the Trustees, The National Gallery, London
71 Camille Pissarro, *Lower Norwood, London: Snow Effect*, 1870, 35.3 x 45.7 (13⅞ x 18). Reproduced by courtesy of the Trustees, The National Gallery, London
72 Alfred Sisley, *The Square at Argenteuil*, 1872, 46.5 x 66 (18¼ x 26). Musée d'Orsay, Paris. © Photo R.M.N
73 Édouard Manet, *Portrait of Berthe Morisot*, 1884 after a portrait of 1872, lithograph, 21.8 x 16.4 (8½ x 6½). Bibliothèque Nationale, Paris
74 Edgar Degas, *Portrait of Madame René de Gas*, 1872–3, 73 x 92 (28½ x 36¼). Chester Dale Collection © 1993 National Gallery of Art, Washington
75 Edgar Degas, *Children on a Doorstep (New Orleans)*, 1872, 60 x 75 (23⅝ x 29½). Ordrupgaardsamlingen, Copenhagen
76 Edgar Degas, *The Ballet from 'Robert le Diable'*, 1876, 76.6 x 81.3 (29¾ x 32). By courtesy of the Board of Trustees of the Victoria & Albert Museum, London
78 Édouard Manet, *Repose: Portrait of Berthe Morisot*, 1870, 155 x 113 (61 x 44½). Museum of Art, Rhode Island of Design, Providence (Bequest of Edith Stuyvesant Vanderbilt Gerry)
Paul Cézanne, *The Artist Engraving beside Dr Gachet*, 1873, drawing, 20 x 13 (7⅞ x 5⅛). Musée du Louvre, Paris (Gift of Paul Gachet, 1951)
79 Pierre-Auguste Renoir, *Riding in the Bois de Boulogne*, 1873, 261 x 226 (102¾ x 89). Kunsthalle, Hamburg
Édouard Manet, *The Trial of Marshal Bazaine before the Council of War at Versailles*, 1873, pencil drawing, 18.5 x 23.8 (7¼ x 9⅜). Fogg Art Museum, Harvard University, Cambridge Mass., Gift of Charles Dudley Porter
Edgar Degas, *The Dancing Examination*, 1873-5, 85 x 75 (33½ x 29½). Musée d'Orsay, Paris. © Photo R.M.N.
81 Jean-Baptiste Faure as Hamlet, photograph by Reutlinger. Bibliothèque Nationale, Paris
Édouard Manet, *Faure in the Role of Hamlet*, 1876, 194 x 131 (76⅜ x 51⅝). Museum Folkwang, Essen
82–3 see p.88
84 Édouard Manet, *Monet Working on his Boat in Argenteuil*, 1874, 81.3 x 99.7 (32 x 39¼). Bayerische Stadtsgemälde-sammlungen, Munich
85 Édouard Manet, *Boy with Dog*, 1868–74, lithograph, 20.9 x 14.8 (8¼ x 5⅞). Bibliothèque Nationale, Paris
86 Title-page of the catalogue of the first Impressionist Exhibition, 1874. Bibliothèque Nationale, Paris
Claude Monet, *Boulevard des Capucines*, 1874, 60 x 80 (23⅝ x 31½). Pushkin Museum, Moscow. Photo Scala
87 Nadar's studio, *c.*1890, photograph. Bibliothèque Nationale, Paris
Pierre-Auguste Renoir, *La Loge*, 1874, 80 x 64 (31½ x 24¾). Courtauld Institute Galleries, London
88 Paul Cézanne, *House of the Hanged Man*, 1873, 55 x 66 (21⅝ x 26). Musée d'Orsay, Paris. © Photo R.M.N.
Claude Monet, *Impression: Sunrise*, 1872–3, 48 x 63 (18¾ x 24½). Musée Marmottan, Paris. Photo Studio Lourmel
89 Berthe Morisot, *The Cradle*, 1872, 56 x 46 (22 x 18⅛). Musée d'Orsay, Paris. © Photo R.M.N.
Edgar Degas, *At the Races in the Country*, 1869, 36.5 x 55.9 (14⅜ x 22). 1931 Purchase Fund. Courtesy, Museum of Fine Arts, Boston.
90 Pierre-Auguste Renoir, *M. Fournaise*, 1875, 55.9 x 47 (22 x 18½). Sterling and Francine Clark Art Institute, Williamstown, Massachusetts
Honoré Daumier, *A Public Sale at the Hôtel Drouot*, woodcut, 1861
91 Édouard Manet, *The Raven*, 1875, transfer lithograph for the poster advertising Edgar Allan Poe's *Le Corbeau*, 16.2 x 15.8 (6⅜ x 6¼). Bibliothèque Nationale, Paris
Armand Guillaumin, *The Seine at Bercy*, 1873–5, 56 x 71.6 (22⅛ x 28½). Kunsthalle, Hamburg
Paul Cézanne, *The Seine at Bercy*, 1876–8, 58.7 x 71.5 (23¼ x28⅛). Kunsthalle, Hamburg
93 Claude Monet, *The Grand Canal, Venice*, 1875, 57 x 48 (22½ x 18⅞). Private Collection
94 Alfred Sisley, *Floods at Port Marly*, 1876, 50.5 x 61 (19⅞ x 24). Musée d'Orsay, Paris. © Photo R.M.N.
95 Marcellin Desboutin, *Portrait of Edmond Duranty*, *c.*1876, etching
Édouard Manet, *Visitors in the Studio*, *c.*1872–76, pencil and watercolour, 14.6 x 9.9 (5¾ x 3⅞). Musée du Louvre, Paris. © Photo R.M.N.
96 Gustave Caillebotte, *The Floor Strippers*, 1875, 120 x 146.5 (40⅛ x 57⅝). Musée d'Orsay, Paris. © Photo R.M.N.
Title-page of Durand-Ruel's exhibition catalogue of the Société Générale des Arts, 1876. Document Archives Durand-Ruel
97 Pierre-Auguste Renoir, *Nude in the Sunlight*, 1875, 81 x 65 (31⅞ x 25½). Musée d'Orsay, Paris. © Photo R.M.N.
Edgar Degas, *Portraits in an Office*, 1873, 73 x 92 (28¾ x 36¼). Musée des Beaux-Arts, Pau
98 Claude Monet, *The Japanese Girl*, 1875–6, 231.5 x 142 (90¼ x 55½). (Anonymous Gift in Memory of Mr and Mrs Edwin S. Webster). Courtesy, The Museum of Fine Arts, Boston
99 Édouard Manet, *Portrait of Stéphane Mallarmé*, 1876, 27.5 x 36 (10⅞ x 14⅛). Musée d'Orsay, Paris. © Photo R.M.N.
Édouard Manet, *The Faun*, 1876, woodcut and watercolour frontispiece for Mallarmé's *L'Après-midi d'un faune*, 1876. Musée Stéphane Mallarmé, Vulaines-sur-Seine
100 Berthe Morisot, *c.*1877, photograph
Front page of *L'Impressionniste*, April 6th, 1877
101 Edouard Manet, *Nana*, 1877, 154 x 115 (60¾ x 45¼). Kunsthalle, Hamburg
Marcellin Desboutin, *Portrait of Degas*, *c.*1876, etching, 22.8 x 14.6 (8¾ x 5¾). The Metropolitan Museum of Art, New York (Rogers Fund, 1922)
Edgar Degas, *The Star*, 1867–7, pastel over monotype, 58 x 42 (22⅞ x 16½). Musée d'Orsay, Paris. © Photo R.M.N.
102 M. Mouchot, *Auction at the Hôtel Drouot*, 1867, engraving.
103 Gustave Caillebotte, *The Pont de l'Europe*, 1876, 124.7 x 180.6 (49⅛ x 71⅛). Musée du Petit Palais, Geneva
Gustave Caillebotte, *A Street in Paris, A Rainy Day*, 1877, 212 x 276 (83½ x 108¾). The Art Institute of Chicago, Charles H. and Mary F. S. Worcester Fund Income
104 Cham, caricatures on the Third Impressionist Show published in *Le Charivari*, 1877
105 Pierre-Auguste Renoir, *Dancing at the Moulin de la Galette*, 1876, 131 x 175 (51⅝ x 68⅞). Musée d'Orsay, Paris. © Photo R.M.N.
106 Claude Monet, *The Gare St-Lazare*, 1877, 75.5 x 104 (29¼ x 40⅞). Musée d'Orsay, Paris. © Photo R.M.N.
107 Paul Cézanne starting out on an open-air painting expedition in Auvers, *c.*1874, photograph
Honoré Daumier, *Landscape Painters: the First copies Nature, the Second copies the First, lithograph*, published in *Le Charivari*, May 12th, 1865
108 Edgar Degas, *Ballet Rehearsal*, 1876–7, pastel and gouache over monotype, 55 x 68 (21¾ x 26¾). The Nelson-Atkins Museum of Art, Kansas City, Missouri (Acquired through the Kenneth A. & Helen F. Spencer Foundation Acquisition Fund)
109 Title-page of Théodore Duret's *Les Peintres Impressionnistes*, May 1878
Edgar Degas, *Singer with Glove*, 1878, pastel and liquid medium on canvas, 52.8 x 41.3 (21 x 16¼). Courtesy of the Harvard University Art Museums, the Fogg Art Museum (Bequest: Collection of Maurice Wertheim, Class of 1906)
Pierre-Auguste Renoir, Illustration for Emile Zola's *L'Assommoir*, 1878, pen-and-ink, 24.8 x 36.8 (9¾ x 14½). Private Collection
110 Pierre-Auguste Renoir, *Portrait of Mme Charpentier and her Children*, 1878, 154 x 190 (60⅝ x 74¾). The Metropolitan Museum of Art, New York (Wolfe Fund, 1907, Catherine Lorillard Wolfe Collection)
111 Paul Cézanne, *The Artist's Father Reading*, 1877–80, pencil drawing in sketchbook
Paul Cézanne, *The Artist's Wife*, *c.*1878–81, graphite drawing. Courtesy of the Harvard University Art Museums, The Fogg Art Museum (Bequest of Marian H. Phinney)
Paul Cézanne, *Portrait of the Artist's Son*, 1877–9, 17 x 15 (6¾ x 5⅞). The Metropolitan Museum of Art, New York, Pearlman Collection
112 Cover of the first issue of *La Vie moderne*, 1879
Poster for the Cirque Fernando, 1879
113 Claude Monet's house in Vétheuil, photograph
Claude Monet, *Camille Monet on her Deathbed*, 1879, 90 x 68 (35⅝ x 26 ¾). Musée d'Orsay, Paris. © Photo R.M.N.
114 Édouard Manet, *In the Conservatory*, 1879, 114.9 x 149.9 (45¼ x 59). Nationalgalerie, Staatliche Museen Preussischer Kulturbesitz, Berlin
115 Edgar Degas, *Miss La La at the Cirque Fernando*, 1879, black chalk with watercolour, 47 x 32 (18½ x 12⅝). The Barber Institute of Fine Arts, The University of Birmingham
Edgar Degas, *Miss La La at the Cirque Fernando*, 1879, 47 x 31 (19½ x 12½). Reproduced by courtesy of the Trustees, The National Gallery, London
116 Poster for the fifth Impressionist exhibition, 1880
Catalogue of recent works by Édouard Manet exhibited at *La Vie moderne*, April, 1880. With reproductions of two lost lithographs. Private Collection
117 Edouard Manet, *Chez le père Lathuile*, 1879, 92 x 112 (36¼ x 44). Musée des Beaux-Arts, Tournai
118 Claude Monet, *Ice Floes on the Seine*, 1880, 97 x 150 (37¾ x 58¼). Shelburne Museum, Shelburne, Vermont
119 Marie Bracquemond, *Young Woman in White*, 1880, 181 x 100 (71¼ x 39½). Musée Municipal, Cambrai
Paul Gauguin, *Bust of Mette*, 1877, 33 (13). Courtauld Institute Galleries, London
120 Berthe Morisot, *Summer (Young Woman by a Window)*, 1878, 76 x 61 (29⅞ x 24). Musée Fabre, Montpellier
121 Edgar Degas, *Portrait of Diego Martelli*, 1879, 108 x 100.3 (42½ x 39½). National Gallery of Scotland, Edinburgh
122 Pierre-Auguste Renoir, *Arab Festival*, 1881, 73.5 x 92 (28⅞ x 36¼). Musée d'Orsay, Paris. © Photo R.M.N.
123 Édouard Manet, *Portrait of Henri Rochefort*, 1881, 81.5 x 66.5 (32 x 26⅛). Hamburger Kunsthalle, Hamburg
Georges Pissarro, *An Impressionist Picnic with Guillaumin, Pissarro, Gauguin, Cézanne, Mme Cézanne and young Manzana*, *c.*1881, pen-and-ink drawing, 21 x 26.5 (8¼ x 10½). Private Collection
124 Pierre-Auguste Renoir, *The Doges' Palace, Venice*, 1881, 53.8 x 66 (21½ x 26). The Sterling and Francine Clark Art Institute, Williamstown, Massachusetts
Édouard Manet, *Portrait of Antonin Proust*, 1880, 129.5 x 95.9 (51 x 37¾). Museum of Art, Toledo, Ohio, Gift of Edward Drummond Libbey
125 Paul Gauguin, *Nude*, 1880, 111 x 79.5 (43½ x 31). Ny Carlsberg Glyptotek, Copenhagen
126 Edgar Degas, *Studies for The Little Dancer of 14 Years*, *c.*1878–80, charcoal heightened with white, 48 x 63 (18⅞ x 24⅞). Private Collection
Edgar Degas, *The Little Dancer of 14 Years*, 1879–81, wax, cotton skirt and hair ribbon, 95.2 (37½). Collection of Mr and Mrs Paul Mellon, Upperville, Virginia
127 Edgar Degas, *The Dance Class*,

Index

285